D1695485

Public Administration and Information Technology

Volume 1

Series Editor

Christopher G. Reddick

For further volumes:
http://www.springer.com/series/10796

Christopher G. Reddick
Stephen K. Aikins
Editors

Web 2.0 Technologies and Democratic Governance

Political, Policy and Management Implications

 Springer

Editors
Christopher G. Reddick
Department of Public Administration
University of Texas
W. Durango Blvd. 501
San Antonio, TX 78207
USA

Stephen K. Aikins
Public Administration Program
Department of Government and
    International Affairs
University of South Florida
4202 E Fowler Avenue, SOC 107
Tampa, FL 33620
USA

ISBN 978-1-4614-1447-6   ISBN 978-1-4614-1448-3   (eBook)
DOI 10.1007/978-1-4614-1448-3
Springer New York Heidelberg Dordrecht London

Library of Congress Control Number: 2012940559

Printed on acid-free paper

Springer is part of Springer Science+Business Media (www.springer.com)

Foreword

Stephen Aikins and I are pleased to introduce this co-edited book as Volume 1 in the Springer Book Series *Public Administration and Information Technology*. Volume 1 is entitled *Web 2.0 Technologies and Democratic Governance*: *Political*, *Policy and Management Implications*, which examines the impact of social media on government. This book discusses one of the most important emerging technologies for government and its application to public administration. It considers the management aspects of Web 2.0 on government, along with the political implications of this technology for governance.

This book series *Public Administration and Information Technology* aims to publish high quality authored and edited books that examine the application of information systems to common issues and problems in public administration. This series examines both the successes of Information and Communication Technology (ICT) adoption and some of the most important challenges to implementation. The books published in this series will address all areas of public administration, through the use of information technology adoption in the public and nonprofit sectors, and in the private sector where important lessons can be learned for public managers and policy analysts. New and emerging technologies that will have a lasting impact on public administration will be featured in this series. Both developed and developing countries will be examined in this series. The research in this series will be able to bridge both theory and practice to provide relevance to public managers. The series will cover all aspects of e-governance/e-government research, and new and emerging trends and issues in this research will be examined. The series publishes edited books, monographs, research handbooks, and upper division textbooks.

Christopher G. Reddick

Preface

This edited volume *Web 2.0 Technologies and Democratic Governance* enhances our understanding of how Web 2.0 technologies are impacting the management of public service delivery, citizen protest, and mobilization against government policies, political campaigning, participatory democracy, and governance processes. In our world today where the Internet provides an avenue for reducing the constraints of time and space, the use of collaborative technologies and social media tools like blogs, YouTube, Facebook, Twitter, and many more are reshaping the landscape of government–citizen interactions regarding public management and democratic governance. Although many argue that Web 2.0 offers a lot of promise to improve the efficiency of public management and the governance process, most of the existing research tends to focus on social networking sites and political participation. Much less attention has been paid to developing a better understanding of the policy and management implications of the uses of Web 2.0 technologies.

This edited volume fills our knowledge gap in the uses and effects of Web 2.0 technologies by helping us to understand their managerial, policy, and political uses in government, some of the existing shortfalls, and by recommending some improvements. Through a rigorous peer review process that focused on relevance, quality, and extent of contribution to the theme of the book, this edited volume presents the works of international experts that make significant contributions to the study of how Web 2.0 affects democratic governance. Collectively, these chapters provide theoretical and practical insights into how social media and related applications can be used to: (1) support a network of public servants to communicate, collaborate, and enhance the management of service delivery; (2) enable government employees and citizens to have online interaction on relevant government programs and policy issues; (3) empower citizens to hold government officials accountable using social networking and user-generated contents; and (4) enable citizens to participate in the democratic process.

The book provides a good source of reference for professors, graduate students, researchers, and professionals in information systems, public administration, and political science fields. In particular, government officials and policy makers interested in how best to use Web 2.0 technologies to improve service delivery and democratic governance will find the book very useful. The editors thank the reviewers for their invaluable service in making this project a success.

Christopher G. Reddick
Stephen K. Aikins

Contents

Chapter 1
Web 2.0 Technologies and Democratic Governance

Christopher G. Reddick and Stephen K. Aikins

In this book, we refer to Web 2.0 as a second generation of the World Wide Web used to describe social media on the Internet—a variety of Web-based platforms, applications, and technologies which exploit the Internet's connectivity to support the networking of people and content. These include social media applications such as blogs, photo and file sharing systems (e.g. Flickr, SlideShare, YouTube) and social networking sites (e.g. Friendster, Facebook, MySpace, SecondLife). Recent innovations in Web 2.0 technologies such as Ajax, XML, Open API, Microformats, and Flash/Flex have enabled the development and use of social media and networking through which individuals can actively create, organize, edit, publish, combine, share, comment, collaborate, and rate Web content. The chapters in this edited volume provide insights into how social media and related applications can be used to enhance the management of public service delivery, to enable online citizen-government interaction and participatory democracy, and to promote accountability.

Technologies in the Web 2.0 domain are appearing rapidly and taking an inventory can be challenging indeed (Dadashzadel 2010). Web 2.0 applications are rapidly transforming citizen–citizen and citizen–government interactions in a manner not seen before. A recent study sponsored by IBM Center for the Business of Government revealed that over the past several years alone, the percentage of US citizens involved in social networking, virtual community activities, and other special interest sites has doubled to over 30 % of the general population (Chang and Kannan 2008). For those in their teens and twenties, this percentage is much

C. G. Reddick (✉)
Department of Public Administration, College of Public Policy, The University of Texas at San Antonio, 501 W. Cesar E. Chavez Blvd, San Antonio, TX 78207, USA
e-mail: chris.reddick@utsa.edu

S. K. Aikins
Public Administration Program, Department of Government and International Affairs, University of South Florida, 4202 E Flower Ave SOC107, Tampa, FL 33620, USA
e-mail: saikins@usf.edu

C. G. Reddick and S. K. Aikins (eds.), *Web 2.0 Technologies and Democratic Governance*, Public Administration and Information Technology 1, DOI: 10.1007/978-1-4614-1448-3_1, © Springer Science+Business Media New York 2012

higher, indicating an ever-increasing trend in the use of the online environment for social networking, exchanging information, creating and building up content, and conducting transactions. Recent developments in the Middle East, especially in Egypt where reliance on social media applications such as Twitter and Facebook served as organizing tools that helped to topple a 30-year-old regime provides further evidence of the growing importance of Web 2.0 applications in the area of democratic accountability.

In recognition of these trends, governments are already taking a close look at Web 2.0 and online communities in order to leverage them for designing products and services and for providing citizen services. The Web 2.0 initiatives—podcasts and virtual worlds—of the Centers for Disease Control (CDC), NASA's internal social networks and virtual worlds, and the US intelligence community's Intellipedia are just a few of the recent efforts launched within the federal government. Given these realities, it is important to find a way to leverage Web 2.0 in the government to strengthen government–citizen relationship and to enable intra- and intergovernmental use in order to improve the policy and public management processes. For this to happen, government organizations need to align their Web 2.0 strategies with their organizational strategic goals for effective outcomes. This calls for clear sets of policy goals and development of Web 2.0 strategies that initiate new interactive ways of policy making, improve data and information management, and stimulate the development and use of knowledge for effective public management. Additionally, it calls for an information strategy aimed at coordinating technology, people, and information exchange in order to add value to the information used in governance and the management of public service delivery. Therefore, an edited book that helps to understand the nature of Web 2.0 applications, their political policy, and managerial implications, as well as how best governments can leverage the applications for effective governance is much needed.

This book, *Web 2.0 Technologies and Democratic Governance,* brings together international scholars to provide the theoretical and practical contexts for understanding the nature of Web 2.0 technologies and their impact on political, public policy, and management processes, and to explore how best Web 2.0 applications can be leveraged and aligned with the strategic goals of government organizations to add value and ensure effective governance. Drawing from experiences from countries around the globe, the book provides the theoretical context of the potential for Web 2.0 applications to transform government services, as well as practical examples of leading public sector institutions that have attempted to use Web 2.0 applications to enhance government operations, policy making, and administration.

1.1 The Context of Web 2.0 for Democratic Governance

Some scholars argue that with Web 2.0 there is a real potential of creating transformational change with a greater degree of transparency, accountability, and collaboration, which will in turn enhance civic engagement (Bertot et al. 2010).

Table 1.1 Essential differences between Government 1.0 and 2.0

Dimensions	Government 1.0	Government 2.0
Operations	Hierarchical	Networked
	Red Tape	Collaborative
	Rule Bound	Flexible
Service delivery	Single mode of delivery	Personalized
	Monopoly	Choice-based
	Single channel choice	Multi-channel
Performance	Inputs	Outcomes
	Line item resourced	Feedback Loop
Information	One-direction flow	Multi-direction flow
Decision Making	Top-down	Participative
		Collaborative
		Open Government

Sources Compiled from ideas from Deloitte (2008); Chun et al. 2010

However, others argue that the long history of studying the institutional context of IT adoption in the public sector indicates that organizations often impede any real reform (Mergel et al. 2009). These institutional pathologies are difficult to overcome, and meaningful change is hard to reach. Essentially, public sector officials and agencies may not want to share information because they fear loss of control which prevents transformative change. Kraemer and King (2003) in the study of technological innovation in government argued that Information Technology (IT) will not lead to new administrative structures, as it is just another path for service delivery. This book examines whether Web 2.0 is different, and does it represent long-lasting change?

In Table 1.1 we compare Government 1.0 with Government 2.0 showing the essential differences between the two typologies. This table shows that with Government 1.0 information is flowing from the top down in the organization with information eventually reaching citizens. Under Government 1.0 there is limited feedback from citizens (Chun et al. 2010). Some of the essential differences between the applications of Web 1.0 and 2.0 are that instead of content on a website being controlled by the administrator, in Web 2.0 users are producers or generators of content (Chang and Kannan 2008). Essentially, users can organize their information in their own way. The basic idea behind Web 2.0 is that the old generations of technologies were unidirectional and citizens were passive receivers of information (Meijer and Thaens 2010). Web 2.0 has created information in a multidirectional format. Web 2.0 gives users greater control over information and its use within a community, something especially important for promoting civic engagement. Much of the e-government research to date has focused on using e-government technology to automate government public service delivery (Norris and Reddick 2012). Web 2.0 technologies can be used to disseminate information and knowledge, thereby integrating information to enhance knowledge management (Dixon 2010).

Denhardt and Denhardt (2000) describe three models of public administration, which are Old Public Administration (OPA), New Public Management (NPM), and

New Public Service (NPS). These three models can be applied to the application of Web 2.0 in government. The traditional model of public administration is OPA, which focuses on bureaucracy, efficiency, and rules. NPS has very close similarities to Web 2.0 in that it offers citizens greater opportunity for civic engagement—a hallmark of NPS. The NPS research shows that governments need to move from merely being responsive (customer-driven) in NPM, to being collaborative with citizens as partners (not clients) in NPS (Vigoda 2002). Some authors have argued that one way to conceptualize e-government is to note that the traditional bureaucracy and new public management are antagonists to one another (Persson and Goldkuhl 2010). By contrast, e-government can be seen as a synthesis of the two opposing strategies, bringing together their best features. Essentially, e-government is able to combine some of the characteristics of OPA and NPM. Brainard and McNutt (2010) discuss the theories of OPA, NPM, and NPS, with NPS being enhanced by the use of e-government and social media to expand civic engagement. Therefore, Web 2.0 can be used as a way for governments to practice NPS.

However, existing research shows that Facebook and other social media technologies cannot be viewed as a way of increasing civic engagement, because they do not change the existing power relations in public organizations (Hand and Ching 2011). In examining three models of citizen interaction with government, Chadwick and May (2003) show that e-government can fall under the participative model, rather than the managerial and consultative models. We can extend this by saying that the Web 2.0 would fit well into the participative model, with its emphasis on user generated content. Social media is also said to be a way of reducing corruption because it provides for greater transparency in government operations (Bertot et al. 2010), an attribute that is increasingly important to enhance trust and confidence in public institutions.

As many of the chapters in this book show, governments employ social media for three reasons: (1) democratic participation, (2) co-production, and (3) crowdsourcing solutions (Bertot et al. 2012). Essentially, they use Web 2.0 for both the political and managerial functions of government. However, we should be cautioned as Millard (2010) states, Web 2.0 should be more aptly called Web. 1.5, since much of the potential for democratic governance has not been fully realized. Web 2.0 technology currently provides some of the new features of collaboration, transparency, and accountability, but there is much room for improvement in its application in government as will be discussed in this book.

1.2 Chapter Overviews

There are three sections in the book *Web 2.0 Technologies and Democratic Governance*. Section I examines government policy and the uses of Web 2.0 for public service delivery. Chapter 2 by Jaeger, Bertot, and Shilton examines social media use and information policy at the federal level in the US One important conclusion that they draw in their case study of federal use of social media was that government usage seemed to favor those already having access to this technology. This suggests that the "digital divide" is an important issue that governments need to address with the implementation of Web 2.0. Chapter 3 by Webb discusses the policies of federal agencies on microblogging, such as Twitter. This author found that agencies typically have policies on social media in particular, but very few agencies had policies regarding microblogging. The results of her paper suggest that oftentimes policy making lags behind the advancement of IT in the public sector. In Chap. 4, Perez, Bolivar, and Hernandez demonstrate the importance of understanding Web 2.0 as a way of reforming public service delivery. This chapter examines the movement from Government 1.0 to Government 2.0 in an analysis of Spanish government websites. In Chap. 5, Gardini, Mattei, and Orelli examine public service delivery and Web 2.0 technology with case studies of four European countries—United Kingdom, France, Germany, and Italy. They are trying to determine whether Web 2.0 has changed public service delivery for these countries. Their results showed that there was much variability in how Web 2.0 has impacted public service delivery. For instance, there is a more user-centered approach to Web 2.0 in the UK, compared with Germany and Italy; where the latter two countries seemed to be using this technology more for efficient public service delivery. In Chap. 6 Anthopoulos and Tougountzoglou examine the concepts of digital cities and how these governments incorporate Web 2.0 into their operations to enhance citizen participation. The digital city can use various collaborative and crowdsourcing tools to enhance citizen participation.

The second section of this book examines Web 2.0 as a tool for mobilization, protests, and governance. In Chap. 7 Agarwal, Lim, and Wigand examine the women's right-to-drive campaign in Saudi Arabia and the impact of social media use on this issue. The findings from this chapter indicate that social media provides citizens with a new voice to be heard, and therefore, encourages greater participation. Social media has a potential to bridge dialog between government and citizens. In Chap. 8, in an examination of Dutch student protests, DeKool found that through Web monitoring, the Ministry of Education was able to determine the reaction of students to a change in education policy. This case shows that governments can use Web 2.0 technology to advert surprises with the implementation of public policies. In Chap. 9 Veljković, Bogdanović-Dinić, and Stoimenov discuss the concept of Web 2.0 in relationship to open government. Open government espouses the three pillars of transparency, collaboration, and participation. These authors believe that with Web 2.0 technologies governments have unprecedented opportunities to engage citizens as partners in public service delivery. In Chap. 10 Mascaro, Novak, and Goggins provide a comparison of the two important political interest groups in the US and their use of Facebook. Their results showed that both groups used social media differently, implying that to understand Web 2.0, one must acknowledge that different groups use it for different forms of political participation. In Chap. 11 Ahn examines whether Web 2.0 is any different from e-government. As Ahn argues, unlike Web 1.0, governments will find it increasingly difficult to control the information that they provide to the public with the use of Web 2.0. This will have an impact on public service delivery, since Web 2.0 will challenge traditional ways of serving the public.

The last section of this book examines the effects of Web 2.0 on political campaigns and participatory democracy. In Chap. 12 Towner notes one of the most important elements of Web 2.0 is for the way political campaigns and elections are run. With Web 2.0 there is a two-way communication between the political candidates and the citizens; this challenges the traditional way that media dominates campaign coverage. As a result, campaigns must invest more time and money into social media to directly reach citizens. Effing, van Hillegersberg, and Huibers in Chap. 13 outline a social media participation model as a way of understanding political participation. This is an important model since much of the research that examines social media and campaigns and elections has very little theoretical understanding of how Web 2.0 impacts political participation. In Chap. 14 Criado, Martinez-Fuentes, and Silvan in an analysis of Twitter in Spanish local elections in 2011 showed that the majority of campaigns for these races simply used Twitter to broadcast information; there were much less responses by candidates to citizens' comments. Therefore, from this case study it appears that Twitter was used more as a one-way communication flow. Chapter 15 by Sandoval-Almazan and Gil-Garcia in an examination of the use of Twitter to increase citizen interactions with the government in Mexico, found that governments are increasingly using Twitter, but there is no overall strategy for its use. Therefore, it is difficult to have meaningful interactions with citizens without an effective strategy. In Chap. 16 Roy examines the use of Web 2.0 in examining Westminster governments. Roy's chapter argues that although social media has the potential to create more citizen interaction and openness in government, only if the underlying institutions of governance support its use will there be meaningful change. Therefore, Roy makes the argument, like many others in the IT and public administration literature, that change from technology does not come without change in the underlying institutional arrangements. In Chap. 17, Papaloi, Staiou, and Gouscos examine the use of social media on parliamentary websites and it impact on e-participation. The findings of this final chapter indicate that there should be a social media readiness framework to determine factors that promote readiness for governments.

References

Bertot, J.C., Jaeger, P.T., & Grimes, J.M. (2010). Using ICTs to create a culture of transparency: E-government and social media as openness and anti-corruption tools for societies. *Government Information Quarterly*, 27(3), 264–271.

Bertot, J.C., Jaeger, P.T., & Hansen, D. (2012). The impact of policies on government social media usage: Issues, challenges, and recommendations. *Government Information Quarterly*, 29(1), 30–40.

Brainard, L.A., & McNutt, J.G. (2010). Virtual government-citizen relations: Information, transactional, or collaborative? *Administration & Society*, 42(7), 836–858.

Chadwick, A., & May, C. (2003). Interactions between states and citizens in the age of the Internet: "e-Government" in the United States, Britain, and the European Union. *Governance*, 16(2), 271–300.

Chang, A., & Kannan, P.K. (2008). *Leveraging Web 2.0 in Government*. IBM Center for the Business of Government. Retrieved from http://www.businessofgovernment.org/report/leveraging-web-20-government

Chun, S.A., Shulman, S., Sandovol, R., & Hovy, E. (2010). Government 2.0: Making connections between citizens, data and government. *Information Polity*, 15(1/2), 1–9.

Dadashzadeh, M. (2010). Social media in government: From eGovernment to eGovernance. *Journal of Business & Economics Research*, 8(11), 81–86.

Deloitte. (2008). *Change your world or the world will change you: The future of collaborative government and Web 2.0*. Retrieved from http://www.deloitte.com/view/en_CA/ca/industries/719ef16bc31fb110VgnVCM100000ba42f00aRCRD.htm

Denhardt, R.B., & Denhardt, J.V. (2000). The new public service: Serving rather than steering. *Public Administration Review*, 60(6), 549–559.

Dixon, B.E. (2010). Towards e-government 2.0: An assessment of where e-government 2.0 is and where it is headed. *Public Administration & Management*, 15(2), 418–454.

Hand, L.C., & Ching, B.D. (2011). "You have one friend request" An exploration of power and citizen engagement in local governments' use of social media. *Administrative Theory & Praxis*, 33(3), 362–382.

Kraemer, K.L., & King, J.L. (2003). Information technology and administrative reform: Will the time after e-government be different? Center for Research on Information Technology and Organizations, Retrieved from http://unpan1.un.org/intradoc/groups/public/documents/APCITY/UNPAN022640.pdf

Meijer, A., & Thaens, M. (2010). Alignment 2.0: Strategic use of new Internet technologies in govenrment. *Government Information Quarterly*, 27(2), 113–121.

Mergel, I., Schweik, C., & Fountain, J. (2009). *The transformational effect of Web 2.0 technologies on government*. Retrieved from http://papers.ssrn.com/sol3/papers.cfm?abstract_id=1412796

Millard, J. (2010). *Government 1.5- is the bottle half full or half empty?* Retrieved from http://www.epractice.eu/en/document/313343

Norris, D.F., & Reddick, C.G. Local E-Government in the U.S.: Transformation or Incremental Change, *American Society for Public Administration*, Las Vegas, NV, March, 2012.

Persson, A., & Goldkuhl, G. (2010). Government value paradigms—Bureaucracy, new public management, and e-government. *Communications of the Association of Information Systems*, 27, 45–62.

Vigoda, E. (2002). From responsiveness to collaboration: Governance, citizens, and the next generation of public administration. *Public Administration Review*, 62(5), 527–540.

Part I
Government Policy and Uses of Web 2.0 for Management of Service Delivery

Chapter 2
Information Policy and Social Media: Framing Government—Citizen Web 2.0 Interactions

Paul T. Jaeger, John Carlo Bertot and Katie Shilton

2.1 Introduction: Policy Goals and Social Media

Web 2.0 technologies, in general, and social media technologies in particular, open new and innovative methods for immediate and ongoing interaction between citizens and governments. The use of these technologies occurs within a broader information policy environment that establishes guidelines for access, use, management, and preservation of information. Government agencies, however, have begun using social media without sufficient consideration of this larger policy environment. Inconsistent goals and practices among related policies, combined with conflicting design values applied to implementations, have created long-term policy conflicts, particularly in approaches to defining and implementing *access*.

The capacities of social media to facilitate information, communication, and interaction between governments and citizens extend many of the principles of information access that have been central to United States policy. Deeply embedded within the founding of the United States is access to government information, beginning with the Declaration of Independence and continuing through e-government programs today (Jaeger and Bertot 2011). "The state is more than an allocator of services and values; it is an apparatus for assembling and managing the political information associated with expressions of public will and with public policy" (Bimber 2003, p. 17). A prevalent thread that weaves

P. T. Jaeger (✉) · J. C. Bertot · K. Shilton
College of Information Studies, University of Maryland,
4105 Hornbake Building, College Park, MD 20742, USA
e-mail: pjaeger@umd.edu

J. C. Bertot
e-mail: jbertot@umd.edu

K. Shilton
e-mail: kshilton@umd.edu

C. G. Reddick and S. K. Aikins (eds.), *Web 2.0 Technologies and Democratic Governance*, Public Administration and Information Technology 1,
DOI: 10.1007/978-1-4614-1448-3_2, © Springer Science+Business Media New York 2012

throughout the nation's information policies is ensuring public access to government information and operations, regardless of socioeconomic status, geographic location, disability, availability of telecommunications technologies, or other factors. Social media can serve to foster new depths of government–citizen interactions; however, information policy must account for unique accessibility issues to make government use of social media truly inclusive.

Social media has quickly become a primary tool to disseminate government information, connect with members of the public, and provide access to services. The US federal government has numerous YouTube channels to distribute videos from Congress, the President, and federal agencies. Many agencies have a presence on Facebook and other social networks, and send out important information via blogging and microblogging channels like Twitter. Large amounts of data are made available for public use through open data sites like www.data.gov. While the relevance and importance of government content distributed through social media can vary widely (Golbeck et al. 2010), the widespread use of social media demonstrates that these tools are likely to be important long-term components of interactions between governments and members of the public.

Given this growing use of social media by governments, traditional information policy considerations of access and inclusion should be central to the formulation and implementation of policies related to social media. If access is not available to segments of the population due to design or implementation, government social media use will create new inequalities in public interactions with government. Although using social media is intended to make government easier to reach, it may instead create new barriers. This problem is particularly pressing as many governments have argued that e-government—and social media in particular— provide reasons to reduce offline communication responsibilities and costs.

Using the US federal government as a case study, this chapter employs policy analysis to explore the laws and policies related to the use of social media by governments and government agencies, with a specific focus on the manifestations of the policies in the implementation of social media strategies. This chapter examines two kinds of evidence to understand government social media implementations. First, it examines existing law and policy for approaches to access that should shape social media implementations. This analysis suggests three predominant perspectives on access: universal service, equity of access, and literacy. The chapter then presents case studies of how these access perspectives, and the values behind them, are implemented in government social media tools.

By analyzing information policy instruments and laws relevant to social media interactions between government and citizens, as well as key memos released by the Obama administration that directly relate to social media use by federal agencies, this chapter illustrates the complexity of the existing legal framework, most elements of which were written and implemented prior to the existence of social media technologies. The policies encouraging citizen-government interaction, and the tools meant to implement this interaction, often lack harmonization with broader information policies, leading to frustrations for both agencies and citizens. By exploring the challenges of dealing with rapidly changing technologies that have outpaced their regulatory framework, the chapter argues for the need to proactively develop policies and tools to address equity of access in a social media context. By harmonizing policy definitions and approaches to access, and using these definitions to redesign social media use by government, this chapter suggests it is possible for those formulating and implementing policies related to government social media usage to encourage equity of access.

2.2 Social Media and Government in the United States

Social media has significant potential for promoting interactions between government and citizens, as agencies increase their use of social media technologies as a way to reach members of the public in new locations, extend government services, and engage members of the public in government efforts. As social media technologies are now regularly employed by a majority of Internet users, these technologies can serve as an appropriate venue through which to promote interactions between governments and citizens:

- 86 % of 18–29 year olds use social media everyday (Madden 2010).
- 72 % of adults and 87 % of teens use text messages everyday (Lenhart 2010).
- Facebook announced that it reached 800 million active users in 2011 (http://www.facebook.com/press/info.php?statistics).

As the number of users has increased there has been a growing interest in applying social media toward addressing national priorities (Pirolli et al. 2010). President Obama became a strong advocate for the use of social media when he was a presidential candidate (Jaeger et al. 2010). Both at the behest of the Obama administration and following the growth in use of social media, federal government agencies have embraced the use of social media. Government agencies are now using a wide range of social media—blogs, microblogs, sharing services, text messaging, discussion forums, collaborative editing tools, virtual worlds, and social networking services—to engage citizens (Bertot et al. 2012; Hansen et al. 2011). These tools vary dramatically in their purposes and approaches, but they rely on user-generated content and enable users to communicate, interact, edit, and share content in a social environment, promoting creation of information resources by geographically dispersed groups.

Much government activity is now focused on social media, with social media becoming a central component of e-government in a very short period of time (Bertot et al. 2010; Chang and Kannan 2008; Osimo 2008). US federal agencies have been using social media to create records, disseminate information, and communicate with the public and between agencies for several years. In addition, the General Services Administration (GSA) has even created a standard agreement for social media providers to allow for government usage of social media services.

Government use of social media offers several key opportunities for agencies and citizens (Bertot et al. 2010):

- *Democratic participation and engagement*, using social media technologies to engage the public in government fostering participatory dialog and providing a voice in discussions of policy development and implementation.
- *Co-production*, in which governments and the public jointly develop, design, and deliver government services to improve service quality, delivery, and responsiveness.
- *Crowdsourcing solutions and innovations*, seeking innovation through public knowledge and talent to develop innovative solutions to large-scale societal issues. To facilitate crowdsourcing, the government shares data and other inputs so that the public has a foundational base on which to innovate.

Though not mutually exclusive, these opportunities offer great promise and pose new challenges in redefining government-community connections and interactions. However, agencies are in large part doing so through an antiquated policy structure that governs agency information flows, access, and dissemination mandates.

Not only is the Obama administration strongly encouraging agencies to use social media to provide information, communicate with members of the public, and distribute services, it has also made a priority of public usage of social media to participate in government (Jaeger et al. 2010). Many members of the public already expect that government services will be available electronically and that government agencies will be accessible via social media technologies (Jaeger and Bertot 2010). The widespread adoption of many of these different social media tools has been emphasized in a number of different White House reports, such as *Open Government: A Progress Report to the America People* (2009), listing numerous uses of social media approaches to promote transparency across many different agencies.

Thus far, the success of government use of social media is mixed. On the positive side, 31 % of Internet users are government social media users (Pew Internet 2010). However, 95 % of these government social media users were already using more traditional government websites, indicating that government use of social media has not attracted much of a new audience. The population of Internet users interacting with government through social media—such as following government agencies or officials on Twitter—is extremely small. At the same time, however, many Internet users rely primarily or exclusively on a Web-enabled cell phone or other type of mobile device to access online content (Pew Internet 2010), indicating that there is an enormous potential population of users of government social media who already favor working through social media platforms on mobile devices.

2.3 Policy, Access, and Government Use of Social Media

The unique nature of social media technologies—and the basis of their mass appeal and strength as a government tool—lies in their ability to create an immediate and interactive dialog. But this nature also creates important policy challenges as these technologies continue to be used more extensively both by governments and the public. Though the current policy environment addresses many issues of privacy, security, accuracy, and archiving, much of the policy related to the use of social media predates the creation of social media technologies. As a result, many of the existing policies do not adequately address the technological capacities or functions of social media. Furthermore, as social media provides new ways to combine previously unavailable and/or separately maintained data, there are now cross-dataset concerns that impact multiple policy issues. Finally, social media comprise private ventures with their own acceptable use, data use, accessibility, and privacy policies that often do not conform to federal requirements.

The Obama Administration is aware of and trying to address at least some of these policy shortcomings. Since April 2010, OMB has issued three significant memos regarding federal agency use of and interaction with social media technologies:

- Memo M-10-22 (Guidance for Online Use of Web Measurement and Customization Technologies) promotes the use of measurement and customization technologies to promote website analytics and customization of the user experience. Consistent with other statements by the Obama administration, this memo emphasizes the perceived benefits of enabling the use of social media technologies. There are still prohibitions such as tracking individual-level activity outside of the website, sharing the data with other departments or agencies, and cross-referencing the data with personally identifiable information.
- OMB Memo M-10-23 (Guidance for Agency Use of Third-Party Websites and Applications) accounts for the increasing amount of Internet activity that occurs on third-party sites, including Facebook, Twitter, YouTube, and other social media. As specific social media sites, such as Facebook, have become important platforms for information exchange, government agencies have created a presence on them. Agencies have also begun including third-party widgets, modules, snippets, and plug-ins on their own websites. These are mini applications with dynamic content or services that are embedded within another Web page. Finally, many social media and related sites offer Application Programming Interfaces (APIs) that allow other programs and sites to call upon their content and services. These support "Mashups" that combine data from different sources into an integrated user experience. M-10-23 encourages the use of all of these sorts of third-party materials, while emphasizing the need to also consider user privacy. Third-party sites, however, raise a range of privacy, security, and accuracy issues, as well as long-term concerns about data usage, records schedules and archiving, and preservation (Bertot et al. 2010, 2012).
- An unnumbered Memorandum (Social Media, Web-Based Interactive Technologies, and the Paperwork Reduction Act) clarifies that "certain uses of social media and Web-based interactive technologies will be treated as equivalent to activities that are currently excluded" from the Paperwork Reduction Act

(PRA). The memo is needed because the vagueness of the original law that specifies that the PRA applies to the collection of information "regardless of form or format," but does not define information. Later OMB regulations excluded three types of activities discussed in the memo that were not considered "information"—general solicitations, public meetings, and like items.

These memos—and the GSA *Social Media Handbook* (2010)—emphasize certain policy issues and bypass others. While issues like privacy, security, web analytics, and definitions of information under the PRA are important to government usage of social media, issues of access, and inclusion in government-to-citizen interactions through social media are utterly missed in these policies. In general, the adoption of social media is affected by education level, age, socio-economic status, gender, and race (Hargittai 2008; Zhou 2010). The area of access and inclusion has been a long-term challenge for e-government development around the world (Jaeger and Thompson 2003, 2004; Powell et al. 2010), and these challenges are not reflected in the memos and handbook related to social media.

2.4 Access in Public Policy

For social media to increase access to government information and services and to successfully facilitate civic participation, members of the public must be able to access and use social media technologies. Public usage of social media is predicated on (Bertot et al. 2010):

- Universal access to the technologies (which at a minimum necessitates a device and Internet access at a speed sufficient to support social media content);
- The development of technology, programs, and Internet-enabled services that offers equity of access to all users; and,
- Information and civics literacy necessary to understand government services, resources, and operations.

These three kinds of access might be summarized as **universal service**, **equity of access**, and **literacy**.

A large amount of existing policy relates to access to government information and services online, and while these policies predominantly predate the existence of social media, their reach extends to agency interaction with and use of social media technologies. These policies establish the requirements of access, but provide no specifics that can be applied to social media. Some are extremely broad; the Telecommunications Act of 1996 and the E-government Act of 2002 both include assertions that access to information and communication technologies being used online and to e-government content should be available to all members of the public. Clearly, government social media interactions fall under these broad directives.

Various populations are also the subject of policies promoting access that predate, but should be applied to, government use of social media. For example, Executive Order 13166—Improving Access to Services for Persons with Limited English Proficiency—requires that agencies provide appropriate access to persons with limited English proficiency, including use of social media technologies to communicate and collaborate with members of the public. This policy objective is meant to address the fact that there are highly pronounced gaps in e-government usage among people who predominantly speak a language other than English, as little e-government content is available in non-English formats. For example, 32 % of Latinos who do not speak English use the Internet, but 78 % of Latinos who speak English use the Internet (Fox and Livingston 2007).

Many policies that establish the precedent for equity of access to e-government relate to persons with disabilities. As the most disadvantaged population in the United States in terms of computer and Internet access, percentages of computer and Internet usage among persons with disabilities have remained at levels below half of the equivalent percentages for the rest of the population since the advent of the Web (Dobransky and Hargittai 2006; Jaeger 2011; Lazar and Jaeger 2011). Yet, one of the laws related to equity of access for persons with disabilities reveals the disjunction between access policies that should apply to government use of social media and the ways in which the government is currently using social media. Section 508 of the Rehabilitation Act requires that electronic and information technologies purchased, maintained, or used by the federal government to meet certain accessibility standards designed to make online information and services fully available to people with disabilities. Social media companies rarely comply with the accessibility requirements of Section. 508, yet this inaccessibility has not been a deterrent to the use of social media by government agencies.

As a result, for persons with disabilities, social media often means a reduced ability to participate (Howard 2011; Lazar and Wentz 2011; Wentz and Lazar 2011). Government agencies are simultaneously trying to reach citizens through inaccessible third-party social technologies, and embedding these technologies in their own sites, negatively impacting the accessibility of their original sites. This disjunction between access policy and social media usage by the federal government demonstrates the need to identify and consider factors that can enable a policy environment to serve all populations in government-to-citizen-social media interactions.

2.5 Policy Harmonization and Social Media

Bringing social media usage by government agencies in line with existing access policies is the first essential step in ensuring that government-to-citizen interactions through social media are inclusive of all segments of the population. To navigate the discrepancies between traditional information policies that govern government information flows, access, and interaction, one suggested solution is a process of harmonization (Shuler et al. 2010). Though the concept of harmonization has been proposed as a general approach for reconciling the laws, regulations, and practices related to e-government, it can be especially useful within the context of access to information, communication, and services through social media. In the government social media context, the long-established core democratic principles intended to foster equity of access should serve as the basis of the harmonization of laws, practices, and regulations (Bertot et al. 2012).

A key example of a problem resulting from the lack of harmonization in the government use of social media can be seen in soliciting comments on proposed regulations. Some agencies now solicit comments through social media about proposed regulations, but are not able to respond to questions people pose in reaction during the notice and comment period due to laws preventing them from responding to questions in the notice and comment period. However, such inaction is antithetical to users' expectations for social media, where they assume that they should receive a response to their questions, creating a direct conflict between two policies. As a result, many of the people posing the questions about the proposed regulations do not understand why no one is responding, which then serves to reduce future participation in government online by making users feel that their input is being ignored.

Existing policies related to access must also receive greater attention when agencies decide to use social media technologies. Agencies may not be aware of the range of policies related to access or the implications of those policies. This situation could be greatly improved by the creation of a guide to provide clear guidance to agencies about the policies that must be considered in the adoption and use of social media. Even with the GSA *Handbook* (2010), there is still need for a cross-agency social media guide specifically devoted to relevant policies and their implications, as the *Handbook* does not encompass the full spectrum of relevant laws and policies, nor does it adequately address user issues, such as equity of access (Bertot et al. 2012).

When the adoption of new technologies by government agencies challenges current information policy, it indicates that the policy development process is not fleet enough for the pace of rapid technological change. As government agencies continue to adopt new technologies, the development of more responsive information policies that is based on principles, rather than tied to specific technologies, will be vital to ensuring that policies can remain relevant. A harmonized policy context will be better positioned to react to and account for technological change. The aforementioned recent memos issued by OMB are a first, insufficient attempt to harmonizing the federal government's policies towards social media technologies.

2.6 Policy Approaches to Social Media Access

Since social media is being used to facilitate governance, provide access to vital government information and services, communicate with the public, and promote civic participation, equity of access to social media will be necessary to prevent citizens from being left out of these new government-to-citizen interactions, particularly as the availability of outlets for conducting similar interactions offline are rapidly diminishing. As the federal government considers ways to regulate its own implementation and usage of social media, the approach to access that is used in policy may result in very differing foci and access outcomes. Social media encompasses dimensions of communication, information, and a range of technologies and can be understood from different perspectives based on these areas. Under terms such as universal service, universal access, universal design, and universal usability, these approaches to access focus on different parts of the connection among the user, the technology, and benefits accrued to society.

The fact that social media relies on the backbone of the telecommunications infrastructure indicates that the **universal service** approach would follow the approach taken in many laws and regulations, most prominently the Telecommunications Act of 1996. The approach of universal service—often used interchangeably with universal access—has been articulated in telecommunication and computer science contexts as the goal of making technology equally available to all, focusing on challenges such as infrastructure and geography (Jaeger 2011; Shneiderman 2000). The language of universal service can be found in government policy documents, business plans of communication companies, and computer science research, among others.

However, universal service overlooks issues of economics and usage. The access that is available has to be affordable to those who need it; otherwise, many people lack meaningful access. Once access is available and affordable to all, citizens still need to be able to use the resources to which they have access. Universal service does not overcome barriers to access like disability, language, literacy, and digital literacy, among others (Kanayama 2003). Given the uses of social media by government, a universal service approach would still leave many citizens unable to participate.

Another potential approach to the regulation of government use of social media is **universal design**. This approach focuses on the inclusive design of the root technologies needed to support government use of social media. Universal design has its roots in making commercial products and architecture more inclusive, taking focus away from the traditional design approach of creating things for an imagined average user. The use of standards in design enables and creates order only for those who meet the standards (Burgstahler 2008; Moser 2006). Instead, universal design focuses on making "products and environments welcoming and useful to groups that are diverse in many dimensions, including gender, race and ethnicity, age, socio-economic status, ability, disability, and learning style" (Burgstahler 2008, p. 3).

Universal design has not been typically applied in information and communication policies, but it is present in many disability rights regulations (Jaeger 2011). For example, policies mandating curb cuts on sidewalks not only support wheelchair access, they help parents with baby strollers, people with rolling luggage and shopping carts, bicyclists, and rollerbladers and many others (Zeff 2007). However, given that universal design does not address issues of affordability of access or digital literacy, it is not a stand-alone policy approach for access to the government use of social media.

Another concept that could be employed in policy to promote government-to-citizen interactions through social media is the concept of **universal usability**. Derived from the study of human–computer interaction, universal usability focuses on the creation and implementation of technologies in ways that they can be accessed and used by most, if not all, people. Established information technologies—postal services, telephones, television—successfully provide universal usability; that is, the vast majority of the population has access to, can use, and regularly does use the technology (Shneiderman 2000). As such, universal usability attempts to bring successful approaches to information access from the physical world to the virtual world, so that information technologies are designed to provide the same kind of widely usable products from the outset.

The concept of universal usability, however, suffers from the fact that it is based on inclusive design. As the government has already widely adopted a range of social media technologies that are based on openly exclusive designs, a policy based on universal usability of social media would also need to require the redesign of many social media technologies before the government can continue using them. In taking such an approach, the government would be following the lead of certain institutions of higher education that refused to adopt certain technologies, including some social media services, until the technologies are made inclusive (Jaeger 2011).

2.7 Design Values Evidenced in Implementation

The current mix of accessibility perspectives shaping e-government social media outreach is evidenced by the various tools in use today. The social values harbored by technologies' designers and hosts are often reflected in their design and deployment (Friedman 1997; Knobel and Bowker 2011). While a broad study of the accessibility values reflected in government social media tools is clearly needed, it is possible to readily identify examples that suggest the diversity of access perspectives currently applied.

The **universal access perspective**, as exemplified by the Telecommunications Act of 1996, emphasizes availability of social media to citizens. The universal access perspective values physical and logistical access to government materials. Key social media features that exemplify the universal access perspective include:

- Providing access to traditionally paper materials;
- Providing search of historical and current materials; and
- Enabling sharing of materials through social media tools.

An example of this perspective in action can be found in the use of Facebook and Twitter widgets in the Federal Register website (https://www.federalregister.gov). The Federal Register is a daily newsletter of proposed rules, public notices, and articles published by federal agencies. The Register's site is meant to increase the availability of agency publications and information. It digitizes each section of the Register and allows for searching of articles dating back to 1994. Under "User Information," the site hosts write that they built the site to "overcome the technical limitations of the official edition and to demonstrate how a new version can more effectively convey regulatory information to the public." The stated goal is to increase availability of information by making the contents of the Federal Register electronic and searchable.

To this end, the site designers include a number of social media tools, including an RSS feed subscription feature and buttons for sharing articles via Facebook and Twitter. Social media tools are employed as part of the Register's outreach to further broadcast the contents of the Federal Register and therefore increase availability of the materials. Social media tools are not explicitly used to increase understanding of the material or to cross social or demographic boundaries that might fetter access. The use of Facebook and Twitter for sharing by the Federal Register is an example of a focus on availability in government information and social media use.

The **equity of access perspective** goes beyond availability to emphasize cultural, language-, or need-based access to social media. The equity of access perspective values access to government information across demographic, cultural, or accessibility barriers (Lievrouw and Farb 2003). Key features of the equity of access perspective include:

- Availability in multiple formats (especially hosting information outside of proprietary and sometimes inaccessible social media formats);
- Access features for users with disabilities;
- Translation into languages other than English; and
- Explanatory materials to help users navigate government resources.

For example, the Disability.gov website (https://www.disability.gov/) provides social content such as videos, forums for public participation in White House conversations and social media news, and resource feeds. The site's designers address the accessibility challenges of these materials directly through both policy and site design. The site's designers describe their social media policy as follows:

> **Social Media Alternate Formats:** Disability.gov understands that third-party social media platforms and websites may not be accessible to all users, including those with disabilities. Therefore, all information posted by Disability.gov on any of its social media accounts will be made available on the site. Please visit the *Disability.gov Social Media* section, located in the Disability.gov *Newsroom*, for alternate formats of information posted on Disability.gov's social media accounts.

Providing a section of the website dedicated to replicating information shared with inaccessible tools illustrates that Disability.gov's designers value access across social and physical barriers. It is likely that site managers' awareness of their user base influenced their values and their equity of access perspective in deploying social media tools.

The **literacy perspective** focuses on helping citizens to use their access to social media. The literacy perspective values education and information about government processes as well as helping users to understand and use technological features. Key features of the literacy perspective help citizens:

- Understand what e-government features do;
- Understand why e-government initiatives are important; and
- Participate in e-government initiatives.

Although many e-government websites include comprehensive civic literacy sections as well as Web tool how-tos, there are fewer deployments of social media tools explicitly devoted to civic or content literacy. Examples of e-government social media tools approached from the literacy perspective are the tools hosted by Regulations.gov (http://www.regulations.gov). Regulations.gov provides social media tools to encourage citizens to participate in the rulemaking process. These include the "Exchange" tool, which is a discussion forum on federal agency initiatives. The Exchange forum allows for customized profiles, so that users can learn about, track, and discuss specific agency initiatives and rulemaking of interest. Citizens can interact with each other as well as agency officials through the Exchange dialog. By using social media tools for explicit citizen involvement, Regulations.gov approaches their task from a literacy perspective, fostering civic engagement rather than simple access to government documents.

Universal access, equity of access, and literacy perspectives are not mutually exclusive perspectives. Indeed, on many government sites, there are sections dedicated to helping users understand e-government materials side-by-side with digitized documents and social media outreach. However, individual social media projects tend to skew towards one values perspective. These examples illustrate how a values-based framework can illuminate the nature of access to government information provided by social media tools. Consciously harmonizing the values built into social media projects across these three spectra would produce the most balanced approach to accessibility of e-government materials.

2.8 Conclusion: Intersections of Law, Access, and Design

The recent development of social media means that many important government usage issues have yet to be fully realized, much less understood. However, the more attention paid to ensuring that government social media initiatives include as many members of the public as possible, the fewer individuals will struggle with barriers to usage once the technologies are entrenched in government operations. As social media becomes an increasingly important channel through which to receive government information services and communicate with government agencies, struggling with access may have large consequences for those with limited or no access. There seems a real possibility that digital divides that currently separate social groups by presence and quality of access to computers, the

Internet, and broadband may be replicated in social media (Jaeger et al. 2012). The development of a social media divide could have significant negative consequences for those on the wrong side.

There are many challenges to policy approaches and design values that will shape access to and usage of social media by members of the public and particularly disadvantaged populations. Early evidence suggests that these challenges are significant. Government agencies have adopted social media, expecting members of the public to begin using them. This approach has led to a user base comprised almost exclusively of people who were already regular users of other e-government technologies, while approximately two-thirds of Internet users do not think government use of social media is a worthwhile use of government funds (Pew Internet 2010). Though hesitancies toward usage may be tied to a range of issues—content, awareness, and interest, among others—the issues discussed in this paper emphasize the first step in adoption: whether social media services will be inclusive or exclusive at the outset. Technological developments historically benefit the already technologically privileged (Hanson 2008; Mackenzie 2010). Government usage of social media seems to favor those who already have access to other technologically based means of government interaction, and those with the information literacy to be comfortable with existing social media.

As polices are created in relation to those tools, there are several key considerations that will shape the inclusivity of social media interactions between the government and the public:

- Development of policies that prioritize the universal usability of government social media activities.
- Emphasis on design values in government social media technologies that address considerations of universal access, equity of access, and literacy.
- Adherence to existing policies intended to ensure equity of access to government information and technologies, such as only employing social media technologies that comply with Section 508 accessibility guidelines.
- Efforts to promote awareness of government social media activities coupled with outreach to members of populations disadvantaged in terms of access.
- Creation of social media programs that reach members of the public on the types of technologies they have access to and literacy using, such as mobile devices.
- Harmonization of policy objectives and design approaches into an across-agency, integrated social media approach that promotes public-government interaction.

As government usage of social media increases, attention to these considerations will take on greater significance, particularly if social media becomes a primary means by which governments want to interact with members of the public.

While examples in this paper have been drawn from the United States, the issues at hand are of consequence to any government currently using, or planning to use, social media as a key means of conducting the business of government. Though policies and implementations will vary between nations, the choices made in policy and implementation will heavily shape the levels of access to, and inclusion in, government activities through social media. The general move internationally toward bringing government information, communication, and services online—while simultaneously reducing offline equivalents—makes access issues an essential consideration in government uses of social media. If certain populations are not included in the implementation, they risk being left out of key government information, communication, and services.

Government usage of social media has rapidly increased in a short period of time, but with little research about implementation, perceptions, and usage. Further, research into the access issues faced by different populations, the policy perspectives on access that shape social media policy, and the design values evidenced by implementations of government social media will be important in documenting, framing, and improving interactions between governments and members of the public in the Web 2.0 environment.

References

Bertot, J. C., Jaeger, P. T., & Grimes, J. M. (2010). Using ICTs to create a culture of transparency? E-government and social media as openness and anti-corruption tools for societies. *Government Information Quarterly, 27*, 264–271.

Bertot, J. C., Jaeger, P. T., & Hansen, D. (2012). The impact of polices on government social media usage: Issues, challenges, and recommendations. *Government Information Quarterly, 29*, 30–40.

Bertot, J. C., Jaeger, P. T., Munson, S., & Glaisyer, T. (2010). Engaging the public in open government: The policy and government application of social media technology for government transparency. *IEEE Computer, 43*(11), 53–59.

Bimber, B. (2003). *Information and American democracy: Technology in the evolution of political power*. Cambridge: Cambridge University Press.

Burgstahler, S. A. (2008). Universal design of technological environments: From principles to practice. In S. Burgstahler & R. C. Cory (Eds.), *Universal design in higher education: From principles to practice* (pp. 213–224). Cambridge, MA: Harvard Education.

Chang A., & Kannan P. K. (2008). *Leveraging Web 2.0 in government*. Washington DC: IBM Center for The Business of Government.

Dobransky, K., & Hargittai, E. (2006). The disability divide in Internet access and use. *Information, Communication & Society, 9*, 313–334.

Fox, S., & Livingston, G. (2007). *Latinos online: Hispanics with lower levels of education and English proficiency remain largely disconnected from the Internet*. Washington, DC: Pew Internet and American Life Project. Available: http://www.pewinternet.org.

Friedman, B. (Ed.). (1997). *Human values and the design of computer technology*. New York: Cambridge University Press.

General Services Administration (2010). *Social media handbook*. Available: http://www.gsa.gov/graphics/staffoffices/socialmediahandbook.pdf.

Golbeck J., Grimes, J. M., & Rogers A. (2010). Twitter use by the US Congress. *Journal of the American Society for Information Science and Technology, 61*, 1612–1621.

Hansen, D. L., Shneiderman, B., & Smith, M. A. (2011). *Analyzing social media networks with NodeXL: Insights from a connected world*, Burlington, MA: Morgan Kaufmann.

Hanson, E. C. (2008). *The information revolution and world politics*. Lanham, MD: Rowman & Littlefield.

Hargittai, E. (2008). Whose space? Differences among users and non-users of social network sites. *Journal of Computer-Mediated Communication, 13*, 276–297.

Howard, A. (2011). Pew: Disability or illness hinders many Americans from using the Internet. Available: http://Gov20.govfresh.com.

Jaeger, P. T. (2011). *Disability and the Internet: Confronting a digital divide*. Boulder, CO: Lynne Reiner.

Jaeger, P. T., & Bertot, J. C. (2010). Designing, implementing, and evaluating user-centered and citizen-centered e-government. *International Journal of Electronic Government Research, 6*(2), 1–17.

Jaeger, P. T., & Bertot, J. C. (2011). Responsibility rolls down: Public libraries and the social and policy obligations of ensuring access to e-government and government information. *Public Library Quarterly, 30*, 1–25.

Jaeger, P. T., Bertot, J. C., Thompson, K. M., Katz, S. M., & DeCoster, E. J. (2012). The intersection of public policy and public access: Digital divides, digital literacy, digital inclusion, and public libraries. *Public Library Quarterly, 31*(1).

Jaeger, P. T., & Thompson, K. M. (2003). E-government around the world: Lessons, challenges, and new directions. *Government Information Quarterly, 20*(4), 389–394.

Jaeger, P. T., & Thompson, K. M. (2004). Social information behavior and the democratic process: Information poverty, normative behavior, and electronic government in the United States. *Library & Information Science Research, 26*(1), 94–107.

Kanayama, T. (2003). Leaving it all up to industry: People with disabilities and the Telecommunications Act of 1996. *Information Society, 19*, 185–194.

Knobel, C. P., & Bowker, G. C. (2011). Values in design. *Communications of the ACM,* July.

Lazar, J., & Jaeger, P. T. (2011). Promoting and enforcing web site accessibility. *Issues in Science and Technology, 17*(2), 68–82.

Lazar, J., & Wentz, B. (2011). Separate but equal web site interfaces are inherently unequal for people with disabilities. *User Experience, 10*(3).

Lenhart, A. (2010). *Cell phones and American adults*. Washington, DC: Pew Internet and American Life Project. Available: http://www.pewinternet.org

Lievrouw, L. A., & Farb, S. E. (2003). Information and social equity. *Annual Review of Information Science and Technology, 37*, 499–540. Information Today.

Mackenzie, A. (2010). *Wirelessness: Radical empiricism in network cultures*. Cambridge, MA: MIT Press.

Madden, M. (2010). *Older adults and social media*. Washington, DC: Pew Internet and American Life Project. Available: http://www.pewinternet.org

Moser, I. (2006). Disability and the promises of technology: Technology, subjectivity, and embodiment within an order of the normal. *Information Communication & Society, 9*, 373–395.

Osimo, D. (2008). *Web 2.0 in government: Why and how?* Washington DC: Institute for Prospective Technological Studies.

Pew Internet (2010). *Government online*. Available: http://www.pewinternet.org/Reports/2010/Government-Online.aspx

Pirolli, P., Preece, J., & Shneiderman, B. (2010). Cyberinfrastructure for social action on national priorities. *Computer, 43*(11), 20–21.

Powell, A., Byrne, A., & Dailey, D. (2010). The essential Internet: Digital exclusion in low-income American communities. *Policy & Internet, 2*(2), article 7.

Shneiderman, B. (2000). Universal usability. *Communications of the ACM, 43*(5), 84–91.

Shuler, J. A., Jaeger, P. T., & Bertot, J. C. (2010). Implications of harmonizing e-government principles and the Federal Depository Library Program (FDLP). *Government Information Quarterly, 27*, 9–16.

Wentz, B., & Lazar, J. L. (2011). Are separate interfaces inherently unequal? An evaluation with blind users of the usability of two interfaces for a social networking platform. Presented at *iConference 2011*, Seattle, WA, United States.

White House (2009). *Open government: A progress report to the America people*. Washington DC: Author.

Zeff, R. (2007). Universal design across the curriculum. *New Directions for Higher Education, 137*, 27–44.

Zhou, T. (2010). Understanding online community user participation: A social influence perspective. *Internet Research, 21*, 67–81.

Chapter 3
Microblogging: An Analysis of Government Issued Policies and Best Practices

Paula Lenor Webb

3.1 Introduction

President Barack Obama's administration opened the doors to the inclusion of social media into the governmental agenda on January 21, 2009—his first day in office. According to the memorandum released his goal was threefold. Government that was previously closed or limited to the citizenship of the United States was to become transparent, participatory, and collaborative. The new administration wanted to foster interaction with citizens by posting interesting, vital, and emergency information using social media to develop cognitive engagement with civic-minded people. This administration entertained a new access point for an old concept; a government that could communicate directly with its people—an important foundational aspect.

In 2009, as a result of the memorandum, the new "open government" movement began a flutter of social networking on behalf of all branches of government. The executive, legislative, and judicial branches actively experimented with social media tools such as Facebook, MySpace, and Twitter. Federal agencies were using recently developed technologies with sophisticated capabilities for interaction with individuals. These technologies allowed agencies and the public to publish comments and to add other forms of media on agency-sponsored, third party social media sites (Wilshusen 2010).

The passage of time has shown that using social media to share information has developed and been integrated into the methodologies in which the government uses to reach out to the community. The dissimulation of information is no longer reliant

P. L. Webb (✉)
Reference and Electronic Resources Government Documents Librarian,
Government Documents Department, University of South Alabama,
5901 USA Drive North, Mobile, AL 36688-0002, USA
e-mail: pwebb@jaguar1.usouthal.edu

C. G. Reddick and S. K. Aikins (eds.), *Web 2.0 Technologies and Democratic Governance*, Public Administration and Information Technology 1, DOI: 10.1007/978-1-4614-1448-3_3, © Springer Science+Business Media New York 2012

upon newspapers, anchormen, or Web-based news sites. Social media, especially microblogging, make these once fast and reliable methods of gathering information appear inert. Twitter and other microblogging platforms are able to broadcast the latest news in a simple text format. In limiting the character count of messages, they can be delivered quickly; thus providing a powerful means to receive government information and network with others who share a similar interest.

Instant feedback is a secondary factor associated with microblogging that cannot be achieved with traditional methods of broadcasting information. The follower, the one who posts and reads a microblog, is able to reply to the information posted instantly. They can request more material, ask a question, or post a comment with their perspective, developing a new form of political interaction. In a quest to meet the public where they are, Twitter, a microblogging tool, is becoming popular among politicians and government agencies to connect with constituents. It is helping to erase the boundaries between the citizens and the government. "Traditional forms of diplomacy still dominate, but twenty first century statecraft is not mere corporate rebranding—swapping tweets for broadcasts. It represents a shift in form and strategy—a way to amplify traditional diplomatic efforts, develop tech-based policy solutions and encourage cyberactivism" (Lichtenstein 2010).

GovTwit, the world's largest Twitter directory, representing all facets of government, lists over 1,200 government agencies using microblogging as a form of communication and the number has continued to grow (The List/Agencies 2011).

"As of May 2011, 13 % of online adults use the status update service Twitter. That represents a significant increase from the 8 % of online adults who identified themselves as Twitter users the first time we asked our "stand-alone" question about Twitter adoption in November 2010" (Smith 2011).

Since many federal agencies are actively using the silicon world of social media and communication, my goal is to analyze organization policies and best practices that the government has specified for microblogging. In most cases they will refer to one specific microblogging tool, Twitter. As a social media form of communication, Twitter has shown itself to be an excellent public relations platform designed to keep citizens of the United States and other countries informed.

The purpose of this analysis is to answer two questions. First, which government agencies have policies and best practices applying directly or indirectly to microblogging? Second, where can other agencies learn from existing policies to use as a guide to build their own?

Most government agencies' policies and best practices have guidelines that only address social media, a general term used to cover all forms of online interaction. This is a key element for investigation. It is my view that instead of combining policies or suggestions for all social interaction tools under the term "social media", each tool should have their own developed guidelines. While an interesting topic, the focus of this paper concerns only microblogging, including Twitter. Other forms of social media should be considered for future research projects.

3.2 Literature Review

During the early days of social media technology, uncertainty of the directions they would develop simplified regulations. However, microblogging has developed into a mainstream governmental activity that should now receive individual treatment in regard to policy and regulation. Layne and Lee stated that e-government is an evolutionary phenomenon and therefore e-government policies and practices should be derived and implemented accordingly (Layne and Lee 2001). Like e-government, microblogging has evolved to the point where such considerations need to be made.

Since a current analysis of government agency policies and microblogging does not exist, we must look to the past to find similar occurrences. Is there another instance when the use of a technology developed before a policy for the technology was considered? In my research, a similar occurrence shows up in the last part of the twentieth and the early part of the twenty-first centuries. Government agencies were beginning to develop "e-government" and Web sites for communication with the public, but not with any sort of unified order. The exponential growth of federal Web sites outpaced federal information management policy guidelines (Eschenfelder and Beachboard 1997). The lack of policy and guidelines for federal agency Web sites was addressed in academic articles at the time.

Based on their observations, Layne and Lee reported that e-government was unmanageable and online transactional services were in their infant stages (Layne and Lee 2001). Until adequate framework becomes available, they proposed a four-stage growth model for e-government: (1) cataloging (2) transaction, (3) vertical integration, and (4) horizontal integration. Their analysis further showed that three issues were fundamental for government consideration if they wanted to evolve into efficient and effective e-government that supports citizens' demands: (1) universal access, (2) privacy and confidentiality, and (3) citizen focus in government management. These three considerations still exist and can be applied to the development of microblogging policies.

Eschenfelder and Beachboard discussed the need to assess US federal government Web sites, showing a concern for federal agency policies (Eschenfelder and Beachboard 1997). They asked a number of important questions regarding policy and federal Web sites. Were new policies needed, or should federal information policies be updated to more realistically reflect the capabilities of this new medium? If so, in what areas were new or updated policies more urgently required? The authors believed that careful consideration should be given to the purpose, structure, and operation of federal Web sites and that federal information policy should be re-examined. The early conclusion to this study suggested that existing policies needed to be modified to promote the most effective use of the Web to disseminate federal information. Policy makers also needed to think through the full implications of existing federal information policies and attempt to assess whether the consequences of these policies actually support the underlying social values as intended.

Wang, Bretschneider, and Gant evaluated e-government services using a different approach; they turned their focus on the citizen. Like the two previous studies, the goal was to develop an evaluation of e-government services using methods derived from analysis (Wang et al. 2005). This study made two important contributions: (1) to provide a general evaluation framework for Web-based e-government services that would be from the perspective of the public and would help answer why Web design leads to success or failure in service delivery, (2) develop instruments to be used with the evaluation model in the real e-government context. The proposed model addressed performance, which is viewed as the transaction between the information user, the task the user was trying to complete, and information itself in regard to the task.

In addition to recognizing the need for the development of policy evaluation methods, e-government policy and assessing government agency Web sites; a fourth perspective concerning transparency was considered when working with information and communication technologies (ICTs) and government agencies.

Research was focused on relationships between information and communication technology use and government transparency, the ability of ICTs embedded within e-government initiative to create a culture of transparency and barriers that ICTs initiatives presented regarding transparency (Bertot et al. 2010). Conference proceedings highlighted blogs, Wikis, Social Networking and Media-sharing, Microblogging, and Mashups as the means for citizens to scrutinize the government. The same proceeding addressed the underlying concept of social media, actively including the user in the process, reflected in the ethos of many e-government transparency efforts even when the social media approaches were not directly incorporated. Numerous transparency efforts relied on citizens collectively monitoring government officials to prevent corruption. People who used social media to communicate and made their wants and needs known to government agencies were the ones following on Twitter.

Bertot, Jaeger, Munson, and Glaisyer conducted a study of social media technology and government transparency that was concerned with policy (Bertot et al. 2010). They ascertained that social media technologies had the ability to transform authority by increasing a government's transparency and its interaction with citizens. This paper provided a selective overview of key issues, questions, and best practice government initiatives regarding social media technologies. They further discussed how this was not a new notion; the Clinton and Bush administration both focused on fostering citizen services through more effective processes and technology. The criteria the authors suggested included democratic participation and engagement, co-production, crowdsourcing solutions and innovations, transparency and accountability. There were examples given of social media and public engagement that fell under the categories of government information and services along with public engagement.

Bertot, Jaeger, Munson, and Glaisyer also pointed out new democratic models of administration with the use of social media. They contended that there needed to be a rethinking of traditional boundaries among individuals, the public, communities, and levels of government. New models included local reporting, local problem-solving, new spheres of authority, redefinition of government processes and operations, and a shift in objectives of participation. Other boundaries they foresaw the need to change concerned redefining governmental boundaries, incorporating participation into governing, a need for new policy structures, processes, frameworks and structures, and risks of polarization. In their conclusion, they listed a number of issues that needed to be further addressed. It is the goal of this paper to answer some of the questions proposed in relationship to microblogging. Questions of interest were: What policy structures and frameworks are necessary for government use of and interaction with social media technologies? How will social media policy change how policy is generally developed?

In considering barriers to social media and e-government transparency there will always be an aspect of disagreement and contention regarding policy. Dawes' paper was a conceptual and empirical exploration of the tensions inherent in the drive to increase openness and transparency in government by means of information access and dissemination (Dawes 2010). She lists three enduring tensions associated with public use of government information, (1) tension between comprehensiveness of the data and its understandability by non-technical oriented citizens, (2) tension between the desires to ensure usefulness of detailed data and to simultaneously protect the confidentiality of data subjects, and (3) the public need and desire to analyze and understand "global" data sets versus the reality that government data is not maintained as a global asset but rather is distributed across scores of organizations and policy domains, at all levels of government. Dawes suggests stewardship and usefulness as two simple principles to use as a framework for working through a variety of goals and challenges inherent in information-based transparency initiatives.

As regards digital access to government information and compliance with the Electronic Freedom of Information Act, (Electronic Freedom of Information Act Amendments of 1996) an analysis was conducted of the content of agencies' electronic reading rooms to determine whether they were compliant with the law (Oltmann et al. 2006). After the signing of the act there was discourse surrounding the EFOIA and many commentators assumed these amendments would improve citizen access to government information. The authors adopted a social informatics perspective to critically examine some of this discourse and found that many of the claims had not borne out in experience. One of the problems discovered with the law was that it provided little incentive for agencies to release information in a timely manner or even to release information at all. The study concluded with few Web sites meeting the legal content requirements according the FOIA. Since the Obama administration has passed the memorandum (Obama 2009) agencies appear to be a lot more relaxed in their sharing of information using social media technologies, such as Twitter. This could be due to the next generation of federal employee who is more familiar with technology. They may be more at ease with sharing data and therefore security is not such a concern. This is an interesting concept that could use further investigation.

Chadwick and May's study concerned the interaction between States and Citizens in the age of the Internet. It focused on three models of interaction, they were termed "managerial," "consultative", and "participatory" (Chadwick and May 2003). They undertook a comparative analysis of the United States, Britain, and the European Union of policy statements on the future role of ICTs in the national government. The examination pointed out policy innovations that soon became dependent upon the key values and discourses that framed them during their early phases. Of all the three models, the one of most interest was the managerial model. In this model of interaction, ICTs are largely seen as a quantitative improvement on previous technologies and increased accountability. This showed the need for guidance and policies in regard to ICTs; this includes social media technologies such as microblogging.

One analysis addressed the idea that e-government often came with a promise to improve public administration efficiency. However, it also had the potential to alter the traditional relationship between government and citizens by creating a new virtual government-and-citizen interface (Wong and Welch 2004). It suggested there were two major sources of change for accountability, (1) global pressure of information technology and (2) an indirect impact of change brought by the domestic context. The authors concluded that as Web-based technologies become widely available and affordable, e-government would become more policy driven than technology and economic driven. Public accountability expressed by e-government would become more and more a conscious policy choice that reflected both national and organizational characteristics. This conclusion is correct and applies to more than e-government. Social media technologies are now at the point where, pressured or not, they need to develop policies.

Those who work for government agencies must place top priority on national security and the position of their individual agency. They must be able to consider what information is to be shared with the public and what is to remain within the confines of the agency. Security can be challenging in a world where everything seems freely available on the Internet. A policy concerning security and protection of government information can be a simple way of safeguarding this sort of information. Security was a very important issue soon after the events of 9/11 and during the development of ICTs during the early part of the twenty-first century.

Lambrinoudakis, Gritzalis, Dridi, and Pernul realized that a rapid technological evolution could not be problem free (Lambrinoudakis et al. 2003). They recognized concerns in respect to the extent 'information security' and 'user privacy' could be ensured and raised. They suggested a new framework for identifying and organizing the security requirements that were common to all information systems that were utilized for the development of an integrated online e-government platform. They demonstrated the feasibility of such an approach by utilizing the 'Organizational Framework for the Security Requirements of e-government services' for identifying the (common) security requirements for an integrated online government service. They recognized that security would increase in necessity as users who accessed services began to view the information from virtually anywhere.

A variety of different ways information could be compromised is discussed in the paper, but the one of interest concerns the security requirements for an e-government platform. The classifications were: actors per service phase, risk levels, and security requirements. There was the interest in adopting protective measures that could effectively satisfy the identified security requirements. It further states that it was feasible to develop a uniform, but also generally applicable and easily expandable, security policy for e-government platforms. They concluded a policy could be built to support the actions needed.

A second study on national security and information rights presented the need to provide a policy, not for the national security, but for the information rights of the citizens (Caidi and Ross 2005). In their article, they advocated for bringing together what were disparate information issues under one label, namely, 'information rights.' Such information rights were to be viewed from a user-centered perspective and have the potential to provide an effective way to view current information issues as they related to policy, security, and civil liberties in the broader sense. They pointed out the lack of a comprehensive information policy from many federal agencies regarding Web sites and contracting out government information services to private firms as a hurdle to access to information. The conclusion was "information rights" must first be considered as more than just another concept but rather as a universally recognized body of rights similar to other accepted models and within the realm of human rights.

Dearstyne explained in his study that mismanagement of information was a central theme in understanding the vulnerability that left the United States open to the terrorist attack of 9/11/01 and the misread clues that led the United States and Great Britain into a war with Iraq (Dearstyne 2005) He listed five strategic approaches from an information management perspective that were very interesting. He suggested: (1) improve understanding of the strengths and limits of intelligence information, (2) intelligence work should draw more extensively on knowledge management and other information management techniques, (3) provide leadership to improve security agencies' information policies, (4) foster more careful, systematic, thoughtful analysis, and (5) actively promote information dissemination and sharing.

It is not uncommon for federal agencies to use technology before policy for that technology is developed. Despite this, policy does develop after the use of the technology in one form or another. It is time to analyze the policies and best practices that have developed for microblogging thus far and apply the knowledge learned to help all agencies develop guidelines to follow.

3.3 Method

Web site design was the closest analysis format discovered in relation to policies developed for microblogging. There were a variety of methodologies used to study policy in regard to Web site design for federal government agencies. These methodologies included the citizen-centric approach, the iterative design strategy, conceptual exploration, empirical exploration, and social informatics.

The focus of the research for this paper was to determine the policies and best practices US government agencies have for microblogging and the social media software that fall under this description. Since this analysis brought into question a number of established social assumptions concerning ICTs and the understanding of what 'information' represented, the author chose to use social informatics as the study design and developed a critical analysis of the material to focus on the associated professional training and discourses (Day 2007). "The critical orientation refers to examining ITs from perspectives that do not automatically and uncritically accept the goals and beliefs of the group that commission, design, or implement specific IT applications" (Kling 2002).

The population sampled in this study was federal agencies who practiced the use of microblogging social media tools. In addition, the author needed to find a comprehensive list of government agencies using social media, but not a current listing. This need was reflected in previous study that suggested policy did not develop until after the agencies had adopted and used the technology (Eschenfelder and Beachboard 1997). Using an older listing would ensure the agency had time to develop a social media or microblogging policy.

A number of resources were investigated to find a sample of government agencies that use social media. Web sites viewed included GovTwit (GovTwit), Listerious (U.S. Government), and Twitter Fan Wiki (Cousins 2010). However, the best sample of agencies using social media could be found in the Government Accountability Office's 2011 Report, "Social Media: Federal Agencies Need Policies and Procedures for Managing and Protecting Information They Access and Disseminate" (Wilshusen 2011). This report analyzed a sample of US government agencies and documented whether they had developed policies and procedures that guided use of social media as a whole including Facebook, Twitter, and YouTube in the overall numbers.

Agencies analyzed for this paper were Department of Agriculture (USDA), Department of Commerce, Department of Defense (DoD), Department of Education, Department of Energy, Department of Health and Human Services (HHS), Department of Homeland Security, Department of Housing and Urban Development (HUD), Department of the Interior, Department of Justice, Department of Labor, Department of State (State Deparment), Department of Transportation, Department of the Treasury, Department of Veterans Affairs, Environmental Protection Agency (EPA), General Services Administration (GSA), National Aeronautics and Space Administration (NASA), National Science Foundation, Office of Personnel Management, Small Business Administration (SBA), Social Security Administration(SSA), U.S. Agency for International Development (USAID).

The search for the social media policy for each of these agencies began by using the new official US Government search engine, www.search.usa.gov. The search was limited to the name of the agency, the abbreviated name of the agency and the term, "social media policy". In an effort to exhaust all possibilities, the search engine, Google was utilized for a general search using the name of the agency and the term, "social media policy". A final search of each agency Web site was conducted using the same terminology. The rationale for finding data in this format

Table 3.1 Microblogging policies and government agencies

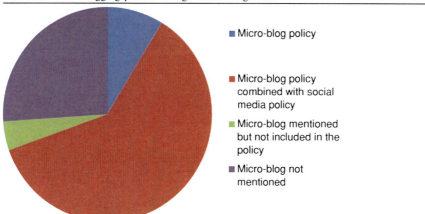

related to the discussing in the literature review that agencies tend to wait till after the use of a technology to analyze use and develop a policy. These meant policies would be neither centralized nor organized. The use of modern research tools was the best method of finding what policies currently do and do not exist.

As a basis for discussing these findings, it was necessary to search for what agencies had microblogging policies and how they were treated in those same policies (Table 3.1). All agencies referenced included blogs or microblogs in one form or another in their social media policies. It is an observation that all agencies studied mentioned "social media" in either their official policy, privacy policy, or comment policy. The strict exclusion of social media technologies and the United States government appears to be an issue of the past.

3.4 Results

In an analysis of the agencies previously listed, there is the mention of blogging but not all agencies addressed microblogging. In addition, policies that were found were not in the same type of agency document and were not always referred to as "policy" or microblogging but the intent was still obvious. Policy guidelines were found in privacy policies, comment policies, open government plans, transparency initiatives, directives, assessments, Web sites, and a variety of other forms of agency documentations. It is noted that policies for social media services as well as those for microblogging were not in similar locations, making the discovering of these policies a challenge.

The initial question asked in this paper was to find what government agencies have polices and best practices applying directly or indirectly to microblogging. In the analysis of the 23 agencies reviewed, the author discovered only two agencies with a policy specifically focused on microblogging: The Department of Health and Human Services (2010) and the Small Business Administration (2011). Each agency provides advice to when their agency should use Twitter. The HHS provides an extensive guide on how the agency should communicate with the public, how not to use the service, how to treat content, how to plan for 'tweeting' on their behalf, and the best uses for Twitter (Department of Health and Human Services 2010). The Small Business Administration has only a privacy policy that focuses specifically on Twitter (Small Business Administration)

Fourteen of the agencies studied included microblogging in their social media policy and discussed Twitter specifically. These agencies include the Department of Commerce (2011), Department of Defense (Deputy Secretary of Defense 2011), Department of Energy (2011), Department of Homeland Security (McShea 2009), Department of Housing and Urban Development (2011), Department of the Interior (2011), Department of Justice (2009), Department of the State (Smith 2011), Department of Transportation (2010), Treasury (2011), Department of Veterans Affairs (2011), Environmental Protection Agency (2011), General Services Administration (2011), and NASA (Hopkins 2011). The EPA provides a very detailed policy for communicating with the public using social media and microblogs (Environmental Protection Agency 2011a , b , c , d). The Department of Transportation (2010) and the Department of Interior (Lee-Ashley 2010), Department of Veterans Affairs (2011) mentions blogs and microblogs in their social media policy concerning their employees and how to communicate online on behalf of the agencies. The weakest area in regarding microblogs with this group seems to concern the security policies.

In analyzing the use of microblogging in agencies there are agencies that mention microblogging but do not include it specifically in its social media policy. Only one agency appeared to fall in this category, the National Science Foundation. The only mention of the microblog tool, Twitter, is in the Chief FOIA Officer Report (National Science Foundation 2010).

Finally, there are those agency policies that do not mention microblogs at all. These six agencies are the Department of Agriculture (2011), Department of Education (2010), Department of Labor (2010), Office of Personnel Management, Social Security Administration and the U.S. Agency for International Development (2010). These agencies mention how they use their blogs and microblogs, but do not provide any guidance to their employees or to those who follow their "tweets."

3.5 Discussion

Each of the agencies analyzed developed their social media policy after the use of social media became a part of their agency. The initial push to include social media, including Twitter, in the standard government agency policies was not a consideration until the 2009 Open Government Directive (Obama 2009) issued by the Obama administration. Many of the agencies followed this directive by creating or modifying their social media policy.

   While research has shown social media policy developing into the horizontal integration of government agencies, references to individual social media tools are still in the transaction stage, but consideration of this need to develop seems to be taking hold in some agencies analyzed (Layne and Lee 2001). Currently, only two agencies have policies specifically for microblogging, but with time and the increasing need to regulate social media and each with their own unique usage formats, some sort of guidance will develop. The Department of Health and Human Services has the most detailed guidance and use policy for Twitter and is an excellent resource for other agencies to view concerning when to use Twitter, approval for tweets, and meeting the 508 accessibility requirements (Department of Health and Human Services). The Small Business Administration only has a Twitter policy concerning privacy issues, but it is extensive and applicable to other agencies (Small Business Administration).

   In analyzing policies concerning microblogging there is a very obvious need to update current policies to address microblogging (Eschenfelder and Beachboard 1997). Out of 23 agencies reviewed, only two addressed microblogging. The rest were either combined under the term social media or did not have a policy. In analyzing microblogging as a part of the agencies that do have a social media policy, in most cases those agencies only need to separate the literature they currently have according to the social media tool, in this case microblogs, and update the material. Those agencies who do not have a microblog policy can review those that do and develop successful guidelines.

   There is a need for microblogs posted on Twitter and an evaluation of the citizens' response to the information. This requires a certain measure of diplomacy on behalf of the agency employee. (Bertot et al. 2010). The tensions can quickly develop because of a lack of policy (Dawes 2010; Wong and Welch 2004). Among those tensions is a lack of transparency and interaction with the citizens. The development of policy guidelines will in turn develop the comfort agency employees need to know what information to post on a microblog. Interaction with citizens over the information posted will reduce tensions.

3.6 Implications

These findings are a step further into integrating microblogging and other social media policies into the standard policy for agencies and their unified communication with citizens. Hopefully, it will become obvious that each type of social media tool needs to develop their own individual policy and not be included under the sum total heading of "social media." Each tool is unique and therefore should be treated as such.

References

Bertot, J. C., Jaeger, P. T., & Grimes, J. M (2010). Crowd-Sourcing Transparency: ICTs, Social Media, and Government Transparency Initiatives. *11th Annual International Conference on Digital Government Research.* Puebla, Mexico.

Bertot, J. C., Jaeger, P. T., Munson, S., & Glaisyer, T. (2010). *Engaging the Public in Open Government: Social Media Technology and Policy for Government Transparency.*

Caidi, N., & Ross, A. (2005). Information Rights and National Security. *Government Information Quaterly,* 663–684.

Chadwick, A., & May, C. (2003). Interaction Between States and Citizens in the Age of the Internet: "e-Government" in the United States, Britain, and the European Union. *Governance: An International Journal of Policy, Administration, and Institutions,* 271–300.

Cousins, M. (2010, June). *USGovernment.* Retrieved September 13, 2011, from Twitter Fan Wiki Web site: http://twitter.pbworks.com/w/page/1779986/USGovernment

Dawes, S. (2010). Stewardship and Usefulness: Policy Principles for Information-based Transparency. *Government Information Quarterly,* 377–383.

Day, R. (2007). Kling and the "Critical": Social Informatics and Critical Informatics. *Journal of the American Society for Information Science and Technology,* 575–582.

Dearstyne, B. (2005). Fighting Terrorism, Making War: Critical Insights in the Management of Information and Intelligence. *Government Information Quarterly,* 170–186.

Department of Agriculture (USDA). (n.d.). *Privacy Policy.* Retrieved September 24, 2011, from Department of Agriculture Web site: http://www.usda.gov/wps/portal/usda/usdahome?navid=PRIVACY_POLICY&navtype=FT

Department of Agriculture. (n.d.). *USDA Comment Policy.* Retrieved September 24, 2011, from Department of Agriculture Web site: http://www.usda.gov/wps/portal/usda/usdahome?contentid=comment_policy.xml&contentidonly=true

Department of Agriculture. (2010, February 24). *USDA Information Quality Activities.* Retrieved September 24, 2011, from Department of Agriculture: http://www.ocio.usda.gov/qi_guide/index.html

Department of Commerce. (2011, June). *Open Government Plan Version 1.5.* Retrieved September 25, 2011, from Department of Commerce Web site: http://open.commerce.gov/sites/default/files/DOC%20Open%20Government%20Plan%20v%201_5%20Final%202011-06-30.pdf

Department of Education. (2010). *Open Government Plan.* Washington D.C.: Department of Education.

Department of Energy. (n.d.). *Social Media.* Retrieved September 26, 2011, from Department of Energy Web site: http://energy.gov/about-us/web-policies/social-media

Department of Health and Human Services. (2010, May 3). *HHS Guidance on When and How to Engage over New Media Platforms.* Retrieved September 26, 2011, from Department of Health and Human Services Web site:http://newmedia.hhs.gov/resources/hhscnm_guidance_on_when_and_how_to_engage_over_new_media_platforms_05032010.pdf

Department of Health and Human Services. (n.d.). *HHS Twitter Guidance.* Retrieved September 26, 2011, from HHS Center for New Media Web site: http://newmedia.hhs.gov/resources/twitter_guidance.html

Department of Housing and Urban Development. (n.d.). *Privacy Policy.* Retrieved September 28, 2011, from Department of Housing and Urban Development: http://portal.hud.gov/hudportal/HUD?src=/privacy_policy

Department of Housing and Urban Development. (n.d.). *Transparency Initiatives.* Retrieved September 28, 2011, from Department of Housing and Urban Development Web site: http://portal.hud.gov/hudportal/HUD?src=/open/plan/transparency-initiatives

Department of Justice. (2009). *Privacy Impact Assessment for Third-Party Social Web Services.* Washington D.C.: Department of Justice.

Department of Labor. (2010). *Open Government Plan Version 1.0*. Washington D.C.: Department of Labor.

Department of Labor. (n.d.). *Privacy and Security Statement*. Retrieved September 28, 2011, from Department of Labor Web site: http://dol.gov/dol/privacynotice.htm

Department of Veterans Affairs. (2011, June 28). *Use of Web-based Collaboration Technologies*. Retrieved October 3, 2011, from Department of Verterans Affairs Web site: http://www.va.gov/vapubs/viewpublication.asp?pub_id=551

Department of Veterans Affairs. (2011, August 16). *VA Publishes Social Media Policy*. Retrieved October 3, 2011, from The Department of Veterans Affairs Web site: http://www.va.gov/opa/pressrel/pressrelease.cfm?id=2150

Deputy Secretary of Defense. (2011). *Directive-Type Memorandum (DTM) 09-026—Responsible and Effective Use of Internet-based Capabilities*. Washington D.C.: Department of Defense.

Electronic Freedom of Information Act Amendments of 1996. (n.d.). Retrieved September 10, 2011, from Thomas Web site: http://thomas.loc.gov/cgi-bin/query/F?c104:1:./temp/~c104OVIIWe:e5787

Environmental Protection Agency. (n.d.). *Privacy and Security Notice*. Retrieved October 3, 2011, from Environmental Protection Agency: http://www.epa.gov/epahome/usenotice.htm

Environmental Protection Agency. (2011a). *Representing EPA Online Using Social Media*. Washington D.C.: Environmental Protection Agency.

Environmental Protection Agency. (2011b). *Should I Respond Online On EPA's Behalf?* Washington D.C.: Environmental Protection Agency.

Environmental Protection Agency. (2011c). *Using Social Media Internally at EPA*. Washington D.C.: Environmental Protection Agency.

Environmental Protection Agency. (2011d). *Using Social Media to Communicate with the Public*. Washington D.C.: Environmental Protection Agency.

Eschenfelder, K. R., & Beachboard, J. C. (1997). Assessing U.S. Federal Government Websites. *Government Information Quarterly*, 173–190.

GovTwit. (n.d.). Retrieved September 13, 2011, from GovTwit Web site: http://govtwit.com/ Hopkins, J. *Social Networking Tools and Web 2.0—Appropriate Use of Web Technologies*. Washington D.C. : National Aeronautics and Space Administration.

Kling, R. (2002, 12 3). *Critical Professional Education about Information and Communications Technologies and Social Life*. Retrieved 9 10, 2011, from Center for Social Informatics Web site: https://scholarworks.iu.edu/dspace/bitstream/handle/2022/168/WP02-06B.html?sequence=1

Lambrinoudakis, C., Gritzalis, S., Dridi, F., & Pernul, G. (2003). Security Requirements for e-government services: A Methodological Approach for Developing a Common PKI-based Security Policy. *Computer Communications*, 1873–1883.

Layne, K., & Lee, J. (2001). Developing Fully Functional E-government: A Four Stage Model. *Government Information Quarterly*, 122–136.

Lee-Ashley, M. (2010, November 18). *Notices—Social Media Policy*. Retrieved September 29, 2011, from Department of the Interior: http://www.doi.gov/notices/Social-Media-Policy.cfm

Lichtenstein, J. (2010, July 16). *Digital Diplomacy*. Retrieved July 13, 2011, from New York Times Magazine Web site: http://www.nytimes.com/2010/07/18/magazine/18web2-0-t.html

McShea, K. (2009). *Government 2.0: Privacy and Best Practices Report on the DHS Privacy Office Public Workshop*. Washington D.C. : Department of Homeland Security.

National Science Foundation. (2010). Chief FOIA Officer Report for 2010. Retrieved October 3, 2011, from the National Science Foundation, http://www.nsf.gov/pubs/2011/ogc11002/ogc11002.pdf

Obama, B. (2009, January 21). *Transparency and Open Government*. Retrieved July 13, 2011, from White House Web site: http://www.whitehouse.gov/the_press_office/TransparencyandOpenGovernment/

Oltmann, S. M., Rosenbaum, H., & Hara, N. (2006). Digital Access to Government Information: To What Extent are Agencies in Compliance with EFOIA? *69th Annual Meeting of the American Society for Information Science and Technology*. Autin, Texas: E-prints in Library and Information Science.

Small Business Administration. (n.d.). *SBA Privacy Policy: Twitter*. Retrieved October 3, 2011, from Small Business Administration Web site: http://www.sba.gov/about-sba-info/21331

Smith, A. (2011). *13% of Online Adults Use Twitter*. Washington, D.C. : Pew Research Center.

State Department. (2010). *U.S. Department of State Open Government Plan*. Washington D.C. : Department of State.

The List/Agencies. (2011, 9 10). Retrieved 9 10, 2011, from GovTwit Web site: http://govtwit.com/list/all/tags/agencies

Treasury Department. (2011, April 1). *Site Policies and Notices*. Retrieved September 29, 2011, from Treasury Department Web site: http://www.treasury.gov/SitePolicies/Pages/privacy.aspx

U.S. Agency for International Development. (n.d.). *Privacy and Security*. Retrieved October 3, 2011, from U.S. Agency for International Development Web site: http://www.usaid.gov/privacy.html

U.S. Department of Transportation. (2010). *U.S. Department of Transportation Open Government Plan Version 1.2*. Washington D.C. : Department of Transportation.

U.S. General Services Administration. (2011, June 28). *Chapter 2. What is Social Media?* Retrieved October 3, 2011, from U.S. General Services Administration: http://www.gsa.gov/portal/content/250041

U.S. General Services Administration. (2011). *GSA's Guide to Official Use of Social Media*. Washington D.C. : U.S. General Services Administration.

U.S. General Services Administration. *Social Media Comments Policy*. Washington D.C. : U.S. General Services Administration.

U.S. Government. (n.d.). Retrieved September 13, 2011, from Listorious Web site: http://listorious.com/GOVsites/u-s-federal-government

Wang, L., Bretschneider, S., & Gant, J. (2005). Evaluating Web-based e-government services with a citizen-centric approach. *38th Hawaii International Conference on System Sciences*.

Wilshusen, G. C. (2010, July 22). *Information Management Challenges in Federal Agencies' Use of Web 2.0 Technologies*. Retrieved July 13, 2011, from Government Accountability Office Web site: http://www.gao.gov/new.items/d10872t.pdf

Wilshusen, G. (2011, June 28). *Social Media: Federal Agencies Need Policies and Procedures for Managing and Protecting Information They Access and Disseminate*. Retrieved September 12, 2011, from Government Accountability Office Web site: http://www.gao.gov/new.items/d11605.pdf

Wong, W., & Welch, E. (2004). Does E-Government Promote Accountability? A Comparative Analysis of Website Openness and Government Accountability. *Governance: An International Journal of Policy, Administration, and Institutions*, 275–297.

Chapter 4
The Use of Web 2.0 to Transform Public Services Delivery: The Case of Spain

Carmen Caba Pérez, Manuel Pedro Rodríguez Bolívar
and Antonio Manuel López Hernández

4.1 Introduction

Increasingly, connected citizens and stakeholders are asking governments to deliver services more rapidly and efficiently (COMNET-IT 2002; IDA 2011; Peedu 2011). In the previous years, European Union governments have been undertaking a specific strategy focusing on public e-Services development (Reggi and Scicchitano 2011). Terms such as access, utilization, availability, and coverage are often used interchangeably in reflections on whether people are receiving the services they need. The implementation of information and communication technologies (ICTs) has helped meet this need and has favored the process of reform and modernization within public administrations (Chan and Chow 2007).

Nonetheless, although there has been gradual progress in e-Government initiatives over the past decade, most of these have focused on putting key services

The research reported in this chapter has been supported by the Andalusia Regional Government through the excellence project "Improving the management, transparency and participation in Local Governments through The Web 1.0 and Web 2.0" (P10-SEJ-06628).

C. Caba Pérez (✉)
Dtpo de Dirección y Gestión de Empresas, University of Almería,
Cañada de San Urbano s/n, 04120 Almería, Spain
e-mail: ccaba@ual.es

M. P. Rodríguez Bolívar · A. M. López Hernández
Dpto de Economía Financiera y Contabilidad, Facultad de Ciencias Económicas y
Empresariales, University of Granada, Campus Universitario de la Cartuja, Granada, Spain
e-mail: manuelp@ugr.es

A. M. López Hernández
e-mail: alopezh@ugr.es

C. G. Reddick and S. K. Aikins (eds.), *Web 2.0 Technologies and Democratic Governance*, Public Administration and Information Technology 1, DOI: 10.1007/978-1-4614-1448-3_4, © Springer Science+Business Media New York 2012

online and publishing websites for government and its agencies. It was based on HTML, which is a static language that simply outlines what a page should look like on-screen. In this regard, an evolution of e-services has been necessary to meet efficiently the needs of stakeholders. The evolution of e-services has been described by the United Nations, pointing out four main stages of online service development (United Nations 2010). In this regard, countries typically begin with an emerging online presence with simple websites, progress to an enhanced state with deployment of multimedia content and two-way interaction, advance to a transactional level with many services provided online and governments' soliciting citizen input on matters of public policy, and finally to a connected web of integrated functions, widespread data sharing, and routine consultation with citizens using social networking and related tools (United Nations 2010).

Therefore, strengthening service delivery has been seen as a key element in public administrations to improve their transparency and accountability. Accordingly, this simplistic model is giving way to a more personalized, outcome-driven, participative, and collaborative model (Table 4.1).

Web 2.0 technologies (Web 2.0) have the potential to change the way government delivers services and its relationship with the public. Among the several ways that Web 2.0 can provide added value to public service organizations are the possibility of enabling more effective social networking, citizens' engagement and collaboration with the community, the provision of valuable Internet applications to make information and services more personalized, faster, easier to use and deliverable, the possibility of enabling effective collaboration and teamwork, and the provision of a development tool for internal staff that offers higher productivity than the Web alone can provide (Accenture 2009).

The use of Web 2.0 applications in the public sector will enable a change in the roles played by users, providing a platform for provider–user interaction, in contrast to non-interactive websites where users can only passively view information (United Nations 2010). In the Web 2.0 era, users have become important actors in almost all aspects of online services (Huijboom et al. 2009) and are expected to provide insight and intelligence that will improve public services. The specific benefits of users taking a proactive role are the improvement of the accessibility and personalization of certain public services (Huijboom et al. 2009) and that this makes government more simple, user-oriented, transparent, accountable, participative, inclusive, joined-up, and networked (Osimo 2008).

Nevertheless, history shows that change is unlikely to happen without the engagement of civil servants (European Commission 2009). If government employees are to have an active presence online, basic Web skills should also be developed such as an understanding of infrastructure tools like blogs, wikis, and microblogs, along with writing skills and online content creation. Therefore, as well as motivation, initiatives to foster literacy and IT skills are needed for citizens in general and civil servants in particular, to ensure active participation and maximum benefits from Web 2.0-based public services (European Commission 2009).

Table 4.1 Differences between Government 1.0 and Government 2.0

Dimension	Government 1.0	Government 2.0
Operating model	• Hierarchical • Rigid	• Networked • Collaborative • Flexible
New models of service delivery	• One-size-fits-all • Monopoly • Single channel	• Personalized • Choice-based • Multi-channel
Performance	• Input-oriented • Closed	• Outcome-driven • Transparent
Decision making	• Spectator	• Participative

Source Deloitte (2008)

In addition, success on a political level is more and more related to the communication ability of managers in e-World (e-Government Academy 2006). In fact, the results of recent surveys made by the e-Governance Academy indicate that although the relevant infrastructure and also quite often the necessary communication tools are already available, there is a low e-Service penetration because top managers do not yet realize that this infrastructure needed for communication and for building e-Services is present (e-Government Academy 2006). Also, up to now, the low penetration of e-Services might be due to the negative perception of public sector e-Service users (TNS Emor 2010), because they believe that e-Services have not helped them to obtain their desired information or answer faster, saved money since they have heightened expectations based on the integration of the Internet into their everyday life and work (Baumgarten and Chui 2009).

Therefore, Government 2.0 is more than simply the adoption of Web 2.0 tools by government. It is about recognizing that conventional governments are unable to address society's challenges alone. To seize the opportunities offered by Government 2.0, the existing public service culture of hierarchical control and direction must change radically, to encourage and reward engagement. Government 2.0 is also a philosophy and a culture that reflects society's new way of interacting and communicating, and one that governments must accept if they wish to keep up (Goldsmith and Eggers 2004).

In addition, Web 2.0 technologies also involve some risks, for example, low levels of participation, or participation restricted to an elite, the low quality of contributions, additional "noise", a loss of control due to excessive transparency, destructive behavior by users, the manipulation of content by interested parties, and privacy infringements (Osimo 2008). In this latter respect, a permission-based system can enable citizens to exercise informational self-determination by applying their online privacy preferences, both as consumers and as creators (Cavoukian 2009). In this regard, legal frameworks appear to be coming under increasing pressure, as current legislation is not keeping up with the burgeoning process of content creation (Huijboom et al. 2009).

Despite the great significance of the future implementation of Web 2.0 technologies in public administration, little research has been done to analyze the use of these technologies to reform public sector service delivery. Over the past few years, only the governments of New Zealand, the United States, and the United Kingdom have shown a strong commitment to integrating Web 2.0 tools into their public governance (Government 2.0 taskforce 2009).

This chapter makes three main contributions: (a) first, we analyze whether, in Spain, regional governments are making use of Web 2.0 applications, such as blogs, Facebook, Twitter, etc., to deliver more personalized, efficient, and participative public sector services; (b) taking into account the importance of the use of Web 2.0 technologies in the delivery of public sector services, we analyze the factors underlying the greater or lesser development of these technologies in public administrations; (c) finally, as an example, we consider the use of social media in eight main public sector services rendered by Spanish regional governments.

As noted previously, this chapter focuses on Spain, and on Spanish regional governments in particular. This approach could be of interest, in view of the legislative reform policies applied to administrative structures in Spain in the 1990s (Gallego and Barzelay 2010), the managerial devolution process implemented in this country (Bastida and Benito 2006), and the rapid introduction of new technologies by these regional governments (Rodríguez et al. 2007). In addition, recent studies indicate that 83 % of Internet users in Spain use some type of social network (Orange Foundation 2011), which could indicate that these citizens are used to utilize these new technologies and could make use of e-Services if regional Governments had introduced Web 2.0 applications.

In short, the aim of this chapter is to determine whether regional governments in Spain have introduced Web 2.0 applications as a tool to improve their accountability and to better meet citizens' needs by providing more personalized public sector services, analyzing this matter not only from a descriptive point of view but also examining factors that are crucial to the use of these applications in the delivery of public sector services by public administrations. To achieve this aim, we analyze whether regional governments in Spain have introduced Web 2.0 technologies in order to personalize public sector delivery and to improve access to and the quality of public sector services.

The rest of this chapter is organized as follows: the next section provides an overview of public policies and legal frameworks at a regional public administration level in Spain. Section 4.3 analyzes how regional governments in Spain are applying the introduction of Web 2.0 technologies. Another question analyzed is that of the main determinants for using Web 2.0 tools to deliver public sector services. In particular, this empirical research examines the particularities of Web 2.0 implementation as a new strategy for innovation in the management of public sector services in terms of improving efficiency and of enhancing interaction with citizens, as part of an ongoing modernization of public sector administrations in Spain. Finally, our main conclusions are presented in Sect. 4.4.

4.2 Public Policies and Legal Frameworks for Web 2.0 Technologies in Regional Public Administration in Spain

According to the results of the United Nations e-Government Survey 2010 (United Nations 2010), governments involve their citizens for feedback and consultation via their websites, and so most such sites contain polls, surveys, comment buttons, or other means of reaction. However, this is believed to be just the tip of the iceberg, and Web 2.0 could enable citizens to have a direct impact on public administrations.

The survey figures show that Europe accounts for 51 % of the countries with the highest uptake of e-participation, followed by Asia with 29 %, the USA with 14 %, and Oceania with 6 %. South Korea is the leading country in the e-participation index, followed by Australia, Spain, and New Zealand.

In the framework of the European Union, many initiatives have been taken to regulate and coordinate the actions of Member States in order to facilitate digital convergence and to meet the challenges of the Information Society. The implementation of the first European e-Government Action Plan (2006–2010) has led to governments of all EU Member States exchanging information about good practice, and has resulted in a number of large-scale pilot projects which are developing concrete solutions for rolling out cross-border e-Government services (ICT PSP from PIC 2011). The second e-Government Action Plan (2010–2015) is intended to meet the targets set out at the 5th Ministerial e-Government Conference, in the Malmö Declaration. According to this ambitious vision, by 2015 European public administrations will be "recognized for being open, flexible and collaborative in their relations with citizens and businesses. They will use eGovernment to increase their efficiency and effectiveness and to constantly improve public services in a way that caters for users' different needs and maximizes public value, thus supporting the transition of Europe to a leading knowledge-based economy".

Let us now focus on the situation in Spain. As described in the 2010 e-Government survey (United Nations 2010), the Spanish public administrations are beginning, albeit slowly, to make use of interactive tools to promote dialog and receive feedback and input from citizens, as well as to provide information and services online. However, while Spain is ahead of many other countries in this respect, e-participation has been less fully developed, being mainly linked to providing information, responding to queries and, to a much lesser extent, decision taking.

Beyond doubt, the definitive impetus to the inclusion of ICTs in the various levels of government—national, regional, and local—both in terms of their relations with citizens and in their internal management, was made by Act 11/2007 of 22 June, governing Citizens' Electronic Access to Public Services (LAECSP), which guaranteed this right to all citizens.

LAECSP is a fundamental measure to encourage e-Government. The most interesting aspect of this legislation is that, apart from the general principles, the legal framework, and the rules and criteria set out, certain specific rights of individual citizens are established, and these automatically become an obligation for the administration. Therefore, the various levels of public administration will have to develop a wide range of Web-delivered services.

Nevertheless, full implementation of the LAECSP—scheduled for 2010—has been uneven, because not all authorities have put the same emphasis on developing ICTs and because in the current economic climate, it is hard to make the financial effort required for the technological infrastructure needed.

Having achieved Spain some of the goals of the first European e-Government Action Plan (2006–2010) through the LAECSP, it has been needed a new strategy for the next few years the "National Strategy 2015" to reinforce the transformation to meet the goals in the Digital Agenda and face Europe's three main challenges in the short term: economic crisis, environmental degradation, and an aging population.

Table 4.2 presents the legislation approved in the Spanish autonomous regions, in most cases following the entry into force of the LAECSP. Nevertheless, not all regional governments in Spain followed the legal requirements and, therefore, a greater risk of digital gap exists between citizens depending on geographical location rather than communications infrastructure—a gap between those governments that have not focused on LAECSP.

4.3 Empirical Research: The Use of Web 2.0 by Regional Governments in Spain

4.3.1 Sample Selection

As noted above, little research has been carried out to analyze the use of Web 2.0 by public administrations in the delivery of public sector services. The empirical research presented in this chapter focuses on Spain in view of the legislative reforms applied to administrative structures in this country in the 1990s (Gallego and Barzelay 2010) and the managerial devolution process implemented in this country (Bastida and Benito 2006). (see Fig. 4.1)

Although all governmental entities within the Spanish public administration have been making significant efforts in e-Government, especially in the past few years with the promotion of a policy of information transparency following the budgetary stability law of 2002, regional governments in Spain have also introduced new technologies to deliver public sector services and to interact with citizens (Rodríguez et al. 2007).

The 17 regional governments play an important role in Spanish public administration, producing social goods and services, especially in educational and health care services, developing infrastructures. Accordingly, they bear a large proportion of the budgetary expenses. Thus, in 2009, regional governments

Table 4.2 Legislation by Spanish regional governments on ICTs and eGovernment

Autonomous Region	Legislation	Description
Andalusia	Act No. 9/2007, of 22 October 2007	Incorporates the principles governing the relations of the different agencies of the Andalusian Government with the public and with other authorities, through open communication networks
Aragon	Order of 29 July 2009	Approves the e-Government Plan of the Autonomous Community of Aragon, providing a roadmap for the modernization of the regional administration in the coming years and complying with LAECSP
Asturias	Decree No. 115/2008, of 20 November 2008	Amends previous regulations on the electronic provision of documents
	Resolution dated 9 January 2009	Publishes procedures adapted for the automatic electronic transfer of data for national ID Cards and Residence Certificates
Balearic Isles	Act No. 4/2011, of 31 March 2011	Sets out the general principles for the use of ICTs
Canary Isles	Act No. 5/2010, of 21 June 2010	Regulates citizens' right to e-participation, and promotion of the latter.
	Decree No. 19/2011, of 10 February 2011	Regulates the use of ICTs by the regional authorities
Cantabria	Decree No. 110/2006, of 9 November 2006	Regulates the e-registration of data by the regional administration, and the provision of electronic notifications and certificates
Castile-La Mancha	Decree No. 12/2010, of 16 March 2010	Regulates the use of ICTs by the regional authorities
Castile and Leon	Resolution No. 29/2009, of 12 March 2009	Approves the 2009–2011 e-Government Introduction Plan
Catalonia	Decree No. 56/2009, of 7 April 2009	In compliance with LAECSP, promotes the implementation of e-Government in the regional administration
	Act No. 29/2010, of 3 August 2010	Regulates the use of ICTs by the regional authorities of Catalonia and in relations between the public sector and citizens in Catalonia
Extremadura	Resolution dated 26 February 2008	Approves the 2008–2011 Plan to Advance Ongoing Improvement and Technological Modernization
Galicia	Decree No. 198/2010, of 2 December 2010	Regulates the use of ICTs by the regional authorities of Galicia and its agencies
La Rioja	Decree No. 57/2006, of 27 October 2006	Sets out the principles regulating the regional administration's presence online
Madrid	Decree No. 62/2009, of 25 June 2009	Regulates the use of ICTs in public procurement by the Madrid regional authorities
Navarre	Act No. 11/2007, of 4 April 2007	Promotes the implementation of effective e-Government to better serve citizens through Internet
Basque Country	Decree No. 232/2007, of 18 December 2007	Regulates the use of ICTs in administrative procedures
	Decree No. 72/2008, of 29 April 2008	Creates and regulates electronic data transfer within the general administration of the Basque Country and that of its agencies
Valencia	Act No. 3/2010, of 5 May 2010	Develops the right of citizens to interact electronically with the public administrations of Valencia and regulates the legal status of e-Government

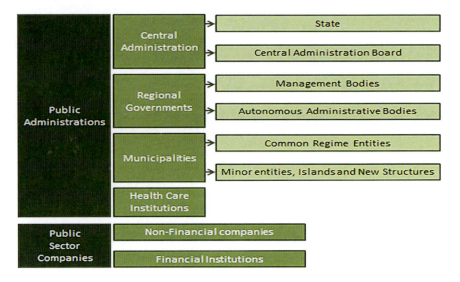

Fig. 4.1 Organizational structure of Spanish Public Administration

represented more than 35.9 % of the consolidated budgetary expenses of Spanish public administrations and 17.3 % of the gross domestic product (Secretaría de Estado de Cooperación Territorial 2009). Therefore, our study sample was based on all 17 Spanish regional governments (Table 4.3), all the Spanish regional departments (152), and all the independent bodies created by the latter to deliver public services, including transfer tax and stamp duty, jobseekers' assistance, employment in the public sector, self-assessed taxation, youth assistance programs, medical appointments system, electronic healthcare card, and job creation grants.

In view of their significant weight in Spanish society and proximity to citizens, this research study focuses on Spanish regional governments, using statistics reported for the period August–September 2011.

4.3.2 Research Methodology

Our analysis of the utilization of Web 2.0 tools and social media by Spanish regional governments to deliver public services is divided into three phases. Initially, we conducted a descriptive study of the use of Web 2.0 tools and social media by each of the regional governments. In the second phase, we analyzed the factors underlying the greater or lesser development of these technologies in the sector. Finally, we analyzed the use of social media in eight public services.

Table 4.3 Spanish regional governments

Spanish regional governments	Government departments	Population
Andalusia	12	6,192,642
Aragon	9	969,685
Asturias	9	800,741
Balearic Isles	7	827,310
Basque Country	11	1,608,275
Canary Isles	8	1,629,929
Cantabria	8	436,125
Castile and Leon	9	1,833,478
Castile-La Mancha	7	1,509,807
Catalonia	11	5,437,239
Extremadura	7	799,039
Galicia	10	2,058,928
La Rioja	7	231,398
Madrid	8	4,799,349
Murcia	8	1,090,153
Navarre	8	457,078
Valencia	13	3,788,069

At the regional level in Spain, public services are provided by the departments. These are usually organized on the basis of separating the powers that are closely related to the direct role of public administration from those concerning the management and delivery of public services. The latter are often exercised through agencies or other public bodies; these bodies maintain the level of autonomy allowed by the rules under which they were created, but report directly to the department. However, as each regional public administration in Spain has jurisdiction over the organization of each department, it can manage the services within its jurisdiction through its own agencies or other bodies, with or without legal personality. Thus, the same public service can be provided through:

- Directorates General: departments are organized into the essential Directorates General that require the specialized services that are integrated within them.
- Independent bodies: independent bodies provide services of a mainly commercial, economic, or financial nature.

The regional government is the body that decides how to structure the official website of its administration, and so each department must decide whether to have its own official website, irrespective of whether a particular Directorate General or independent body has an official website of its own, and so on. In consequence, there are administrations that decide:

- The official information about each department forms part of the regional government's official website, and so information about public service is obtained through a single regional government website.

- The departments each have an official website that offers information about the public services offered.
- The independent bodies or Directorates General each have an official website with information about the public services offered.

Thus, Spanish regional governments, in using Web 2.0 tools, may opt to use any or all of the following:

- Official interdepartmental communication channels in which information is provided about the various public services of the regional administration.
- Official Presidential communication channels in which information is provided about the various public services of the regional administration.
- Communication channels exclusive to each department, providing news on any public service it provides.
- Communication channels exclusive to each independent body or Directorate General.

For these reasons, before beginning our analysis of departmental websites, we examined how many had their own official website, independent of the one posted by the regional government. This revealed that only three of the 17 regions have an independent official website for each department, and so the online management of public services, in most cases, is effected through the regional government's official website. Having established this, we then proceeded to analyze the official website of each regional government.

1. Stage one

For the analysis of Spanish regional governments' use of Web 2.0 applications, we examined the official website of each government, in search of the following items: (1) podcasts; (2) vodcasts; (3) RSS; (4) widgets; (5) facilities to share; (6) mashups; (7) webcasts. The items are rated on a dichotomous scale: if the item is available, it is scored with a 1, otherwise, with a 0 (Table 4.4).

To analyze Spanish regional governments' use of social media, we examined the existence of the social media link in the official website of each regional government. In this regard, we have observed in the official website of each regional government if the social media link is managed by the regional Government, by the Presidential of the regional Government, or by the different regional Departments. We did not wish to make a search of a closed list of social networks, but rather to identify all those used. Therefore, data were added as their existence was confirmed by the link in the official website analyzed. The three most commonly used social media—Twitter, Facebook, and YouTube—were evaluated in terms of specific items, such as the number of groups, the number of followers, or the number of visits. For Twitter, the following items were examined: (1) existence of an official Twitter account; (2) number of followers; (3) number of tweets; (4) number of lists; (5) number being followed. In Facebook, we examined: (1) existence of an official Facebook page; (2) number of pages-groups of which the regional public administration is a follower; (3) number of followers;

Table 4.4 Web 2.0 application

Podcasts	The distribution of audio files, usually in mp3 format, via a system of RSS syndication by which users can subscribe and use a program that downloads the podcast content for subsequent listening
Vodcasts	The concept is similar to that of podcasting, but instead of having only audio it also includes video
RSS (Really Simple Syndication)	Used to transmit frequent updates to users who have subscribed to the content source. The format makes it possible to distribute content without a browser, using software designed to read these RSS feeds, although a browser can also be used to view RSS feeds
Widgets	Small applications or programs, usually presented in small files or folders, which are executed by a widget engine. Intended basically to provide easy access to frequently used functions and to provide visual information
Facilities to share	Applications that allow a user to share information in a website with other users
Mashup	An application that uses and combines data from one or more sources to create new services
Webcast	A live Internet transmission, similar to that offered by a television or radio station

(4) number of people talking about the public department. In YouTube, we examined the following: (1) existence of an official channel on YouTube; (2) number of subscribers; (3) number of videos; (4) number of videos viewed in 1 month; (5) maximum number of viewings of a video.

2. Stage two

The second stage of the analysis is that of explanation. In order to analyze the influence of independent factors on the development of Web 2.0 technologies for Spanish regional governments, we need first to quantify the level of use of these applications. For this purpose, each regional government was classified according to an index of visibility (IV) consisting in calculating the sum of all the Web 2.0 tools and social media used by the departments, the regional governments and the President of each government. The IV of each regional government was calculated as the ratio of the sum of the items available (scored with a 1) and the total number of Web 2.0 tools and social media that has been found over the different governments. Thus, the IV is based on both the analysis of the official website of the public regional administration and on the presence of the latter in the most important social communication media.

Having defined the dependent variable (IV), taking into account prior research on transparency, visibility, websites, and social networks (Bertot et al. 2010; Bonsón and Flores 2011; Celaya et al. 2009), we selected the factors that may promote the development of Web 2.0 tools and social communication media for regional governments. These were tested using a multiple regression model. The explanatory factors considered are summarized in Table 4.5, showing the units of measurement used and the expected relations with the IV.

Table 4.5 Explanatory factors

Factor	Measurement parameter	Expected relation
Population (POP)	Population of the region (2010)	Positive
Fiscal pressure (FP)	Total income/Population (2010)	Positive
Debt (DEB)	Financial expenditure/Population (2010)	Positive
Social network penetration (SNT/P)	Level of social network penetration in the region (2010)	Positive
Government internet penetration (GINT/P)	Level of internet penetration in the public administration of the region (2010)	Positive

3. Stage three

Finally, this study analyzes eight public services managed by the Spanish regional governments, selected from the 26 analyzed in the study by CapGemini (2011). The latter chapter considers the average degree of online availability of public services provided by Spanish regional governments, highlighting the regions that are achieving full electronic development, by facilitating online documentation and management. These services were scored using the scale used in the e-Europe (CapGemini 2009) study, with development levels ranging from 0 to 4: 0 %, stage 0; 25 %, stage 1; 50 %, stage 2; 75 %, stage 3; 100 %, stage 4. *Some of the presented services are beyond the 20 European ones that have been defined by the EU strategies for e-delivery, concretely health relative services; income tax, corporate tax, VAT, job search.*

The following public services are analyzed in-depth, in addition to the official websites of independent agencies and Directorates General, regarding their use of social networks.

- Transfer tax and stamp duty
- Self-assessed taxation
- Jobseekers' assistance
- Employment in the public sector
- Job creation grants
- Medical appointments system
- Electronic healthcare card
- Youth assistance programs

4.3.3 Analysis of the Results

1. Stage one

As shown in Table 4.6, Spanish regional governments and their departments make a moderate use of Web 2.0 tools and social communication platforms. RSS feeds and vodcasts are used by over 70 % of the regional governments, making these the most commonly used tools. Just over half of the webs analyzed contain podcasts and mashups. Only five regional governments use widgets, and only one uses live Internet transmission. Finally, no more than six items are used by any single regional government, and only four utilize over 70 % of the items. Finally, one regional government does not use any of the Web 2.0 tools.

Of the official interdepartmental social communication media pages, the microblogging platform Twitter is most commonly used by Spanish regional governments (58.82 %) followed closely by Facebook (52.94 %) and YouTube (52.94 %), with half of the sample also having an official page on this social network. Third, 35.29 % have an official Flickr page in which users have access to all photos posted by the regional governments. As stated in the methodology section, we also observed other platforms such as LinkedIn, Tuenti, Blogs, Ivoox, Slideshare, Delicious, Friendfeed, which are used by the regional public administrations. In all, 11 different platforms are used. Nevertheless, it is remarkable that seven of these regional governments have not created an official interdepartmental page on a social network to enable citizens' participation.

As official Presidential social communication media pages, Twitter and Facebook are most commonly used by the Presidents of Spanish regional governments (17.65 %) followed closely by Flickr (11.76 %) and YouTube (11.76 %). In total, four regional governments have established official websites where citizens can interact directly with the President of the region on issues of public interest, via five different social platforms. Two of these four governments enable interaction with the region's President, while the other two opt for both an official interdepartmental website and a Presidential one.

Of the official departmental social communication media pages, as above, Facebook and Twitter are the most commonly used, although the percentages are very low (around 8 % of the 152 departments). Only two of the three regional governments whose departments have their own official website use a social network to address areas of their competence, but most of the departments in each region do not use any network (74 %). Among the seven channels of communication used, it is noteworthy that one of the regions has chosen to create a new social network on professional issues regarding public services. A total of 13 different social communication media are used by Spanish regional governments.

As can be seen, many regional governments have an official page in Facebook, Twitter, and/or YouTube, the three most popular social communication media; 64.7 % have an official account in one or more, and over 47 % are present on all three. In addition, there is a high average number of subscribers, especially on Twitter, with an average of 4,713 followers, and Facebook, with 3,023 (Table 4.7).

Other important items reflecting the relevance of the use of social media by Spanish public administration include the average number of tweets (3847.7). For each public administration, on YouTube, an average of 7995.5 videos is viewed and 18 new videos are posted each month during the 2 years that the channel has been available.

Table 4.6 The use of Web 2.0 tools and social communication platforms

Web 2.0 tool	Regional governments (%)	Presidents (%)	Departments (%)
Podcasts	58.82		
Vodcasts	70.59		
Really simple syndication (RSS)	88.24		
Widgets	29.41		
Facilities to share	17.65		
Mashup	52.94		
Webcast:	5.88		
Social media			
Facebook: a social networking site	52.94	17.65	8.55
LinkedIn: a business-related social networking site	5.88		
Tuenti: a Spain-based, invitation-only private social networking website that has been referred to as the "Spanish Facebook"	5.88	0.00	
Blogs: regularly updated websites that chronologically compile texts or articles by one or more authors, where the author retains the freedom to publish whatever he/she sees fit	11.76	0.00	0.00
Flickr: a tool enabling users to share photos	35.29	11.76	2.63
IVOOX: a tool enabling users to share music	11.76		
Slideshare: a tool enabling users to share presentations	5.88		2–63
YouTube enable users to share videos	52.94	11.76	3.95
Del.icio.us: a social bookmarking web service for storing, sharing, and discovering web bookmarks	5.88		1.32
Twitter: a microblogging platform based on 140-character messages	58.82	17.65	7.89
Friend feed: a real-time feed aggregator that consolidates the updates from social media and social networking websites, social bookmarking websites, blogs and micro-blogging updates	5.88		
Own public administration social network: a public administration-related social networking site			1.97
Formspring: a social website that allows its users to set up a profile page, follow other users and ask questions of other users		5.88	

Finally, let us must make special mention of the latest Facebook metric "*n* People Are Talking About This," launched in September 2011. This new indicator has quickly become the best reference of a page's level of interaction with the community. It counts the number of unique individuals that have generated diverse interactions with the page, which tells us how interesting it is for viewers and at what level it is connected with the community. The success of a page (previously calculated only by the number of followers) is now measured as the "*n* People are talking about this" divided by the number of followers, with a

Table 4.7 Data on social communication media used in official web pages

	Social communication media	Mean	Standard deviation
Twitter	Official account in Twitter	(58.82%)	
	Number of followers	4713	6443.16
	Number being followed	1321.7	2965.61
	Number of tweets	3847.7	3434.73
	Number of lists	232.6	319.01
Facebook	Official page in Facebook	(52.94%)	
	Number of page-groups followed by the government	10	8.23
	Number of followers	3023	2435.63
	Number of people talking about this regional government	64.5714286	66.84
YouTube	Official channel in YouTube	(52.94%)	
	Number of subscribers	121.88	137.55
	Age of the official channel (years)	2.5	2.562
	Total videos posted on the official channel	173.28	132.13
	Maximum number of viewings	7995.5	11355.39
	Videos posted in the last month	18.11	16.90

value above 5 % being considered a good one. For Spanish regional governments, this ratio, compiled from average data, was 2.13 %, which confirms that they have yet to achieve real importance in Facebook.

2. Stage two

The second phase of this study was to examine the influence of certain independent variables in the use of Web 2.0 tools and social communication media by Spanish regional governments. To do this, we applied a multiple regression analysis; assuming that the variables under study presented a linear relationship, the statistical technique selected was that of multiple linear regression. The critical value of Fisher's F statistic ($F = 5.544$, $Sig = 0.009$) confirmed the existence of a significant linear relation between the dependent variable and the set of independent variables.

After confirming compliance with the initial assumptions of the model (linearity, homoscedasticity, normality, independence, and collinearity), the Pearson correlation matrix was created (Table 4.8). As can be seen, the matrix shows that there are no problems of multicollinearity among the independent variables.

According to our analysis (see Table 4.9), the explanatory power of the resulting model, as measured by the adjusted R-squared value, is 58.70 % and so the fit is moderate. As for the significance of the variables, only three of the five independent factors are significant.

In relation to the budget of the regional public government, the results show there is a significant negative relationship between this factor (measured as the tax income obtained each year) and the dependent variable (-2.447^{**}). In other words,

Table 4.8 Pearson's correlation matrix

	IV	POP	FP	DEB	SNT/P	GINT/P
IV	1					
POP	0.599[a]	1				
FP	−0.478	−0.265	1			
DEB	0.293	0.247	0.417	1		
SNT/P	0.449	0.032	−0.173	0.053	1	
GINT/P	0.208	0.001	−0.147	−0.163	0.477	1

[a] The correlation is significant at the level of 0.05 (bilateral)

the regional public administrations that impose the lightest tax burden tend to present the greatest development of Web 2.0 applications and social platforms. This result is contrary to our initial hypothesis that this relationship would be positive.

In terms of debt, the analysis shows this to be positively related to the visibility index, with a high level of significance ($p < 0.01$). Therefore, the higher the level of debt of the region, the greater the use of Web 2.0 tools and social communication media. The region's population is the third significant variable identified, and the relationship was found to be positive (1.963^{*}).

For the other independent variables analyzed, there is insufficient evidence to suggest a significant relation with the level of use of Web 2.0 applications and social communication platforms by regional governments.

3. Stage three

Finally, we examined the use of social networks by the agencies responsible for eight basic public services provided by Spanish regional governments, grouped in the following main areas: finance; health; employment; young people.

For the two services analyzed in the area of Finance (transfer tax and stamp duty, and self-assessed taxation), most regional governments have created an independent body responsible for their management. However, neither the official websites of these agencies nor those of the departments to which they belong use any channel of communication between citizens and the administrations' finance staff. This is contrary to the policy followed by this department, which has enabled these services to be processed almost entirely online, achieving an average of 0.933 with respect to a maximum value of 1 (Table 4.10).

In the employment area, three services were selected: jobseekers' assistance, job creation grants and employment in the public sector. As in the previous case, practically all the regional governments have created an independent body to manage these services. Five independent agencies have created at least one official page on a social network. The only social networks on which an official website has been opened are Facebook (3), Twitter (5), and YouTube (3), with only two of these independent agencies making use of all three channels. Although these services are gradually introducing social communication channels, in accordance with the departments to which they belong, they still fail to comply with the policy of the corresponding departments, which have enabled these services to be

Table 4.9 Results of regression analysis

Model	Non-standardized coefficients		Standardized coefficients	T
	B	Standard error	BETA	
(Constant)	−35.344	29.74		−1.188
POP	0.000	0.00	0.360	1.963[a]
FP	−5.428	2.22	−0.490	−2.447[b]
DEBT	2.417	1.21	0.402	2.003[c]
SNT/P	13.169	8.18	0.305	1.609
INT/P	1.896	6.37	0.056	0.297
R	R squared	Adjusted R squared	Standard error of the estimate	Durbin–Watson
0.846[a]	0.716	0.587	2.59735453	2.638

[a] The correlation is significant at the level of 0.10 (bilateral)
[b] The correlation is significant at the level of 0.05 (bilateral)
[c] The correlation is significant at the level of 0.01 (bilateral)

processed almost entirely online, achieving an average of 0.911 with respect to a maximum value of 1.

In the area of health services, in providing the two services included in the Cap Gemini Report (2011)—the medical appointments system and the electronic healthcare card—the Spanish regional governments have established independent agencies which have their own website. However, only four of these agencies have chosen to use a social network, with a maximum of two different networks being used (Facebook in four cases, and Twitter in three). These services usually have a lower level of online development than those discussed above, and so these agencies need to progress further in both directions.

For the last of the services analyzed, Youth Aid Programs, the departments, in most cases, have not created independent agencies, and so each program reports directly to a Directorate-General. However, for this group the departments have considered it appropriate to create their own portals. While this service has advanced least in total online processing of documentation, as regards social networks the opposite is true, with 12 departments making use of them, with up to five different networks. The networks used are Facebook (11) and Twitter (12) followed by YouTube (7) and Tuenti (6)—this latter network has been termed the Spanish Facebook, and it is widely used by young people in Spain. Also used are Blog (1) and media sharing platforms such as Ivoox (1), Slideshare (1), Flickr (2), and Del.icio.us (1).

4.4 Conclusions

Spanish regional governments are affected by the development of ICTs and the information requirements of today's society. According to the results of our study, although regional departments' use of Web 2.0 tools is only moderate, their

Table 4.10 Analysis of the public service areas addressed by Spanish regional governments

Area	Finance			Employment			Health			Young people		
	Government tax office	Social communications network (mean score)		Employment service	Social communications network (mean score)		Health	Social communications network (mean score)		Programmed Aid	Social communications network (mean score)	
		Ind. agency/D. Gen.	Department		Ind. Agency/D. Gen.	Department		Ind. agency/D. Gen.	Department		Ind. agency/D. Gen.	Department
Andalusia	1	0	0	1	3	3	0.87	0	0	1	4	1
Aragon	1	0	0	0.83	2	0	0.75	0	0	0.5	5	0
Asturias	1	0	0	1	0	0	1	0	0	1	0	0
Balearic Isles	1	0	0	0.92	0	0	1	0	0	0.5	0	0
Basque Country	1	0	0	0.83	2	0	1	2	0	0.5	5	0
Canary Isles	1	0	0	0.75	0	0	0.62	0	0	0.5	3	0
Cantabria	1	0	0	0.83	0	0	0.37	0	0	0.5	4	0
Castile and Leon	1	0	0	1	0	0	1	1	0	1	0	0
Castile-La Mancha	0.5	0	0	1	0	0	1	0	0	1	2	0
Catalonia	1	0	0	1	1	3	1	0	0	1	4	0
Extremadura	0.5	0	0	0.83	3	0	1	2	0	0.5	3	0
Galicia	1	0	0	0.83	0	0	1	0	0	0.5	3	0
La Rioja	1	0	0	0.92	0	1	1		1	1	2	1
Madrid	1	0	0	1	0	0	1	0	0	1	0	0
Murcia	1	0	0	0.75	0	0	0.62	2	0	0.5	3	0
Navarra	1	0	0	1	0	0	0.62	0	0	0.5	0	0
Valencia	0.87	0	0	1	0	0	0.62	0	0	0.5	5	0
	0.93	0	0	0.91	0.65	0.41	0.85	0.44	0.06	0.71	2.53	0.12

presence in social networks and the use of the latter for increasing e-participation is more widespread.

Good visibility for a website indicates that it is perceived as important by users. However, Spanish regional governments in general do not seem to be aware of these benefits, and our analysis shows that much remains to be done in their use of Web 2.0.

Moreover, it seems unlikely, at least for the moment, that Web 2.0 applications will generate any significant revolution in relations between Spanish regional governments and society. To all appearances, they have taken a relatively minor step in the use of ICTs as a means of providing information and services to the general public, but they have not achieved significant advances in processes of interactive dialog.

As for social communication media, with the popularity of social networking, online forums and blogs, many Spanish regional governments have rushed to create a Facebook page and open a Twitter account, but this is by no means sufficient. It is not merely a question of creating a presence and a reputation, it is also necessary to manage an online presence using a well-considered social media strategy, to make regional governments visible to citizens. Our results show that regional governments have recognized the benefits of social platforms as a means of increasing their visibility, and 64.7 % now have an official account in one or more of the three communication media that are most commonly used, and the items and ratios reflecting the interest and relevance of social networks testify to this.

Those regional governments which are not present in social networks face a double handicap: in the first place, they are less aware of their citizens' opinions, and so may miss out on an important source of information; second, even if a regional department has no official page on a social network, people do speak about regional governments, and so opportunities to participate in conversations about themselves are being lost.

Regarding the factors that influence the use of social communication media and Web 2.0 tools by Spanish regional governments, our regression analysis shows that those with higher levels of debt, a lower fiscal burden and a larger population are where Web 2.0 applications are most highly developed.

Finally, we observe that Spanish regional governments are making great efforts to provide fully digitized public services, and so further work is needed for greater social interconnection to be achieved.

References

Accenture (2009). Web 2.0 and the Next Generation of Public Service. Driving high performance through more engaging, accountable and citizen-focused service.

Bastida, F. J. & Benito, B. (2006). Financial Reports and decentralization in municipal governments. *International Review of Administrative Sciences*, 72(2): 223–238.

Baumgarten, J. & Chui, M. (2009). E-government 2.0. *Mc-Kinsey on Government*, 4: 26–31.

Bertot, J. C., Jaeger, P. T. & Grimes, J. M. (2010). Crowd-sourcing transparency: ICTs, social media, and government transparency initiatives. In Proceedings of the *11th Annual International Conference on Digital Government Research*, Pueblo, Mexico, May 17–20.

Bonsón, E. & Flores, F. (2011). Social media and corporate dialogue: the response of the global financial institutions. *Online Information Review*, 35(1), 34–49.

Capgemini (2009). *Benchmark Measurement of European eGovernment services*. Available at http://www.capgemini.com/insights-and-resources/by-publication/2009-egovernment-benchmark

Capgemini (2011). *Estudio Comparativo 2011 de los Servicios Públicos online en los 20 mayores Ayuntamientos españoles*. Available at http://www.informeeespana.es/docs/Estudio_Comparativo_Ayuntamientos_2011.pdf

Cavoukian, A. (2009). *Privacy and Government 2.0: The Implications of an Open World*. Ontario: Information & Privacy Commissioner.

Celaya, J., Vázquez, J.A., Saldaña, I. & García, Y. (2009). Visibilidad de las ciudades en la Web 2.0. Grupo BPMO.

Chan, H. S. & Chow, K. W. (2007). Public Management Policy and Practice in Western China: Metapolicy, Tacit Knowledge, and implications for Management Innovation Transfer. *American Review of Public Administration,* 37 (4): 479–497.

Commonwealth Network of Information Technology for Development Foundation (COMNET-IT) (2002). *Country profiles of E-governance*. Paris: UNESCO.

Deloitte (2008). *Change your world or the world will change you. The future of collaborative government and Web 2.0.* Quebec: Deloitte & Touche LLP and affiliated entities.

E-Government Academy (2006). *E-Government actions in Europe. Best European e-practices.* Project part-financed by the European Union. Estonia: Tallinn.

e-Government Action Plan (2006). *eGovernment Action Plan 2006, COM 2006/173 of 25.04.2006.* Available at http://ec.europa.eu/information_society/activities/egovernment/library/ index_en.htm

European Commission (2009). *Public services 2.0. Web 2.0 from the periphery to the centre of public service delivery*. Report from the ePractice workshop. Brussels: European Commision.

Gallego, R &Barzelay, M. (2010). Public Management policymaking in Spain: The Politics of Legislative Reform of Administrative Structure, 1991–1997. *Governance*, 23(2): 277–296.

Goldsmith, S. & Eggers, W. D. (2004). *Governing by Network: The New Shape of the Public Sector*. Washington: Brookings Institution Press.

Government 2.0 taskforce (2009). E*ngage Getting on with Government 2.0*. Report of the Government 2.0 Taskforce. Canberra: Australian Government Information Management Office.

Huijboom, N.; Van den Broek, T.; Frissen, V.; Kool, L.; Kotterink, B.; Nielsen, M. & Millard, J. (2009). *Public Services 2.0: The Impact of Social Computing on Public Services*. Institute for Prospective Technological Studies, Joint Research Centre, European Commission. Luxembourg: Office for Official Publications of the European Communities.

ICT PSP from PIC (2011). *ICT Policy Support Programme*. Available at http://ec.europa.eu/ information_ society/activities/egovernment/implementation/ict_psp/index_en.htm

International Development Association (IDA) (2011). *Information and Communication Technology Agency of Sri Lanka (ICTA)*. Volume 3, Colombo-05: Sri Lanka.

Orange Foundation (2011). eEspaña. *Informe anual sobre el desarrollo de la sociedad de la información en España 2011*. Madrid: Orange Foundation.

Osimo, D. (2008). *Web 2.0 in Government: Why? and How?* Institute for Prospective Technological Studies, Joint Research Centre, European Commission. Luxembourg: Office for Official Publications of the European Communities.

Peedu, G. (2011). *Enhancing Public Service User Experience in Information Society*. Master Thesis. Estonia: Tallinn University.

Reggi, L. & Scicchitano, S. (2011). *European Regions Financing Public e-Services: the Case of EU Structural Funds*. Working Papers 1110, Rome: University of Urbino Carlo Bo.

Rodríguez Bolívar, M.P., Caba Pérez, C. & López Hernández, A.M. (2007). E-government and public financial reporting. The case of Spanish Regional Governments. *American Review of Public Administration*, 37(2): 142–177.

Secretaría de Estado de Cooperación Territorial (2009). *Informe Económico-Financiero de las Administraciones Territoriales 2009*. Madrid: Secretaría de Estado de Cooperación Territorial, Dirección General de Cooperación Autonómica.

TNS Emor (2010). Konadike rahulolu riigi poolt pakutavate e-teenustega. Available at http://www.riso.ee/et/files/kodanike_ rahulolu_avalike_eteenustega_2010.pdf.

United Nations (2010). *E-Government Survey 2010. Leveraging e-government at a time of financial and economic crisis*. New York: United Nations.

Chapter 5
Toward a Gov 2.0 Society for All: European Strategies for Public Service Delivery

Silvia Gardini, Marco Maria Mattei and Rebecca Levy Orelli

5.1 Introduction to Gov 2.0 in the Public Administration

Gov 2.0 is a term that refers to a new phase of the evolving and extended Internet, and it is more than a mere set of technologies. It includes a social dimension with user-generated content, increased simplicity in design and features as well as participatory, decentralized models and processes. The three key components of Gov 2.0 are web-based technology and architecture, technologies built around communities and social networks, and content generated by stakeholders, and it consumes and remixes data from multiple sources (Wigand 2007, p. 276). The paradigm shift enabled by Gov 2.0 is from end users consuming information to produce information and to facilitate interaction and collaborative work.

To what extent the shift to Gov 2.0 technologies, embedded in the latest European governments' strategies, is changing public service delivery in practice? Gov 2.0 technologies provide numerous opportunities for governments to create efficiencies and better serve the public. With the public sector facing intense scrutiny of its budgets it should clearly be exploring where these tools can ease financial pressure, guarantee democratic governance, and improve public service delivery. The interactive and collaborative nature of Gov 2.0 should be encouraged

S. Gardini · R. L. Orelli (✉)
Department of Management, University of Bologna,
15 piazzale della Vittoria, 47121 Forlì, FC, Italy
e-mail: rebecca.orelli@unibo.it

S. Gardini
e-mail: silvia.gardini@unibo.it

M. M. Mattei
Department of Management, University of Bologna,
34 via Capo di Lucca, Bologna, BO, Italy
e-mail: marcomaria.mattei@unibo.it

C. G. Reddick and S. K. Aikins (eds.), *Web 2.0 Technologies and Democratic Governance*, Public Administration and Information Technology 1,
DOI: 10.1007/978-1-4614-1448-3_5, © Springer Science+Business Media New York 2012

given the fact that public interaction is quickly moving to center stage on the public governance agenda, as it is increasingly recognized as a primary driver for innovation and value creation in both the private and public sectors.

For the past decade, the adoption of electronic governmental services has increased in different countries to provide public services and e-government has been the key tool for the government offices in order to provide efficient and effective public services. E-government can be defined as "The use of information and communication technologies (ICT), particularly the Internet, as a tool to achieve better government" (OECD 2003, p. 23).

Building upon basic components, i.e., technologies, concepts of communities and networks, and the production, consumption, and remixing of data, Gov 2.0 can be distinguished from Gov 1.0 on a number of characteristics (Chang and Kannan 2008, p. 16; Drapeau and Wells 2009, p. 2; Wigand 2010, p. 168): the control is decentralized and democratic, the content is created by end users and not published by government, communication is multidirectional and interactive, data are dynamic, and users are networks of individuals and communities are collaborating and producers of content. This paradigm shift from a controlled and static web environment characterizing Gov 1.0 to a dynamic, decentralized, and networked environment implies numerous challenges for governments at all levels. The Gov 2.0 environment is user-centric and offers multiple channels, so that governments need to consider engaging users in their social network sites and online communities.

Eight Gov 2.0 technologies can be considered as means for comparing the adoption by government in European countries, namely blogs, microblogs, mashups, podcasts, RSS feeds, social networking sites, video sharing, and wikis (Chang and Kannan 2008, p. 11). Each of these technologies demonstrates one or more of the basic concepts of Gov 2.0, as to enhance user-generated content, to extend the reach of communications to new audiences, to build relationships via social networks, to create collaborative environments with internal and external stakeholders, and to increase stakeholder engagement.

This chapter is structured as follows: The second section presents an overview of the strategic plans launched by the EU over the last decade in order to strengthen e-government services for citizens and analyzes to what extent the four major European countries have defined strategic objectives which imply the use of Gov 2.0 technologies. The extent to which the shift to Gov 2.0 technologies are changing public service delivery in practice is presented in the third section. Finally, in the conclusion we summarize the analysis highlighting advantages and challenges of Gov 2.0 development in Europe.

5.2 Gov 2.0 and European Strategies

In this section, we focus on the last decade of EU strategies adopted to strengthen e-government services for citizens (Orelli et al. 2010a) and how the four major European countries have implemented those strategies at national level.

In particular, we try to understand whether EU and the four Member States have posed strategic objectives which explicitly or implicitly imply the use of Gov 2.0 technologies.

In 2000, the Member States approved the eEurope initiative, which aimed at exploiting the advantages offered by the Internet and new ICT, and started the first structured European policy on ICT for governments. This initiative helped Member States to achieve the ambitious strategic goal declared at the European Council held in Lisbon for making the EU "the most dynamic and competitive knowledge-based economy in the world." To implement the eEurope initiative the European Commission issued two different action plans. The first one, named eEurope 2002, was lunched in 2000 and basically intended to promote the use of Internet in the EU. The second action plan, called eEurope 2005, was approved in 2002 and focused on using broadband technologies to provide online services in both the private and public sector, to create new jobs and growth opportunities. In particular, eEurope 2005 proposed that "by end 2004, Member States should have ensured that basic public services are interactive" (p. 11). However, it seems that with the adjective "interactive" the European Commission meant that a citizen could complete the full processing of a public service on Internet, but not necessary with any kind of online active support from the administrative unit. To what extent eEurope 2005 was effective in improving the online availability of public services is still not clear, but it is sure that in 2005 the European Commission decided to reconsider the strategic goal proposed in Lisbon, given the modest progress made so far, and to refocus on more specific and urgent goals: growth and job creation.

After the revision of the Lisbon strategy, the European Commission launched the new initiative on ICT, called "i2010—an European information society for growth and employment" that identified three new objectives. First, Member States had to carry out the completion of a single European information space, in order to promote an open and competitive internal market for information society and media. Second, they had to increase their investments in ICT research to promote innovation and technological leadership. Third, Member States had to support better public services and quality of life through innovative use of ICT, and ensure that all citizens, including socially disadvantaged groups, benefit from e-government. The European Commission took the responsibility to prepare an i2010 e-Government Action Plan 2006–2010 in order to precisely identify all the actions necessary to achieve the new objectives. On the other hand, the Member States had to preset National Reform Programs covering the 3-year period, coherent with the i2010 and i2010 e-Government Action Plan.

i2010 e-Government Action Plan 2006–2010 recognized three (out of five) strategic priorities that related to public services for citizens or e-democracy and e-participation. In particular, the first strategic priority *No citizen left behind* was about the delivery of services that were more easily accessible and increasingly trusted by all users within the Member States. Moreover, public administrations had to increase the use of ICT-enabled public services among people with disabilities that could become major beneficiaries of e-government. The second strategic priority *Making efficiency and effectiveness a reality* highlighted how e-government services could make citizens and public administrations save time and money promoting economic growth. Finally, the last strategic priority was *Strengthening participation and democratic decision-making*, through the implementation of innovative tools. ICT could help to promote an effective public debate and enlarge participation in democratic decision-making. Although all the above-mentioned strategic priorities may be addressed involving citizens in the process, the Action Plan mainly focused on the supply side and identified actions that did not really push European public administrations toward a closer interaction with users.

As scheduled, in 2010 the European Commission launched the "Digital Agenda for Europe", which is the successor of i2010 and one of the first flagship initiative of the renew EU economic strategy adopted in the same year by the European Council (Europe 2020–A strategy for smart, sustainable and inclusive growth). The Digital Agenda for Europe presents the objectives for the next 10 years to promote "sustainable economic and social benefits from a digital single market based on fast and ultra fast Internet, and interoperable applications." With specific reference to e-government, however, the European Commission issued another document, the European e-Government Action Plan 2011–2015, which aims at achieving the ambitious objectives proposed at the 5th Ministerial e-Government Conference in Malmö (the so-called Malmö Declaration). According to the Malmö Declaration and the European eGovernment Action Plan 2011–2015, there are four political priorities that all European public administrations have to focus on within the next 5 years. First, citizens and businesses have to be empowered by e-government services, which should be designed around users' needs. Second, Member States have to provide seamless e-government services to increase mobility of people and businesses in the EU. Third, public administrations have to improve the efficiency and the effectiveness of their organizational processes and to reduce the administrative burden by using ICT. Forth, Member States have to create the necessary legal and technical preconditions in order to allow public administrations at any level to enhance e-government services. All those political priorities relate public services to citizens, and the first one makes an implicit reference to the Gov 2.0 philosophy. Setting out the specific targets and actions to empower citizens, in fact, the European e-Government Action Plan 2011–2015 states that "Social networking and collaborative tools (e.g. Web 2.0 technologies) enable users to play an active role in the design and production of public services" (p. 7) and, although they are still used by a relatively still small number of organizations, it is important to understand "which are the most suitable tools and how best to apply these to effectively engage businesses, civil society and individual citizens." The European eGovernment Action Plan 2011–2015, then, is the first official document on the EU e-Government policy that calls for the Gov 2.0 technologies and sets out a strategy which explicitly requires Member State public administrations to move forward a bidirectional interaction with citizens on the Internet.

To conclude, for the last 10 years the European Commission has been promoting the use of ICT to improve the quality and efficiency of public services. In those years, on the one hand, the European policy on e-Government has been inspired by the best practices developed across Europe and, on the other hand, it has been stimulating all the Member States to achieve common standards in providing public services. Moreover, the priorities have been moved forward as long as the identified targets were reached and citizens became more aware of new technologies. Given the number and the heterogeneity of the Member States, it is not surprising that the Gov 2.0 has been explicitly required by the European guidelines only recently.

Furthermore, it is worth saying that, according to the European legal system, the Member States can choose the path to implement the strategies identified by the Commission, since the action plans are guidelines that do not cope with the differences in legal environments and administrative traditions existing within the EU. For this reason we think that it is interesting to investigate how the four major Member States, which have different cultural traditions, have put into operation the e-Government European strategies so far and to what extent those countries have been employing Gov 2.0 technologies, even though the EU did not really require them until recently.

In *France*, the first e-Government strategy was lunched in 2004 with ADELE program (French e-Government Factsheets, Ed. 10.0; 13.1; and 14.0). ADELE consists of a strategic plan and an action plan (2004–2007), which are audited and eventually updated every year. ADELE appeared to be more ambitious than the European strategies at that time, since its main objective was to make e-Government accessible to all and move from simply providing information to delivering interactive services that enabled users to perform full administrative procedures remotely. This objective was articulate in three strategic points: (1) make life easier for citizens; (2) generate confidence in ICT; and (3) contribute to the modernization of public administration. The French strategy on e-Government did not change until late 2008 when a new plan (Development Plan for the Digital Economy by 2012) was presented. The plan identifies more than 150 actions and focuses more on efficiency and cost savings, but the general objectives are substantially unchanged from those of ADELE.

In 2000, the *German Federal Government* defined the e-Government strategy for the next 5 years (BundOnline 2005) (German e-Government Factsheets, Ed. 10.0; 13.0; and 14.0). The BundOnline's 2005 main objective was to make available online all the services of the federal administration which could be provided electronically. This plan was quite innovative and gave an important contribution against bureaucracy, since it emphasized the importance of focusing on citizens' needs when implementing ICT systems. In 2006, the Federal Cabinet launched a comprehensive strategy "Focused on the Future: Innovations for Administration", aiming at the modernization of the federal state administration and the e-Government 2.0 program, which was developed in compliance with the European action plan i2010. In particular, drawing on BundOnline 2005 experience, e-Government 2.0 set out new targets in order to enhance of the quantity and quality of federal e-Government service. Recently, a new one-year plan has been approved (The National E-Government Strategy) in cooperation with a broad spectrum of stakeholders and in the light of the framework proposed at the 2009 National IT-Conference of the Federal Chancellor. The National E-Government Strategy starts from the idea that an efficient use of ICT in public administrations is a relevant growth driver and aims at bringing Germany into a leading position in Europe by 2015. The plan also gives great importance to social participation of citizens and businesses in improving efficiency and usefulness of e-Government services.

The *Italian* strategy on e-Government has been following the European initiatives. In 2000, the Italian e-Government Action Plan (2000–2002) was approved and, as required by eEurope 2002, its main objectives were to promote the use of ICT within public administrations and to provide online public services to both citizens and businesses (Italian e-Government Factsheets, Ed. 9.1; 13.1; and 14.0). Moreover, annual guidelines identifying e-Government priorities have been issued since 2001. In 2005, the Italian Parliament passed a new set of laws called e-Government Code, which aimed at providing a clear legal framework for the development of e-government and set out several rules and targets for public administrations. However, after EU issued i2010 Action Plan in 2006, the newly appointed Italian Government revised the national e-Government strategy to focus on the renewed Lisbon strategy priorities. Recently, the Italian Government has introduced a new strategic plan (i2012—Innovation Strategies) which promotes the citizens' engagement in order to improve the quality of public services and recognizes the role of e-Government in promoting innovation within the country.

In 2005, the *UK government* launched its strategy on e-Government (Transformational Government-Enabled by Technology) and one year later issued the Transformational Government Implementation Plan (UK e-Government Factsheets, Ed. 10.0; 13.0; and 14.0). The main objective was to exploit the opportunity provided by technology to transform and improve the "business of government". The Implementation Plan set out three main strategies. First, e-Government services had to be designed around citizens and businesses. This required public administrations to be customer oriented and, on the other hand, could help improving efficiency by reducing duplication and routine processing. Second, public administrations had to move to a shared services culture, in order to release efficiencies across the system and support delivery more focused on customer needs. Third, the implementation of ICT had to be the opportunity for a step change in government professionalism in providing public services. The UK strategy, then, has always focused on citizens, even though it has not explicitly defined the strategy of interaction with them. In 2011, the Cabinet Office issued the new "Government ICT Strategy", which has confirmed the UK's effort to promote and improve e-Government services in order to cope with contemporary challenges.

To conclude, likewise the EU Commission, the national governments of the four major Member States do not explicitly mention the Gov. 2.0 approach and technologies in their e-Government strategies, nevertheless those countries have posed different emphasis on citizens' needs and interaction with public service users over time (Orelli et al. 2010b). Specifically, French and UK governments seem to have been pushing their administration units toward a citizen-centered implementation of ICT, whereas Germany and Italy appear to have focused more on the modernization and efficiency of public services through the use of ICT from a "supply side" perspective. Thus, in the following part of this chapter, we will empirically investigate the extent to which those differences in the strategic emphases have been reflected in the way the four countries analyzed actually provide ICT-enabled public services.

5.3 Gov 2.0 and European Practices

To understand the extent to which the shift to Gov 2.0 technologies, embedded in the latest European governments' strategies, is changing public service delivery in practice, an empirical analysis of four European countries' practices is carried. In the following sections we illustrate the methodology employed, and then the research findings.

5.3.1 Research Methodology

The purpose of this chapter is to create a composite snapshot of the current adoption patterns of Gov 2.0 technologies, in comparison with declared strategies of adoption, within the four different countries. For this reason, it is proposed a framework to examine the use of the eight selected Gov 2.0 tools previously presented within the context of central governments. Such analysis requires the use of several sources of data derived from multiple reports on the use of specific Gov 2.0 technologies as well as direct observation on governments' websites.

We chose to perform the analysis on four European countries, the ones that have been traditionally distinguished as the major European economies, namely Germany, France, Italy and the United Kingdom (Orelli et al. 2010b).

The analysis is focused on the four following areas of information: (a) *e-government portal* for citizens, as reported on the e-Government Factsheets, Infrastructure section (www.epractice.eu/en/factsheets) of each country that represents the main channel through which citizens can access public services online; (b) *e-identification and e-authentication system* for citizens that allows people to be identified inside governmental websites, and that represents a prerequisite in order to access online service delivery. The most typical electronic identification systems and online authentications analyzed are electronic identity card, certified mail, electronic passport, and are reported within each country's e-Government Factsheet, Infrastructure section; (c) *status of inclusive e-Government*, as reported on the e-inclusion Factsheets (section Status of inclusive e-government) that provides information about the level of efficiency and transparency of public administrations obtained through the implementation of technological innovation (www.epractice.eu/en/factsheets); and last, (d) *online availability and sophistication of public services* for citizens, based on the common list of 20 basic public services (12 for citizens and 8 for businesses) used by the EU for its annual report about the status of online public services (see for all European commission, European Commission, i 2010a). The 12 services for citizens are (1) Income taxes: declaration, notification of assessment; (2) Job search services by labor offices; (3) Social security benefits; (4) Personal documents (passport and driver's licence); (5) Car registration (new, used, imported cars); (6) Application for building permission; (7) Declaration to the police (e.g., in case of theft); (8) Public libraries (availability of catalogs, search tools); (9) Certificates (birth and marriage) request and delivery; (10) Enrolment in higher education/university; (11) Announcement of moving (change of address); (12) Health-related services (interactive advice on the availability of services in different hospitals; appointments for hospitals). All such information can be retrieved from e-Government Factsheet (Services for citizens section). Within this work the analysis focuses on the area of services for citizens due to impossibility of evaluating business online services, the access to whom is restricted to subjects that can prove their status of firm.

While the first three dimensions provide a general overview of the interoperability between digital public administrations and citizens, and contain the necessary prerequisite for the development of Gov 2.0 in each of the four European selected cases, the fourth dimension gives insights into the effective online interaction between citizens and governments thought the eight typical Gov 2.0 tools delineated in our framework. In order to measure Gov 2.0 tools in a homogeneous way among the four countries, the analysis was conducted considering only the websites indicated by each central government within its e-Government Factsheet. For each of the 12 citizen services we verify the presence (highlighted in gray) of each of the eight Gov 2.0 tools considered in the framework.

5.3.2 Research findings

This section presents the state of the art in adopting Gov 2.0 tools in delivery services for citizens in the four countries considered, namely France, Germany, Italy, and the UK. For each country, using the presented analytical framework, we describe the e-government portal and its online services and features, the digital identification and authentication supports, and the specific availability and sophistication of public service digital delivery, according to the methodology presented.

5.3.2.1 France

The e-Government portal for citizens www.service-public.fr is the main access point to practical information focused on the daily life events of public service users. It provides orientation, documentation, online forms, and links to public

Table 5.1 Gov 2.0 tools for citizens in France

Web 2.0 tools	Services for citizens											
	[1] IncTax	[2] JobSea	[3] SocSec	[4] PerDoc	[5] CarRe	[6] BuiPer	[7] DecPol	[8] PubLib	[9] Cert	[10] HigE	[11] AnnM	[12] Hea
Blogs												
Microblogs												
Mashups												
Podcast								■			■	
RSS		■										■
Social networking sites												
Video sharing				■								
Wikis	■	■		■						■	■	

IncTax Income taxes: declaration, notification of assessment, *JobSea* Job search services by labor offices, *SocSec* Social security benefits, *PerDoc* Personal documents: passport and driver's licence, *CarRe* Car registration (new, used, imported cars), *BuiPer* Application for building permission, *DecPol* Declaration to the police (e.g. in case of theft), *PubLib* Public libraries (availability of catalogs, search tools), *Cert* Certificates (birth and marriage): request and delivery, *HigE* Enrolment in higher education/university, *AnnM* Announcement of moving (change of address), *Hea* Health-related services (interactive advice on the availability of services in different hospitals; appointments for hospitals)

services online. The portal has been improved with 'Mon.Service-Public.fr', aimed at offering a set of Government services available online. The users of the portal can create a personal account which enables them to securely manage their administrative procedures online, accessing personalized and customized information. Regarding digital identification and authentication, the electronic services provided online are supported by one common electronic signature solution. The legal basis for this solution is the 2005 ordinance on electronic interactions between public services users and public authorities and among public authorities. Only the electronic certificates provided by 'qualified' Certification Service Providers (CSPs) are eligible for the online interactions of citizens and businesses with the Government. Another identification tool is the latest generation of health cards that started being issued at the beginning of 2007. The card also contains a wide range of essential medical information. The main advantage for users is the general online overview of ongoing administrative formalities, the interaction via a personal account, and alerts on the state of progress of any relevant administrative procedure. In addition, personal data spaces for electronic documents (e.g., certificates, income tax declarations, birth certificate extracts) and other files are also provided to registered users (French e-Government Factsheets, Ed. 14.0; French e-inclusion Factsheets, Ed. 1.0).

Regarding the specific availability and sophistication of public service digital delivery, the analysis of the 12 services shows a use of Gov 2.0 tools mainly due to RSS, podcast, and wikis (Table 5.1). There is no evidence of blogs, microblogs, mashups, and social networking sites, even if there is the chance of tagging websites on social networks.

Table 5.2 Gov 2.0 tools for citizens in Germany

	Services for citizens											
	[1] IncTax	[2] JobSea	[3] SocSec	[4] PerDoc	[5] CarRe	[6] BuiPer	[7] DecPol	[8] PubLib	[9] Cert	[10] HigE	[11] AnnM	[12] Hea
Blogs												
Microblogs	X			X								
Mashups												
Podcast												
RSS			X	X								
Social networking sites	X									X		
Video sharing												
Wikis	X	X	X	X								

For abbreviations please refer see Table 5.1 footnote

5.3.2.2 Germany

The e-Government portal for citizens www.bund.de provides central access to the online services. In March 2005, the Federal Government presented a common e-card strategy for digital identification and authentication. The strategy provides a common framework to develop different electronic cards projects, such as the electronic identity card, the e-health insurance card, and the ELENA procedure (job card). This approach is based on the features of qualified electronic signatures and of electronic authentication, which shall be implemented on the various electronic cards. Germany's new Identity Card (e-id) provides additional functions than the traditional one (photo id, identification document, and travel document) so that the new card facilitates the reciprocal identification in the Internet. The card provides an (online) authentication functionality through a microchip applicable to online transactions in order to promote the usage of electronic signatures. Finally, the electronic health card, based on a smart microchip, is being implemented and will support both administrative and medical applications. All these activities are aimed at providing citizen inclusion (German e-Government Factsheets, Ed. 14.0; German e-inclusion Factsheets, Ed. 2.0).

If we consider the specific availability and sophistication of public service digital delivery, the analysis of the 12 services shows a limited use of Gov 2.0 tools, restricted to RSS, social networking sites, microblogs, and wikis (Table 5.2). Moreover, we did not find any blog, mashups, podcast, and video sharing.

5.3.2.3 Italy

The e-Government portal for citizens is www.italia.gov.it. It has been described as an engine of change for all online public services by Italian government, which aims at improving electronic participation through a more intense use of digital communication technologies. This portal helps citizens to access directly to the

Table 5.3 Gov 2.0 tools for citizens in Italy

Web 2.0 tools	Services for citizens											
	[1] IncTax	[2] JobSea	[3] SocSec	[4] PerDoc	[5] CarRe	[6] BuiPer	[7] DecPol	[8] PubLib	[9] Cert	[10] HigE	[11] AnnM	[12] Hea
Blogs		X										
Microblogs		X										
Mashups												
Podcast												
RSS	X	X	X					X				X
Social networking sites				X								X
Video sharing			X									X
Wikis	X	X				X	X			X		X

For abbreviations see Table 5.1 footer

sites through which they can interact with public administrations. About digital identification and authentication, the Italian electronic ID card comprises a microchip, an optical memory, and an ICAO machine readable zone for the use of the card as a travel document. It contains a set of personal data, including the holder's fiscal code, blood group, and fingerprint scans. The microchip makes online identification possible, enables transactions between citizens and providers, including e-payments, and it can also store digital signature certificates. Moreover, the service of certified e-mail is available that enables citizens to exchange messages with the public administrations in a legal compliant manner. The Italian Government has launched several special projects that aim to provide a more inclusive e-Government, improving the efficiency and the transparency of the public administration and the quality of the Administration-to-Citizen relationship. For instance, the *Linea Amica* project is designed to enhance citizens' trust, collecting the degree of citizens' satisfaction and making it public, the *Mettiamoci la faccia* project allows the citizens-customers to assess in real-time the public services they have used, and the *Reti Amiche* project aims at multiplying the access points and reducing the waiting time (Italian e-Government Factsheets, Ed. 14.0; Italian e-inclusion Factsheets, Ed. 2.0).

Considering the specific availability and sophistication of public service digital delivery, the analysis highlights (Table 5.3) a reasonable use of Gov 2.0 tools, mainly due to the use of RSS, wikis, and video sharing. More limited is the use of blogs, microblogs, and social networking sites. Last, mashups and podcast are never used.

5.3.2.4 The United Kingdom

The e-Government portal for citizens www.direct.gov.uk provides easy and effective digital access to all public services and related information. The portal is organized on the basis of major public services areas (e.g., health, education, employment)

Table 5.4 Gov 2.0 tools for citizens in the United Kingdom

Web 2.0 tools	Services for citizens											
	[1] IncTax	[2] JobSea	[3] SocSec	[4] PerDoc	[5] CarRe	[6] BuiPer	[7] DecPol	[8] PubLib	[9] Cert	[10] HigE	[11] AnnM	[12] Hea
Blogs												
Microblogs	▓	▓					▓		▓			
Mashups												
Podcast												
RSS					▓							
Social networking sites	▓	▓	▓			▓			▓	▓		
Video sharing	▓											
Wikis	▓	▓	▓						▓	▓		▓

For abbreviations see Table 5.1 footer

and on target customer groups (e.g., parents, disabled people, youth). The breadth of information presented is vast, reducing the need for users to navigate further sites. About digital identification and authentication, the Government Gateway is the main central UK identification platform and a central registration and authentication engine. Users are required to register in order to use online services and subsequently transact securely with the respective departments. User identification is based either on a digital certificate issued by an accredited certification authority, or on a user ID (supplied by the Government Gateway) and a password for services that do not require the level of security provided by digital certificates. About e-inclusion, the portal (DirectGov) is a multi-channel service across Web, TV, and mobile. To increase and widen digital engagement, DirectGov acts as an enabler offering easy access to public services across its TV and mobile platforms offering services such as 'Find my nearest' UK online center database across its multi-channel service of Web, TV, and mobile. Finally, sections provided by the portal have a customer feedback in order to collect the citizens-customers' assessment of the usefulness of the information given in the website (UK e-Government Factsheets, Ed. 14.0; UK e-inclusion Factsheets, Ed. 2.0).

Considering the availability and sophistication of public service digital delivery, the analysis shows (Table 5.4) a high use of Gov 2.0 tools, mainly due to the use of microblogs, social networking sites, video sharing, and wikis. On the other hand, we did not find any blogs, mashups, and podcasts.

Gathering together all the results, it is possible to assess the degree of Gov 2.0 in the four European countries analyzed. For each country, Table 5.5 shows in the first column the number of services (out of the 12 public services considered) that make use of at least one Gov 2.0 tool for service delivery, and the second column reports the corresponding percentage.

There is a massive presence of Gov 2.0 tools, particularly of microblogs, social network sites, video sharing, and wikis. It seems that the UK efforts have been focused only on a limited number of tools, but they use them extensively. France and

Table 5.5 Gov 2.0 tools for citizens in France, Germany, Italy, and the UK

	France		Germany		Italy		UK	
	n.	%	n.	%	n.	%	n.	%
Blogs					1	8		
Microblogs			2	17	1	8	8	67
Mashups								
Podcast	5	42						
RSS	8	67	2	17	6	50	1	8
Social networking sites			2	17	1	8	8	67
Video sharing	1	8			3	125	9	75
Wikis	10	67	4	42	7	17	10	17
Total	24	25	10	10	19	20	36	38

Italy presents a more limited use of Gov 2.0 in comparison to the UK, with France that replicates the UK ideas of development of Gov 2.0 on limited number of tools, namely podcast, RSS, and wikis and Italy that presents a more diversified composition that involves all the Gov 2.0 tools except for mashups and podcast. Last, Germany presents a very scarce use of Gov 2.0 technologies, even if condensed among four areas, namely microblogs, RSS, social networking sites, and wikis.

Referring to the theory of innovations diffusion, according to Rogers and Shoemaker (1971), at present the major EU countries have understood the potential of Gov 2.0 tools (*knowledge* stage) and demonstrated a positive attitude toward the innovation (*persuasion* stage); nevertheless, there is a lack of explicit *decision* (*decision stage*) to adopt Gov 2.0 tools at a strategic level, even if practices demonstrate to different extents such adoption. Maybe a reinforcement for the decision to adopt Gov 2.0 technologies (*confirmation* stage) would help to strengthen both strategies and practices in the EU.

Considering the five adopter categories of Rogers and Shoemaker (1971) the UK represents an *innovator* country, being the first one largely adopting Gov 2.0, while France and Italy can be seen as *early adopters,* acting as the second group to adopt Gov 2.0; Germany seems to represent the kind of adopter defined as *early majority* that demonstrates cautious and slower progress in the Gov 2.0 adoption process.

5.4 Conclusions

The aim of this chapter was to analyze the extent to which the shift to Gov 2.0 technologies, embedded in the latest European governments strategies, is changing public service delivery in practice. After having setup the scenario of Gov 2.0 within public administration, providing context, incentives, and theoretical framework for Gov 2.0, it was presented an overview of the strategic plans launched by the EU in order to strengthen e-Government services for citizens. One of the major changes enabled by Gov 2.0 technologies is the sharing of information with citizens and expanding the communication outreach to the citizenry. Along with the benefits of these technologies, challenges such as security and privacy issues have to be confronted and addressed.

The analysis of the four major European countries, namely Germany, France, Italy, and the UK showed that even if they did not mention Gov. 2.0 in their official e-Government strategies, they posed an implicit emphasis on citizens' needs of interaction with public service using ICT technologies end e-Government tools. In particular, the French and UK governments have been pushing their administration units toward a citizen-centered implementation of ICT, whereas Germany and Italy have focused more on the modernization and efficiency of public services through the use of ICT from a "supply side" perspective.

We investigated the extent to which such differences in the strategic emphases reflected on the way the four European countries delivered public service through Gov 2.0 technologies in practice. The results of our empirical analysis show that the use of Gov 2.0 technologies by central administrations differ among the four countries analyzed. The UK shows a larger use Gov 2.0 tools, focused on a limited number of tools (microblogs, social network sites, video sharing and wikis). France and Italy show a more limited use of Gov 2.0 tools. France presents a development of Gov 2.0 on a limited number of tools (mainly podcast, RSS and wikis), as well as the UK, whereas Italy has all the Gov 2.0 tools (except for mashups and podcast). Germany presents a rather scarce use of Gov 2.0 technologies, condensed within the areas of microblogs, RSS, social networking sites, and wikis. Considering the five adopter categories in the framework of innovations diffusion by Rogers and Shoemaker (1971) the UK represents the *innovator*, being the first country largely adopting the Gov 2.0, France and Italy can be considered as *early adopters*, while Germany seems to represent an *early majority*, due to the slower progress in the Gov 2.0 adoption process. All in all at present the major EU countries seems to be placed between the decision and the confirmation stage of the innovation diffusion theory, position caused by the lack of an explicit *decision* to adopt Gov 2.0 tools at a strategic level, even if the practices clearly demonstrate to different extents such adoption. Maybe an explicit reinforcement for the decision to adopt Gov 2.0 technologies would help to strengthen both strategies and practices in the EU.

The reason for such a heterogeneity may be found in the different strategic focus with which the four countries analyzed have implemented ICT to provide public services over the last decade. For instance, Italy and Germany seem to be more focused on exploiting the advantages of e-Government in order to improve the efficiency of public administrations and reduce bureaucracy. On the other hand, France has always set out strategies more ambitious than the EU guidelines on e-Government, trying to achieve both modernization of public administrations and improvement in the quality of public services for citizens. Finally, since the beginning the UK e-Government strategy has been centered on customers' needs and engagement, more than on simply increasing the efficiency of processes. Thus, it is not surprising that the ICT-enabled public services provided by central government in the UK tend to be more interactive and user oriented than those in Germany and Italy.

The results of the analysis have to be viewed in light of its limits. In particular, within this work the analysis focuses on the area of services for citizens due to impossibility of evaluating business online services, the access to whom is restricted to subjects that can prove the status of firm. Moreover, to guarantee comparability among different countries we investigated Gov 2.0 tools inside a limited number of sites, the ones directly identified by each country as the best cases of e-government development and listed in the Factsheets. Last, at this stage of analysis we were able to measure the presence of different Gov 2.0 tools, but not the intensity of use. This represents the main area of interest for further research.

The importance of this chapter for public administrators is realized in that it helps them to make certain the relevance of these Gov 2.0 applications for governmental organizations. For researchers this effort opens new research streams to ascertain how to measure these applications determining the effectiveness and efficiency for the delivery of public services.

References

Accenture. (2009). *Web 2.0 and the next generation of public service*. Retrieved from http://www.accenture.com.

Baumgarten, J., & Chui, M. (2009). E-government 2.0. *McKinsey on Government, Summer* (4). Retrieved from www.mckinseyquarterly.com/E-government_20_2408.

Chang, M., & Kannan, P. (2008). *Leveraging Web 2.0 in government*. IBM Center for the Business of Government. Retrieved from www.businessofgovernment.ort/pdfs/ChangReport2.pdf.

Council and the European Commission, eEurope 2002: An Information Society For All, 14.6.2000, Brussels.

Drapeau, M., & Wells, L. (2009). *Social software and national security: An initial net assessment*. Center for Technology and National Security Policy, National Defense University. Retrieved from http://www.ndu.edu/ctnsp/Def_Tech/DTP61.

European Commission, A Digital Agenda for Europe, 26.8.2010, COM(2010) 245 final/2, Brussels.

European Commission, Directorate General, Information Society and Media (2010) 'Digitising Public Services in Europe: Putting ambition into action–9th Benchmark Measurement', December.

European Commission, eEurope 2005: An Information Society For All, 28.5.2002, COM(2002) 263 final, Brussels.

European Commission, i2010—An European information society for growth and employment, 1.6.2005, COM(2005) 229 final, Brussels.

European Commission, i2010 eGovernment Action Plan: Accelerating eGovernment in Europe for the Benefit of All, 25.04.2006, COM(2006) 173 final, Brussels.

European Commission, The European eGovernment Action Plan 2011–2015: Harnessing ICT to promote smart, sustainable & innovative Government, 15 December 2010, COM(2010) 743, Brussels.

French eGovernment Factsheets, Ed. 10.0, 13.1, 14.0, from June 2008 to January 2011. Retrieved from www.epractice.eu/en/factsheets.

French eInclusion Factsheets, Ed. 1.0, October 2010. Retrieved from www.epractice.eu/en/factsheets.

German eGovernment Factsheets, Ed. 10.0, 13.0, 14.0, from July 2008 to January 2011. Retrieved from www.epractice.eu/en/factsheets.

German eInclusion Factsheets, Ed. 2.0, October 2010. Retrieved from www.epractice.eu/en/factsheets.

Italian eGovernment Factsheets, Ed. 9.1, 13.1, 14.0, from June 2008 to March 2011. Retrieved from www.epractice.eu/en/factsheets.

Italian eInclusion Factsheets, Ed. 2.0, April 2010. Retrieved from www.epractice.eu/en/factsheets.

McKinsey Global Survey Results. (2008). *Building the Web 2.0 enterprise*. Retrieved from http://McKinseyquarterly.com.

O'Reilly, T. (2007). What is Web 2.0: Design patterns and business models for the next generation of software? *Communications & Strategies*, 65(1), 17–36.

Orelli R.L., Padovani E., Scorsone E., (2010a), "Information Systems, Accountability, and Performance in the Public Sector: A Cross-Country Comparison", in Garson D., Shea C. (eds.), Handbook of Public Information Systems, CRC Press/Routledge, pp. 453–78.

Orelli R.L., Padovani E., Scorsone E., (2010b), "E-Government, Accountability, and Performance: Best-In-Class Governments in European Union Countries", in C. G. Reddick (ed.), Comparative E-Government: An Examination of E-Government Adoption across Countries, Springer, New York, pp. 561–86.

Organisation for Economic Development and Cooperation (OECD). (2003). OECD. *The e-government imperative*. Paris: OECD e-government studies.

Rogers, E. M. with Shoemaker, F. (1971). *Communication of innovation: A cross-cultural approach* (2nd ed.). New York: Free Press.

UK eGovernment Factsheets, Ed. 10.0, 13.0, 14.0, from October 2008 to July 2010 (retrieved from www.epractice.eu/en/factsheets).

UK eInclusion Factsheets, Ed. 2.0, July 2010 (retrieved from www.epractice.eu/en/factsheets).

Venkatesh, V., Morris, M. G., Davis, G. B., & Davis, F. D. (2003). User acceptance of information technology: Toward a unified view. MIS Quarterly, 27(3), 425–478.

Wigand F. D. L., (2010), 'Adoption of Web 2.0 by Canadian and US Governments', in C. G. Reddick ed., Comparative E-Government: An Examination of E-Government Adoption across Countries, Springer, New York. 161–82.

Wigand, R. T. (2007). Web 2.0: Disruptive technology or is everything miscellaneous? In A. Huizing & E. J. de Vries (Eds.), Information management: Setting the scene (pp. 269–284). Oxford, England and Amsterdam, the Netherlands: Elsevier Scientific Publishers.

Chapter 6
A Viability Model for Digital Cities: Economic and Acceptability Factors

Leonidas G. Anthopoulos and Theologis E. Tougountzoglou

6.1 Introduction

Various notions such as "digital cities", "smart cities", "knowledge spaces", etc. refer to limited geographic spaces (e.g. cities, peripheries, neighbors, clusters) where information and communication technology (ICT) infrastructures and applications are installed and offer various forms of e-services. In this chapter, the term "digital city" (Anthopoulos and Fitsilis 2010) will be used to refer to all the above notions. The scope of the deployed e-services is extensive and many of them are based on Web 2.0 applications in order to achieve social participation. The components of a digital city usually concern "smart people", "smart environment", "smart economy", "smart governance", "smart mobility" which generally constitute the notion of "smart living" (Giffinger et al. 2007). On the other hand, according to Caragliu et al. (2009), a city can be "smart" *"when investments in human and social capital combined with traditional and modern ICT infrastructure fuel sustainable economic development and a high quality of life, with a wise management of natural resources, through participatory governance"*. This last approach suggests the significance of "sustainability" in "smart living".

Digital cities are being evolved for more than 15 years and introduce new ways for peripheral and urban development, which are based on the simultaneous evolution of the ICT solutions in the urban space. According to Ishida and Isbister (2000), in 1994 more than 100 European organisations started to discuss and

L. G. Anthopoulos (✉) · T. E. Tougountzoglou
Project Management Department,
Technological Education Institute (TEI) of Larissa,
41110 Larissa, Greece
e-mail: lanthopo@teilar.gr

T. E. Tougountzoglou
e-mail: tougount@yahoo.gr

C. G. Reddick and S. K. Aikins (eds.), *Web 2.0 Technologies and Democratic Governance*, Public Administration and Information Technology 1, DOI: 10.1007/978-1-4614-1448-3_6, © Springer Science+Business Media New York 2012

debate over digital cities, while similar initiatives were undertaken in the USA and in Japan during the same period. The objectives of these initiatives concerned the utilization and the exploitation of the ICT in order to reinforce the local stability, sustainability, and economy, and improve the everyday life in the cities. However, each initiative faced different challenges and priorities that lead to different objectives and to ways for evolution. The primary objectives of a city concern the improvement of the residents' everyday life, the development of knowledge-based societies, the "close" of the "digital divide" -in terms of ICT literacy, in the creation of free-of-charge e-services, and in encouraging social participation via the ICT, and the simplification of the public services (Anthopoulos and Fitsilis 2010). Moreover, some digital cities (e.g. Dubai and Amsterdam smart cities) prioritize e-commerce services and fee-based public services, while others (e.g. Trikala Greece, Barcelona, Hull) deploy free of charge the entire set of the deployed services. Others focus on the local quality of life, while others prioritize the viability of the digital city.

The social dimensions, the extensive scale and the diversity of the various digital cities, suggest a careful investigation on the economic and social needs that lie beneath such a project. The identification of these local needs will secure a careful and sustainable urban growth. Moreover, the deployment of Web 2.0 applications is critical since they establish social participation in decision making over the definition and the review of the digital city's objectives, which consider environmental, renewable resources', and health's issues. Finally, the success of such a project has to be secured, since huge funding supports its implementation and various social implications accompany its deployment.

In the following section, a domain analysis and a digital cities' classification constitute the background of this chapter. Section 6.3 concludes on the sets of e-services that are provided by the most important digital city cases, and considers the digital city as a unique Web 2.0 application where citizens can participate, deliberate, and contribute with various forms of sources via the available e-services. In Sect. 6.4, the sustainability and the viability considerations of a digital city are summarized and a viability model that can be adaptive by various different cases is structured and proposed. In the final section, some conclusions are extracted and some future thoughts are discussed.

6.2 Background

Cities around the world cover 2 % of the entire Earth's surface and host the 55 % of the global population. This rate is estimated to reach 75 % (6.4 billion people) until 2050. In fact, 450 cities have a population of more than a million people, while 20 of them have a population that exceeds 10 million people (OECD 2008). In 1975, only three megacities existed (Tokyo, Mexico City, and New York with 53 million people population) while in 2009 this number exceeded the 21 (Tokyo and New Delhi hosted 320 million people). According to McKinsey Global

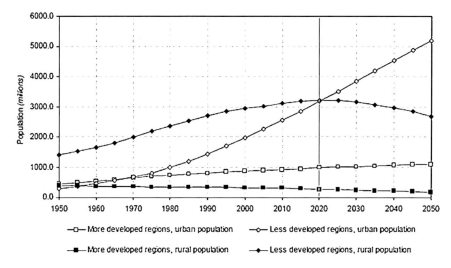

Fig. 6.1 Urban and rural populations per regional growth rate (U.N. Department of Economic and Social Affairs—Population Division 2010)

Institute (2009), it is estimated that a population of 350 million people will move from rural to urban areas, structuring an unprecedented poverty within the urban centers. It is expected that the world in 2025 will create refugees mainly from Asian countries that will move to Western cities as an attempt for employment and for political stability (European Commission 2010). By 2009, the 51 % of the world's population lived in cities. United Nations (UN) Secretary–General Ban Ki-moon stated that "*we are living in an 'urban century'*" (Ban Ki-moon 2009). Urbanization presents variation according to the national tendencies, the political affairs, the market transformations within and outside countries, and the realization of the growth and prosperity, which are all presented on (Fig. 6.1).

On the other hand, digital cities' evolution does not necessarily follow urbanism, since many cases occurred in small cities. In Fig. 6.2, the existing cases of various digital cities are classified according to their definition and to their objectives. In Fig. 6.2 the cities' names are mostly presented with the exception of Eurocities, of Portugal Cities and of Telecities, where the projects' titles are used. *Web cities* virtualized urban spaces and provided citizens with local information via the Web. *Digital and Smart cities* combine both the physical and the digital space in order to provide with e-services via extensive metropolitan infrastructures, while any smart city may be digital, but digital cities are not necessarily smart (Komninos 2002). Digital cities seem to mainly deploy public services designed by the State, while in smart cities collaboration between citizens and the State designs the kinds of e-services and forms of the digital space. *Ubiquitous cities (U-cities)* deploy ubiquitous computing around the city, which offers e-services from anywhere to everyone. On the other hand, *Broadband cities* use various communication technologies (fiber optic, Wi-Fi and Wi-Max networks, etc.) that enable connection to the

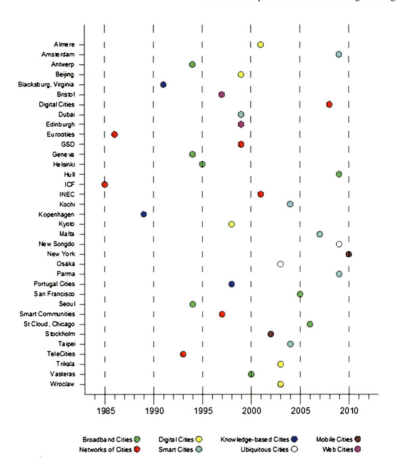

Fig. 6.2 Classification of major cases and their evolution

internet and to local e-services to citizens and enterprises. *Mobile cities* concern wireless networks installed in the city, via which residents and visitors access various types of applications and services. *Knowledge-based cities* utilize the ICT for their development. Databases collect local information and structure empirical knowledge bases of domains of interest in the areas, which are accessible by citizens and local authorities. Finally, *networks of cities* are structured via the ICT in order to face common challenges or to create opportunities for common growth by different cities in the same or in different countries.

As it was mentioned before, in this chapter the term *digital city* covers and describes all the above mentioned forms in order to not confuse the reader. In this context, the above classification gives the dimensions to a digital city that vary from metropolitan ICT infrastructures, to virtual representations of a city. The first dimension of *broadband and wireless cities* transforms a city to an extensive worksite, where all its physical features may be updated in order for the ICT to be incorporated and to support urban living. Moreover, ubiquitous infrastructure is installed and provides the decision makers with tools and methods to monitor and perform sustainable urban planning. Like in other large-scale projects, a transitional period until the completion mediates until the city transforms to digital.

The second dimension of *web cities* classifies cities in commercial, governmental, community networks, and virtual cities according to project's priorities. Commercial cities are driven by market and they offer guides and catalogs with information -such as sightseeing, restaurants and hotels, shops, etc.—for the residents and the visitors. An alternative web form concerns a network of similar information called Community Network, which was introduced by the *Free-Nets* in Cleveland (USA). The rationale that lies behind Free-Nets is the connection of similar web cities and the composition of a digital community. This community intends to collect and organize information in a consistent manner and to create websites for the communication of its members. Non-profit organisations are created and they operate through donations and governmental grants. The viability of Community Networks is not ensured since they provide free-of-charge services.

The third dimension concerns the *digital and the smart city* and it is supported by the local Government and/or the local market, as a means to develop e-Government and e-Commerce services and information. E-Services of the four e-Government levels are observed in various cases; while in some of them e-Democracy applications enable public consultations and social dialog. E-Services are grouped according to their users—e.g., the services provided by the municipality could be grouped under the name "city hall, while citizens can actively contribute and to participate in city's transformation.

6.3 Digital City's Services and Applications

In March 2010, the European Commission proposed the "Europe 2020 Strategy" in order to overcome the economic crisis and to support the European member countries for the upcoming decade. New jobs, productivity growth, and social cohesion have been identified as the primary challenges, while the Commission has determined the axes of precedence to achieve in particular objectives. The Digital Agenda suggests the cornerstone of the European policy, which presents the contribution of the ICT to various European challenges (European Commission 2010). In this context, the European digital cities capitalize funding opportunities provided by the European e-strategies in order to align their environments in order to:

- establish information flow cross-border services and create a common digital market,
- create secure networks and preserve privacy,
- install fast networks to support innovative services,

- use ICT for energy saving, for health and care services' provision and for the improvement of public services,
- promote research and innovation via the transformation of goods and services, and
- offer learning opportunities, and utilize human resources with the ICT.

Digital cities have to become viable through a two-stage phase (Schaffers, et al. 2011) in order to deal with above mentioned challenges. The first stage concerns the installation of (a) fiber optic network and wireless networks that will provide high speed connectivity, (b) sensors and smart devices around the city in order to collect and deliver data, and (c) appropriate applications to handle the collected information. The second stage concerns the structure of groups of central administrative members and of ordinary citizens that will monitor and review digital city's progress.

The components of a digital city are grouped in multitier (n-tier) architecture (Anthopoulos and Fitsilis 2010) and determine the structure and the features of new products and services. *Ubiquitous computing* can offer broadband connection in competitive prices. *Modern portable devices* provide ease-of-access to information and services. *Handheld devices* enable remote control of distributed infrastructures. *Open access* contributes to decision-making over issues of common interest. *Mining and statistical analysis methods* support decision makers. *The Internet of Things* concerns the wireless interconnection of sensors and other devices, in order to collect and process data from anywhere, and to contribute with energy saving, distant healthcare, weather prediction, atmospheric, and water pollution, etc. *Cloud computing* can support delivery of software as a service and of hardware as a service solutions of low cost. *Geospatial platforms* enable the visualization of the above information and support decision makers.

The transformation of applications into consuming services is vital for the development and improvement of the above mentioned components, and hence for the viability of digital cities. Utilizing applications should arise as a result of thorough planning and programing. The cooperation between the provider and the receiver of the service is considered even more crucial in order to improve the product and ensure the viability of initiatives.

Moreover, the role of Web 2.0 technologies (social networks, wikis, blogs, Podcasts, Enhanced events, extended networks, cloud services, etc.) is predominant. Via Web 2.0 applications the transparent information flow among the participants is enhanced, while there are no restrictions of the communication channels. Web 2.0 is a powerful and advanced technology, but in any case, the ICT are still evolving rapidly (O'Reilly and Battelle 2009). The adoptions of new technologies, business strategies, and social trends have to be effective (Murugesan 2007) in order for a smooth transformation to be established in the city. In (Fig. 6.3) the evolution of Internet technologies is presented, in order to describe how rapid the evolution is, and how critical the adoption of technological evolution is for the sustainability of the digital city.

The above considerations and the potential digital city's e-services could be summarized as follows:

1. Digital city's infrastructures provide information exchange from everywhere to anyone.
2. Numerous e-services (e.g. e-dialoguing, e-health, tele-care services, crowd sourcing, and knowledge bases) concern the composition of social networks and crowd sourcing via Web 2.0 technologies.
3. Various social networks can be deployed in the city, which can focus on local particular needs (e.g. Smart Communities).
4. The entire digital environment that the digital city structures can offer global e-Government and various e-services, both from local and national authorities (Anthopoulos and Tsoukalas 2006).
5. The implementation model for a digital city (Anthopoulos and Tsoukalas 2006) considers various Web 2.0 issues such as privacy and ethics.

The above remarks show that a digital city can be considered as an entire Web 2.0 application, which offers various e-services and provides with crowd sourcing tools for social participation and for information collection across the city or a network of cities. This Web 2.0 environment could support local communities in addressing economic and social challenges. Moreover, this Web 2.0 environment can be effectively used only if it is adopted by the local community and by various stakeholders (enterprises, Non-Governmental Organizations (NGOs), and local Government).

Furthermore, various aspects concern Web 2.0 applications. From the citizen point of view, the adoption of Web 2.0 services is based on their contribution to the particular local needs. Particularly the governments can focus on collaborative decision-making and strategic planning (Reddick 2011). In this context, the constructive interactivity and interventionism with the citizens can reinforce democracy and participatory governance (Macintosh and Whyte 2008). Urban rapid growth that was mentioned above requires the transition from the traditional models of high resource demanding to modern ones, especially today where municipal budget are constantly truncated due to current economic conditions. However, like any other innovative project, there are risks that should be undertaken. Low participation, poor input quality, managerial inefficiencies, and trust, question the viability of digital cities (Osimo 2008).

On the other hand, from the business point of view, Web 2.0 in combination with the consumers' attitudes has brought huge profits to the private sector, which is enabled to easily collect information about consumers' preferences and satisfaction. Moreover, managers have reinforced marketing and sales strategies with improved and focused methods in order to extend their market share. Web 2.0 applications are low cost, effective and user friendly, and in this context they have been adopted by many enterprises. Additionally, Web 2.0 applications enable businesses to approach international markets.

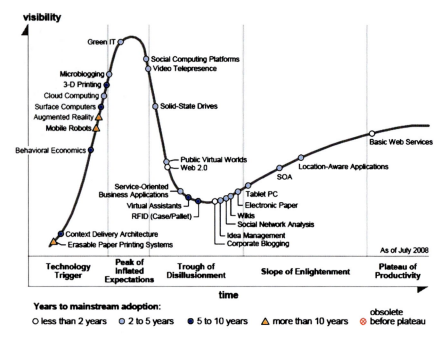

Fig. 6.3 Internet evolution (Gartner Research 2009)

6.4 Viability and Sustainability Aspects

During the second half of the tewntieth century, large-scale projects concerned transportation networks at national and supranational levels (railways, highways, and airports) and the improvement of everyday life (e.g. water supply and sewerage networks). On the other hand, during the last 15 years, cities around the world tend to capitalize knowledge and innovation via the ICT utilization in an effort to improve urban life (Komninos 2002). However, large infrastructure projects for digital cities constitute a novel challenge. Extensive funding is allocated on engineering projects, either by the public or the private sectors. These projects affect urban life and cause major problems in traffic and in environmental condition during their construction. Therefore, potential failure of these projects has to be avoided.

A definition of the term sustainable development has been given by the prime minister of Norway, Gro Harlem Brundtland in her 1987 report to the UN as chairman of the World Commission on Environment and Development: "*the development that meets the needs of the present without compromising the ability of future generations to meet their own needs*" (World Commission on Environment and Development 1987). At the Rio Earth Summit in 1992, from which the Agenda 21 for sustainable construction arose, sustainable development was defined as "*the development which in the long run provides economic, social and environmental benefits meeting the needs of present and future generations*". The attention that international organizations (Organization for Economic Cooperation and Development (OECD), European Union (EU), United Nations (UN), etc.) and scientists paid on sustainability about its contribution for future social evolution, the term has been supported by legislation, while it has been integrated within the international law and the European Union's law.

Today, the notion of sustainability differs across countries and it is accompanied by a plethora of standards, while it reflects national economic growth. The most developed countries aim in upgrading their existing infrastructures and buildings, as well as their technological automation, in order to become innovative in implementing construction projects. Developing countries on the other hand, aim in developing digital cities of hybrid forms, based on the experience of best cases, and in an effort to capitalize funding opportunities by framework programmes. Various indices and factors can measure the viability of a digital city, while they can play a vital role in its planning and definition. These factors concern geographic, financial, socio-political, cultural, legal, technical, environmental, and social perspectives.

6.4.1 Recent Challenges that Affect Digital City's Viability

The composition of a viability model for digital cities should satisfy three primary parties: the client—usually the local Government—, the contractor, and the end users (Project Management Institute (PMI), 2008; Construction [sic] Project Management (Federal Transit Administration 2007). In this context, the OECD, the EU and the UN behave as regulatory authorities, and they define strategies and objectives to be followed by national Governments. These organizations are responsible for equal opportunities, for red tape bureaucratic elimination, for corruption treatment, for market competition and, in this context they offer funding opportunities to the Governments.

According to the declaration for the future of the Internet Economy that took place in Seoul (OECD 2008), the digital content is a key factor toward the formation of social and economic growth. Some primary principles were defined that support the implementation of various digital initiatives, the installation of ICT infrastructures and the encouragement of private investment in creation, deployment, and maintenance of digital content (OECD 2008). In June 2011, a meeting of the Internet Economy took place in Paris, in order to review and identify the reasons that caused failures in the aforementioned efforts. The participants noted that the delay in measuring the end users' expectations from the ICT initiatives led to unused and inactive projects. Moreover, it was highlighted that the Internet's power and vitality depend on high-speed networks, on transparency and on trust (OECD 2011).

6.4.2 Implementation Models for Digital Cities

On the other hand, the digital cities are modern projects and therefore insufficient data are available for decision makers. However, serious argument concerns the economic and the social dimensions of these projects, since the number, the types and the applicability of the offered e-services are unknown during the planning and the implementation phases. It is also difficult to predict the acceptance and the profit of these services. Moreover, ICT infrastructures alone will not contribute to (New Millennium Research Council 2005):

1. closing the "digital divide",
2. the economic growth, since they do not affect the key factors toward this direction (urban income growth, reduction of unemployment, etc.),
3. the economic viability.

The capitalization of infrastructures by e-services and applications is the only means to increase the value of the digital cities. Social networking and participation can contribute via composing an open digital space. In this context, the Government should act as a key-role market player, without abusing its power to act as a regulator and a service provider simultaneously.

As already mentioned, social participation during the stage of definition and planning of a digital city is critical. In this context, it is not determined whether the selected e-services in the digital city initiatives meet user expectations (Ishida et al. 2009). This occurs due to the existence of gap between computer science and social sciences (Ishida, Aurigi, and Yasuoka 2005). Technology offers opportunities, which are eventually evaluated concerning their practicality by the end users. For instance, collaborative environments of Web 2.0 applications are preferred due to their contribution in interoperability and in knowledge transfer. On the other hand, the insufficient end users' ICT skills will lead to overestimation of the available e-services. From technical perspective, insufficient requirements engineering is performed that demands extensive funding for infrastructure, while only a few e-services are deployed (e.g. digital city of Trikala). This ineffective requirements analysis results in huge infrastructure maintenance costs without citizens enjoying e-services. Standardization accompanied by a proper legal framework could lead to funding capitalization and to successful digital city projects (Anthopoulos et al. 2010). Other reasons of failure concern the inability to ensure the source of incomes/revenues or even to secure the initial funding, as well as its future maintenance and expansion (Iowa Communications Network, California's CALNET system, etc.).

The evaluation and review of a digital city concern the identification of viable solutions for the particular case. Evaluation plays a vital role in innovative projects since they involve uncertainty and complexity. A flexible evaluation process that enables management and correction of any divergence through the setting of metrics and goals has to be identified. Moreover, the space where digital cities are developed is dynamic, and it is formed under the interaction between local stakeholders (Fig. 6.4).

Fig. 6.4 Local stakeholders participating for effective management (Naphade et al. 2011)

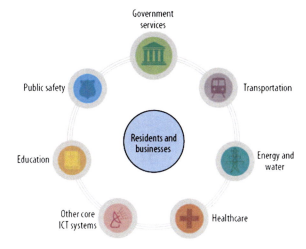

Therefore, the implementation model of a digital city consists of three levels (IBM 2009). *Planning* utilizes the information that is collected from users and/or the existing city services. It supports the management team to define and align strategies to the local priorities, and to make use of best practices. *Management* enables the implementation of coordinated tasks for the implementation of infrastructures and for the association with the future urban development. *Functions* embody multiple data sources that represent the real time coordination of city's components.

The satisfaction of various parameters that are defined by the involved stakeholders under a bottom-up procedure (Anthopoulos 2005) is necessary in order to the digital city to be successful and adopted. For the purposes of this chapter, these factors are classified in the following categories (Van Bastelaer and Lobet-Maris 1999), which affect requirements engineering process (Anthopoulos 2005).

Geographic factors refer to the geopolitical conditions in the country, city or region where the digital city will be located. They are influenced by the national strategies and framework programs. *Economic and market factors* refer to wealth, enterprises, and growth level in the particular area. A flavor economic environment for households and firms typically secures technology acceptance. Additionally, regional funding opportunities support innovative initiatives. *Sociopolitical factors* concern the intention of local community to participate in project definition, development, and use. The political factors mainly focus on the level of transparency in public procedures, and on the encouragement for projects' initiation. *Legal factors* refer to the legal framework that prevails in the region. The flexibility and the absence of bureaucratic procedures support e-service deployment and use. *Cultural factors* concern social attitudes and indicate the existence of communities of common interests, which could potentially support innovative initiatives. *Technological factors* refer to the technologies that are involved in the project, and to the existence of the appropriate ICT industry to provide and support them. *Human factors* indicate the existence of supervisors and executives with proper skills. Finally, *Environmental factors* identify project's environmental implications, and means to establish sustainable urban planning with the ICT.

The above factors can compose a suitable viability model, which with appropriate alignments can lead to a viable digital city. A digital city can be considered large scale due to its implications and duration—since large-scale projects are usually concerned with a budget of more than $1 billion, with timeframe of more than 5 years, with significant implications for the society, the environment, and the economy (Flyvbjerg et al. 2003). Moreover, digital city is affected by a variety of factors, some of which were potentially considered under project's planning, but others rise during project's implementation and cause delays or even project's abandonment. In this context, sufficient management and continuous project evaluation by the project team are necessary to secure project's completion.

6.4.3 The Determination Process for a Viability Model

The proposed viability model requires stakeholders' involvement during all implementation phases (design, development, operation, maintenance, and expansion). However, this is a complex procedure since stakeholders see project from different perspectives, while they have different levels of duties during the lifecycle of the project (PMI 2008). Their involvement varies from participation in surveys to full involvement in development and management. Moreover, the involvement of the end users in the development and the operation of a digital city is critical. Additionally, an effective collaboration between project team, end users, and society has to be established during project's lifecycle, with identified limits for social participation. Furthermore, the development of a digital city requires the private–public sector involvement, in order to the funding to be secured. The involvement of the above stakeholders structures a complex project organization, which can be optimized with the identification of limits and of relations among each other. End users for instance are involved to secure adoption; they have to be approached during project design and must be kept informed during project development.

The viability of a large-scale project—like a digital city—is influenced by quantitative and qualitative parameters. The proposed model incorporates the most important qualitative factors that affect the development, and influence quantitatively its viability. Moreover, the model has been flexible in order to align to different cases. In this context, Ozdoganm and Birgonul (2000), introduced a model that was based on a list of qualitative factors, which were aggregated according to whether they were project, country, or government policy related. Nevertheless, due to the subjectivity of judgment, their model does not measure the precise influence of qualitative factors on project development and it cannot support decision making process. Dias and Ioannou (1996) introduced a model that returns an index of attractiveness of projects via qualitative factors, which relate to the project and the national characteristics. However, their model requires time for structure and application, and it is limited to construction projects. The proposed model is inspired by the work performed by (Salman et al. 2007), which concerns concession projects (Built-Operate and Transfer (BOT) projects).

6.4.4 The Proposed Viability Model

In this chapter, only the construction procedure is presented, and an indicative form of the model is given on (Fig. 6.4). The presented indexes are indicative too, the actual implementation method, and data collection and process for this model are beyond the purposes of this chapter. The proposed model was structured in two phases: during the first phase the determination of viability critical factors is performed with literacy review (Tiong 1990, 1995a, b, 1996; Centre of Regional Science 2007; Dias and Ioannou 1996; Levy 1996; UNIDO 1996; Gupta and Narasimham 1998; Ranasinghe 1999; Ozdoganm and Birgonul 2000; Salman, Skibniewski and Basha 2007) and with the contribution of experts in large-scale ICT projects. During the second phase, the selected indices were determined with the contribution of senior ICT project managers and academics, via the Delphi method (Björn 2011).

The Delphi method is designed to support decided during the process of planning for the future, priority setting, and decision making. Delphi can be used to create hypotheses about the development of scenarios and their socio-economic impacts. For example, it has been widely used for the provisioning in the field of technology, education, and other sectors. These procedures are not easily supported by statistical models because it requires the inclusion of human crisis, as shaped by economic, technical and historical data (Björn 2011).

During the second phase, the income from the first phase was analyzed and classified in initial categories of factors. Initially, the qualitative factors were distinguished in two levels: the country level and the project level. In this context, the model becomes flexible and adaptable to a variety of different cases. On the other hand, the model has to be tested concerning the environmental performance of the project, its alignment to national policies, and to legal or other restrictions. Practice shows that the viability factors at this level are fuzzy and the evaluation procedures are usually defined by the international organizations (UN, World Bank, etc.), through annual reports and future forecasts. At project level, three (3) hierarchical levels structure the model (Dias and Ioannou 1996): the *first* hierarchical level concerns the objectives of the viability model; the *second* defines three or more primary categories of factors; and the *third* contains the qualitative factors (Fig. 6.5). These qualitative factors are determined under a Delphi method (Schmidt 1997), which has to be performed on senior ICT project managers, and/or experts, and/or academics. The Delphi method uses questionnaires that are structured, responded, and reviewed in at least two cycles: the first cycle intends to highlight, to aggregate and to prioritize critical factors for project viability (collected by domain analysis as well as from the individual recommendations).

The collected information is analyzed and submitted for evaluation to the respondents. The evaluation results are collected and used to update the initial model. The updated model can be reviewed similarly in other cycles. At the beginning of each cycle, the respondents are informed about the results of the previous round. Various cycles are executed until the "criterion of agreement" will be obtained, which achieves a minimum matching of 66 %. One of the Delphi method's advantages is the ability to capture expected future developments (Daniel and White 2005), such as research challenges and their implementation in a research agenda. After the collection of data from the executed cycles the final version of the hierarchical model is structured (Fig. 6.5).

After model's composition, model's validation is required in order for its relevance and adaptability to be tested. According to Dias and Ioannou (1996), several methods have been applied in an effort to validate results of multi-factor models because of the subjectivity's amount. For the purposes of the presented model, the Delphi method was applied on a panel of four academics, and on a panel of ten senior ICT project managers. These experts were questioned about their opinion on suggested viability model. The collected information was evaluated with a Chi-square test, in order for differences in the responses to be identified (SPSS 16.0 Software Package was used for this test). The results returned no significant differences between the two panels of experts.

6.5 Conclusions

In this chapter, the context of the digital city was analyzed as an attempt to determine sustainability and viability factors and to answer economic and social considerations on Web 2.0 applications. Various types of digital cities were identified and classified, together with their e-services and more specifically their Web 2.0 services. The entire digital city was considered as a Web 2.0 application that offers collaboration and crowd sourcing services.

Moreover, recent challenges and new technologies suggest participatory methods and applications to secure digital city's viability. Regardless the consideration of citizens', businesses' and State's perspectives during project's design, the viability of digital cities is critical. In this context, general guidelines offered by International Organizations were investigated, which will contribute failures' estimation and avoidance.

Finally, a viability model for digital cities was introduced, which incorporates several qualitative factors that can affect the evolution of a large-scale project. The development of the presented model was based on domain analysis for factors' proposition, and on a performed Delphi method on senior ICT project managers and academics for model's determination and testing. The subjectivity in factors' selection cannot be avoided, and returns weaknesses to the model. However, the above model provides the decision maker with the possibility (a) to determine the development of the project and focus on strengthening the factors that will assist

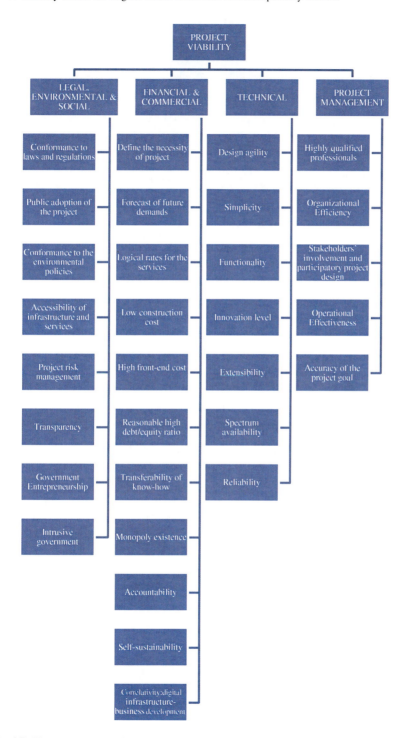

Fig. 6.5 The proposed viability model for digital city

project's success; (b) to specify the qualitative factors influencing digital city projects; (c) to incorporate new factors that rise during project's development, via the testing of the viability indices and the prioritization of factors; and (d) gives the opportunity for adding further categories that evaluates project's viability. Our future thoughts, concern the further testing of the proposed viability model on digital city's project managers around the world, in order to provide with as secure as possible viability indices to recent and to future digital cities.

References

Anthopoulos, L. (2005). Collaborating environments in e-government. PhD Thesis. Retrieved from Aristotle University of Thessaloniki–Psifiothiki. (GRI-2005-690).

Anthopoulos, L., & Fitsilis, P. (2010). *From Digital to Ubiquitous Cities: Defining a Common Architecture for Urban Development*. Paper presented at the Proceedings of the 6th International Conference on Intelligent Environments- IE'10, Malaysia. Retrieved, Sept. 2011 from: http://ieeexplore.ieee.org/stamp/stamp.jsp?tp=&arnumber=5673950

Anthopoulos, L. & Tsoukalas, I. (2006). The Implementation Model of a Digital City: The Case Study of the Digital City of Trikala, Greece. *Journal of E-Government, 2 (2)*, 91–109.

Anthopoulos, L., Gerogiannis, V. & Fitsilis, P. (2010). *Enterprise Architecture for e-Strategy Standardization and Management: Lessons Learnt from Greece*. International Journal of Digital Society (IJDS), Volume 1, Issue 4, December 2010.

Ban Ki-Moon, (2009). *Better, More Equitable Urban Planning is Essential* (On World's Habitat Day). Vienna: UN Information Service.

Björn, N. (2011). Iceberg ahead: On electronic government research and societal aging. *Government Information Quarterly, 28(3)*, 310–319.

Caragliu, A., Del Bo, C. & Nijkamp, P. (2009). Smart cities in Europe. *Series Research Memoranda 0048*. VU University Amsterdam, Faculty of Economics, Business Administration and Econometrics.

Centre of Regional Science (SRF). (2007). *Smart cities–Ranking of European medium-sized cities, Final Report*. Vienna: Centre of Regional Science.

Daniel, E. M., & White, A. (2005). The future of inter-organisational system linkages: Findings of an international Delphi study. *European Journal of Information Systems, 14*, 188–203.

Dias, A. Jr. & Ioannou, G. Ph. (1996). Company and project evaluation model for privately promoted infrastructure projects. *Journal of Construction Engineering and Management, 122 (1)*, 71–82.

European Commission. (2010). *Digital Agenda for Europe: Communication from the Commission*. Retrieved, Sept. 2011 from: http://eur-lex.europa.eu/LexUriServ/LexUriServ.do?uri=COM:2010:0245:FIN:EL:PDF

Federal Transit Administration. (2007). *Construction Project Management Handbook*. New York: FTA's Office of Technology. Retrieved, Sept. 2011 from: http://www.fta.dot.gov/documents/Construct_Proj_Mangmnt_CD.pdf

Flyvbjerg, B., Bruzelius, N., & Rothengatter, W. (2003). *Megaprojects and risk: an anatomy of ambition*. Cambridge: Cambridge University Press.

Gartner Research. (2009). *Hype Cycle for Emerging Technologies*. Stamford: Gartner Inc. Retrieved, Sept. 2011 from: http://bhc3.com/tag/gartner/

Giffinger, R., Fertner, C., Kramar, H., Meijers, e. & Pichler-Milanovic, N. (2007). *Smart Cities: Ranking of European medium-sized cities*. Retrieved, December, 2011 from: http://www.smartcities.eu/download/smart_cities_final_report.pdf

Gupta, M. C. & Narasimham, S. V. (1998). Discussion of 'CSFs in competitive tendering and negotiation model for BOT projects. *Journal of Construction Engineering and Management, 124 (5)*, 430.

IBM. (2009). *How Smart is your city? Helping cities measure progress.* New York: IBM Global Business Services.

Ishida, T., & Isbister, K. (2000). *Digital Cities: Technologies, Experiences, and Future Perspectives.* Germany: Springer.

Ishida, T., Aurigi, A., & Yasuoka, M. (2005). World Digital Cities: Beyond Heterogeneity. In P Van den Besselaar & S.Koizumi (eds), *Digital Cities 3: Information.technologies for social capital* (pp.271–314). Germany: Springer.

Ishida, T., Aurigi, A., & Yasuoka, M. (2009). The Advancement of World Digital Cities. In Nakashima, H., Aghajan, H., & Augusto, J.C. (eds.), *Handbook on Ambient Intelligence and Smart Environments* (pp.23). New York: Springer.

Komninos, N. (2002). *Intelligent Cities: Innovation, Knowledge Systems and Digital Spaces* (1st eds.). London: Routledge.

Levy, S. M. (1996). *Build, operate, and transfer: Paving the way for tomorrow's infrastructure.* New York: Wiley.

Macintosh, A., & Whyte, A. (2008). Towards an evaluation framework for e-Participation. *Transforming Government: People, Process and Policy, 2 (1),* 16–30.

McKinsey Global Institute. (2009). *Preparing for China's urban billion.* Shanghai: McKinsey & Company.

Murugesan, S. (2007). Understanding Web 2.0. *IT Professional, 9 (4),* 34–41.

Naphade, M., Banavar, G., Harrison, C., Paraszczak, J. & Morris, R. (2011). Smarter Cities and Their Innovation Challenges. *Computer, 44 (6),* 32–39.

New Millennium Research Council. (2005). *Not In The Public Interest—The Myth of Municipal Wi-Fi Networks.* Washington: New Millennium Research Council.

O'Reilly, T., & Battelle, J. (2009). Web *Squared: Web 2.0 Five Years On.* Retrieved, January, 2012 from: http://assets.en.oreilly.com/1/event/28/web2009_websquared-whitepaper.pdf

OECD (Organisation for Economic Co-operation and Development). (2008, June). *Policy Guidance for Digital Content.* Paper presented at the OECD Ministerial Meeting on the future of Internet Economy, Seoul. Retrieved, Sept. 2011 from: http://www.oecd.org/dataoecd/20/54/40895797.pdf

OECD (Organisation for Economic Co-operation and Development). (2011 June). *The Internet Economy: Generating Innovation and Growth.* Paper presented at the OECD High Level Meeting, Paris. Retrieved, Sept. 2011 from: http://www.oecd.org/dataoecd/40/21/48289796.pdf

Osimo, D. (2008). *Web 2.0 in Government: Why and How?* Retrieved from Institute for Prospective Technological Studies (IPTS) website: http://ipts.jrc.ec.europa.eu/publications/pub.cfm?id=1565

Ozdoganm, I. D. & Birgonul, M. T. (2000). A decision support framework for project sponsors in the planning stage of build-operate-transfer (BOT) projects. *Journal of Construction Engineering and Management, 18,* 343–353.

PMI. (2008). *A Guide to the Project Management Body of Knowledge: Pmbok Guide* (4th ed). Pennsylvania: Project Management Institute Inc.

Ranasinghe, M. (1999). Private sector participation in infrastructure projects: A methodology to analyze viability of BOT, *Journal of Construction Engineering and Management, 17,* 613–623.

Reddick, G. C. (2011). Citizen Interaction and e-government: Evidence for the managerial, consultative and participatory models. *Transforming Government: People, Process and Policy, 5 (2),* 167–184.

Salman, A. F. M., Skibniewski, M. J. & Basha, I. (2007). BOT viability model for large-scale infrastructure projects. *Journal of Construction Engineering and Management, 133 (1),* 50–63.

Schaffers, H., Komninos, N., Pallot, M., Trousse, M., Nilsson, M., & Oliveira, M. (2011). Smart Cities and the Future Internet: Towards Cooperation Frameworks for Open Innovation, In J. Domingue et al. (Eds.), *Future Internet: Achievements and Promises* (pp.431–446), Heidelberg: Springer.

Schmidt, R. C. (1997). Managing Delphi surveys using nonparametric statistical techniques. *Decision Sciences, 28(3),* 763–774.

Tiong, R. L. K. (1990). Comparative study of BOT projects. *Journal of Construction Engineering and Management, 6 (1)*, 107–122.

Tiong, R. L. K. (1995a). Competitive advantage of equity of BOT tender. *Journal of Construction Engineering and Management, 121 (3)*, 282–289.

Tiong, R. L. K. (1995b). Impact of financial package versus technical solution in BOT tender. *Journal of Construction Engineering and Management, 121 (3)*, 304–311.

Tiong, R. L. K. (1996). CSFs in competitive tendering and negotiation model for BOT projects. *Journal of Construction Engineering and Management, 122 (3)*, 202–211.

U.N. Department of Economic and Social Affairs, Population Division. (2010). *World Urbanization Prospects: The 2009 Revision*. New York: United Nations.

UNIDO. (1996). *Guidelines for infrastructure development through build-operate-transfer (BOT) projects*. Vienna: UNIDO.

Van Bastelaer, B., & Lobet-Maris, C. (Eds). (1999). *Social Learning regarding Multimedia Developments at a Local Level: The Case of Digital Cities*. Namur: CITA—University of Namur.

World Commission on Environment and Development. (1987). *Our Common Future*. Oxford: Brundtland, Gro Harlem et al.

Part II
Web 2.0 as Tools for Mobilization, Protests and Governance

Chapter 7
Online Collective Action and the Role of Social Media in Mobilizing Opinions: A Case Study on Women's Right-to-Drive Campaigns in Saudi Arabia

Nitin Agarwal, Merlyna Lim and Rolf T. Wigand

7.1 Introduction

Citizens and government alike may benefit from many facets of Web 2.0, especially social media developments comprising social networking sites, such as Facebook, Twitter, various forms of crowd-sourcing, as well as the usage and mining of blogs. Social media sites are attractive places and two-way channels to gather information not only about citizens but also for citizens to gather information about government-related issues and strategies. Social media has become integral to the political realm. Consequently, social movements such as recent Tunisian and Egyptian revolts as well as urban anarchic actions such as the London riots can neither be solely seen as social media nor as a non-social media event. To frame such revolts as a "Facebook revolution" or a "people's revolution" is an oversimplification (Lim 2012, p. 232). People and social media are not detached from each other as in some nations such as Tunisian and Egyptian social media has been an integral part of political activism for years (Lim 2012, p. 232). "The power of networked individuals and groups who toppled" authoritarian regimes "cannot be separated from the power of social media

N. Agarwal (✉) · R. T. Wigand
Department of Information Science, University of Arkansas at Little Rock,
2801 S. University Ave, Little Rock, AR 72204, USA
e-mail: nxagarwal@ualr.edu

R. T. Wigand
e-mail: rtwigand@ualr.edu

M. Lim
Consortium of Science, Policy and Outcomes (CSPO), School of Social
Transformation—Justice and Social Inquiry, Arizona State University,
1120 S. Cady Mall, Tempe, AZ 85287, USA
e-mail: Merlyna.Lim@asu.edu

C. G. Reddick and S. K. Aikins (eds.), *Web 2.0 Technologies and Democratic Governance*, Public Administration and Information Technology 1, DOI: 10.1007/978-1-4614-1448-3_7, © Springer Science+Business Media New York 2012

that facilitated the formation and the expansion of the networks themselves" (Lim 2012, p. 232).

However, regardless of the prominent role of social media platforms in such revolts, there is a scarcity of online collective action (CA) research. Mere journalistic accounts on such actions tend to be based on anecdotes rather than rigorously designed and examined research. Existing computational studies focusing on capturing and mapping social media interactions and issues manage to identify the very manifestations of CA. These studies, unfortunately, rarely go beyond a mere descriptive tendency. Our study aims to provide a methodological approach to understand processes involved in the formation of online CAs.

This chapter is organized as follows: First we present a review and discussion of CA theory, as this is the theoretical framework guiding our research. We then address the existing efforts of mapping social media to motivate the need for a more systematic and foundational analysis modeling CA in social media. The following section describes computational social networks analysis (CSNA) and demonstrates how CSNA provides a rich set of social network methodologies to observe and explain various useful patterns such as community extraction, expert identification, and information diffusion. Next, a case study is presented, i.e., the Women's Right to Drive Campaign in Saudi Arabia that demonstrates the formation of collective sentiment and its manifestation in the form of CA. Our overall research effort is then addressed in three phases: individual, community, and transnational perspectives. The utilized research methods and design are described, including data collection, by examining experiments and presenting our analysis. Lastly, our conclusions are offered by highlighting our major findings, we suggest ideas for future research and we present some research implications for governance.

7.2 The Theory of Collective Action

Collective action refers to the pursuit of a common goal by more than one person. Presumably, the achievement of the goal will then benefit all of society (e.g., Sandler 1992). The term dates back to some of the work by Vilfredo Pareto in the 1930s and Mancur Olson (1965) in *The Logic of Collective Action: Public Goods and the Theory of Groups*. CA problems arise when each individual in a group pursues a rational strategy, yet the collective outcome is bad for all of those same individuals, thus, in effect, creating "collective irrationality" (Wheelan 2011). Accordingly, transaction costs, especially those pertaining to the cost of organizing of such CA, for a majority attempting to achieve the utility of the goal (typically a public good) are disproportionately higher than the transaction costs for a small minority. An additional problem of CA is the benefit gained by those who do not participate in its achievement. This is generally referred to as the *free rider problem*, elegantly explained by Vilfredo Pareto (1935). The concept of CA has been used extensively also by several scholars in the standards evolution, standards diffusion, as well as the standards adoption literature (e.g., Markus et al. 2006; Wigand et al. 2005).

New ICTs, especially the Internet, "have completely transformed the landscape of collective action" (Friedland and Rogerson 2009, p. 2). Facilitated online communications within the network of CAs can be executed with low or nearly no cost, making the success of CA less reliant on the size of the groups. However, "some experts believe the collective action effects of the Internet are overstated and may prove ephemeral" (Friedland and Rogerson 2009, p. 2). A capacity to communicate globally or internationally does not automatically translate into successful international CAs as the online environment is not sympathetic to the formation of strong interpersonal ties needed to build successful CA (Lim 2009; McAdam 1996). Etzioni and Etzioni (1999) argue that online-based communications are less stable than those built with face-to-face interaction. Among the successful CAs, however, many of them were substantially organized online or related to the Internet such as the 1996 Zapatista rebellion in Mexico (Cleaver 1998; Bob 2005), the 1998 Indonesian political revolution (Lim 2006, 2004), and the recent Tunisia, Egypt (Lim 2012), Libya, and Syria revolts.

The pervasive usage of ICT also influences the ways citizens relate with the government by providing a new tool for participation and engagement. The socio-political information provided online has impacted citizens' decision to participate in politics (Margetts et al. 2011). Internet's "ability to provide real-time information on the participations of others" (Margetts et al. 2009, p. 17), in particular, has stimulated individuals' participation in a political CA. Online CAs have expanded the sphere of engagement and participation for citizens in communicating with, monitoring, and even challenging the government.

Using both available successful and unsuccessful online CA "research has now begun identifying aspects of the collective action process that can succeed online as well as shortcomings and disadvantages of online collective action" (Bimber et al. 2005, p. 366). However, such research has not answered many other questions related to the emergence of various forms of CA in the online world. Lupia and Sin (2003) urge to critically assess whether the traditional CA paradigm is even appropriate for explaining contemporary phenomena. Such phenomena have prompted us to examine some fundamental aspects of CA that remain theoretically undeveloped (Bimber et al. 2005, p. 366) and called for innovative fundamental research that can provide insights into reconceptualizing online CA.

7.3 Mapping Social Media

In this section, we assess some of these fundamental efforts to map the social media that motivate the need for a more systematic and foundational analysis modeling CA in social media settings.

Adamic and Glance (2005) mapped the U.S. political blogosphere and observed the dichotomy between liberal and conservative blogs. Examining the link graph between and across these blogs, these authors observed certain interblog citation behavior patterns such as conservative bloggers tend to link more often than the liberal bloggers, but there is no uniformity in the news or topics discussed by conservatives. However, the study fell short of suggesting a theory to explain these patterns. In a similar study, Kelly and Etling's (2008) analyzed 60,000 Iranian blogs using social network analysis and content analysis. They identified a wide range of opinions representing religious conservative views, secular and reform-minded ones, and topics ranging from politics and human rights to poetry, religion, and pop culture. In yet another study, Etling et al. (2009) analyzed 35,000 active blogs primarily from Egypt, Saudi Arabia, Kuwait, and other Middle-Eastern countries. The authors identified major clusters organized by countries, demographics, and discussion topics around domestic, politics, and religious issues.

These studies show that individuals discuss varied topics in multiple forms of social media. However, there is a lack of methodologies enabling the analysis of how the discussions converge to central themes and a rigorous and fundamental analysis that explains online CAs. In addressing this gap, the proposed efforts will leverage CA theory and computational mapping in order to explain and predict the underlying processes involved in online CAs.

7.4 Computational Social Network Analysis

CSNA provides a rich set of SNA methodologies to observe and explain characteristic patterns, such as community extraction, expert identification, and information diffusion, among others. Here, we review community extraction and expert identification, two methods that are most relevant to the proposed research.

Community extraction—Communities play a vital role in understanding the creation, representation, and transfer of knowledge among people, and are the essential building blocks of all social networks. How does one exactly extract communities from a social network? There are three dominant approaches for community extraction: network-centric, content-centric, and hybrid approaches (Agarwal and Liu 2009). Network-centric approaches leverage network structural properties to identify communities within a social network (Fortunato 2010). Assuming members of a community tend to talk about similar topics, content-centric approaches (Li et al. 2007) extract communities based on the similarity of members' content. Hybrid approaches leverage both content and network information to extract communities. The central tenet behind such an approach is: a set of blogs that are highly linked and tend to share similar content reflect tighter communities (Java et al. 2008).

Expert identification—Influential blog sites exert influence over the external world and within the blogosphere (Gill 2004). The blogosphere, however, follows a power law distribution (Faloutsos et al. 1999) with very few influential blog sites that form the short head of the distribution and a large number of non-influential sites that form the Long Tail (Anderson 2006). Influence is often studied from an information diffusion perspective by identifying the key members who maximize the information spread by leveraging theories from epidemiology (Gruhl et al. 2004), viral marketing

(Richardson and Domingos 2002), cascade models (Goldenberg et al. 2001), greedy models (Java et al. 2006), and submodularity-based models (Leskovec et al. 2007). The casual environment of the blogosphere, where not many blogs cite the actual source, presents significant challenges to employ the above-mentioned purely link analysis-based approaches. Song et al. (2007) define opinion leaders as those who generate novel ideas and opinions, which is estimated using cosine similarity between their posts and the ones they refer. Goyal et al. (2010) showed that the influence probabilities between users can be learned based on their community affiliation logs. Further, a few blogs list most active bloggers for a particular time window based on the number of submitted posts, comments received, etc. (Gill 2004). Such statistics could easily mistake voluble bloggers for influential bloggers (Agarwal et al. 2008). The research mentioned here and other similar efforts provide computational capabilities to analyze online social networks and the various phenomena (such as community formation, affiliations, influence) that can help in modeling online CAs.

7.4.1 Women's Right-to-Drive Campaigns in Saudi Arabia: A Case Study

Saudi Arabia's political system is an absolute monarchy without elected institutions or political parties, where the King is both the head of state and the head of government. Decisions are made by the King mostly based on consultations with the senior members of the royal family and the religious leaders. The systems of governance, the rights of citizens, and the roles of the state are set out based on the Basic Law which declares both the *Koran* and the *Sunna* (tradition of the Prophet Muhammad) as the country's constitutions. In this country, *Sharia* (Islamic law) and tribal customs influence the ways in which gender roles are assigned in society. Women's rights are thus defined by the (strict) interpretation of these laws and customs. Saudi women predominantly do not see Islam as the main hindrance to women's rights. They see the cultural interpretation—patriarchal and traditional—as the chief obstacle for any struggles aiming for women's equality. As Saudis like to say "It's the culture, not the religion." "If the Qur'an does not address the subject, then the clerics will err on the side of caution and make it haram [forbidden]. The driving ban for women is the best example."[1] Saudi Arabia is the only country in the world prohibiting women from driving. While there is no written ban on women driving per se, locally issued licenses are required to drive. The problem is that such licenses are not issued to women, thus driving is effectively illegal for women. In reference to this situation, we choose to study Saudi women's right-to-drive campaigns. The early version of this

---

[1] https://sites.google.com/site/roblwagnerarchives/saudi-female-journalist-defies-stereotypes, last accessed on 04/29/2012.

campaign was initiated by Wajeha Al-Huwaider in 2008.[2] The latest one, called Women2Drive campaign,[3] was held in June 2011 with Manal Al-Sharif as one of the prominent leaders.

The Al-Huwaider Campaign refers to the series of online campaigns for women's rights originally initiated by Saudi writer and journalist Waheja Al-Huwaider and later became a regional phenomenon.[4] Her YouTube campaign started in 2007. On International Women's Day 2008, Al-Huwaider drove a car in the Kingdom of Saudi Arabia (KSA), where it is forbidden for women to do so, while videotaping a plea to Saudi officials. She posted the video on YouTube attracting international attention. Despite the obstacles placed by the Saudi government, Al-Huwaider continues to promote her ideas, through her writings online. Her articles analyze the Arab social situation, criticize the status of human rights, and vehemently protest discrimination and violence against women. Her online campaign has not only become an inspiration but also an influential voice for CA, calling for reform, among Middle Eastern women. Al-Huwaider's campaign was mostly centered around YouTube videos and propagated through the blogosphere.

Her actions have motivated other social reformists and women's rights activists to join the cause. In the beginning of 2011, a well-known Saudi blogger Eman Al Nafjan decided to initiate a campaign encouraging women to drive on June 17, 2011 called Women2Drive. As part of the campaign, Manal al-Sharif, one of the Women2Drive activists decided to drive and posted videos of driving a car that were filmed by Wajeha al-Huwaider.[5] Manal al-Sharif herself did not join the campaign on June 17, 2011 as she was arrested while doing the test drive. After being released, she pledged not to drive. Her arrest, though, propelled the movement to the mainstream media, nationally, regionally, and globally. The arrest also drove the global audience to pay attention to the June 17 Women2Drive campaign. The campaign itself, in addition to YouTube and blogs, also uses social networking platforms, such as Facebook and Twitter (see Tables 7.1 and 7.2). The hashtag #Women2Drive was used for all tweets related to the campaign. On June 17, 2011, there was no mass movement but about 40 Saudi women across the country took the wheel and challenged the ban. These women tweeted from the cars and spread the message all over the world. In short time the movement gained significant attention and traction from national and international audiences as well as received coverage from prominent media such as *Al-Jazeera*, *CNN*, *The Guardian*, and the *Huffington Post*.

---

[2] http://www.thenation.com/article/161224/conversation-saudi-womens-rights-campaigner-wajeha-al-huwaider, last accessed on 04/29/2012.

[3] http://www.guardian.co.uk/commentisfree/2011/jun/03/saudi-arabia-women2drive-women-driving, last accessed on 04/29/2012.

[4] http://articles.cnn.com/2010-09-07/world/saudi.arabia.women_1_saudi-women-wajeha-al-huwaider-saudi-arabia, last accessed on 04/29/2012.

[5] http://observers.france24.com/content/20110523-saudi-woman-arrested-defying-driving-ban-manal-al-sharif-khobar, last accessed on 04/29/2012.

Table 7.1 Data collection statistics from Facebook, Twitter, and YouTube (as of 10/27/2011)

Group page name	Group page web link	Number of subscribed users
Facebook		
Support #Women2Drive	http://www.facebook.com/Women2Drive	17,256
Women2drive—Manal and Bertha—Woman2drive—17 June Saudi Arabia	http://www.facebook.com/pages/Women2drive-Manal-and-Bertha-Woman2drive-17-June-Saudi-Arabia/176962935691371	7,643
Saudi women spring	http://www.facebook.com/SaudiWomenSpring	7,432
Saudi women to drive	http://www.facebook.com/pages/Saudi-Women-To-Drive/227817097234537	4,430
Saudi women driving campaign	http://www.facebook.com/pages/Saudi-Women-Driving-Campaign-%D8%AD%D9%85%D9%84%D9%84%D9%84%D9%84%D9%84%D9%84%D9%84%D9%82%D9%84%D8%A9%D8%A9%D8%A7%D8%A7%D8%A7%D8%AF%D8%A9-%D8%A7%D7%D9%84%D9%84%D8%A9%D8%85%D8%B1%D8%A3%D8%A9%D8%A9/215739848446522	1,984
Let woman drive in Saudi	http://www.facebook.com/pages/Let-Woman-Drive-in-Saudi/105530276205410	592
Saudi women 2 drive	http://www.facebook.com/pages/Saudi-Women-2-Drive/209028675799595	304
The campaign to let women drive in Saudi Arabia	http://www.facebook.com/pages/The-campaign-to-let-women-drive-in-Saudi-Arabia/189629577752570	206
Let the Saudi women drive	http://www.facebook.com/pages/Let-the-Saudi-women-drive/158019944263799	83
Twitter		
@W2Drive	http://twitter.com/#!/W2Drive	13,054
@Women2Drive	http://twitter.com/#!/Women2Drive	2,772
@gwnwiki	https://twitter.com/#!/gwnwiki	1,109
@honk4W2D	http://twitter.com/#!/honk4W2D/	201
YouTube		
KSAWomen2Drive	http://www.youtube.com/user/ksawomen2drive	1,250
Honk for Saudi women	http://www.youtube.com/user/HonkforSaudiWomen	233
SaudiWomen2Drive	http://www.youtube.com/user/SaudiWomen2Drive	409
I support Saudi women driving	http://www.youtube.com/user/Sarah1978Jaber	47

Table 7.2 Data collection statistics from blogs (as of 10/27/2011)

Search keyword	Number of blogs	Number of overall search results
Saudi women drive	4,710,000	6,040,000
KSA women drive	249,000	6,060,000
Women2drive	35,100	521,000

While not yet radically changing the traditions that prohibit women from driving, the movement itself has scaled up to the transnational level and gained international recognition and support. The international coverage of the movement has at least put the Saudi government in the national and international spotlight. When a Saudi court found Shaima Jastaina, one of the women who joined the Women2Drive campaign on June 17, guilty of violating the driving ban, Saudi King Abdullah overturned the sentencing.[6] Arguably, this act is very much related to the global pressure on the issue. In the latest development, Manal al-Sharif and another woman from the campaign had filed the lawsuits for being refused driver's licenses and now are urging judicial authorities to follow-up on the case (In The News 2012).

This case demonstrates how individual sentiment diffuses within the network, shapes into collective sentiment, and transforms into CA. The overarching question anchored in this case is: How are decentralized online individual actions transformed into online CA?

7.5 A Three-Phased Research Approach

In order to cogently address the research question posed above, we propose a three-phased approach: phase 1, Individual Perspective; phase 2, Community Perspective; and phase 3, Transnational Perspective. Figure 7.1 shows the overall architecture of this approach, which highlights the interdependencies and outcomes of the three phases. As illustrated in Fig. 7.1, our data collection strategy focuses on social media and open data sources. The data sources primarily include individual and group owned blogs and statistics derived from search engines and various social media sites. The data collection strategies including the preprocessing are explained in detail in the Experiments and Analysis section. The core of the model analyzes the data from the three different perspectives with findings from each perspective laying the foundation for the next. We delve into the details for each perspective next and summarize how the outcomes from each phase are coupled to address the higher level research questions.[7]

---

[6] http://www.guardian.co.uk/world/2011/sep/29/saudi-woman-lashing-king-abdullah, last accessed on 04/29/2012.

[7] A primitive version of the proposed model has been introduced in the authors' earlier publications (Agarwal et al. 2011a, b).

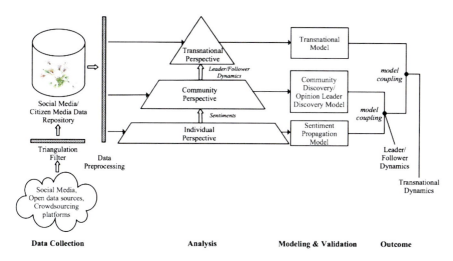

Fig. 7.1 Overall envisioned research design

7.5.1 Individual Perspective

Individual causes/issues can be transformed into collective cause. To understand and model this process, we need to study how personal issues and concerns evolve and propagate in social networks and how they converge and form collective concerns. We begin with preprocessing the blogs, identifying issues and concerns representing individual cause; and then modeling their diffusion in the network, and analyzing their convergence to collective cause.

Preprocessing and extracting cause: For each event, blog reactions are analyzed. Topic modeling techniques (such as Latent Semantic Analysis) assist in identifying, segregating, and teasing out relevant topics. Blog posts containing relevant topics are summarized to reduce off-topic chatter narrowing in on the key information (Coombs et al. 2008). The summarized text is used to extract representative keywords using Wordle that renders words with font sizes proportional to their frequency in the text. Starting from the seed blog, the above process is repeated for all other blogs that are connected to the seed blog. Blogs connected to the seed blogs are termed adjacent blogs. This demonstrates whether the issues and concerns mentioned in the seed blog were diffused to the adjacent blogs.

Modeling the diffusion of cause: We analyze the extracted issues and concerns representing a certain cause and study their propagation. Specifically, we explore how network ties affect an individual's concerns. The proposed diffusion model extends the existing information diffusion models by considering concerns as the information chunks that propagate over the social network of bloggers. Since the underlying social network remains the same, the structural properties of the concern diffusion are no different than information diffusion characteristics. In other words, leaders of the community responsible for the fastest information diffusion also tend to be the major influencing factors on the individual's issues and concerns and, hence, it follows the collective concerns of the community.

7.5.2 Community Perspective

Community leaders often exert significant influence over fellow members in transforming individual opinion and shaping into collective sentiment. To model this phenomenon, we analyze the community of bloggers and identify the opinion leaders of the community. This enables us to address the following issues: Do followers consistently follow the same leader(s)? Or, is the influence of opinion leaders time-variant and/or topic-variant? To address these questions, first, we extract and analyze the community of bloggers and then identify the opinion leaders.

Community identification: Often in the blogosphere users do not explicitly specify their community affiliation. The discovery of communities through network-centric approaches has been extensively studied (Lancichinetti and Fortunato 2009); however, as pointed out in Kritikopoulos et al. (2008), blogs are extremely sparsely linked due to a casual environment that does not necessitate users to "cite" sources that inspire them. Moreover, spam links generated by malicious users could connect unrelated and/or irrelevant blogs, affecting community discovery processes. Further, spam may also adversely affect content-oriented community identification approaches. We identify their implicit community affiliations and orientations leveraging the network structures (social ties, participation in other forms of social media) and issue/cause diffusion characteristics identified in the individual perspective phase. The content-induced interactions approach, leveraging issues, and concerns diffusion characteristics extracted from the individual perspective phase, not only guides the network-centric community extraction (while considering the relevant links and ignoring the spam/irrelevant links) but also complements it through revealing new potential links. Leveraging the insights from our prior study (Agarwal et al. 2010), the purpose of which is to identify communities from blog networks by examining the occurrence of shared concerns on particular events/causes, we unveil interactions through the observation of individual concerns. If the concerns of these blogs were similar, we assume the blogs are themselves similar. Mathematically, the similarity between any two blogs can be computed using cosine similarity as follows:

$$\text{Sim}(B_\mathrm{m}, B_\mathrm{n}) - \frac{P_\mathrm{m} \cdot P_\mathrm{n}}{||P_\mathrm{m}||P_\mathrm{n}||}$$

where, $\text{Sim}(B_\mathrm{m}, B_\mathrm{n})$ is the cosine similarity between blogs B_m and B_n. The concerns of B_m and B_n on an issue is represented by the column vectors P_m and P_n, respectively. The data mining clustering algorithm, k means, is used to extract communities.

Identifying Influentials: After identifying the communities from the social media, we set out to identify the leaders. We examine how social gestures of "influentials" could be approximated by collectable statistics from the social media. We gather network-based statistics from various indexing services such as Technorati and the Google search engine. These statistics use the linking knowledge gleaned from the graph of who cites whom and leverage prestige-based stochastic models to evaluate influence of each node in the graph. Knowledge from prior work on identifying influential bloggers, iFinder (Agarwal et al. 2008), enables us to model community leaders factoring in socio-cultural traits of the community that bootstraps our understanding of opinion leaders. The model analyzes how issues and concerns travel across the network. Tracking the diffusion of issues across the network helps discounting viral blogs as a form of CA. Longitudinal analysis could be further performed to address questions such as, whether followers consistently follow the same leader(s), or is the influence time-variant, offering deeper understanding of group dynamics. An individual perspective provides an understanding of how issues and concerns propagate along the network. The outcome of the community perspective enlightens us with a deeper understanding of leader–followers dynamics. Together, outcomes from both phases lend insights into the emergence of online CAs in socio-culturally diverse environments.

7.5.3 Transnational Perspective

In this phase, we study and analyze whether collective concerns in communities transcend nation-state barriers and converge into transnational online CA or not. Social networking platforms have undoubtedly intensified the degree of connectivity by building up capacity to circulate ideas and to transfer content very quickly across all barriers. Consequently, these platforms have favored a complex array of coordinated mobilization at the global level. Analyzing the emergence of transnational actors and networks, structures relating to fluidity, and boundless organizational architecture, are key to a deeper understanding of transnational underpinnings of online CAs. The issue can be geographically mapped periodically to detail the development of the issue network. The mapping process can identify each individual and classify her in one or more clusters. The issue networks and mapped clusters can also be studied longitudinally over a chronological sequence of various events, to identify and track how they merge/expand/split and to discern other interesting patterns, regardless of their geographic dispersion and at local or global scales (Fig. 7.2).

7.6 Experiments and Analysis

Next, we present our data collection efforts to analyze our proposed methodology for the Women2Drive case study.

Fig. 7.2 Search keyword volume for the three most popular keywords using Google Trends (Results were obtained using Google Trends at http://www.google.com/trends/ as of 10/27/2011.)

7.6.1 Data Collection

In this section the authors employed a multi-faceted data collection strategy, due to the role of a multitude as well as variety of social media sites identified and observed in various online CAs. Data from blogs and other social media sites were collected and anonymized in a completely observational and non-obtrusive manner. We started the data collection using the Google search engine and the keywords/ tags related to the campaign such as 'women2drive,' 'Manal Bertha Woman2d-rive,' '17 June Saudi Arabia,' 'Saudi Women Drive,' and 'KSA women drive.' The search keywords were enriched by the suggestions provided from the search engine. We performed both a generic search and a focused search. The generic search was conducted on the entire Web and the focused search was limited to specific social media sites using the search engine's advanced search parameters. The results were analyzed to identify the fan pages, Twitter groups, and YouTube channels. These identified groups were further investigated to find the number of subscribed users. Table 7.1 summarizes these findings. The sheer volume of blog results made it impossible to analyze the links individually. This is indicated by the number of blog hits versus overall web hits for the different search keywords. Table 7.2 summarizes these findings for the top three search keywords. The numbers presented in Table 7.2 could be an overestimation of actual search results due to redundancy. However, the redundancy exists in both the Web search results as well as the blog search results thereby making the comparison between the two fair. Figure 7.3 illustrates the search volume index on Google for the keywords, which indicates spikes on June 18, 2011 indicating the celebration of Women2Drive Day in Saudi Arabia[8] and another spike on September 25, 2011 indicating the announcement of Women's Right to Vote in Saudi Arabia.[9]

---

[8] http://www.thelinguist.com/en/en/library/item/131557/, last accessed on 04/29/2012.

[9] http://www.bbc.co.uk/news/world-us-canada-15052030, last accessed on 04/29/2012.

Note that 'KSA Women Drive', although mentioned in the blogs and on Web pages, was not used as a keyword for searches. This is indicated by the no search volume of 'KSA Women Drive' as compared to the other two search keywords.

Next we present our analysis and findings on the collected data using the proposed research methodology.

7.6.1.1 Individual Perspective

In analyzing the individual perspective on the Al-Huwaider driving campaigns, we started with the original narrative of Wajeha Al-Huwaider's cause to lift the ban of driving for Saudi women as a source of issues and concerns. Representative keywords were then extracted using a tag cloud generator. We repeated the extraction for each blog within Al-Huwaider's network to seek whether Al-Huwaider's issues and concerns were diffused to these blogs. Our findings (Fig. 7.3) show the occurrence of similar keywords representing similar issues and concerns across these blogs (e.g., Saudi, women, cars, drive/driving, right/rights). Figure 7.3 shows how an individual cause of Al-Huwaider was propagated in social networks (Fig. 7.4).

Next, the same method is applied to the three formal statements delivered by the 2011 Women2Drive campaign management to seek the connection between this later action with the 2008 Al-Huwaider driving campaign. As this campaign is about women's right to drive, expectedly (as can be seen in Fig. 7.5) dominant keywords of the statements generally mimic those of Al-Huwaider original statement. However, we also see the occurrence of a different set of keywords representing different subissues. In the second statement launched immediately after the arrest of Women2Drive leader Manal al-Sharif, we see 'Manal,' 'al-Sharif,' 'Women2Drive,' 'campaign,' and 'management' as being more prominent than keywords representing the issue (rights, driving). Indeed, the statement was issued mostly to clarify the existence of the movement despite the withdrawal of Al-Sharif's participation in the campaign. Closer to the date of the campaign, in the fourth and fifth statements, the keywords central to the issue (women, rights, driving) came back to dominate the narratives (Fig. 7.6).

7.6.1.2 Community Perspective

Al-Huwaider was a major factor in mobilizing individual bloggers with similar concerns (toward various issues) into a community and in leading the movement, i.e., transitioning individual cause to collective cause and ultimately manifesting into a cyber-collective movement. This also correlates with our findings in the individual phase, where the community leader was identified as the most significant influence over the individuals' concerns. We followed the proposed methodology analyzing our data by extracting communities and opinion leaders and observing leader–follower dynamics.

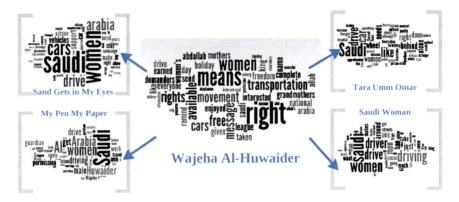

Fig. 7.3 Issue analysis of Al-Huwaider campaign

Fig. 7.4 Women2Drive second statement

Fig. 7.5 Women2Drive fourth statement

Continuing with the example presented in Fig. 7.3, we identified the occurrence of various Al-Huwaider's causes in three blogs, "Tara Umm Omar," "Saudi Woman," and "Sand Gets in My Eyes." If the concerns of these blogs were similar we assume the blogs were themselves similar. We illustrate our analysis in

Fig. 7.6 Women2Drive fifth statement

Table 7.3, where we aggregate the concerns from these three blogs (denoted in columns) for each cause/issue (denoted in rows).

Once communities of bloggers are extracted, our next step is to identify the influentials. We analyzed a community of 75 blogs that shared similar concerns for Al-Huwaider's campaigns and identified top 10 influential blogs, as illustrated in Table 7.4. Due to space limitations we could not present the analysis of other blogs. However, all 75 blogs had an average influence score of 198.306, a maximum influence score of 833, a minimum influence score of 1, and a standard deviation of 269.892. The influence score for each blog is provided by Technorati indexing service, which is directly proportional to the number and authoritativeness of blogs and other media that cite/link to the blog in question. The distribution indicates the expanse of the blogs in terms of the influence or authoritativeness. Representative tags extracted using Wordle are specified next to the blog posts to give contextual background and the topical keywords. The analysis demonstrates a feasible approach to identify influential blogs for an event.

7.6.1.3   Transnational Perspective

Analyzing the emergence of transnational actors and networks, structures relating to fluidity and boundless organizational architecture, is key to a deeper understanding of the transnational underpinning of cyber-collective movements. One such actor identified in our analysis was Wajeha Al-Huwaider. Despite the cultural, ethnic, political, social, and geographical diversity of Al-Huwaider's supporters as illustrated in Fig. 7.7 below, the sense of community superseded differences and nation-state barriers and converged individual concerns into CA. Figure 7.7 illustrates the geographical distribution of the transnational support for Al-Huwaider's campaigns and Fig. 7.8 shows the actual geographical locations of the links supporting the Women2Drive campaign obtained from analyzing the data.

Transnational communities can also be analyzed by clustering pages from blogs/sites based on issues discussed in those blogs and websites. In Fig. 7.9 we can see that conversations around Al-Huwaider campaigns are diffused in various blogs, websites, news portal, and social media sites. Identified communities here are not always

Table 7.3 Occurrence of shared issues and concerns in each blog for the women's right-to-drive cause

Al-Huwaider's causes	Tara Umm Omar	Saudi woman	Sand gets in my eyes
Women's right to drive	Drive, car, like, wheel, right, behind, alone, needs (+)	Driving, drive(r), want, around, make, men, ban, sense, king, right (+)	Cars, drive, vehicles, right, support, make, issue, allow, campaign, right, changed (+)

Table 7.4 Top-10 influential blog posts discussing Wajeha Al-Huwaider's campaign along with their influence scores and representative tags extracted using Wordle.net

Blog	Representative tags	Influence score
http://hotair.com/archives/2009/07/12/saudi-feminist-blocked-from-leaving-country/	Saudi, Al-Huwaider, Arabia, border, male, passport, permission, activists, rights, guardian	833
http://jezebel.com/5552458/japan-likely-to-reject-ban-on-sexualization-of-minors-playboy-model-jailed-for-boob+grope	Women, minors, drinkers, Japan, Yousef, freedom, infected, prisoners, police, jail, charges, allegations	824
http://volokh.com/posts/1245159018.shtml	Saudi, Arabia, HRW, Human, rights, links, mail, organization, government, Israel, workers	739
http://thelede.blogs.nytimes.com/2009/03/12/saudi-woman-drives-for-youtube-protest/	Saudi, Huwaider, driving, BBC News, Arabia, Arab, women protest, video, Fattah, car, YouTube	702
http://www.memeorandum.com/100418/p4	Saudi, women, driving, Arabia, raped, reform, issues, populace	695
http://www.moonbattery.com/archives/2007/10/the_nobel_joke.html	Afghanistan, Navy, Murphy, bad, gore, Arafat, combat, killed, Marxist	690
http://latimesblogs.latimes.com/babylonbeyond/2010/06/saudi-women-use-fatwa-in-driving-bid.html	Women, Saudi, drive, Islamic, Wajeha, maternal, breastfeed, Obeikan, cars, ban, campaign	665
http://www.hrw.org/english/docs/2006/10/20/saudia14461.htm	Saudi, human, rights, police, detained, government, Mabahith, Arabia, Khobar, freedom	644
http://www.hrw.org/en/news/2006/10/30/saudi-arabia-lift-gag-order-rights-campaigner	Rights, Al-Huwaider, Saudi, Arabia, human, September, Mabahith, Khobar, Abdullah, interrogated, police, officers	644
http://globalvoicesonline.org/2008/08/12/saudi-arabia-bans-women-from-olympics/	Feminist, Burundi, Olympics, Wajeha, Macha, Women, Muharram	627

necessarily linked to each other, but they represent clusters of individuals and/or groups of individuals who share similar conversations. For example, individual blogs such as saudiwomen.wordpress.com and daughterofarabia.blogspot.com share

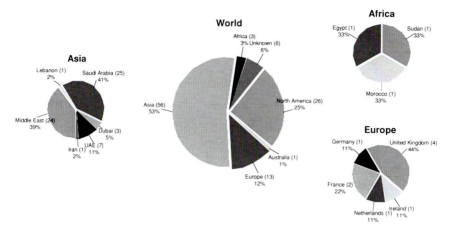

Fig. 7.7 Transnational support for Wajeha Al-Huwaider's campaign

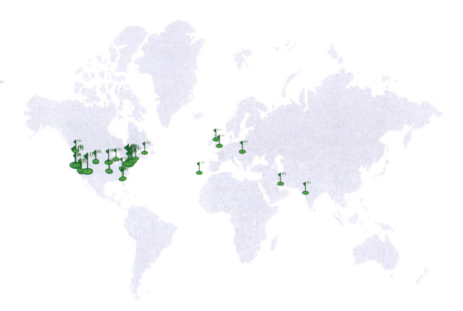

Fig. 7.8 Transnational support for Women2Drive campaign

conversations around the profile of Wajeha Al-Huwaider with transnational organizational blogs such as TheMemriblog.org and cyberdissident.org, as well as with *BoingBoing* and global news portals such as *CNN, The Nation, Reuters,* and *Washington Post.* Meanwhile, daughterofarabia.blogspot.com and BoingBoing also share another community with mypenmypaper.wordpress.com, wikigender.org, *the New York Times'* blogs, and autoguide.com by the narrative on the significance of the

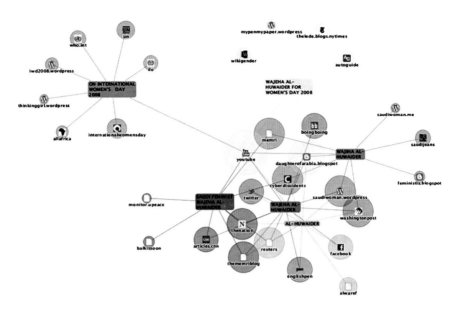

Fig. 7.9 Transnational networks of issue clusters in Al-Huwaider Campaign

driving campaign on the 2008 International Women's Day. By identifying clusters of conversations/contents, we can map the diffusion networks of issue and discover disparate communities that essentially share the similar issues even without physical links. From the size of its node, we can also see how central YouTube was in the Al-Huwaider campaign. We can see that YouTube is connected to all communities that discuss the campaign from various angles/perspectives. From Fig. 7.9 we also learn that in the 2008 Al-Huwaider campaign, issues are propagated mostly in the blogosphere and international news portals. We can spot that an individual blog of daughterofarabia.blogspot.com is central in such propagation.

We repeated the same method for the 2011 Women2Drive campaign and found a significantly denser network and a larger number of immediate communities/clusters. Interestingly, while YouTube is still prominently central to the network, there are some new dominant actors coming into play. We see that *The Guardian* is the most dominant node in the network. It connects to the majority of clusters. Meanwhile, *Al-Jazeera, Huffington Post,* and *CNN* have also become prominent. In addition, we also observe the emergence of Facebook as one of the leading nodes in the network of clusters. As expected, the usage of social networking such as Facebook was not so popular in 2008. The 2011 Women2Drive campaign was carried out after the wave of social media-driven Arab Spring, understandably the movement attempted to make good use of social media in diffusing the issue. As we can see in Table 7.1, with over 13,000 subscribers each, Facebook and Twitter are indeed the two most popularly used media in the campaign.

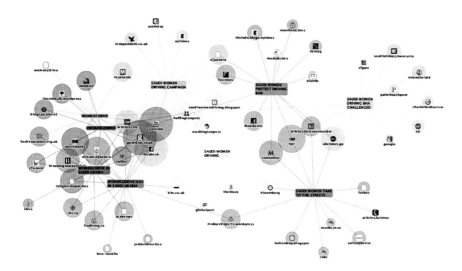

Fig. 7.10 Transnational networks of issue clusters on Women2Drive

In light of the centrality of YouTube in the transnational networks above, we also analyzed the top 60 videos for Women2Drive campaign posted by different users on YouTube over time. The analysis as illustrated in Fig. 7.10 demonstrates the significance of recency in determining influence. Few observations that jump out from the analysis are:

1. It is more likely that newly posted videos are more influential or garner more views. This is evident from a large number of videos in the top-right quadrant. These are all recent videos.
2. Certain videos such as the one in the top-left quadrant remain influential even after a long period of time (Fig. 7.11).

Videos that remain influential regardless of the time period (top-left quadrant) could be leveraged as 'hooks' to study the long-term opinions of the viewer community on possibly various issues. Videos in the top-right quadrant that are both influential and recent could offer insights about how the transnational community relates to the incident captured in the video. These insights could be contrasted with the findings from the videos in the lower right quadrant to suggest correlations between the type of incidents and community's reflections. Essentially this analysis could possibly help to advance our understanding of how and to what extent various media or incidents reflect the community's opinions transnationally. This analysis could also be used to filter out videos that are old and non-influential, i.e., those in the lower left quadrant.

The findings from the transnational perspective prompts us to seek answers for further questions such as, Can transnational social movements be autonomous from national constraints in terms of discourses, strategies, and resources? Can the

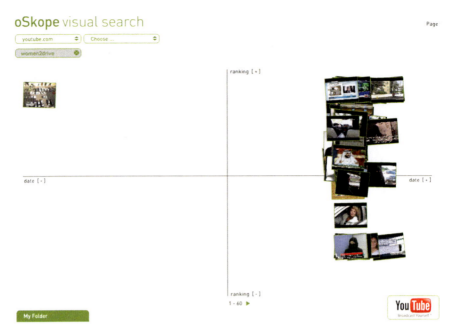

Fig. 7.11 Visualization of top 60 YouTube videos for Women2Drive campaign over time

shifting scale (from local and national to global and transnational) also bring about a change of culture and identity of these movements? With respect to outcomes and goals, can the transnational social movements deliver concrete strategies to overcome the unpredictability of their mobilizations? With respect to their internal dynamics, can the transnational social movements encourage their perpetuation through mitigating the individual convictions of the CAs/movements?

Social media has played a key role and irreversibly transformed organization and mobilization of collective movements. The three-phased approach, individual—community—transnational perspective, offers a great vantage point to analyze the collective movements via ICTs. Specifically, the findings from the individual perspective indicate the affect of social ties on the diffusion of issues in the network. The issue diffusion network is further analyzed in the community perspective to identify the naturally emerging communities and the leaders within. The findings indicated that the leaders of the community tend to be the major influencing factors on the individual's issues and concerns and hence the collective concerns of the community. The transnational perspective helped in analyzing how the communities distributed globally that shared similar concerns helped in the convergence of individual and community concerns into a collective movement.

7.7 Conclusions

In this chapter the authors sought to understand the fundamentals, complexity, and dynamics of online CA. Through this research we highlight the need to revisit the traditional CA theories. Our methodology continues to embrace the conventional CA theories and further helps to reshape the traditional theories to better understand the implication of new forms of communication (facilitated by social media) for CA. As pointed out earlier, the capacity to communicate globally does not automatically translate into successful transnational CAs; the proposed methodology enables a three-phased systematic analysis of how the discussions converge to central themes from individual, community, and transnational perspectives. Specifically, the proposed efforts leverage traditional CA theory and CSNA in order to explain and predict the underlying processes involved in CAs in social media.

7.7.1 Major Findings

As conceptualized, utilized, and illustrated in the case studies of the Al-Huwaider and the Women2Drive campaigns, our novel methodological approaches highlight several key contributions to the fundamental research on online collection actions as well as computational studies on social media in general, as follows:

1. By employing multiple perspectives (individual, community, and transnational), we offer a modus operandi to understand (a) the evolution of online CA networks and (b) the diffusion of issue in multi-scales online environments.
2. By focusing on the formation of issues (such as shared narratives), our approaches offer a powerful explanatory model that goes well beyond a mere descriptive tendency of most computational studies on social media, such as simply mapping the blogosphere.
3. By comparing two different yet related events, our study suggests that in a networked online environment one CA cannot be studied as a mere independent event isolated from other actions. The nature of an online environment presents a high likelihood for CAs to be connected and, further, to mutually influence and shape each other.
4. By utilizing a comparative study encompassing two different periods of time, our study also demonstrates the relationship between online CAs and the rapidly changing online media environment. Our findings (i.e., the importance of YouTube in both campaigns, the importance of blogs in the 2008 Al-Huwaider campaign vis-à-vis the surfacing of Facebook and Twitter, and the importance of mainstream media outlets in the 2011 Women2Drive campaign) display that the centrality and importance of online platforms significantly influence and shape the evolution and expansion of online collection actions.

7.7.2 Further Research

The findings in this chapter also show some future possibilities to develop predictive models of CAs in the blogosphere by combining social network analysis methods as well as focusing methodologically on information flows, issues, sentiments, and communities as well as opinion leadership that, in turn, provide a considerably deeper and more penetrating understanding of CA Theory.

For the future research agenda, we propose to longitudinally analyze the extracted issues, concerns, and sentiment and to identify the factors involved in their propagation. We also propose to utilize existing cognitive and behavioral theories to gain deeper insights into the adaptation of individual behavior stemming from social interaction and cultural ties. These theories will form the basis of our exploration, aided by the development of novel statistical and stochastic diffusion models focusing on the transformation and propagation of sentiments along network ties over time. The model will help in advancing sociological as well as computational understanding of how collective sentiment shapes and will be improved upon in later phases of the analysis by incorporating community and transnational factors.

The longitudinal transnational map of issue networks and clusters can be correlated with intrinsic factors (e.g., demographic, economic, and political statistics) and extrinsic factors (e.g., uprisings in socio-demographically similar regions), which could offer deeper insights into the structural dynamics of certain key factors (viz. primary, secondary, and tertiary relations) that create 'affordance' for successful uprisings.

7.7.3 Research Implications on Governance

Looking at the broader picture, our research lends some insights into the relationship between social media and governance. The case studies presented in this chapter—the Al-Huwaider and Women2Drive campaigns in Saudi Arabia—show that the CA to push government to look at certain issues (that are otherwise overlooked) is a form of engagement, especially citizen engagement, that acts a corrective mechanism and it is in itself a part of a governance system. In addition, such actions often also enable new organizational forms as well as refreshingly new forms of citizen and government engagement. We also posit that valuable information and data may be collected and mined from the ever-growing social media that is of considerable potential benefit to citizens and governments. And, as discussed earlier, social media outlets can potentially provide two-way communication channels between citizens and government for effective information dissemination.

Some of the ideas proposed here might be conjecture. Yet, in reflecting on some discussions in this chapter, we can observe that various ongoing citizen participatory efforts through social media (such as in online citizen journalism) can inform the government in pursuing a better governance, for better decision making and policies toward civic amenities, public safety, and political transparency. Some examples of such efforts include FightBack,[10] HarassMap,[11] and Ushahidi,[12] among others.

When viewed from a top strategic level these new forms of communication also offer novel forms of transparency or even accountability for governments. Social media lend themselves to give citizens a new voice to be heard and, conversely, encourage citizens to engage and participate. Social media can potentially be a bridge to connect the government and its citizenry as well as a place where the two parties communicate, have dialogs, and together pursue a democratic form of governance. The authors hope to have made a contribution that advances research in this significant area of interest by offering novel methodological approaches permitting a deeper and more penetrating analysis within a CA Theory framework.

Acknowledgments This research was funded in part by the National Science Foundation's Social-Computational Systems (SoCS) and Human Centered Computing (HCC) programs (Award Numbers: IIS-1110868 and IIS-1110649) and the US Office of Naval Research (Grant number: N000141010091). Their support is gratefully acknowledged. Any opinions, findings, and conclusions or recommendations expressed in this material are those of the authors and do not necessarily reflect the views of the funding agencies.

References

Adamic, L., & Glance, N. (2005). The political blogosphere and the 2004 US election. *Proceedings of the Third International Workshop on Link Discovery*, 36–43.

Agarwal, N., Galan, M., Liu, H., & Subramanya, S. (2010). WisColl: Collective wisdom based blog clustering. *Journal of Information Science*, **180**, 39–61.

Agarwal, N., Lim, M., & Wigand, R. T. (2011a). Finding her master's voice: The power of collective action among female muslim bloggers. *Proceedings of the 19th European Conference on Information Systems (ECIS)*. Helsinki, Finland, June 9–11, Paper 74. http://aisel.aisnet.org/ecis2011/74.

Agarwal, N., Lim, M., & Wigand, R. T. (2011b). Collective Action Theory meets the blogosphere: A new methodology. In S. Fong (Ed.), *Networked Digital Technologies—Third International Conference, NDT 2011, Proceedings*. Macau, China, July 2011. Berlin—Heidelberg: Springer Verlag, 224–239.

Agarwal, N., & Liu, H. (2009). *Modeling and data mining in blogosphere*. Bonita Springs, FL: Morgan & Claypool Publishers.

Agarwal, N., Liu, H., Tang, L., & Yu, P. (2008). Identifying influential bloggers in a community. *Proceedings of the First International Conference on Web Search and Data Mining (WSDM)*, February 10–12, Stanford, CA: Stanford University, 207–218.

Anderson, C. (2006). *The long tail: Why the future of business is selling less of more*. New York: Hyperion Books.

---

[10] http://www.fightbacknews.org/, last accessed on 04/29/2012.

[11] http://harassmap.org/, last accessed on 04/29/2012.

[12] http://ushahidi.com/, last accessed on 04/29/2012.

Bimber, B., Flanagin, A. J., & Stohl, C. (2005). Reconceptualizing collective action in the contemporary media environment. *Communication Theory*, **15**, 365–388.

Bob, C. (2005). *The marketing of rebellion: Insurgents, media, and international activism.* Cambridge, MA: University Press.

Cleaver, H. (1998). The Zapatistas and the electronic fabric of struggle. In J. Holloway, E. Pelaez and E. Pelaez (Eds.) *Zapatista!: Reinventing Revolution in Mexico.* London: Pluto Press, 81–103.

Coombs, M., Ulicny, B., Jaenisch, H., Handley, J., & Faucheux, J. (2008). Formal analytic modeling of bridge blogs as personal narrative: A case study in grounding interpretation. *Proceeding of the Workshop on Social Computing, Behavioral Modeling, and Prediction (SBP)*, Phoenix, AZ, 207–217.

Etling, B., Kelly, J., Faris, R., & Palfrey, J. (2009). Mapping the Arabic blogosphere: Politics, culture, and dissent. Internet & Democracy Project, Berkman Center for Internet & Society. Cambridge, MA: Harvard University.

Etzioni, A., & Etzioni, O. (1999). Face-to-face and computer-mediated communities, a comparative analysis. *The Information Society*, **15**, 241–248.

Faloutsos, M., Faloutsos, P., & Faloutsos, C. (1999). On power-law relationships of the Internet topology. *ACM SIGCOMM Computer Communication Review*, **29**, 251–262.

Fortunato, S. (2010). Community detection in graphs. *Physics Reports*, **486**(3–5), 75–174.

Friedland, J., & Rogerson, K. (2009) How political and social movements form in the Internet and how they change over time. IHSS Reports, Institute for Homeland Security Solutions, Research Triangle Park, NC.

Gill, K. E. (2004). How can we measure the influence of the blogosphere? Paper presented at WWW2004, New York.

Goldenberg, J., Libai, B., & Muller, E. (2001). Talk of the network: A complex systems look at the underlying process of word-of-mouth. *Marketing Letters*, **12**, 211–223.

Goyal, A., Bonchi, F., & Lakshmanan, L. V. S. (2010). Learning influence probabilities in social networks. *Proceedings of the Third International Conference on Web Search and Data Mining*, 241–250.

Gruhl, D., Guha, R., Liben-Nowell, D., & Tomkins, A. (2004). Information diffusion through blogspace. *Proceedings of the 13th International Conference on the World Wide Web*, 491–501.

In The News. (2012, February 6). Manal al-Sharif. *Arkansas Democrat-Gazette* (Little Rock, AR), 1A.

Java, A., Joshi, A., & Finin, T. (2008). Detecting communities via simultaneous clustering of graphs and folksonomies. *Proceedings of the Tenth Workshop on Web Mining and Web Usage Analysis (WebKDD)*.

Java, A., Kolari, P., Finin, T., & Oates, T. (2006). Modeling the spread of influence on the blogosphere. *Proceedings of the 15th International World Wide Web Conference*, May 22–26, Edinburgh, UK.

Kelly, J., & Etling, B. (2008). Mapping Iran's online public: Politics and culture in the Persian blogosphere (Vol. 1). Berkman Center for Internet & Society. Cambridge, MA: Harvard University.

Kritikopoulos, A. Sideri, M., & Varlamis, I. (2006). Blogrank: ranking weblogs based on connectivity and similarity features. *Proceedings of the 2nd international Workshop on Advanced Architectures and Algorithms for Internet Delivery and Applications*. Pisa, Italy, October 10—10, AAA-IDEA '06.

Lancichinetti, A., & Fortunato, S. (2009). Community detection algorithms: A comparative analysis. *Physical Review E*, 80, 056117.

Leskovec, J., Krause, A., Guestrin, C., Faloutsos, C., VanBriesen, J., & Glance, N. (2007). Cost-effective outbreak detection in networks. *Proceedings of the 13th ACM SIGKDD International Conference on Knowledge Discovery and Data Mining*, 420–429.

Li, B., Xu, S., & Zhang, J. (2007). Enhancing clustering blog documents by utilizing author/reader comments. *Proceedings of the 45th Annual Southeast Regional Conference, New York*, 94–99.

Lim, M. (2012). Clicks, Cabs, and Coffee Houses: Social Media and Oppositional Movements in Egypt (2004–2011). *Journal of Communication*, **62**(2), 231–248.

Lim, M. (2009). Global Muslim blogosphere: Mosaics of global-local discourses. In M. McLelland and G. Goggin (Eds.) *Internationalizing Internet Studies: Beyond Anglophone Paradigms*. London: Routledge, 178–195.

Lim, M. (2006). Cyber-urban activism and the political change in Indonesia. *Eastbound*, **1**, 1–21.

Lim, M. (2004). Informational terrains of identity and political power: the Internet in Indonesia. *Indonesian Journal of Social and Cultural Anthropology*, **27**, 1–11.

Lupia, A., & Sin, G. (2003). Which public goods are endangered?: How evolving communication technologies affect the logic of collective action. *Public Choice*, **117**, 315–331.

Margetts, H., John, P., Escher, T., & Reissfelder, E. (2011). Social information and political participation on the internet: An experiment. *European Political Science Review*, **3**(3), 321–344.

Margetts, H., John, P., Escher, T., & Reissfelder, S. (2009). Can the internet overcome the logic of collective action? An experiment of the impact of social pressure on political participation. *Political Studies Association Annual Conference*, April 7–9, Manchester, UK: University of Manchester.

Markus, M.L., Steinfield, C.W., Wigand, R.T. & Minton, G. (2006). Industry-wide IS standardization as collective action: The case of the US residential mortgage industry. *MIS Quarterly*, **30**, 439–465.

McAdam, D. (1996). The framing function of movement tactics: Strategic dramaturgy in the American civil rights movement. In D. McAdam, J. D. McCarthy & M. N. Zald (Eds.), *Comparative Perspectives on Social Movements: Political Opportunities, Mobilizing Structures, and Cultural Framings*. New York: Cambridge University Press, 338–356.

Olson, M. (1965). *The logic of collective action*. Cambridge, MA: Harvard University Press.

Pareto, V. (1935). *The Mind and Society*. London: Jonathan Cape.

Richardson, M., & Domingos, P. (2002). Mining knowledge-sharing sites for viral marketing. *Proceedings of the Eighth ACM SIGKDD International Conference on Knowledge Discovery and Data Mining*. 61–70.

Sandler, T. (1992). *Collective action: Theory and applications*. Volume 4. Ann Arbor, MI: University of Michigan Press.

Song, X., Chi, Y., Hino, K., & Tseng, B. (2007). Identifying opinion leaders in the blogosphere. *Proceedings of the Sixteenth ACM Conference on information and Knowledge Management*, 971–974.

Wigand, R. T., Steinfield, C.W. and Markus, M.L. (2005). Exploring interorganizational systems at the industry level of analysis: Evidence from the US home mortgage industry. *Journal of Information Technology*, **20**, 224–233.

Wheelan, C. (2011). *Introduction to public policy*. New York: W.W. Norton.

Chapter 8
Web Monitoring and Strategic Issue Management: Dutch student protests against the 1040-hour norm

Dennis de Kool

8.1 Introduction

Social media provides individuals and small groups with powerful resources for rapid political mobilization online or what has been called 'E-mobilization' (Chadwick 2006). Social media have for example played an important role in the anti-government protests sweeping the Middle East and North Africa.

New social network technologies challenge the existing patterns of consultation and negotiation between classical intermediary organizations and policy makers. This new reality makes it necessary for governments to develop a new strategy to deal with 'strategic surprises' that occur when individuals and small groups use social media to protest against governmental policies or trying to influence the public debate about controversial issues, for example climate change.

In the Netherlands, the ministry of Education, Culture, and Science was one of the first to be confronted with the mobilization power of social media in the Netherlands. In 2007, Dutch students used social media as a mobilization tool to protest against the government's enforcement of the 1040-hour norm. This norm refers tot the total amount of teaching hours that students are required to follow each year during the first and second years of secondary education. At the ministry of Education, Culture and Science policy makers and the Deputy Minister in charge were surprised by the scale of the protests, the speed of organization of the protest actions, and the mobilization force the Internet provided to the protesting students. As a result of these experiences, the ministry of Education, Culture, and Science has developed a 'webmonitoring' strategy as a strategic tool to deal with social media.

D. de Kool (✉)
Center for Public Innovation, Erasmus University Rotterdam,
P.O. Box 1738, Room T11-17, 3000 DR, Rotterdam, The Netherlands
e-mail: dekool@publicinnovation.nl

C. G. Reddick and S. K. Aikins (eds.), *Web 2.0 Technologies and Democratic Governance*, Public Administration and Information Technology 1, DOI: 10.1007/978-1-4614-1448-3_8, © Springer Science+Business Media New York 2012

This chapter explores the nature of the possible strategic surprises that (can) occur when individuals and small groups use social network technology in political mobilization and how policy makers in government organizations deal with these surprises by analyzing a concrete case in the Netherlands. First, we address a number of relevant theoretical notions, namely web monitoring and strategic issue management (Sect. 8.2). Then we explain the research strategy and present the empirical results of the case study analysis. The students' protests against the 1040-hour norm are not only interesting because it is one of the first Dutch examples of mobilization by using social media, but also because the ministry of Education, Culture, and Science has developed a new strategy to deal with social media (Sect. 8.3). Section 8.4 contains some conclusions and reflections.

8.2 Theoretical Framework

The two central theoretical concepts in this chapter are strategic issue management and web monitoring. This section will discuss these concepts in more detail.

8.2.1 Web Monitoring

Monitoring activities have become a strong tradition within the public sector (Bouckaert et al. 2003; De Kool 2007, 2008). An important goal behind 'traditional' monitoring activities is reducing uncertainties in the policy environment. 'Traditional' monitoring is signalizing relevant and specific developments in the visible environment, for example on the domains of nature-, safety-, education-, and water policies. The results of these monitoring activities are being published regularly. Because of the time space between signalizing and publishing many of these data are not up-to-date.

In recent years public organizations face the emergence of social media. Social media is a label for many new Internet technologies that are used to share information (pictures, movies, music, and expertise) with other people. Social media can facilitate and stimulate bottom-up participation and self-organization (Boulos and Wheelert 2007). Examples of social media are Linked-in, Twitter, Yammer, and blogs. With the expansion of social media, monitoring activities have become both simpler and more complex (Sutton 2009). This development makes it necessary for governments to develop new monitoring strategies to deal with the social media usage of citizens. These approaches include strategies to search for breaking news, processes to access and follow communication in online forums, choosing which media to monitor, and decision making about how to address misinformation online (Sutton 2009). Against this background many governments are currently developing tools to monitor the social media usage of citizens in relation to policy relevant issues. Social media monitoring involves the identification, observation, and analysis of content produced by and transmitted between social media users.

Social media monitoring tools generally fall under the category of 'reputation management' of 'buzz monitoring' (Sutton 2009). This is partly true for private companies who are using social media for marketing, sales and services, and to deal with complaints (Social Media Monitor, Social Embassy 2011). But for government organizations legitimacy and acting responsively (including gaining public support for policies) are more important then reputation management.

In this chapter, we will also make a distinction between 'webmonitoring' and 'webcare' (Bekkers et al. 2011a). Web monitoring can be, but is not necessarily, the first phase of 'webcare' that includes 'talking back' in online dialogs with citizens (Bekkers et al. 2011a) These 'early warning tools' are aimed at signalizing relevant discussions online and to monitor the digital 'national mood' about policy programs or plans. Web monitoring can have a narrow and a broad scope. Within the narrow scope Croll and Power (2009) distinguish three ways to monitor visitors, namely web analytics, web interaction analytics, and real user monitoring. Web analytics records visitor requests and shows what visitors did on the website of a company or governmental agency. Web interaction analytics shows how (these) visitors interacted with (these) pages and digital forms. Real user monitoring involves watching actual user interactions with public or private websites (Croll and Power 2009). Business or governments can also broaden their scope by monitoring relevant issues elsewhere on the Internet to track the topics that matter for them. Complete web monitoring implies complete web alerting, bringing all of the problems detected by all monitoring tools into a single, central place, where companies or governmental agencies can analyze and escalate them appropriately (Croll and Power 2009: 565).

Unlike traditional monitoring (see Table 8.1), web monitoring is real time and continuously preoccupied with relevant issues throughout the year. This also means a continuous 'surveillance' for relevant discussions and signals on the Internet and, when such issues arise, activating an early warning system.

8.2.2 Strategic Issue Management

In modern information societies governments face new challenges and changes. A new challenge is dealing with social media. Web monitoring can be a promising tool to deal with 'surprises' in the virtual world. Dealing with new challenges and surprises is an important part of strategic issue management (Ansoff and McDonnel 1990; Heath and Palenchar 2009). Strategic issue management (SIM) is "a systematic procedure for early identification and fast responses to surprising changes both inside and outside an enterprise" (Ansoff and McDonnel 1990: 370).

Unlike traditional monitoring, SIM is real time and continuously preoccupied with relevant issues throughout the year. This also means a continuous

Table 8.1 Traditional monitoring and web monitoring

	Traditional monitoring	Webmonitoring
Focus	Visible environment	Virtual environment
Intensity	Regularly	Permanently
Goal	Signalizing relevant developments (selection before)	Signalizing potentially relevant developments (selection and interpretation during the process)

surveillance for relevant discussions and signals on the Internet and, when such issues arise, activating an early warning system. Web monitoring contains several steps, because both companies and governmental agencies cannot watch everything all the time. The first step in issue analysis is issue identification. The procedure is to cross-out the issues which are not relevant for the organization and to add others which are identified from scanning of the virtual world (webmonitoring). Digital environmental surveillance should be supplemented by identification of important internal trends and events which are expected to have important impact on organizational performance. Based on the trends and events, threats and opportunities can be traced and an impact analysis can take place to estimate the impact and urgency of issues. Social media events with minor impact can result in no further action. Events with modest impact can result in delayed action and urgent issues with big impact will make immediate action necessary.

8.3 Case Study Analysis

8.3.1 Research Strategy

The research strategy is based on a case study approach. The advantage of a case study is that it recognizes the complex nature of social phenomenon in a coherent and integrated way, thereby acknowledging the complex, and meaningful interaction between relevant social processes and actors instead of limiting the study of social phenomenon to a very specified set of variables and the relations between them (Yin 2003). The case refers to the protests of secondary school students against the so-called 1040 norm in 2007 and the lessons that the ministry of Education, Culture, and Science has learned since then (Bekkers et al. 2011a, b). This case is interesting because the ministry of Education, Culture, and Science can be seen as 'pioneer' on the domain of web monitoring in the Netherlands. This policy department was one of the first to be confronted with the mobilization power of social media in the Netherlands.

We have used different research techniques to collect the empirical data, namely a combination of desk research and semi-structured interviews with key players.

8.3.2 Case Description

The introduction of major reforms in primary and secondary education during the last decade caused the quality of education to be a widely discussed issue in the Netherlands. In 2007, discussion focused on one particular issue: the government's enforcement of the '1040-hour norm'. This norm refers to the total amount of teaching hours that students are required to follow each year during the first and second years of secondary education. Although required by education inspectors to comply with this norm, many schools were unable to do so, because of teacher shortages. Such schools were forced to take a variety of "phony" or "misleading" measures (for example, hours for "self study" in the class rooms) suggesting students were receiving education. Students complained that they were forced to be at school, without taking classes. In November 2007, students across the country revolted against the perceived absurdity of this norm.

The initial mobilization actor in this case was the National Student Action Committee (*Landelijk Actie Komitee Scholieren*, LAKS), which was established in 1984 with government support and acts as the trade union for secondary school students. In early November 2007, LAKS launched several protest actions, including strikes and demonstrations. LAKS was able to draw the attention as well as the support of many school boards. As framed by LAKS, the 1040-hour norm was detrimental to school quality, claiming that "if you are in favour of quality, you are opposed to the 1040-hour norm". These words made it quite easy to understand why the students were angry. Other terms that were used were "kennel requirement" or "kennel hours" (in Dutch, *ophokoplicht* or *ophokuren*). From then on, these 'frames' dominated the discussion, and they were adopted by most of the involved actors, including the media (Bekkers et al. 2011b).

8.3.3 Case Analysis

One key figure in the expansion of the issue was one individual student, Kevin. On Friday morning 23 November 2007, strikes and demonstrations took place in many cities. Throughout the country, thousands of students came into action, which in some incidents cause for orderly disturbance. One day before, Kevin had forwarded the following MSN message to his friends: '*All students in the Netherlands are going on strike because the number of lessons is increased to 1040 h. As a result, we have to stay in school longer, and a ninth hour is added to the schedule. Therefore, the whole Netherlands will strike on 23-11-07, immediately after the first break, simply on the school playground, and ignore the lessons. FORWARD THIS TO ALL*'. And these friends forwarded the message to their friends and the wheel was set in motion. Kevin also setup a site on Hyves (a Dutch equivalent of Facebook) entitled 'Away with the 1040', which grew to about 50,000 members. Postings were made to announce strikes on schools. Many of the actions were recorded by pupils with their mobile phones and uploaded to YouTube. For instance between November 26th and December 7th 2007 the amount of videos made available on the course of the protest had risen from 800 until more than 1600 (Bekkers et al. 2009).

In a statement, LAKS declared it had not organized these protests. However, LAKS was glad the students had raised their voices, although for some days LAKS was not able to control the local demonstrations. On Wednesday 28 November, the House of Representatives met for an emergency debate. When a large majority of the Representatives still continued to support the compliance of the norm, LAKS summoned the students to demonstrate on Friday 30 November in Amsterdam, thereby trying to regain control over the protests. About 20,000 pupils participated in this demonstration. This demonstration ended the campaign for the time being, and LAKS announced it was planning to enter negotiations with the ministry. It also stated it would resume its actions in February 2008 if the government refused to take measures. No further action was necessary. In mid-January, 20 secondary schools announced their refusal to comply with the norm. More schools followed. At the same time, LAKS incited students to be absent during all school hours in which no teaching took place (Bekkers et al. 2011a).

The norm received new attention on 13 February 2008, when the parliamentary inquiry committee, named after its chair (J. Dijsselbloem) published its report 'Time for education' (*Tijd voor Onderwijs* in Dutch). The Committee Dijsselbloem severely criticized the role of the politicians who had been responsible for the reforms in recent decades. The Committee concluded that "politics had overloaded the field of education with ambitions and trampled the freedom of the schools" (Commissie Dijsselbloem 2008). In its recommendations, it argued the present 1040-hour norm was "much contested" and should be reconsidered. In the House of Representatives, the State Secretary expressed agreement with this recommendation and promised an investigation. Although the norm was not formally withdrawn, it became clear it would not be enforced during the investigation. The ministry reacted in a traditional way by appointing a special committee ('Commissie Cornielje') to address the 1040-hour norm in relation to the broader discussion concerning improving secondary education quality. The outcome meant the norm itself would not be changed substantially (to 1000 hours), while the quality issue itself was hardly discussed (Commissie Cornielje 2008). Finally, the Committee Cornielje 'pacified' the issue.

At the ministry policy makers and the Deputy Minister in charge were surprised by the scale of the protest and the speed of organization of the protest actions in November 2007 and the mobilization force the Internet provided to the protesting students. With the help of a trainee, they acquired information about the places and the contents of these Internet discussions in which the students participated. Before then, Internet discussions had not been seen as relevant sources of information. Policy makers were primarily focused on the opinions and information that were expressed by the vested organizations in the field of secondary education as well as the coverage of the events in the traditional media. They were also surprised by the massive use of social networks by the students. They were also confused on "whether and how they should react and which media they should use to inform students and the wider public on their views". In the end, they decided to use the traditional media. Policy makers within the ministry feared, once the opinion of the deputy minister was posted, students would "manipulate the message", given the open and flexible character of the content in Web 2.0 environments. They feared that the Deputy Minister might eventually become "a joke". For policy makers it was also difficult to "pin point the locations of the discussions". Although policy makers in the end were able to locate some relevant websites and networks, like Kevins Hyves page "wegmet1040" and some YouTube-related discussions, they had the impression that the use of, for instance, MSN made the discussion not only very fluid, but it was also not visible.

8.3.4 Lessons Learned

This event has resulted in the development of a new strategic issue management tool, namely web monitoring, an online communication strategy and some experiments with 'webcare'.

Web monitoring as new strategy
No procedures were available at the policy department on how to react to these new, social network-driven forms of protest politics. We also notice that within the ministry no knowledge and staff were available to deal with these kinds of protests. During the peak of the revolt policy makers adhered to the established standard operating procedures, thereby relying on their access to the traditional media, to counterbalance the claims of the students. As a result of these experiences, the ministry of Education, Culture, and Science initiated an evaluation by Young Works (2008). The goal behind this evaluation was to get insight into the social media that young people use, their online behavior, and the digital information culture they live in. Another step was developing a new 'online monitoring' strategy to signalize what is going on in the virtual world about education-related issues in an early stage. Online early warning systems can reduce the risk that the department will be confronted with new issues and unforeseen protests. Online monitoring provides the department with a digital 'scan' about virtual discussions and is seen as a useful extra source of information.

The protests of secondary school students against the 1040 norm have been a 'wake up-call' for developing a web monitoring strategy withtin the new division "Knowledge about the environment and communication (Afdeling Omgevings-kennis en Communicatie in Dutch). However, web monitoring is not only a point of attention for this division. Generally speaking, civil servant have become more aware about the need to monitor the physical and virtual policy environment permanently to find out what people say and think about policy programs and policy intentions. Policy-related discussions in the virtual world are no less important than debates in the physical world or expressed opinions in newspapers or respected television programs. For that reason civil servants state that they follow relevant news sites and monitor the websites of relevant actors on the policy domain of education (for example, LAKS and the General Unions of Education and the Education Council of the Netherlands).

Web monitoring is not only a strategy of the Ministry of Education, Culture, and Science but also a point of attention within other policy departments in the Netherlands. Civil servants from the Ministry of Infrastructure and the Environment monitor social media to signalize relevant developments in an early state under the label of 'clever listening'. The Dutch Tax Administration (Belastingdienst in Dutch) is currently exploring the possibilities of Twitter to communicate and interact with their digital clients.

Online communication strategy
Different factors made the development of an adequate communication strategy very difficult. First, civil servants from the department were seen as 'natural opponents' of students from the perception that they represent the group who support the maintenance of the norm. Second, the matter of time is a relevant point of attention. The speed of social media can also collide with the meticulous and therefore 'delaying' procedures, regulations, and rules which have to be taken into account in government communication. Third, the ministry has a traditional focus on the classical media (like newspapers) to explain the vision of the department. During the student protests the department had some resistance to use new social media and to 'penetrate' into the virtual networks of students. Finally, the department chose not to use Hyves or MSN, because it could be counterproductive to communicate in the 'private' virtual students networks. Nevertheless, a You Tube movie has been made in which the Deputy Minister explained her vision. Nowadays, the department has become less reserved by using social media to communicate with students. The current consideration is that the government should 'be where they (the students) are'. The virtual world has become more important for students, so online communication has become more important for the departments. Against this background the spokespersons of the department are nowadays using Twitter to discuss with their stakeholders, to correct wrong information (for example about child care). Another example is a website launched on Hyves in which the (former) deputy minister asked students about their experiences with their temporary placements at non-profit or voluntary organizations.

8.4 Conclusions and Reflections

8.4.1 Conclusions

Individuals and small groups can use social media as a powerful mobilization tool for protesting against government policies. In 2007, Dutch students used social media to protest against the so-called 1040-hour norm. At the ministry of

Education, Culture, and Science policy makers and the Deputy Minister in charge were completely surprised by the scale of the protests and the speed of organization of the protest actions and the mobilization force the internet provided to the protesting students. The protests of secondary school students against the 1040 norm have been a 'wake up-call' for the ministry of Education, Culture, and Science for developing an online early warning system to signalize relevant discussions about education topics on Internet ('webmonitoring') and an online communication strategy. These strategies are aimed at reducing 'strategic surprises' in the modern information society. At the same time this department is taking some steps toward 'webcare', by using Twitter and Hyves to interact with students.

8.4.2 Reflections

The virtual world has become a dynamic reality. Web monitoring is being developed as an early warning system to anticipate virtual discussions about policy issues. Web monitoring brings new challenges. The first challenge is to select the relevant and representative signals from the mass of many online interactions. It can be very difficult to judge if statements represent individuals or a broader group. Another challenge is that students and civil servants often do not speak the same language. Students can use informal words instead of formal policy labels for the same discussion. Both government and students usually do not speak a 'common grammar'. Tracing relevant online discussions implies having attention for this and getting insight into online behavior of students. Finally, the dynamic character of social media makes it very difficult to trace the relevant virtual platforms. Virtual discussions can shift from one platform to another community. A potential risk of web monitoring is that attention of policy departments will go to (react to) current events in daily life ('waan van de dag' in Dutch) instead of long-term policy making. Another risk is that web monitoring can result in 'information overload' and collecting virtual data becomes a goal in itself. Permanent digital surveillance by web monitoring can also be perceived in society as Orwellian control in which 'Big Brother' is permanently observing the virtual moves of citizens on the Internet. For that reason web monitoring can be perceived as (or result in) unacceptable intrusions into the private sphere of citizens (Chadwick 2006). Finally, web monitoring can feed the (naive) idea that all strategic issues can be anticipated. However, it is a misperception that information can be controlled in our digital society (Sutton 2009).

Although web monitoring is on the agenda of many policy departments, the (inter)active part of it, namely web care, is still rare. Web care implies not only collecting information online, but also using these signals to react to and interact with citizens online. The first explanation is that online interaction can bring several risks for government agencies (De Kool 2010). A weakness of social media is that digital content (almost) always remains present and that politicians and civil

servants thus can be confronted with their 'digital footprint' for many years.
Furthermore, social media can distribute and enlarge news very quickly, in
practice this often leads to lots of attention for incidents and misconceptions of the
day. The reliability and quality of information used in virtual discussions can also
be a doubtful factor (Beer and Burrows 2007). In practice the level of online
discussions is mostly varying and noncommittal. Another risk is that it is often
unclear whether in social media the participants are representative for a larger
group. This could lead to a situation in which the voice of an empowered citizen
with digital skills is heard better than the voice of those people who are not
participating in the digital debate.

Web monitoring also brings some challenges and risks to citizens being virtually monitored on the internet. Web monitoring can stimulate a responsive dialog
between citizens and government agencies, in which the government takes into
account the ideas, suggestions, sorrows, and complaints being expressed by citizens on the social media. However, permanent digital surveillance by government
agencies can also result in (the perception of) Orwellian control in which 'Big
Brother' is permanently observing the virtual moves of citizens on the internet
(Chadwick 2006). For that reason civil servants are often not yet a regular and
accepted group of users on the internet. Second, social media monitoring can be
perceived as (or result in) unacceptable intrusions into the 'private' sphere of
citizens (Chadwick 2006). So the privacy of social media users should be an
important topic of attention (Eggers 2007; Beer and Burrows 2007).

References

Ansoff, I. & McDonnel, E. (1990). *Implanting Strategic Management*. New York et al.: Prentice
  Hall (2nd Edn).
Beer, D. & Burrows, R. (2007). Sociology and, of and in Web 2.0: Some initial considerations.
  URL http://www.socresonline.org.uk/12/5/17.html.
Bekkers, V.J.J.M., Beunders, H., Edwards, A.R. & Moody, R. (2009). *De virtuele lont in het
  kruitvat. Welke rol spelen de oude en nieuwe media in de micromobilisatie van burgers en hun
  strijd om politieke aandacht?* Den Haag: Uitgeverij Lemma.
Bekkers, V.J.J.M., Straten, G., Edwards, A.R. & Kool, D. de (2011a). *Spraakmakende burgers,
  sociale media en het strategisch vermogen van de overheid*. Rotterdam: Erasmus Universiteit
  Rotterdam.
Bekkers, V.J.J.M., Edwards, A.R., Moody, R. & Beunders, H. (2011b). New Media,
  Micromobilization, and Political Agenda Setting: Crossover Effects in Political Mobilization
  and Media Usage. *Public Management Review, 27* (4) 209–219.
Bouckaert, G., Peuter, B. de & Dooren, W. van (2003). *Meten en vergelijken van lokale
  bestuurlijke ontwikkeling: een monitoringsysteem voor het lokaal bestuur in Vlaanderen*.
  Brugge: Die Keure.
Boulos, K.. & Wheelert, S. (2007). The emerging Web 2.0 social software: an enabling suite of
  sociable technologies in health and healthcare education. *Health Information and Libraries
  Journal, 24* (1) 2–23.
Chadwick, A. (2006). *Internet Politics: States, Citizens, and New Communication Technologies*.
  New York and Oxford: Oxford University Press.

Commissie Dijsselbloem (2008). *Tijd voor onderwijs.* Den Haag.
Commissie Cornielje (2008). *De waarde van een norm: advies van de Commissie Onderwijstijd.* Den Haag.
Croll, A. & Power, S. (2009). *Complete Web Monitoring.* Sebastopol: O'Reilly.
Eggers, W.D. (2007). *Government 2.0: using technology to improve education, cut red tape, reduce gridlock, and enhance democracy.* Lanham et al.: Rowman & Littlefield Publishers.
Heath, R. & Palenchar, M. (2009). *Strategic issues management.* Thousand Oaks: Sage.
Klandermans, B. (1984). Mobilization and participation: social-psychological expansions of resource mobilization theory. *American Sociological Review, 49*, 583–600.
Kool, D. de (2007). *Monitoring in beeld: een studie naar de doorwerking van monitors in interbestuurlijke relaties.* Rotterdam: Erasmus Universiteit Rotterdam (thesis).
Kool, D. de (2008). Rational, political and cultural uses of performance monitors: the case of the Dutch Urban Policy. In: W. van Dooren & S. van de Wall (Eds), *Performance Information in the Public Sector: How it is Used* (pp. 174–191), New York: Palgrave Macmillan: New York.
Kool. D. de (2010). Ambtenaren en sociale media: kansen, risico's en dilemma's, *Bestuurskunde, 20* (3), 35–43.
Social Embassy (2011). *Social Media Monitor 4.* Hilversum.
Sutton, J.N. (2009). Social Media Monitoring and the Democratic National Convention: New Tasks and Emergent Processes, *Journal of Homeland Security and Emergency Management, 6* (1), article 67.
Yin, R. (2003). *Case study research: design and methods.* Thousand Oaks: Sage Publications (3rd ed).
Young Works (2008). *Digitale media, digitale politiek?* Den Haag (evaluation).

Chapter 9
Web 2.0 as a Technological Driver of Democratic, Transparent, and Participatory Government

Nataša Veljković, Sanja Bogdanović-Dinić
and Leonid Stoimenov

9.1 Introduction

Information and communication technologies have set unprecedented opportunities and challenges that governments will have to deal with over the next few decades. With the emergence of a broadband Internet access, and smart mobile devices with the capability for accessing data over the Web, citizens, and governments gained an opportunity to access and consume information via multiple channels. Since number of Internet users expands rapidly (United Nations 2011), government is leveraged to use Internet as a medium to engage citizens in a variety of functions, redefine relationship with the public, create customized and customer-focused services, encourage public participation, and in this way transform itself into transparent and accountable entity.

With the rise of Web 2.0 applications and technologies new opportunities were presented for the public and the private sector to redefine and modernize their procedures, processes, and internal and external relationships. It is especially interesting to consider the impact Web 2.0 technologies have on government today. The former government model, characterized by static and rather exclusive relationship with the citizenry, in which they were only considered as passive observers, is no longer sustainable. Instead, new governmental concept is born, as a natural consequence of the changing technologies and the raising need of the society to participate more actively in the government (Anthopoulos et al. 2007).

N. Veljković (✉) · S. Bogdanović-Dinić · L. Stoimenov
University of Niš, Faculty of Electronic Engineering, A. Medvedeva 14,
18000 Niš, Serbia
e-mail: natasa.veljkovic@elfak.ni.ac.rs

S. Bogdanović-Dinić
e-mail: sanja.bogdanovic.dinic@elfak.ni.ac.rs

L. Stoimenov
e-mail: leonid.stoimenov@elfak.ni.ac.rs

C. G. Reddick and S. K. Aikins (eds.), *Web 2.0 Technologies and Democratic Governance*, Public Administration and Information Technology 1, DOI: 10.1007/978-1-4614-1448-3_9, © Springer Science+Business Media New York 2012

The Open Government concept brings innovations in the current government model. The attribute open relates to the main features of the new governmental concept that is reflected through the notion of open data, open access to governmental information, transparency, and user participation in government (Orszag 2009). Government is becoming more oriented toward citizens as they have the possibility to interact with it and thus state their opinion. Citizens are becoming requestors and creators of electronic services (Bekkers & Moody 2009) and moreover, they are participating in government decisions by giving their opinions and attitudes toward important matters (European Commission 2010a).

Citizens already have active participation in Web 2.0 technologies, which is a mitigating circumstance for governments to fully exploit Web 2.0 potential in relation to key issues of transparency, accountability, communication, and collaboration and to promote civic engagement in the public sector (Mergel et al. 2009). Use of social networks would allow governments to include users to give valuable feedback, reviews, and improvement suggestions in an open and spontaneous manner. Having government officials address their opinions over blogs could generate valuable public reactions and online discussions. Each government employee could use wiki to document how his activities relate to the government goals and objectives. Usage of video networks as channels for informing citizens enables putting valuable information and videos about various matters that concerns citizens. Government could utilize innovative and engaging method of Web 2.0 applications in order to increase efficiency and effectiveness, gain faster response rate, and achieve greater accountability in addition to empowering and engaging citizens. All mentioned Web 2.0 assets could also help users to take more active role in government, to participate in services' design and delivery, in commenting and reviewing current, or laws and regulations that are in creation, in sharing, and shaping different governmental data toward their own needs and in every other governmental aspect that concerns them as citizens.

Almost a decade after the first sparks appeared in the process of forging and shaping of something that we know today as e-government, it is an appropriate time to reflect on the past and present in order to better understand its future development. There is a need to look upon technological environment surrounding e-government today, to better understand why and how do evolutionary e-government models of the past became redundant. Accordingly, the purpose of this chapter is twofold: first, to provide historic overview of e-government models; and second to explore transformative power of Web 2.0 technologies, their influence on e-government transformation and their contribution to the Open Government model.

9.2 Web 2.0 Contribution to Government Evolution

With the emergence of the World Wide Web, in the early 1990s, possibilities were opened for governments at all levels to reinvent their external operations and efficiency. Before the 1980s, governments were focused on improving internal efficiency and communication (Ho 2002), but since the invention of the Internet, they were able to shift the focus to the external relationship with citizens and businesses. The initiative known as electronic government (e-government) was raised with an aim to improve the way governments deliver services, engage constituents, and perform overall governance (European Commission 2003). The United Nations Public Administration Network (UNPAN) defined e-government as "utilizing the Internet and the world-wide-web for delivering government information and services to citizens" (2005). Worldwide, e-government was promoted as the use of information and communication technologies for enhanced access and delivery of government services to citizens, businesses, and government employees (Silcock 2001). The e-government was expected to become a new form of governance and to show willingness to implement the transformation of public sector, internal, and external relationships through the Internet-enabled operations, internet technology, and communications.

As part of e-government initiatives and strategies, governments were required to do businesses online. They started to adopt this by creating websites, which at first played only an informative role. This can be characterized as the Information stage of e-government 1.0 model, the first out of four stages: Information, Interaction, Transaction, and Transformation (Seifert 2003; Baum & Di Maio 2000). This stage meant government presence on the Web, providing the public with relevant information including government structure, public announcements, and contact information. However useful, this was not facilitating the completion of users' tasks with public administration. It was merely the beginning of e-government introduction. In the second stage of e-government 1.0 model progress, interaction between the government and the public was stimulated with various applications. Citizens were able ask questions via e-mail, use search engines, and download forms and documents.

Soon, government agencies and public bodies started creating and promoting online services for citizens and businesses, which were to reduce the administrative costs and the time needed for completing administrative procedures. This allowed government to enter the Transaction stage. The idea of one stop shop of public services appeared as an alternative to functional departmentalization (Ho 2002) and it was moved to the forefront of e-government initiatives. Serving citizens and businesses from a single point, 24 hours a day and in a user-friendly manner became a foremost goal of every government. E-services were delivered at citizens' doorstep, and the only thing expected from them was to open the door. However, the expectations were different than the reality. Although governments supplied services electronically, their consumption was low. In the European countries, for instance, where the Internet is available to a broad population there was a disproportion between e-services supply and consumption (Wauters & Lorincz 2008). According to the Eurostat's data, the availability of e-services reached 58% in 2007 (Eurostat 2011). Still, at the same time only 30% of Europeans were using the Internet for interaction with public authorities (Eurostat 2011). Low consumption of e-government services was a real concern for governments. One way to deal with this problem was to promote electronic services and talk about innovations in government. Transformation, as the last stage of the model (Seifert 2003), was introduced to bring redesign in government functions and organization and help achieving better and more efficient governance.

Around the turn of the millennium, when a new generation of technologies, applications, and concepts appeared on the Internet under the name Web 2.0, it became apparent that they will change the prior way of communication between citizens and the public sector. Web 2.0 appeared as a consequence of various combinations of Web innovations over the last decade, including new technologies, applications, and concepts (Osimo 2008). As perceived by Murugesan, Web 2.0 is both a usage and a technology paradigm (Murugesan 2007). It allows users to access and contribute to web content by using new technologies such as AJAX, XML, Flex, Microformats. These technologies allow building applications for easy content creation and publishing. Blog, Wiki, Social networks, Virtual networks are just some examples of the Web 2.0 technologies legacy. Web 2.0 applications, otherwise known as social media (Kaplan & Haenlein 2011), bring new possibilities for user involvement in what makes up the Internet (Crook et al. 2008). They are all built on the same concept—user is the creator of content. This concept has opened infinite possibilities for users by allowing them to contribute to the Web as much as they consume it (Anderson 2007). Formerly casted as the consumer, now as the creator of content, every user is able to make more meaningful contribution to the society.

In contrast to Web 1.0 which was limited to users with high technical skills, Web 2.0 offered possibilities even for the less skilled individuals. Most of the Web 2.0 applications are free to use and do not require installation, meaning that anyone with a basic IT skills and any computing device (PC, mobile phone) can easily access them. Before Web 2.0, typical methods for sharing government information with the public included static Web sites, telephone information lines and printed publications. The problem with these methods was that information was often outdated. Web 2.0 brought possibilities for governments to publish information via dynamic Web portals keeping it current and up-to-date. Within the social media environment governments gained an opportunity to transform citizens into public servants, offering them two-way channels for interaction, collaboration, and information exchange with the governments. The next generation of government Web portals is bringing people closer to governments with more services, new designs, and Web 2.0 social media capabilities (Chun & Kim 2010). The great number of the previously mentioned Web-based applications demonstrates the foundations of the Web 2.0 concept. These applications are already being used to a certain extent in governments (Huijboom et al. 2009).

E-government 2.0 has emerged as a new term reflecting government transformation driven by the Web 2.0 impact. As a technologically enhanced model of government, e-government 2.0 reflects government attempts to renew and modernize its operations and relationship with public sector using Web 2.0 technologies. Di Maio noticed that in e–government 2.0, technology blurs the roles of individuals, who are both information providers and information consumers, employees, and citizens and the distinction between internal and external collaboration becomes artificial (Di Maio 2009). By using Web 2.0 tools and applications, governments have opportunity to improve and strengthen their communication with businesses and citizens, enhance internal cooperation, and provide transparent, open, and seamless services. Web 2.0 capabilities can be used for the internal government operations such as cross-agency collaboration and knowledge management as well as for the soft issues as political participation and transparency, service provision, and law enforcement (Osimo 2008).

9.3 Open Government

Since the development of the Internet and understanding of its impact on society, e-government has started entering the virtual scene and making its place in the virtual community. At first, e-government meant simple presence of state government on the Web, in the form of an informative website (Seifert 2003), but in time the concept of e-government has evolved.

Open Government is the new governmental concept that raised many discussions in the academic society. The debate is whether it is a new concept or is it just the government 2.0 with a new name. Di Maio (2010) sees Open Government as a subset of government 2.0. Many authors argue over this statement. Jenn Gustetic (2010) explains that Open Government would not be possible without the outcomes of government 2.0. From his perspective Open Government is the evolution of government 2.0. Tim O'Reilly (2010) delivers the vision of government as a platform and in this vision government 2.0 is the next release. According to Microsoft (2010) Open Government is interoperable government in which people and systems communicate freely.

The Open Government movement started in 2009, when the President of the United States of America, Barak Obama, set creating an unprecedented level of openness in government as a primary goal (2009). According to Obama (2009), the goal of Open Government would be achieved by transforming government into a transparent, participatory, and collaborative entity. The Obama Administration released an Open Government Directive (OGD), in order to present detailed instructions for departments and agencies on how they are to implement the principles of transparency, participation, and collaboration (Orszag 2009). Encouraged by the USA government example, the European countries started creating their own initiatives for government openness. The EU Member States have ratified the Malmoe Declaration on the joint e-Government strategy until 2015 (EU Member States Ministers 2009). A year after signing the Malmoe declaration, the EU Member State ministers responsible for e-government agreed on an Action Plan that will set out the path for the field of e-government up until 2015 (European Commission 2010b). The Action Plan aims to transform current e-government model, which implies the creation of a new generation of open, flexible and collaborative e-services at local, regional, national, and European level. The European Commission's main responsibility in conveying this plan will be to

Fig. 9.1 3D and 4D
government

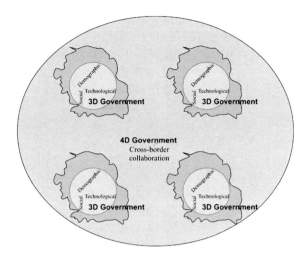

improve the conditions for the development of cross-border e-government services provided to citizens and businesses regardless of their country of origin. This further implies ascertaining preconditions (interoperability, e–Signature, e-Identification) that will help strengthen the internal market and complement EU legislative acts and their effectiveness in domains such as procurement, justice, health, environment, and others. In order to achieve these highly set goals, the Action Plan defines four political priorities: user empowerment, internal market, efficiency and effectiveness of government, and administrations and preconditions for developing e-government, followed by actions identified as means for their achievement. According to this Plan, the main focus of e-government for the next 4 years will be on increasing user involvement, improving transparency and data reusability, and most importantly, improving internal markets and implementing cross-border e-government services. From this point of view, the definition of Open Government can again be rephrased, and now we can say that Open Government represents four-dimensional government, where one dimension is technical, the second one is social, the third one is demographic, and the fourth refers to collaboration between different state governments through cross-border e-government services. Taking this definition into further consideration, we can conclude that Open Government, analyzed on the one state government level, can be seen as a 3D e-Government, but on the Europe, or even the World level, from the aspect of collaboration among governments, it can definitely be considered as a 4D e-Government. So, at the same time we can talk about 3D and 4D Open Government, just from the different perspectives (Fig. 9.1).

As previously stated, we can look at Open Government on the state level as the three-dimensional e-government. One dimension is technical and it refers to technologies that will enable its development. Technological revolution and the ubiquitous Internet have instilled unsettling transformations in many organizations, both public and private. Government is not excluded from these transformations. On the contrary, under the technological influence it is forced to transform its internal procedures in order to achieve stronger and better-trusted relationship with both public and private sectors. With the rise of Web 2.0 technologies governments gained possibilities to offer more interactive content, deliver value and communicate more efficiently with its users. Static websites are no longer satisfying the new technological criteria, and therefore a new generation of government portals is rising with features such as: active user involvement, user orientation, and customization.

The second dimension is social and it concerns citizens and their relations to government and governmental data. Social networking has changed the way people interact electronically. It has provided ground structure for government to reinvent its relationship with citizens and businesses. Online collaboration enables participation of millions of users in government, which is more than what a simple government information counter can provide. Within the social media environment governments gained an opportunity to transform citizens into public servants, offering them two-way channels for interaction, collaboration, and information exchange.

The third dimension is demographic, as there are new types of Internet users who drive the innovation and change that affects government online presentation and services. The Internet is the most recognizable signature technology of our time, since it has changed the way people live and socialize. With the social networks, interactive image galleries, blogs, and other Web 2.0 tools present online, it is no wonder that the Internet gained popularity very quickly, at first among the younger population, and later its popularity spread on the whole demographic structure of society. There are no more passive readers and viewers on the Internet. Almost every user is an active participant in the creation of content (Pascu 2008). The so-called Net Generation of users (Tapscott 1998) or digital natives (Prensky 2001) are the young people of today who use technology both for education and entertainment. The virtual presence, embraced by the younger population, is starting to permeate across all aspects of everyday life of all generations. This overall acceptance of Web 2.0 applications is affecting not only the way people communicate with one another, but also the way they interact with the government. They tend to participate, give suggestions, initiate changes, and involve in e-government services delivery.

Through the lens of technological and social and demographic evolution we can observe a completely new stance on electronic governance: Open Government. Its main characteristics are: transparency and openness, participation, collaboration, efficiency, and effectiveness.

9.3.1 Transparency and Openness

The people's right to know is a fundamental component of a democratic society, and a necessary variable in an Open Government equation. It can be achieved by injecting transparency and openness in government. Transparency in government is an idea which gained considerable momentum with the emergence of computing and the Internet in general. Internet technologies have enabled governments to open up their internal procedures and inform general public where and how their money is spent. More transparency means better governance, more efficiency, and legitimacy. Letting people see the internal government flows and investigate whether or not their representatives have met their expectations is an important step for governments to empower citizens. By enabling them to contribute more to the government and to the decision-making process, citizens will build a long and steady trust in government.

Transparency is a basis for democracy in which giving the people right to know is essential. Transparency is related to information openness, which is in all cases underpinned by a legislative framework. The right of access to the information held by public authorities fulfills three important goals of democratic society. It enables citizens' participation in the government, strengthens citizens' control and thus prevents corruption, and finally it guarantees a greater legitimacy of the administration (Savino 2011).

> The history of free access to information held by public authorities can be seen as the history of state democratization and its transformation from the instrument of governance of subjects into an institution at the service of citizens. (Fund for an Open Society 2006)

Without the freedom of information, citizens cannot hold their government accountable. Noticeably, the principles of government openness and accountability are essentially contained in the Freedom of Information Act (FOIA). FOIA empowers citizens to request that the government discloses a wide range of information. Twenty years ago, only ten countries had a law that guaranteed their citizens the legal right to have access to information possessed by the authorities (Ackerman & Sandoval-Ballesteros 2006). Since then the situation has dramatically changed. Many countries have adopted FOIA providing citizens and other interested parties with an access to information of public interest. By 2010, 80 national FOIAs, 184 subnational FOIAs, and two international FOIAs have been adopted (Vleugels 2010). Information of public importance, within the meaning of almost every FOIA is information held by a public authority body, created during the work or related to the work of the public authority body, contained in a document, and related to everything that the public has a justified interest to know. This law obliges all public sector organizations to actively and promptly publish all information related to political and administrative processes on all levels of administration. The availability of government information that is of public importance should help increase the accountability and steer the paths for innovative and new uses of this data.

In 1996, the Electronic Freedom of Information Act (EFOIA) was enacted in the USA. By this act FOIA disclosure and dissemination obligations extend to electronic formats. Entities and agencies at every level of government were required to make a minimum amount of information available to citizens over the Internet and in this way actively engage citizens in the policy making process. The fact that FOIA, EFOIA, and other acts have been enacted suggests that the democratic governments are determined to accomplish information disclosure by the government, and by that achieve the goal of transparency. However, the acts per se do not promise more openness and transparency, yet they are the crucial step on the way to an Open Government (Savino 2011).

While the USA is embracing the Open Government concept and bringing the necessary legislative framework to support it, the European Union and its Member States are slowly moving toward this new concept. In the European Union, the Council of Ministers adopted the European Directive on the reuse of public sector information (PSI) that deals with the way public sector bodies should enhance the reuse of their information resources. It sets minimum rules for the reuse of public sector information (PSI) throughout the European Union and encourages Member States to move the boundaries and adopt open data policies, allowing a broad use of documents held by public sector bodies. Most of work in this area is done by the U.K. The U.K. Centre for Technology Policy Research published a report (Centre for Technology Policy Research. (May 2010) entitled "Open Government some next steps for the UK" giving steps for implementation of Open Government in the U.K. The U.K. Government Licensing Framework (UKGLF) provides a policy and legal overview for licensing the reuse of public sector information both in central government and a wider public sector. It sets out best practice, standardizes the licensing principles for government information, and recommends the use of the U.K. Open Government License (OGL) for public sector information. The U.K. has also launched the open data website data.gov.uk that offers free access to a huge amount of public sector data for private or commercial reuse under the OGL.

Open data portals are rising all over the world. The initiative started with the U.S. government data portal (data.gov). It reflected key Open Government and Web 2.0 principles, namely that data is at the heart of Internet applications. Data.gov has a large community which is constantly contributing to portal's growth by taking part in discussions, developing different kinds of applications for data analyses, and data interlinking that helps generating more useful information from the existing data sets. Soon after the U.S. government opened data portal, other countries also followed the initiative for opening the governmental data and started deploying their own portals: U.K. (data.gov.uk), Kenya (opendata.go.ke), Norway (data.norge.no), Australia (data.norge.no), Austria (data.gov.au), and other countries (Open data portals 2011).

Besides opening data, there are also other efforts aimed at improving transparency in government. U.K.'s Web portal *TheyWorkForYou* (www. theyworkforyou.com) provides information on what members of parliament and other parliamentary bodies are doing in the name of citizens. The site brings together content from Hansard of the House of Commons, House of Lords, Scottish Parliament, and the Northern Ireland Assembly, together with details about MPs, their interests, voting records, and election results. Citizens can read debates, see what is currently happening in the Parliament, sign up for email alerts, and communicate more easily with MPs. In the U.S., there are many examples of government attempts to promote transparency and accountability. *GovTrack*

(govtrack.us) is a Web portal which provides the public with information on the activities in the U.S. Congress. It provides comprehensive legislative tracking, voting records exploring, writing petition,s and addressing the U.S. Congress collectively. *Recovery.gov* is a Web portal created by the U.S. government with an intention to provide taxpayers with user-friendly tools to track how and where recovery funds are spent. Data is presented in a useable form so that people can utilize it to gain information about how government is working.

9.3.2 Participation

The interaction between government and the governed is, as stated by Gant & Turner-Lee, a core pillar of democratic society (2011). This interaction, now empowered by modern technology, is happening in a way that has never previously been practicable. One-way design of public services by governments solely is abandoned. Instead, the idea of a co-creation, where services are designed in collaboration between consumers and providers is rising as a powerful tool for participation in government. Collaborative nature of modern technology has provided a way for governments to empower users and include them in the process of services creation. This participative approach is becoming primary in service delivery, but it can spread by involving citizens in receiving valuable feedback on various matters and involving them in the policy making process. Participation in government is in general about government asking people how to solve their problems, engaging them in policy making, service delivery, political decisions, and political opinions on all levels. In this way, more sophisticated, seamless, proactive, and citizen-centered services can be offered. In this way we can look at the new concept of democracy in which sustainable participation is fostered.

A number of initiatives in the world have appeared to provide a more participative way of thinking about public services. There are many prominent examples of participation. In the U.K. a Web portal *FixMyStreet* (www.fixmystreet.com) is designed to provide citizens information about their community by giving them the ability to browse, file new problems, or subscribe to information on the already reported problems in their neighborhood. The site enables visitors to enter any postcode (or street name and area in Great Britain), locate the problem on the map, provide details of the problem, and then entrust FixMyStreet to notify the local council of the problem. Another example from the U.K. is the *PatientOpinion* (www.patientopinion.org.uk). It represents a feedback platform for health services. PatientOpinion enables patients to write their own impressions about how they were treated or what happened to them or their family when they were ill. PatientOpinion tries to ensure that people receive the feedback on their impressions. Their comments are aimed at improving the future health system and relationship between patients and health employees. On the European Union level, a Web-based system has been promoted, under the name TodayIDecide (tidplus.net) that enables discussion between the government and the society. It allows citizens to leave comments, vote on draft law,s or present their own ideas for future laws. Another example is the *EuropeanCitizensConsultations* (www.european-citizens-consultations.eu), a Web portal for invoking citizens from the EU Member States to involve in the debate on the future of the EU across the boundaries of geography and language. It provides an opportunity for the public to discuss their concerns and ideas with each other but also with the EU policy makers. In the U.S. there are many participation examples. Hereby, we will mention only a few. The first one is *AmericaSpeaks* (america-speaks.org). This website is promoted as a neutral advocate for public participation. It includes citizens into the process of public decision making by enabling them to discuss problems concerning politics and presenting this discussions to the decision makers. Another one is *Regulations.gov*, the U.S. government Web portal that helps in gathering public opinion on regulations in the United States. Through this portal more than 300 U.S. Federal agencies post government regulations on which public can give their comments.

9.3.3 Collaboration

There are different types of collaboration: internal collaboration within government itself, intracollaboration between government and nonprofit organizations, businesses, and individuals in the private sector, and finally external collaboration between government and the public. The first two types of collaboration involve exchange of documents, coordination of work, communication with third parties, decision making, and knowledge management. Collaboration between government and the public is aimed at improving the use of information assets that will enable more responsive decision making based on the collaborative work and feedback information. In the ancient Greece meetings were conducted in the public square (Greek. agora). The agora represented a single place for gathering, asking questions, presenting ideas, commenting, rating, or criticizing (Kovač & Dečman 2009). Today, people are too busy to gather at public squares to discuss civic issues and drive policy decisions. Instead, they have moved this to the social tools, i.e., agoras of our time. Modern and agile Web 2.0 technologies brought social tools that can be used for meetings and discussions. Twitter, Facebook, and other social media tools can improve coordination between policy makers, government employees, and the general public. They have integrated feedback mechanisms that enable better and more open communication with citizens and business. Social networks are places where people gather to communicate, share opinions, find solutions for their problems. Governments can utilize this social media tools to bring people closer and include them to work collaboratively on the matters that concern them directly.

There are many living examples on how governments collaborate both internally and externally. *GovLoop* (www.govloop.com) is a social network for governments that contributes to knowledge exchange among government employees and professionals and serves as a platform for expertise, opinion, and news network. Since its establishment in 2008 until today, GovLoop has grown to over 40,000 users from all around the world. *Intellipedia* (www.intelink.gov) is a wiki-based platform for collaborative data sharing between intelligence officials of the U.S. government. GovGab (blog.usa.gov) is a blog written by the U.S. Federal Citizen Information Center. It serves as a formal channel for information and communication between citizens. *PeerToPatent* (www.peertopatent.org) engages citizens to provide input on the pending patent applications that are published on the U.S. Patent Office website. It invites public to share information, knowledge, and expertise with patent examiners about the patent applications. After registration, interested users are able to review online patent applications and provide information on the already existing patents. In this.way they help the patent examiner and increase the quality of patents.

9.3.4 Efficiency and Effectiveness

The traditional silos approach for the development of public services is not sustainable in the open governmental model. Instead, a new approach for the development based on the workflows and citizens demands needs to be adopted. This can lead to considerable efficiency gains and lessening of administrative burdens. Besides the changes in the development, the delivery of services is another issue. Public services need to be delivered through multiple channels and through diverse intermediaries and devices. For this to happen, both human and infrastructure capacity should be strengthened.

Behind services delivery is government administration that needs to be efficient enough to serve more citizens in less time, without sending them to wonder through the different branches of government. The internet can help make public services and the interaction points with the government ubiquitous, and in this way improve government effectiveness. Reduction of administrative burden includes the horizontal integration of government processes across the government departments as well as vertical integration of back- and front-end processes and collaboration inside and outside government departments. To ease this process the use of ICT is preferred and necessary. Government employees need to have adequate knowledge of ICT and ability to learn and improve that knowledge in order to follow new trends and innovations. Web 2.0 tools and applications such as learning and file sharing platforms as well as wikis offer significant efficiency gains and can contribute greatly to internal knowledge management (OECD 2009).

By achieving the newly set goals of Open Government: user participation, collaboration between the government and the governed, and the transparency in government, governments could strengthen the pillars of democratic societies and introduce more efficient and effective governance.

9.4 Conclusion

Web technologies have experienced immense changes over the last few years. More importantly, innovations in Web technologies, particularly Web 2.0, have influenced transformations in business procedures and in operations of both private and public sector. Web 2.0 technologies are widely accepted by many organizations for the introduction and modernization of their internal and external workflows and relations with partners and customers. Same can be achieved in governments. Moreover, Web 2.0 tools and applications could help governments to achieve set objectives in a timely, cost-effective and in a manner appealing and understandable for the users. With the usage of Web technologies governments have an unprecedented opportunity to engage with citizens, consider them as partners in the creation and delivery of online public services, and to include them in the decision-making process.

In the government domain we have experienced a change in a governmental model that appeared as a natural consequence of technological innovations and the rising needs of the society to collaborate more actively with the government. The new model, known as Open Government promotes transparency, participation and collaboration as strategic goals that will enable more efficient and effective government. Having citizens using social media applications and other Web 2.0 tools to request new electronic services, participate in government, discuss over various topics, and leave their opinion and attitude toward important matters is a great satisfaction for every government which strives toward Open Government model.

References

Ackerman, J., & Sandoval-Ballesteros, I. (2006). The Global Explosion of Freedom of Information Laws. *Administrative Law Review*, *58*(1), 86.

Anderson, P. (2007). What is Web 2.0? Ideas, technologies and implications for education. *JISC Technology and Standards Watch*, 7–12.

Anthopoulos, L., Siozos, P., Nanopoulos, A., & Tsoukalas, I. A. (2007). Applying participatory design and collaboration in digital public services for discovering and re-designing e-Government services. *Government Information Quarterly*, *24*(2), 353–376.

Bekkers, V., & Moody, R (2009) Visual Culture and Electronic Government: Exploring a New Generation of E-Government. In M.A. Wimmer et al. (Eds.), *EGOV 2009 Proceedings* (pp. 257–269), LNCS 5693. Berlin Heidelberg.

Baum, C. H., & Di Maio, A. (2000). *Gartner's Four Phases of E-government Model*. Retrieved from http://www.gartner.com

Centre for Technology Policy Research. (May, 2010). *Open Government some next steps for the UK*. London.

Chun, H., & Kim, D. (2010). Web 2.0 Applications and Citizen Relations through E-Government Websites. In E. Downey, C. Ekstrom & M. Jones (Eds.), *E-Government Website Development: Future Trends and Strategic Models* (pp. 266–283).

Crook, C., Fisher, T., Graber, R., Harrison, C., Lewin, C., Logan, C., Luckin, R., Oliver, M., & Sharples, M. (2008). *Web 2.0 technologies for learning: The current landscape–opportunities, challenges and tensions*. BECTA Research Report. Retrieved from http://dera.ioe.ac.uk/1474/1/becta_2008_web2_currentlandscape_litrev.pdf

Di Maio, A (2009) *Government 2.0: Gartner Definition*. Industry Research. Retrieved from http://dc.gov/DC/OCTO/Publication%20Files/government2_0_Gartner_Definition_G00172423.pdf

Di Maio, A. (2010). *How Do Open Government and Government 2.0 Relate to Each Other?*, Gartner Blog, Retrieved from http://blogs.gartner.com/andrea_dimaio/2010/09/03/how-do-open-government-and-government-2-0-relate-to-each-other

EU Member States Ministers (2009) *Ministerial Declaration on eGovernment*. Retrieved from http://www.egov2009.se/wp-content/uploads/Ministerial-Declaration-on-eGovernment.pdf

European Commission. (2003). *The role of eGovernment for Europe's Future*, COM(2003) 567, Brussels.

European Commission. (2010a). *A Digital Agenda for Europe. Communication from the Commission to the European Parliament, the Council, the European Economic and Social Committee and the Committee of the Regions*, COM (2010) 245, Brussels

European Commission. (2010b). *The European eGovernment Action Plan 2011–2015. Harnessing ICT to promote smart, sustainable & innovative Government*, COM(2010) 743, Brussels.

Eurostat (2011) http://epp.eurostat.ec.europa.eu

Fund for an Open Society. (2006). *Implementation of the Law on free access to information of public importance*, Monitoring Report, Belgrade, Retrieved from http://www.fosserbia.org/view_file.php?file_id=104

Gant, J., & Turner-Lee, N (2011) *Government transparency: Six strategies for more open and participatory government*. Washington, D.C: The Aspen Institute.

Gustetic, J. (2010). *E-Gov versus Open Gov: The Evolution of E-democracy*, Retrieved from http://www.phaseonecg.com/docs/egov-opengov-whitepaper.pdf

Ho, A. T. (2002). Reinventing local governments and the e-government initiative. *Public Administration Review*, *62*(4), 434–444.

Huijboom, N., van den Broek, T., Frissen, V., Kool, L., Kotterink, B., Nielsen, M. M., et al. (2009) *Public Services 2.0: The Impact of Social Computing on Public Services*. Luxembourg. European Commission, Joint Research Centre.

Kaplan, A., & Haenlein, M (2011) The early bird catches the news: Nine things you should know about micro-blogging. *Business Horizons*, *54*, 105–113.

Kovač, P., & Dečman, M (2009), Implementation and change of processual administrative legislation through an innovative web 2.0 solution. *Transilvanian Review of Administrative Sciences*, *28*, 65–86.

Mergel, I., Schweik, C., & Fountain, J (2009) The Transformational Effect of Web 2.0 Technologies on Government, *Social Science Research Network*, Retrieved from http://ssrn.com/abstract=1412796.

Microsoft. (2010). *U.S. Government white paper: Democratizing data for open government Meeting the goals of the Open Government Directive: The national strategy for improving adult literacy and numeracy skills*, Microsoft Corporation.

Murugesan, S. (2007). Understanding Web 2.0. *IT Professional*, *9*(4), 34–41.

Obama, B (2009) *Memorandum for the Heads of executive Departments and Agencies: Transparency and Open Government, White House*, Retrieved from http://www.whitehouse.gov/the_press_office/Transparency_and_Open_Government.

Organisation for Economic Development and Cooperation—OECD (2009) *Focus on Citizens: Public Engagement for Better Policy and Services*, OECD Studies on Public Engagement, OECD Publishing.

Open data portals (2011) http://www.data.gov/opendatasites/#mapanchor

O'Reilly, T. (2010). Government as a platform. In D. Lathrop & L. Ruma (Eds.), *Open Government: Collaboration, Transparency, and Participation in Practice* (pp. 11–39). O'Reilly Media.

Orszag, P. (2009) December 8 *Memorandum for the heads of executive departments and agencies, Open Government Directive*, Executive Office of the President, M-10-06, Retrieved from http://www.whitehouse.gov/sites/default/files/omb/assets/memoranda_2010/m10-06.pdf

Osimo, D (2008) *Web 2.0 in Government–Why and How?*. JRC Scientific Technical Reports, Seville.

Pascu, C. (2008). *An Empirical Analysis of the Creation, Use and Adoption of Social Computing Applications*. JRC Scientific and Technical Report. Retrieved from http://ftp.jrc.es/EURdoc/JRC46431.pdf.

Prensky, M. (2001). Digital natives, digital immigrants. *On the Horizon, 9*(5).

Seifert, J. (2003). *A primer on e-government: Sectors, stages, opportunities, and challenges of online governance*. Washington, DC.: Congressional search Service, Retrieved from http://www.fas.org/sgp/crs/RL31057.pdf.

Savino, M (2011) *The Right to Open Public Administrations in Europe: Emerging Legal Standards*, SIGMA Papers No. 46.

Silcock, R (2001) What is e-government?. *Parliamentary Affairs*, *54*(1), 88–101.

Tapscott, D (1998) *Growing up digital: The rise of the Net Generation*. New York: McGraw-Hill Companies.

United Nations (2011) *The Millennium Development Goals Report*, Retrieved from http://www.un.org/millenniumgoals/pdf/(2011_E)%20MDG%20Report%202011_Book%20LR.pdf

UNPAN. (2005). *Global e-Government Readiness Report: from e-Government to E-inclusion*, Retrieved from http://unpan1.un.org/intradoc/groups/public/documents/un/unpan021888.pdf

Vleugels, R. (2010). *Overview of all FOI laws*. Fringe Special.

Wauters, P., & Lorincz, B. (2008). User satisfaction and administrative simplification within the perspective of eGovernment impact: Two faces of the same coin?. *European Journal of ePractice*, *4*, 1–10.

Chapter 10
Emergent Networks of Topical Discourse: A Comparative Framing and Social Network Analysis of the Coffee Party and Tea Party Patriots Groups on Facebook

Christopher M. Mascaro, Alison N. Novak and Sean P. Goggins

10.1 Introduction

Political action has become increasingly rooted on the Internet. During the 2010 election season, 73% of adults in the United States used the Internet to acquire political information and 23% of individuals used social networking sites, such as Facebook or Twitter, to actively participate in the political process (Rainie 2011). This represents a significant increase from 2008, illustrating that technology is playing an increasingly important role in engaging citizens in the political process.

Social media is becoming a new center in the political process, but little is known about how political groups function online. Often, it is group administrators who set the agenda that guides discourse. Agenda setting and framing is thoroughly examined in traditional media (McCombs and Shaw 1972; McCombs 1994; Nelson et al. 1997), but there is limited examination of the agenda setting activities of online groups. Group administrators have a noticeable effect on the discourse in these groups through selection of the topics for discussion and as a result of this influence it is necessary to understand how groups select and promote certain topics of discourse.

C. M. Mascaro (✉) · S. P. Goggins
Drexel University, College of Information Science and Technology,
3141 Chestnut Street, Philadelphia, PA 19104-2875, USA
e-mail: cmascaro@gmail.com

S. P. Goggins
e-mail: outdoors@acm.org

A. N. Novak
Drexel University, College of Arts and Sciences,
3141 Chestnut Street, Philadelphia, PA 19104-2875, USA
e-mail: ann37@drexel.edu

C. G. Reddick and S. K. Aikins (eds.), *Web 2.0 Technologies and Democratic Governance*, Public Administration and Information Technology 1,
DOI: 10.1007/978-1-4614-1448-3_10, © Springer Science+Business Media New York 2012

This chapter presents findings from a comparative analysis of two politically oriented groups on Facebook, "Join the Coffee Party Movement" and the "Tea Party Patriots". We examine how administrators frame issues through article links and topic selection in parent posts on a group's social media page. Parent posts are those posts included on the main page for the Facebook group that are managed by the group administrators. We couple this framing analysis with social network analysis to identify how group members participate differently depending on the topic. Our findings identify how administrators of two ideologically distinct groups are able to affect participation and how our novel methodological approach applies social network analysis to identify salient actors by topic area.

First, we present a brief overview of the relevant literature pertaining to agenda setting, framing, and political groups. Next, we introduce the Coffee and Tea Party groups followed by an in-depth description of our methodological approach. We then present the findings of our study in three parts to illustrate how the agenda setting activity of the administrators affects participation by group members. We finish with a discussion of the implications for citizen engagement and technology design for political engagement.

10.2 Literature Review

10.2.1 Agenda Setting/Framing

Agenda setting is conceptualized as the ability for the media to influence what items the public thinks are important based on its coverage (or lack of coverage) of certain issues (McCombs and Shaw 1972). Previously, agenda setting analysis was used for studying the ways that the news media focused on certain issues (McCombs 2005). Because the Internet provides a variety of news and information sources to every user, it is difficult to study using traditional media analysis techniques and tools. McCombs (2005) states that "there are many agendas in contemporary society and many more of these are now available to a large segment of the population" (p. 544). In the case of online groups controlled by a subset of administrators, we argue that it is possible to study agenda setting by analyzing the topical inclusion of stories within a group's social media presence.

Framing is related to agenda setting. Unlike agenda setting, framing can be studied on an interpersonal or one-to-one level and is related to how a message is delivered (Goffman 1974). Issues can be framed negatively or positively by using keywords with positive or negative connotations. Framing has specific effects on the way that a message's receiver interprets information. For example, the terms "freedom fighter" and "terrorist" are used to ascribe values to a group (Hughes 2007). It is in this subtle way that the frames used by mass media can influence public opinion as not all frames are interpreted the same.

Due to the significant number of information sources on the Internet, agenda setting and framing analysis now have new roles as modern research tools

(McCombs 2005). One of the newest areas of research is the occurrences of these concepts within blogs and forums that encourage political discussion and action. Woodly (2008) builds on previous work (Farrell and Drezner 2008) to suggest that blogs in particular draw upon traditional agenda setting techniques to influence reader's opinions. Through frame analysis, Woodly was able to investigate the ways the Internet allowed for new forms of political engagement with fellow citizens and government and

how the Internet was being used to help frame public viewpoints about certain issues. We apply similar techniques to our analysis of two Facebook groups.

10.2.2 Groups and Social Movements

Research on online groups has shown that political discourse occurs more frequently than other forms of discourse in non-politically focused online communities (Hill and Hughes 1997; Gonzalez-Bailon et al. 2010). When individuals participate in politically focused groups they do so to engage with other supporters (Sweetser et al. 2008) and to share information with other individuals who share their viewpoint (Kavanaugh et al. 2010; Robertson et al. 2010). This prior research has also illustrated the ways that technology facilitates the discourse.

Facebook first openly supported political discourse in 2006 by creating a part of its website called *Election Pulse*. Many candidates and groups adopted Facebook as a component of their campaign's communication strategy, with mixed results (Williams and Gulati 2007, 2009). Social media and the Internet also played an integral part in the 2008 and 2010 election cycle as candidates began to rely on the technology to engage with individuals more and individuals understood the power of technology to communicate with others (Rainie 2011).

Technologically mediated groups empower administrators and participants to engage in a shared discourse space. The electronic trace data of an online group like the Coffee Party and Tea Party Patriots make it easier to identify and analyze leadership and participation. Bebbe & Masterson (2009) identify leadership as "communication that influences, guides, directs, or controls a group." In an online group the leadership role is taken on by administrators and highly prolific participants as administrators set the initial agenda and participants then take control in the discourse stream (Hersey and Blanchard 1992; Cassell et al. 2006). In previous research (Mascaro and Goggins 2011a), we have used social network analysis to understand leadership and control of political groups on social networking sites (Mascaro et al. 2012).

In this chapter, we apply the constructs of agenda setting and framing along with social network analysis to examine the presentation of information and discourse in the Coffee Party and Tea Party Patriots groups on Facebook. We identify differences in the activity of participants and how the agenda setting power of the administrators within each group influences individual participation. We do not speculate on how these activities within the groups are reflected in the physical world (Karpowitz et al. 2011); instead we identify important factors of online group activity.

10.3 Coffee/Tea Party

The Coffee Party was established by Annabel Park, a documentary filmmaker, in response to the Tea Party Movement in the United States in January 2010. Park established the group as a virtual place for civil deliberation among individuals (Park 2010). The Coffee Party moved quickly from a virtual to physical presence by holding numerous "National Meeting Days", during which groups of individuals organized at local coffeehouses to discuss issues facing the country. These activities helped the organization gain momentum and lead to the first Coffee Party Convention in September 2010 that drew 350 participants from all over the world (Zak 2010).

The Tea Party Patriots (teapartypatriots.org), a faction of the larger Tea Party, was established in a much different fashion than the Coffee Party. The Tea Party Patriots group is a self-identified national grassroots organization that promotes fiscal responsibility, constitutionally limited government, and free markets. The Tea Party first became recognized in 2009 for sponsoring and organizing the September 12, 2009 "Taxpayer March on Washington" along with the citizen opposition at the town hall meetings for healthcare reform in 2009 (Urbina 2009). The movement was also established with some political support from members of the Republican Party who had become frustrated with the party. This is a distinctly different formative trajectory than the Coffee Party.

During the 2010 mid-term election, the Coffee Party fielded one candidate in a US House of Representatives election that received over 200 write in votes, while the Tea Party fielded 139 candidates for House of Representative contests, winning a number of them (Spillius 2010). The Coffee Party is rooted online but directed toward activity in the physical world. In contrast, the Tea Party is affiliated with a traditional political organization and utilizes social media to organize and garner support in both the physical and virtual space. Both organizations use their online presence to facilitate discourse, but as illustrated in the findings section, they each utilize different topics and strategies to engage their group members.

10.4 Methods/Dataset

Our sample includes parent posts with more than 25 comments from each group's main Facebook page between 25 October 2010 and 12 January 2011; enabling analysis of interaction networks within the parent posts. The total sample included 345 parent posts with 52,774 comments from the Coffee Party and 245 parent posts with 47,167 comments from the Tea Party Patriots group. As of October 1, 2011 the Coffee Party Facebook group had just over 400,000 followers and the Tea Party Patriots had just over 840,000 followers.

We bound our analysis to this time period because it represents a politically active time period in the United States. Our data set begins the week before the election and ends the week after the newly elected Congress is seated. In addition to these events, there was significant debate surrounding key pieces of legislation, including immigration reform, social issues, and economic policy. The time period also includes the days immediately following the shooting of Arizona Representative Gabrielle Giffords.

We follow a previously established method of categorizing the topics of the parent posts (Mascaro and Goggins 2011a, b; Mascaro et al. 2012) by utilizing a process of open coding (Glaser and Strauss 1967; Charmaz 2006) to identify one salient theme for each parent post. We identify 17 discrete codes for the Coffee Party, which we apply to 345 parent posts; and 16 codes for the Tea Party Patriots, which we apply to 245 parent posts.

Our methodological approach builds a weighted social network from the electronic trace data for each parent post category. In our construction of the network, each comment in a thread has some relationship to all the comments before it, but the strength of that relationship decays with time. The strength of connection between a comment and the comments immediately before it are strongest (Goggins et al. 2010). After constructing the network, we calculated betweenness for each actor within the parent post category network using the TNET package (Opsahl 2009) in the statistical software program, R. We use betweenness centrality (Freeman 1979) as a social network analysis measure to identify individuals who act as information brokers in conversational discourse similar to our previous work on political discourse (Mascaro and Goggins 2011a, b).

10.5 Findings

In the following sections we present specific findings in three parts. First, we present an agenda setting and framing analysis of the topical content of the parent posts to understand the administrator controlled activity in the groups. Second, we present the distribution of comments versus the distribution of parent posts from a categorical perspective. We operationalize the construct of role disparity by looking at parent post percentages. Finally, we use social network analysis to analyze the individuals with the highest betweenness in each of the parent post categories to identify the differences in discourse between the two groups.

One of the most significant overall findings is the difference in participation by the administrators for the Coffee and Tea Parties. The time period contained 345 parent posts (average 153/comments per parent post) from the Coffee Party and 245 parent posts (average 192/comments per parent post) from the Tea Party Patriots. Within the discourse, the Coffee Party contributed 521 times whereas the Tea Party Patriots administrators only contributed 12 times. Neither of the group administrators posted in the other group. The Coffee Party participated in discourse as a facilitator, whereas the Tea Party Patriots used their comments to clarify misunderstandings. These actions illustrate different levels of involvement in each of the respective groups.

10.6 Topical Analysis of Parent Posts

The topical focus of the two Facebook groups varied significantly. Table 10.1 illustrates the percentage of the categories coded in each of the groups determined through a process of open coding explicated in the methods sections (Glaser and Strauss 1967; Charmaz 2006). The topics bolded with 0% represent a code not applied to that specific group. The Coffee Party was identified as having 17 categories of parent posts and the Tea Party was identified as having 16 parent post categories. In total, the two groups shared nine categories of parent posts, illustrative of organizational activities and temporally specific to the studied time period. These shared categories include: Defining the Platform, Economy, Election 2010, Giffords, Immigration, Mobilization, Security, Social, and Tax. Though the groups shared some categories, the manner in which the issues were presented differed significantly.

10.6.1 Organizationally Focused Parent Posts

The codes of Defining the Platform and Mobilization were used differently in the two groups and help to illustrate the organizational differences in the groups. The Coffee Party had very limited access to traditional media and relied on Facebook to establish their group identity. One example of a Coffee Party parent post coded as "Defining the Platform," said: "We the People Speak Out! … Yes, we know you're frustrated, but let's keep this discussion civil. Let's listen to one another and strive to understand." This post helps to identify and further proliferate the Coffee Party's interest in facilitating open discourse and lead to a threaded discussion about the importance of such discourse.

In contrast, the Tea Party used "Defining the Platform" messages on Facebook to refer physical activities that were serving as the primary vehicle for proliferating their message. In one parent post, the Tea Party Patriots administrators posted a link to a documentary about the Tea Party. This documentary served to further explain the roots of the group and define the views of the group.

The other shared, organizationally focused code was "mobilization"; parent posts were coded as mobilization if they included a member call to action. One of the greatest focuses of the Coffee Party in the early part of the time period was to get individuals to vote in the 2010 mid-term election, and participate in physical rallies such as the "Rally to Restore Sanity and/or Fear" hosted by Comedians Jon Stewart and Steven Colbert. Mobilization messages in the Coffee Party group were also often coupled with references to specific legislation that was about to be voted on with instructions on how to reach members of Congress and what should be said in support or dissent of the legislation.

While many of the Coffee Party "Mobilization" parent posts were focused on supporters coming out to rallies or calling Congress to stop certain legislation, the Tea Party Patriots mobilized support differently. One of the most significant

Table 10.1 Topical distribution of parent post categories

Parent post category	Coffee (%)	Tea (%)
Campaign finance	10	0
Congress	4	0
Current congress	0	7
Defining the platform	12	9
Economy	11	3
Election 2010	4	8
Employment	4	0
Environmental	3	0
Future planning	0	3
Giffords	5	4
Get out the vote	0	6
Health	4	0
Immigration	2	4
Media	3	0
Mobilization	5	7
New congress	0	12
Organizational	0	9
Political atmosphere	6	0
Quotes	8	0
Security	6	5
Social	6	4
Spending	0	9
Tax	7	7
Voter fraud	0	3

mobilizations drives for the Tea Party during the time period was to call the incoming Tea Party Congressional Freshmen to voice their support and clarify policy stances of the Tea Party. The Tea Party also provided phone numbers of members of Congress that were voting counter to the Tea Party interests before the new Congress was seated. In a non-politically directed illustration of mobilization capabilities, the Tea Party group encouraged voting for Bristol Palin on the television show "Dancing with the Stars." These similar mobilization actions, with different purposes, illustrate the differences in the groups.

10.6.2 Shared Parent Posts of Discourse

The other shared parent post categories concentrated on specific external events salient to the group. One of the most interesting sets of parents posts were those coded as "Giffords", which all occurred in the last 4 days of the data set and pertained to the attempted assassination of Representative Gabrielle Giffords in Arizona on January 8, 2011. The Tea Party was blamed by many in the media for the shooting as a result of what some perceived as the promotion of violent rhetoric. Many of the posts coded as "Giffords" on the Tea Party Patriots page were defensive and linked to articles or interviews where individuals defended the group. On the other hand, the Coffee Party utilized the shooting to further their platform of promoting open discourse and not resorting to violence. In one parent post, the Coffee Party administrators were retrospective: "Friends, this is not the moment to justify anger and hatred directed at our own perceived opponents. This is the time to unite in our love for peace and the wellbeing of our community, country and humanity..." This illustrates the different framing of the same issue within the two groups.

The categories of Economy, Immigration, Security, Social ,and Tax were all specific to external events ongoing in the American political environment. Parent posts in the Coffee Party coded as Economy (11% of the total) pointed fingers at the bankers and Wall Street as to why the economy was in its current state. In one parent post, the Coffee Party explicitly identified the problem from their perspective, "As you know, the current concentration of power and wealth is not only morally wrong, it is politically and economically unsustainable..." On the other hand, the Tea Party Economy parent posts were limited (3%) and were mostly focused on criticizing the economic policies of the Obama administration. The different framing of the economic problems in the country illustrate the ideological differences in the groups.

The immigration-focused parent posts in the two groups mostly focused on the December 2010 legislative action of the Development, Relief, and Education for Alien Minors (DREAM) act that afforded certain categories of illegal immigrants permanent residency and benefits. The bill passed the House of Representatives, but not the Senate. The framing of the bill on the two groups illustrates the vastly different ideological stances of the groups. The parent posts on the Tea Party Patriots group were focused on educating the members of the group about the bill and calling Senators to ensure a filibuster. On the other hand, the Coffee Party posted many things during the time period alluding to the positives of the DREAM act. One such positive aspect of the bill that was identified in a parent post was, "The CBO estimates this measure would reduce our deficit by $1.4 billion over the next 10 years due to increased tax revenue." This illustrates the different framing and ideological stances of the groups on a specific issue.

10.6.3 Parent Posts Unique to Each Group

Analyzing how similarly coded parent posts are framed in the previous section allows for an analysis of the differences in framing of issues. In this section, we analyze the parent post categories that are not shared between the groups. The different topical content of the two groups illustrates the distinctly different ideological stances of the two groups and helps to illustrate the ability of Facebook to mobilize individuals utilizing political issues. It also highlights the interests of the group and the intended discourse by the administrators.

Although different codes emerged from the two groups, the Congressional elections were a salient issue. The Coffee Party mostly focused on Congress in general, whereas the Tea Party focused much of their posts on distinguishing between the "Current Congress" and trying to stop the passage of certain bills before the newly elected members took office and the "New Congress" which discussed committee assignments and legislative agenda for the newly elected members. In addition to posts categorized as "New Congress", the Tea Party had many posts categories as general future planning that took things beyond just the incoming congressional members to future elections and platform decisions.

The framing of the problems with the political system and election was one of the most salient findings in analysis of the parent posts. The Coffee Party blamed electoral issues with campaign finance deregulation and the Citizen's United decision, but the Tea Party attempted to highlight the possibility of voter fraud as an issue with the elections. The Coffee Party was created on January 26, 2010 right after the Supreme Court ruling about Citizens United, which allows for unlimited corporate donations to candidate campaigns. Almost 10% of the Coffee Party posts were related to Campaign Finance issues and most discussed the problems surrounding money in campaigns. The Coffee Party identifies this issue as being at the core of political problems and influence: "...The decision to abandon public financing in presidential elections and recent Supreme Court rulings, particularly the Citizens United case early this year that gave unions and corporations a greater voice in politics, will push the boundaries further."

In contrast, the Tea Party Patriots group does not discuss campaign finance issues at all. The group is mostly focused on getting candidates elected which they see as a legitimizing action of the group. Analysis of the Tea Party parent posts indicates that Citizens United is mentioned within the group. Instead, the Tea Party believes that the sanctity of elections is at stake as a result of "voter fraud" (3%) and the belief that individuals would try to usurp possible electoral gains of the Tea Party. In the week leading up to the election, the administrators attempted to solicit 2000 volunteers to monitor voting. The different framing of the problems with elections and the political systems illustrates the differences in groups at different stages in the political environment.

10.6.4 Parent Post Category Participation Levels

In the following section, we present a descriptive analysis of the distribution of comments based on parent post category. We calculate a measure of comment disparity, which is the total percentage of parent posts of a particular category minus the percentage of total comments within that parent post category. The disparity between the two provides the researcher a lens to analyze the interest in specific categories of discourse. A positive number indicates a greater interest in the topic from the group administrator whereas a negative number indicates greater interest from the participants.

In Fig. 10.1, we see the disparity between the percentage of parent posts and the percentage of overall comments in the Coffee Party. The parent posts with the greatest disparity of interest from the administrators are Campaign Finance,

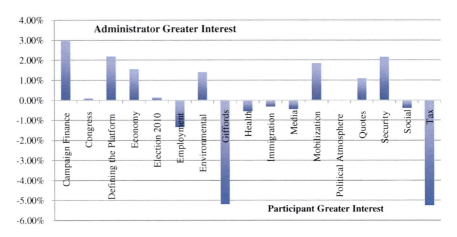

Fig. 10.1 Topical distribution of parent post categories in the coffee party

Defining the Platform, and Security. On the other hand, the parent post categories with the greatest interest from the participants are Giffords and Tax.

The higher interest in Campaign Finance and Defining the Platform for the administrators are correlated because one of the most significant issues for the Coffee Party was the Citizens United decision. The Coffee Party used these parent posts more as an informational broadcast mechanism and as a result facilitated less discourse from participants. Parent posts coded as Security mostly focused on foreign policy and defense. The limited amount of discourse from the participants is likely attributable to the prevailing discursive focus on domestic issues.

The higher interest on behalf of the participants in the Coffee Party group in the parent posts pertaining to the Giffords shooting and issues of Tax are likely a result of the contentious nature of both of the parent post categories. The Giffords shooting marked a highly active time in both the Coffee and Tea Party groups and the discourse in the Coffee Party group focused on furthering the fundamental message of the Coffee Party, open and civil discourse, instead of promoting violence. The message of civil discourse was widely discussed in the comments of the parent posts and significant blame for the shooting was placed on those who did not promote such ideals. The increased interest in the issue of parent posts related to the category Tax is a result of the possible expiration of the Bush era tax cuts that was being highly debated in Congress in fall 2010.

In Fig. 10.2, we see the disparity between the percentage of parent posts and the percentage of overall comments in the Tea Party. The parent posts "Get out the Vote", "New Congress", and "Organization" illustrate the greatest disparity between administrators and participants in the Tea Party group. Participants in the group focused more on commenting on posts coded as Giffords, Immigration, and Social.

Similar to the Coffee Party, the Tea Party administrators mostly focused on organizational issues of getting individuals out to vote and promoting the Tea Party message to the newly elected members of Congress. The less interest in

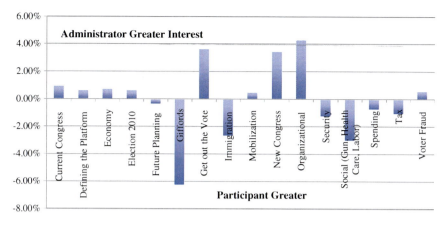

Fig. 10.2 Topical distribution of parent post categories in the tea party patriots

organization parent posts from the group members is likely the result of the fact that many of these parent posts were informational in nature and did not spark significant discourse among individuals. The high interest in parent posts associated with the Giffords shooting is similar to the Coffee Party. The increased participation during that time period may be the result of the supporters of the Tea Party defending against many dissenters who participated in the group to blame the shooting on the Tea Party's activities. The high interest in Immigration and Social issues was the result of significant legislation relating to these issues during the time period as explained in the previous section.

The comment disparity figures of the Coffee and Tea Parties allow for a high-level analysis of the activity within the group at a topical level. The presence of electronic trace data allows for a granular analysis such as this to be conducted. Understanding which topics the members of the group are more interested in informs the administrators what topical areas are generating the most interest from participants. We now present a detailed analysis of user activity in the parent post categories by identifying individuals who had the highest betweenness measure in each parent post category. We conceptualize these individuals as topical leaders of discourse within the groups that act as information brokers and can influence the direction of the discourse.

10.6.5 Identifying Topical Expertise Through Social Network Analysis

Our prior empirical work in various domains demonstrates that individuals high in betweenness centrality act as information brokers (Goggins et al. 2010). Research in political discourse by the authors (Mascaro and Goggins 2011a) has further connected those individuals highest in betweenness in electronic trace data to the concept of "issue entrepreneurs (Agre 2004)," individuals who specialize in discourse focused on a specific issue.

Through our network analysis, the Coffee Party administrator account has the highest betweenness actor in 6 of the 17 parent post categories (Quotes, Defining the Platform, Security, Campaign Finance, Mobilization, and Economy) and in the top 15 in betweenness in 5 other categories. This position illustrates the Coffee Party Administrator's important role in those categories indicating that they are able to propose the initial agenda and then shape it over time. The Coffee Party administrators are not in the top 15 in betweenness in Tax, Media, Election 2010, Environmental, Health, and Congress. The users who are the highest in betweenness in the other 11 categories that the Coffee Party is not the highest in betweenness are all unique illustrating that discourse participants concentrated on one topical area in the overall context of the network and acted as "issue entrepreneurs."

The limited participation in the discourse of the Tea Party Patriots administrators did not put them in the top 15 of betweenness in any of the parent post categories. Instead, there were two individuals who were the highest in betweenness for more than one category. "Frank" was the highest in betweenness in Defining the Platform, Spending, and Tax and "Jason" was the highest in betweenness in Economy, Election 2010, and Voter Fraud. At least one of these individuals finished in the top 15 in betweenness in all but four parent post categories, Giffords, Immigration, Security, and Social. The other individuals who were the highest in betweenness were all unique.

Analysis of Frank and Jason's activity in the group indicates that they are the two most prolific commenters in the Tea Party Patriots group. Analysis of their comments indicates that though they are high in betweenness in these topical areas, they express dissent with the views of the Tea Party group and use negative-worded comments to illustrate their displeasure in the way that the Tea Party addresses issues. Many of the comments from these two individuals are directed toward other individuals in the discourse arguing specific points that Frank and Jason believe are misguided. These findings illustrate that the most prolific individuals in a group are not necessarily supportive of the overall group message and viewpoint. In the case of Frank and Jason, we see that they are most influential in some of the more controversial topics, the fundamental organization of the Tea Party and issues that that the Tea Party is trying to champion.

One of the interesting findings in the Tea Party Patriots group was the presence of "Rebecca" as the second highest actor in betweenness in the categories Spending and Social. Rebecca is an individual who posted in both the Tea Party and Coffee Party groups and tended to debate issues with individuals in the Tea Party and voice a general dissatisfaction with the state of politics in the United States in discourse in the Coffee Party group. The presence of Rebecca as being highly between in the Spending and Social parent post categories in the Tea Party Patriots group helps to further narrow down the areas of discourse in which the individual debated the most with Tea Party group members. These two areas also tended to be the categories where the Tea Party defined their platform the most in cutting spending and changing social programs.

The identification of individuals high in betweenness in certain categories is important for identifying subject matter or topical issue leaders. The difference in the type of actors who are high in betweenness illustrates the difference between the two groups. The high participation of the Coffee Party illustrates both a topical- and discourse-based leadership, whereas the Tea Party does not participate in the discourse, but instead relies on others to lead the discourse. In this case, many of the more prolific leaders are those individuals who do not agree with the overall viewpoint of the group and end up high in betweenness because they argue with others in the group.

10.7 Implications for Future Research of Technologically Mediated Political Groups

Our analysis of two politically focused groups on Facebook illustrates how technology facilitates mobilization and discourse in an open online space. The group administrators of the Coffee and Tea Parties set the agenda for discussion, resulting in different levels of discourse in each group. The focus on similar topics in the two groups such as Mobilization and Defining the platform illustrate traditional group processes enacted in distinct ways and represent the different structure and interests of the two groups. Through analysis of the unique topics that the administrators chose to include, it is possible to identify the agendas of the groups.

Understanding how group participants react to the inclusion of different topics in a group space enables groups or candidates to better tailor the message or the issues being addressed in the open forum. The second set of findings related to topical comment disparity highlight the fact that sensational events, like the shooting of a political figure, can lead to variations in interaction levels. Social network analysis combined with how certain issues are framed in a virtual discourse group can highlight the power that administrators have in setting an agenda. Analyzing the specific activities of the participants and how they respond to certain parent posts or messages included in a group for discussion can help groups or political candidates better decide to include specific stories to develop more engagement in the technological space.

The administrators of the two groups engaged in the social networking space in two distinct capacities. The Coffee Party administrator's high involvement in the group discourse was representative of the group wanting to engage with individuals who had shared viewpoints or debating with those who may have dissented with the views of the Coffee Party. This activity was in line with the stated purpose of open and civil dialog. In contrast, the absence of the Tea Party administrators except to further highlight events or points within the discourse illustrates the lack of focus on participating in the online discourse of the group. This distinction also represents the more traditional structure of the Tea Party in which they were originally developed as a physical group with an augmenting presence as opposed to a virtual group that moved to the physical world.

The identification of individuals who participate in specific forms of topical discourse also has many implications for groups or candidates who wish to influence the message within technologically mediated discourse. The Coffee Party administrators were able to influence the discourse through both setting the agenda and actively participating in topical areas of greatest interest to them, while allowing others to take on key roles in other topical areas. On the other hand, the Tea Party administrators only participated in the discourse a small number of times, contributing very little to the evolving threads of comments. This allowed dissenters to play a significant role in the discourse stream and may have lead to limited activity by supporters in some topical areas. Understanding how to both set the initial agenda and then influence the agenda as discourse carries on is important to understand from the perspective of a group administrator.

10.8 Conclusions

This study represents an initial foray into comparing the agenda setting and discourse practices in two political groups on Facebook. The reliance of groups and candidates on using technologically open spaces, such as Facebook, for discourse and mobilization means that more understanding needs to be developed with respect to how individuals participate and interact with others in the group. We have shown in other research that the administrators of a group can censor individuals who do not support the viewpoint of the group without notifying the group at large (Mascaro et al. 2012). This has significant negative implications for open discourse. The fact that Facebook requires a real identity and as a result individuals have some physical social capital at stake makes individuals accountable for their contributions. Therefore, the activity that occurs within the group is likely to be able to be moved outside of the group and still have some level of effect in the "real" world.

As technology evolves, understanding how to design and use systems for civic engagement will be important. Building open spaces with the hope that individuals will participate may not be enough. Designers must understand how groups and individuals utilize these technologies and provide the appropriate affordances to facilitate and increase the productivity of these interactions. This is likely to be an iterative process requiring more understanding of the activities and requirements inside of the variety of systems currently in existence.

References

Agre, P. E. (2004). The Practical Republic: Social Skills and the Progress of Citizenship. In A. Feenberg (Ed.), *Community in the Digital Age* (pp. 201–224). Rowman and Littlefield.

Bebbe, S. A., & Masterson, J. T. (2009). *Communicating in Small groups: Practices and Principles* (9). Boston: Pearson Education.

Cassell, J., Huffaker, D., Tversky, D., & Ferriman, K. (2006). The language of online leadership: Gender and youth engagement on the Internet. *Developmental Psychology, 42,* 436–449.

Charmaz, K. (2006). *Constructing Grounded Theory: A Practical Guide through Qualitative Analysis (Introducing Qualitative Methods series).* London: Simon & Schuster.

Farrell, H., & Drezner, D. (2008). The Power and Politics of Blogs. *Public Choice, 134,* 15–30.

Freeman, L. C. (1979). Centrality in social networks conceptual clarification. *Social Networks, 1*(3), 215–239.

Glaser, B. G., & Strauss, A. L. (1967). *The discovery of grounded theory.* Chicago: Aldine.

Goffman, E. (1974). *Frame Analysis: An Essay on the Organization of Experience.* Lebanon: University Press of New England.

Goggins, S., Galyen, K., & Laffey, J. (2010). *Network Analysis of Trace Data for the Support of Group Work: Activity Patterns in a Completely Online Course.* Proceedings from ACM Group, Sanibel Island, FL.

Gonzalez-Bailon, S., Kaltenbrunner, A., & Banchs, R. E. (2010). The structure of political discussion networks: a model for the analysis of online deliberation. *Journal of Information Technology, 2010,* 1–14.

Hersey, P., & Blanchard, K. (1992). *Management of organizational behavior: Utilizing human resources* (6). Englewood Cliffs, NJ: Prentice Hall.

Hill, K. A., & Hughes, J. E. (1997). Computer-Mediated Political Communication: The USENET and Political Communities. *Political Communication, 14*(1), 3–27.

Hughes, J. (2007). The Chechnya Conflict: freedom fighters of terrorists? *Demokratizatsiva, 15,* 293–311.

Karpowitz, C. F., Monson, J. Q., Patterson, K. D., & Pope, J. C. (2011). Tea Time in America? The Impact of the Tea Party Movement on the 2010 Midterm Elections. *PS: Political Science and Politics, 44*(2), 303–309.

Kavanaugh, A., Perez-Quinones, M. A., Tedesco, J., & Sanders, W. (2010). Toward a Virtual Town Square in the Era of Web 2.0. *International Handbook of Internet Research, 2010,* 279–294.

Mascaro, C., & Goggins, S. (2011a). *Brewing Up Citizen Engagement: The Coffee Party on Facebook.* Proceedings from Communities and Technologies, Brisbane, Australia.

Mascaro, C., & Goggins, S. (2011b). *The Daily Brew: The Structural Evolution of the Coffee Party on Facebook During the 2010 United States Midterm Election Season.* Proceedings from 2011 Political Networks Conference at The University of Michigan, Ann Arbor, Michigan.

Mascaro, C., Novak, A., & Goggins, S. (2012). *Shepherding and Censorship: Discourse Management in the Tea Party Patriots Facebook Group.* Proceedings from Hawaii International Conference on System Sciences (E-Government Track), Grand Wailea Maui, Hawaii.

McCombs, M. (1994). News Influence on our pictures of the world. In J. Bryant & D. Zillmann (Eds.), *Media Effects: Advances in Theory and Research* (pp. 1–25). Hillsdale, NJ: Lawrence Elbraum Associates.

McCombs, M. (2005). A look at agenda-setting: Past, present and future. *Journalism Studies, 6,* 543–557.

McCombs, M., & Shaw, D. J. (1972). The agenda-setting function of the mass media. *Public Opinion Quarterly, 36,* 176–187.

Nelson, T. E., Oxley, Z. M., & Clawson, R. A. (1997). Towards a psychology of framing effects. *Political Behavior, 19,* 221–246.

Opsahl, T. (2009). *Structure and Evolution of Weighted Networks.* Ph.D. University of London, London, UK.

Park, A. (2010). Why I started Coffee Party USA. Retrieved October 15, 2010, from http://www.cnn.com/2010/OPINION/03/18/park.coffee.party

Rainie, L. (2011). The Internet and Campaign 2010. Retrieved from http://www.pewinternet.org/Reports/2011/The-Internet-and-Campaign-2010.aspx

Robertson, S. P., Vatrapu, R. K., & Medina, R. (2010). Off the wall political discourse: Facebook use in the 2008 U.S. Presidential election. *Information Polity, 15*, 11–31.

Spillius, A. (2010). US Midterms: Coffee Party Emerges to take on the Tea Party. Retrieved October 28, 2010 from http://www.telegraph.co.uk/news/worldnews/northamerica/usa/us-politics/8088024/US-midterms-Coffee-Party-emerges-to-take-on-the-Tea-Party.html

Sweetser, K. D., & Weaver Lariscy, R. (2008). Candidates Make Good Friends: An Analysis of Candidates' Uses of Facebook. *International Journal of Strategic Communication, 2*(3), 175–198.

Urbina, I. (2009). Beyond Beltway, Health Debate Turns Hostile. *New York Times,*.

Williams, C., & Gulati, G. J. (2007). *Social Networks in Political Campaigns: Facebook and the 2006 Midterm Elections*. Proceedings from American Political Science Association, Chicago.

Williams, C., & Gulati, G. J. (2009). *Facebook Grows Up: An Empirical Assessment of its Role in the 2008 Congressional Elections*. Proceedings from Midwest Political Science Association, Chicago.

Woodly, D. (2008). New Competencies in Democratic Communication: Blogs, agenda setting and political participation. *Public Choice, 134*, 109–123.

Zak, D. (2010). Coffee Party activists say their civic brew's a tastier choice than Tea Party's. *Washington Post.*

Chapter 11
Whither E-Government? Web 2.0 and the Future of E-Government

Michael J. Ahn

11.1 Introduction

Broadly defined as the provision of government services and information using the Internet and other digital means (Gant et al. 2002; Holden et al. 2003; Moon 2002; West 2004), e-Government promised increasing efficiency and effectiveness in providing government services to citizens (Grönlund 2002), and showed potential in improving government transparency, accountability, and democratic responsiveness by facilitating greater citizen participation and communication with the government (Applebaum 2002; Edmiston 2003; Furlong and Kerwin 2005; La Porte et al. 2002). Governments around the world have embraced e-Government where there exists significant variation in quality and performance (West 2008). Here in the US, governments at various levels have invested in e-Government with an emphasis on providing online services, while it tends to lag behind in utilizing the technology to improve citizen participation, and online dialog with the government (Edmiston 2003; Ho 2002; Scott 2006; Thomas and Streib 2005; Torres et al. 2006; West 2005). This has had an effect of identifying the term e-Government narrowly with online services such as driver's license renewal, income tax filing, and parking fine payment as other potentials of e-Government are mostly overlooked.

In its relatively short history, e-Government development has been a government initiated and government-centered process where the government—the sole supplier of e-Government services—plans, develops, and manages e-Government website and its various online applications. Although in many case, e-Government

M. J. Ahn (✉)
Department of Public Policy and Public Affairs, University of Massachusetts Boston,
McCormack Hall 3rd Floor, Rm. 422, 100 Morrissey Boulevard,
Boston, MA 02125-3393, USA
e-mail: Michael.Ahn@umb.edu

C. G. Reddick and S. K. Aikins (eds.), *Web 2.0 Technologies and Democratic Governance*, Public Administration and Information Technology 1, DOI: 10.1007/978-1-4614-1448-3_11, © Springer Science+Business Media New York 2012

applications are developed with the help of private vendors, it is the government that defines the breadth and scope of the e-Government services and the government has the ownership, as well as the responsibilities associated with its e-Government applications. The private sector vendors simply take orders and take part in the development and the management of the software, hardware, and technical expertise necessary to operate the e-Government applications. Although there is a "make or buy decision" to be made in e-Government development (Scholl 2003), the government is solely responsible for the content of e-Government as it determines which services are to be provided online and consequently invest in the development and management of these services. In other words, the government is the sole and therefore monopolistic supplier of e-Government and citizens, businesses, and NGOs are the recipients of the service.

This chapter suggests that such trend may be changing with the emergence of Web 2.0 that allows nongovernmental actors such as citizens, businesses, and NGOs to become capable of developing applications that traditionally would have been considered e-Government services. The lowering of the technical barrier by Web 2.0 was complemented by increasing availability of public information sources and data, based upon which e-Government type applications can be created by nongovernmental actors. This would inadvertently shift the traditional role of government as a single developer and supplier of e-Government services to a new mode of production where various actors including nongovernmental actors such as citizens, businesses and NGOs develop, and provide various kinds of e-Government services. Unlike the previous monopolistic mode of production, the new mode of e-Government production may facilitate a burst of new and innovative e-Government applications—applications that may indeed bring about the fundamental transformation that some scholars envisioned of e-Government.

This chapter explores the changing landscape of e-Government development where the essential role of the government is shifting from that of a developer of e-Government to a provider of public data, based upon which nongovernmental actors develop e-Government type applications. This potentially signifies a passing of a baton from the government to citizens as the primary developer of e-Government and lead to a new kind of e-Government that may be richer in diversity, functionalities, and innovativeness.

11.2 Traditional Models of E-Government Development

Before examining this shift, it is useful to examine the path that e-Government has followed in its developmental history to see the trajectory of e-Government development and its likely destination, from which, this chapter suggests, we may be witnessing a shift from. As mentioned in the introduction, since its initial adoption, e-Government has been a government initiated and government-centered process where the government is the sole supplier and producer of e-Government services and citizens, businesses, and NGOs are the "customers" of the services.

Here, what determines the final product of e-Government is the combination of various processes of planning, developing, and managing e-Government applications. That is, e-Government is provided in an environment where the government is the single supplier, and therefore it was government that defined and shaped what
e-Government was. Government could choose which services and information to provide and which services and information not to (Table 11.1).

As shown in Table 11.1, there exists a number of "models" or "stages" of e-Government development that explain a developmental path of e-Government. These models of e-Government, with small variation, describe and predict "the linear development or evolution of e-Government from a basic online presence to full integration, seamlessness, and transformation." (Coursey and Norris 2008) and they are useful tools for "assessing, comparing, and benchmarking the progress and success of e-Government implementation in the public sector organizations" (Andersen et al. 2011). According to Coursey and Norris (2008):

> These models all predict the linear, stepwise, and progressive development of e-government. Governments begin with a fairly basic, in some cases even primitive, Web presence. They pass through predictable stages of e-government, such as interactivity, transactions, and integration, and then arrive at an e-government nirvana. This final step is described variously as either the seamless delivery of governmental information and services, e-participation, e-democracy, governmental transformation, or some combination of the above.

These models of e-Government development envision a gradual progress in the quality of e-Government, starting from simple Web presence to increasingly sophisticated online services that eventually transcend functional and hierarchical boundaries of the government. The only distinctive variation comes as some authors envision that e-Government would not only provide "fully integrated" online transactions, but also transform the relationship among citizens, as citizens "participate" in government affairs through e-Government (denoted as e-participation or e-democracy).

That is, two kinds of the final stages of e-Government are predicted according to these models—models that envision fully integrated comprehensive one-stop online public service transaction and models that envision e-democracy or e-participation where citizens are empowered to participate in public affairs online through e-Government applications, and hence a transformation in the relationship between citizens and the government. However, these models do not seem to accurately predict the development of e-Government as most local e-Government remain in the informational stage with few transactional services (Coursey and Norris 2008) and according to Dawes (2008) "citizen engagement receives much less attention in practices than services or management concerns" who assessed e-Government in the US state and local governments. Nevertheless, these models of e-Government are insightful in envisioning what an ideal e-Government should be—a vision of e-Government that we aspire to achieve. Then would we ever be able to achieve the final stage of e-Government envisioned in various models of e-Government?

Table 11.1 Steps of e-Government development

	Step 1	Step 2	Step 3	Step 4	Step 5	Step 6
Layne and Lee (2001)		Catalog	Transaction	Vertical integration	Horizontal integration	
Baum and Di Maio (2000)		Presence	Interaction	Transaction	Transformation	
Ronaghan (2001)	Emerging presence	Enhanced presence	Interactive	Transactional government	Seamless	
Hiller and Belanger (2001)		Information dissemination	Two-way communication	Integration	Transaction	Participation
Wescott (2001)	E-mail and internal network	Enable interorganizational and public access to information	Two-way communication	Exchange of value	Digital democracy	Joined-up government
West (2004)		The Billboard stage	Partial-service-delivery stage	The portal stage	Interactive democracy stage	
Common stage of development	Web presence, Information display		Presence of online service and transactions			Integrated, full online transactions, online citizen participation, and communication with government

The Model's Steps, adopted and modified from Coursey and Norris (2008)

To begin with, none of the authors behind these models of e-Government development saw the final stages of their models materialize. It is a commonly held view that the future of e-Government is most likely to resemble e-Government of today except that it will be more sophisticated and has better-quality services and the e-Government sites would look better, sophisticated, and easy to use (Norris 2010). No transformation seems to have risen out of two decades of technology innovation in government as "IT (Information Technology) itself does not drive reform but instead foster incremental change within traditional structures of power and authority." (Dawes 2008) and the "key services" that some scholars expected to facilitate meaningful transformation in the government, such as e-Democracy and e-Communication type applications, are not likely to appear (Norris 2010). Several authors concur this observation where there is distinctive lack of online public dialog or e-participation while government has been relatively successful in making government services available online (Edmiston 2003; Ho 2002; West 2005; Thomas and Streib 2003, 2005; Scott 2006).

It seemed that e-Government was bound to follow the trend of development as observed by several authors above—the continued addition of government websites and services, while continuing to lack any key applications that may transform the government. However, this would have been true if one assumption underlying all these models remain true in the future. That is, most models of e-Government development made an assumption that government will continue to be the sole developer of e-Government services. However, this chapter suggests that this may be changing as nongovernmental actors are increasingly becoming an important factor in developing e-Government applications. This, we suggest, will change the future outlook of e-Government in a dramatic way than currently predicted.

11.3 The Rise of Citizen and NGO-Initiated E-Government Through Web 2.0

This chapter proposes that another, more optimistic future of e-Government is emerging where we see much invigorated development and outburst of various kinds of innovative e-Government applications by nongovernmental actors such as citizens and NGOs. The shift from the government as the sole provider of e-Government to the inclusion of the nongovernmental actors is made possible by two factors. One is the continued advancement in the Information and Communication Technologies (ICTs) that gave rise to the emergence of Web 2.0, making it easier and cheaper for nongovernmental actors to develop e-Government type applications and the other is increasing availability of public information and data, based upon which e-Government applications can be developed.

First, since its initial introduction to the general public, the Web has become increasingly sophisticated over time. Websites, 10 years ago and now, look considerably different and the functionalities of the Web have greatly expanded over time. While the Internet in its early stage was used mainly to communicate basic text information either on the webpage or through e-mail, it is now capable of far more functionalities. In particular, terms such as Blogs, Mashup, Really Simple Syndication (RSS), Open-source software, Social Networking Sites (Facebook, Linked), Microblogging (Twitter), Podcasts, vlogs, and Wikis became increasingly common on the Web and came to be called Web 2.0, to denote the new trend from conventional Web 1.0 (Chang and Kannan 2008; Chun et al. 2010; Nam 2012). While there are some disagreements surrounding the definition of the term (O'Reilly 2005), Web 2.0 signals a break from traditional Web technology with distinctive differences (O'Reilly 2005). Web 2.0 can be defined as a net-worked platform and a collection of social media that support individuals to create, share, edit and comment on content individually, and collectively, resulting in content that in the "permanent beta" status using diverse devices and technologies. (Chang and Kannan 2008; Chun et al. 2010).

In addition, with the introduction of smart phones such as iPhone and Blackberry, and more importantly, the emergence of "Apps" (short for application software), the Internet's functionality improved even further where people can access and contribute to the Web away from their computer stations. Broadly speaking, Apps fall under the definition of Web 2.0 as they are created primarily by individuals and businesses and there has been an explosion of various kind of Apps available as people seek to gain profit by developing innovative and useful Apps. The software necessary to create an Apps is readily available online at a relatively low or no cost, and some of these software are designed so that individuals with not enough knowledge in computer language can develop them (Business Insider, February 26 2011; Komando 2011; Popular Mechanics, September 1 2011), significantly lowering the technical barriers to Apps development.

As the web evolves over time, the amount of information available on the Internet has also increased exponentially (IDG Press Release 2003; White and Dorman 2000; Williams 2007). Included in this surge of information are var-ious public information, records, and data that were previously unavailable to general public. In the early part of the e-Government history, it was the government that had the monopoly over public information and data as no one else had access to this information and the Internet was in its early stage of adoption where such information was not yet available online. This, however, began to change as more information has become available online provided either by the government or by nongovernmental actors, mostly NGOs and news media, who collects the information from various sources, and make them available to general public.

For instance, *Open Government Initiative* by the Obama administration seeks to increase government transparency by making various public information and data available to the general public. *Open Government Initiative* was started with the signing of the Memorandum on Transparency and Open Government by President Obama in 2009 that laid out the principles of transparency, participation, and collaboration (Executive Office of the President 2009). The resulting Open

Government Directive entailed actions for the executive departments and agencies to make public information and data available to the public and solicit public input and participation and seek collaboration from nongovernmental actors such as nonprofit organizations, businesses, and individuals in the private sector. This initiative has opened the gate to government data that was previously unavailable to general public. For instance, *Data*.gov is created exclusively to provide various public data, held by the Federal Government to general public.

In addition to increasingly available government data, individual citizens, NGOs, or news media with diverse interests and agenda, investigate and provide information online that becomes available to the general public. From these, increasing sources of public information, nongovernmental actors are increasingly able to develop e-Government type applications. For example, as it is elaborated more later in this chapter, website such as *Opencongress.org*—that enables people to research and track a bill, a Member of Congress, or an issue area—draws information from a multiple public, private, and nonprofit sources such as U.S. Library of Congress, Google News, YouTube, opensecrets.org, sunlightlabs.com, daylife.com, Google blog, to name a few. In addition, increasing use of social networking applications such as Twitter, Facebook and YouTube allow various information to flow freely over the Internet. The U.S. Geological Survey recognized that many citizens use Twitter to share information about earthquakes in populated regions and sometimes Twitter reports often precede the USGS's publically—released, scientifically—verified earthquake alerts. Based on this, USGA created the Twitter Earthquake Detector (TED)[1] to draw on citizens' updates—that is, data produced voluntarily by citizens—as an early warning system of seismic activity. Information based upon various social networking sites is increasingly becoming important sources of news and information as they go directly, unfiltered, and uncensored to general public.

These two elements—increasingly available Web 2.0 applications and the amount of information and data online—combined together, creates a synergy from which various innovative e-Government applications may sprout from numerous nongovernmental actors with diverse incentives and agenda.

11.4 Emerging Trends

Here, some examples are presented that reflect the new trend in e-Government development suggested in this chapter. They are *Open Data Initiative Project* (in Massachusetts), *OpenCongress.org, Challenge.gov,* and *Data.gov.*

---

[1] http://twitter.com/usgsted.

11.4.1 Open Data Initiative (In Massachusetts)

As a part of Open Government Initiative pushed forward by President Obama, the state of Massachusetts began making public data available to citizens of the Commonwealth online. The data provided on its website[2] are machine-readable and free of copyright, patent and trademark for various uses, and applications. Currently, the data are provided in 14 categories[3] including education, health, population, environment, energy, and transportation data. The site states "collaboration among citizens and across agencies" as one of the open data initiative's strategic goals and, in fact, since the launch of the website professional and amateur enthusiasts got together to create new applications and data visualizations using the databases (Noveck 2009). There has been a surge of Apps that are designed to help citizens locate the positions of buses and subways ("the T") operated by the Massachusetts Bay Transportation Authority (MBTA) on a real-time basis. The MBTA website[4] showcases 31 Apps that are constructed by various individuals and organizations at the time of writing. This is an initiative that is in its early developmental stage and its full effects are yet to be materialized. However, this is an example of how publishing government information online facilitates "collaboration between government and the public to transform dry data into the tools that improve people's lives" (Noveck 2009). Since this type of application did not appear until the real-time public data became available, it is possible that these services may never have materialized or it may have taken a considerable amount of time until the government decide to develop them (which would require identifying the needs, securing the political support and various financial, technical, and human resources to develop them). However, when the public data sets were released, the demand for locating buses and subways was captured immediately that led to a number of helpful and easy to use Apps. This exemplifies how the new model of e-Government development—where the public sector "releases" public sector data and the nongovernmental actors develop the e-Government applications—can amount to a surge of innovative e-Government applications in a relatively short period of time with minimum costs to the government.

11.4.2 OpenCongress.org

As briefly mentioned before, opencongress.org is a website launched publicly in 2007 by two NGOs—the Participatory Politics Foundation (PPF) and the Sunlight

---

[2] https://wiki.state.ma.us/confluence/display/data/Data+Catalog.

[3] These are economic, education, energy, environmental, financial, geographic, health, housing, licensing, municipal, population, public safety, technology, and transportation data.

[4] http://www.mbta.com/rider_tools/apps/.

Foundation—with a goal of bringing the legislative-related information such as viewing and tracking information and the status on bills, senators, representatives, and votes closer to citizens. In addition, as NGOs with an agenda of improving transparency in the legislative process, the website features "the Money Trail" which draws connections between campaign "contributions, the content of bills, and important votes by Members of Congress."[5] It displays the amount of contributions received by the Members of Congress under various sectors and industries. OpenCongress's website integrates information from these sources to provide easy-to-use and easy-to-understand legislative information, which previously had been considered long, arcane and hard-to-understand, and navigate. If e-Government on the legislative branch of government is considered to lag behind compared to its executive counterpart (West 2004), this is a case where a nongovernmental actor—an NGO—takes the baton and supply the innovative and customer-friendly services to public that, for various reasons, escaped the radar of the legislature. Here the NGO has the technology, access to public information and sufficient political incentive—their political agenda of providing more legislative information available to the general public—to provide an e-Government application.

11.4.3 Challenge.gov

While this is not exactly the case of nongovernmental actors providing e-Government applications in a technical sense, challenge.gov illustrates how the same philosophy of incorporating the innovativeness of nongovernmental actors can translate into the public policy arena. Challenge.gov is a website administered by the U.S. General Services Administration (GSA) that allows the general public to provide solutions to "challenges." Challenges are various problems, issues, and tasks that require solutions and they are posted by various government agencies, such as the Federal Communications Commission, Federal Emergency Management Agency, and Department of Transportation. Topics range from simple matters such as submitting ideas, creating logos, videos, and mobile Apps to "proofs of concept, designs, or finished products" that address the challenges. Government agencies create challenges on challenge.gov where they provide the details of the problems, issues, and tasks with deadlines and essentially anyone who signs upon the site can take on the challenges and propose a solution or product (depending on the challenge). Those whose solutions are selected by the proposing agency will earn the reward proposed with the challenge. Rewards are both monetary and nonmonetary (honorary) depending on the nature, as well as complexities of the challenges posted.

---

[5] http://www.opencongress.org/money_trail.

Challenge.gov is inspired by a call from President Obama to "increase their ability to promote innovation by using tools such as prizes and challenges to solve tough problems"[6] and on March 2010, the OMB issued memorandum on the use of challenges/contests and prizes to improve government and encourage innovation. This memo provided a policy and legal framework to guide agencies in using prizes to stimulate innovation and advance their core missions. The OMB tasked GSA to select an online challenge platform, which in turn selected ChallengePost, out of eight organizations who responded to RFI by the GSA. The platform has since been available at no cost to all federal agencies (U.S. General Services Administration 2011a).

A few examples at the time of writing include a challenge by FEMA to provide ideas on "how we can all help prepare our communities before disaster strikes and how the government can support community-based activities to help everyone be more prepared." The challenge indicates that ideas can come from across a broad spectrum, from within whichever field people work. For instance, if you are a doctor, what role can the medical community play and if you are an artist, how can his/her medium contribute? The reward in this case is nonmonetary as the selected idea will be highlighted on FEMA's website. Another interesting example would be a challenge with monetary awards. This challenge, posted by U.S. Department of Education, asks the participants to post the most pressing classroom problems ($1,000 if selected) and propose solutions ($2,500 if selected). Lastly, a simpler example would be a call for a calendar by U.S. Department of Health and Human Services (with no monetary reward).

11.4.4 Data.gov

Data.gov is a government website that provides access to various government data that are generated and held by the Federal Government and makes it easy to find, download, and use the datasets. As a part of Obama administration's Open Government Initiative, this site was launched in May 2009 with 47 datasets online (Kundra 2010) and as of January 2010, it features more than 168,000 datasets. Data.gov was developed by the Federal CIO council as an interagency Federal initiative and is hosted by the General Services Administration (U.S. General Services Administration 2011b).

The goal of the site is to increase the accessibility and availability of high-value data to "increase agency accountability and responsiveness; improve public knowledge of the agency and its operations; create economic opportunity; or respond to need and demand as identified through public consultation." (Kundra 2010). The US Open Government Directive of December 8, 2009 requires that all agencies post at least three high-value data sets online and register them on

---

[6] http://challenge.gov/about.

data.gov within 45 days. Datasets can be used to build applications, conduct analysis, or perform research (Kenyon, November 27 2010). Apps have been developed from the data sets posted on Data.gov and the site features nine such Apps.[7] For instance, FlyOnTime.us is developed by private citizens to allow travelers to find the most on time flights and is based on data sets from the Bureau of Transportation Statistics (from Data.gov), the Federal Aviation Administration, the National Oceanic and Atmospheric Administration, the National Weather Service, and twitter feeds from citizens (FlyOnTime.us 2011). Employment Market explorer App is designed to help people understand local employment market, to allow them to compare local, regional, and state unemployment rate.[8] Lastly, Clean Air Status and Trend Network (CASTNET)[9] allow people to check the status of air quality in their area by displaying the ozone level.

Additionally, there are other similar cases where the government provides data that citizens can download and use in ways that are useful for them. Recently, the Department of Health and Human Services began providing to the public vast amounts of data on community health performance such as smoking rates and obesity rates as well as determinants of health, hospital quality, nursing home quality and other information free of charge, and without intellectual property constraint. The department states that the goal of the initiative is to facilitate a wave of innovative applications being built by entrepreneurs, companies, NGOs, and advocacy groups that would help consumers, care providers, employers, local officials and community leaders to make better decision, and improve health (The Department of Health and Human Services 2011). The DHHS aims to replicate what the National Oceanic and Atmospheric Administration (NOAA) had accomplished with weather data. By making its data available on the Internet in downloadable, machine-readable form, NOAA was able to facilitate the development of an array of weather websites, newscasts, Apps and research from nongovernmental developers.

11.5 Discussion and Conclusion

If the current vision of the future of e-Government is that e-Government will continue to be what we have now, only looking better with more sophisticated services, but nothing that would transform the government, this chapter presents a more optimistic vision of e-Government in which the real change or the transformational potential of e-Government is just beginning to materialize. As Web 2.0 emerges and as more public information and data become available to

---

[7] FlyOnTime, National Obesity Comparison Tool, Fix My City DC, Employment Market Explorer, Check it and See, DataMasher, Visualizing Community Health Data, Clean Air Status-Ozone, Plant Hardiness Zone Map (more details available at http://www.data.gov/developers/showcase).

[8] http://pujaplicaciones.javeriana.edu.co/Employment/.

[9] http://www.data.gov/semantic/Castnet/html/exhibit.

the general public, the government will find it increasingly difficult to dictate which services are to be provided and which not, as a monopolistic supplier of e-Government. If there is a need, nongovernmental actors are increasingly able to just develop them—whether it is website or an App—and provide them between themselves that may not have typically been supplied by the government.

With e-Government, the government has done an admirable job of bringing some government transactions available online as the number of e-Government applications has increased consistently over time at various levels of government in the US. However, key e-Government applications that some argued would bring transformation in the relationship between citizens and the government and bring greater accountability, transparency, responsiveness, and democratic participation in government affairs have lagged behind due to limited resources, lack of incentive, and leadership support in the government (Scott 2006; Vigoda 2002; West 2005). Here, the shift, as suggested in this chapter, from the government to nongovernment actors to develop e-Government services may help overcome such limitation. The new paradigm, so to speak, is that if government does not provide, the people will, whether government find it desirable or not.

This may signify a fundamental shift in the role of government from developer of e-Government to the provider of public and government data, based upon which various innovative e-Government type applications may be developed. In this new role, the government should be able to provide relevant, accurate, and up-to-date data in a real-time basis to the public. Consequently, another important role of government as provider of public data would be to ensure that the nongovernmental developers do not intentionally distort the public data for illegal gains or mislead or manipulate the public using the public data sources, which will undermine the credibility of citizen and NGO-initiated e-Government applications. The government must ensure and safeguard the "truthfulness" of public data that is being used by various nongovernmental actors with various intentions and agenda.

One cannot help but feel the initial enthusiasm about e-Government has greatly diminished over time as the term has come to be equated with driver's license renewal and online income tax filing—simple administrative services—and no real transformation seems to be taking place from e-Government as anticipated. The new trend that began to emerge in America is encouraging and exciting as it mean the beginning of a new chapter in e-Government history and signify a beginning of a fundamental shift in the role of government in e-Government.

References

Andersen, K. N., Medaglia, R., Vatrapu, R., Henriken, H. Z., & Gauld, R (2011) The forgotten promise of e-government maturity: Assessing responsiveness in the digital public sector. *Government Information Quarterly, 28*, 439–445.

Applebaum, A. I. (2002). Failure in the cybermarketplace of ideas. In E. C. Kamarck, & J. S. Nye (Eds.), *Governance.com : Democracy in the information age* (pp. 17–31). Washington, D.C.: Brookings Institution Press.

Baum, C. H., & Di Maio, A. (2000). *Gartner's four phases of E-government model.* from http://www.gartner.com

Business Insider (February 26, 2011). *Make your own mobile apps for the android market.* Retrieved 1/26, 2012, from http://articles.businessinsider.com/2011-02-26/tech/30068937_1_android-apps-app-inventor-mobile-website

Chang, A., & Kannan, P. K. (2008). *Leveraging web 2.0 in government.* Washington, DC: IBM Center for The Business of Government.

Chun, S. A., Shulman, S., Sandoval, R., & Hovy, E. (2010). Government 2.0: Making connections between citizens, data and government. *Information Policy, 15,* 1–9.

Coursey, D., & Norris, D. F. (2008). Models of E-government: Are they correct? an empirical assessment. *Public Administration Review, 68*(3), 523.

Dawes, S. S. (2008). The evolution and continuing challenges of E-governance. *Public Administration Review, 68,* S86–S102.

Edmiston, K. D (2003) State and local E-government: Prospects and challenges. *American Review of Public Administration, 33*(1), 20–45.

Executive Office of the President. (2009). *Transparency and open government—memorandum for the heads of executive department and agencies.* Retrieved 2/1/2011, 2012, from http://www.whitehouse.gov/the_press_office/TransparencyandOpenGovernment/

FlyOnTime.us. (2011). *About FlyOnTime.us.* Retrieved 02/01, 2011, from http://www.flyontime.us/about

Furlong, S. R., & Kerwin, C. M. (2005). Interest group participation in rule making: A decade of change. *Journal of Public Administration Research and Theory, 15*(3), 353–370.

Gant, D., Gant, J., & Johnson, C. C. (2002). *State Web Portals: Delivering and Financing E-service.* Washington, DC: IBM Center for the Business of Government. From http://www.businessofgovernment.org/report/state-web-portals-delivering-and-financing-e-service

Grönlund, Å. (2002). *Electronic government : Design, applications, and management.* Hershey, PA: Idea Group Publishing.

Hiller, J., & Belanger, F. (2001). *Privacy strategies for electronic government.* Washington, DC: IBM Center for the Business of Government. from http://www.businessofgovernment.org/report/privacy-strategies-electronic-government

Ho, A. T. (2002). Reinventing local governments and the E-government initaitive. *Public Administration Review, 62*(4), 434–444.

Holden, S., Norris, D. F., & Fletcher, P. D (2003) Electronic government at the local level. *Public Performance and Management Review, 26*(4), 325–344.

IDG (2003). *IDC Finds that Broadband Adoption Will Drive Internet Traffic Growth,* accessed 09/18, 2009, http://www.idc.com

Kenyon, H. (November 26, 2010). Data modeling for the masses. *Government Computer News,* accessed 02/01/2011, from http://gcn.com/articles/2010/11/26/federal-site-offers-data-modeling-for-the-masses.aspx

Komando, K. (September 8, 2011). Make your own smartphone apps. *USA Today,*

Kundra, V. (2010). *They gave us the beatles, we gave them data.gov.* Retrieved 02/01, 2011, from http://www.whitehouse.gov/blog/2010/01/21/they-gave-us-beatles-we-gave-then-datagov

La Porte, T., Demchak, C. C., & De Jong, M. (2002). Democracy and bureaucracy in the age of the web—empirical findings and theoretical speculations. *Administration & Society, 34*(4), 411–446.

Layne, K., & Lee, J. (2001). Developing fully functional E-government: A four stage model. *Government Information Quarterly, 18,* 122–136.

Moon, M. J. (2002). The evolution of E-government among municipalities: Rhetoric or reality? *Public Administration Review, 62*(4)

Nam, T. (2012). Suggesting frameworks of citizen-sourcing via government 2.0. *Government Information Quarterly, 29,* 12–20.

Norris, D. F. (2010). E-government 2020: Plus ça change, plus c'est la meme chose. *Public Administration Review, 70*(Special)

Noveck, B. (2009). *Open government laboratories of democracy.* Retrieved 02/01, 2011, from http://www.whitehouse.gov/blog/2009/11/19/open-government-laboratories-democracy

O'Reilly, T. (2005). *What is web 2.0: Design patterns and business models for the next generation of software.* Retrieved 1/26, 2012, from http://oreilly.com

Popular Mechanics. (September 1, 2011). *How to make your own apps.* Retrieved 1/26, 2012, from http://www.popularmechanics.com/technology/how-to/software/how-to-make-your-own-apps

Ronaghan, S. A . (2001). *Benchmarking E-Government: A Global Perspective.* New York : United Nations Division for Public Economics and Public Administration and American Society for Public Administration. From http://unpan1.un.org/intradoc/groups/public/documents/UN/UNPAN021547.pdf

Scholl, H. J (2003) Electronic government: Make or buy? In *Electronic Government: Second International Conference, EGOV 2003 proceedings Prague, Czech Republic.*

Scott, J. K. (2006). "E" the people: Do U.S. municipal government web sites support public involvement? *Public Administration Review, 66*(3), 341–353.

The Department of Health and Human Services. (2011). *The community health data initiative.* Retrieved 02/01, 2011, from http://www.whitehouse.gov/open/innovations/CHDI

Thomas, J. C., & Streib, G. (2003). The new face of government: Citizen-initiated contacts in the era of E-government. *Journal of Public Administration Research and Theory, 13*(1), 83–102.

Thomas, J. C., & Streib, G. (2005). E-democracy, E-commerce, and E-research. *Administration & Society, 37*(3), 259–280.

Torres, L., Pina, V., & Acerete, B. (2006). E-governance developments in european union cities: Reshaping Government's relationship with citizens. *Governance, 19*(2), 277–302.

U.S. General Services Administration. (2011a). *About challenge.gov.* Retrieved 02/01, 2011, from http://challenge.gov/about

U.S. General Services Administration. (2011b). *Data.gov—FAQ.* Retrieved 02/01, 2011, from http://www.data.gov/faq

Vigoda, E. (2002). From responsiveness to collaboration: Governance, citizens, and the next generation of public administration. *Public Administration Review, 62*(5), 527–540.

Wescott, C. (2001). E-Government in the Asia-Pacific Region. *Asian Journal of Political Science 9*(2): 1–24.

West, D. M. (2004). E-government and the transformation of service delivery and citizen attitudes. *Public Administration Review, 64*(1), 15–27.

West, D. M. (2005). *Digital government : Technology and public sector performance.* Princeton: Princeton University Press.

West, D. M. (2008). *Improving technology utilization in electronic government around the world.* Washington DC: Brookings Institution.

White, M., & Dorman, S. M. (2000). Confronting information overload. *Journal of School Health, 70*(4)

Williams, A. (November 11, 2007). Too much information? ignore it. *New York Times*

Part III
Effects of Web 2.0 on Political Campaigns and Participatory Democracy

Chapter 12
Campaigns and Elections in a Web 2.0 World: Uses, Effects, and Implications for Democracy

Terri L. Towner

12.1 Introduction

Political campaigns are inherently social, as they encourage communication among voters and candidates. In the nineteenth century, campaigning in the US consisted of pamphlets, songs, banners, editorials, stump speeches, and whistle-stop train tours. But as technology changed, so did campaigns. The advent of radio and television brought campaign communications to new heights, with sound bites, spot ads, debates, and political conventions transmitted directly into voters' homes. In the past few decades, candidates and parties have depended heavily on radio, television, and hard copy newspapers to communicate with voters. As a result, campaign communication flowed from candidates to the public in a single direction through the mainstream media's filter. Yet, just as technology revolutionized campaigns with television in the 1950s and 1960s, technology has given us the Internet as a new medium for political communication.

12.1.1 The Rise of the Internet in Campaigning

Emerging in the 1990s, the Internet has had a major influence on US campaigns. Bill Clinton's 1992 presidential campaign was the first to contact voters via email and listserv. In 1996, candidates for US president, Bill Clinton and Bob Dole, were the first major party candidates to have political websites. Soon, major party candidates at all levels had a website (e.g., Kamarck 1999, 2003; D'Alessio 2000).

T. L. Towner (✉)
Department of Political Science, Oakland University,
426 Varner Hall, Rochester, MI 48309, USA
e-mail: towner@oakland.edu

C. G. Reddick and S. K. Aikins (eds.), *Web 2.0 Technologies and Democratic Governance*, Public Administration and Information Technology 1,
DOI: 10.1007/978-1-4614-1448-3_12, © Springer Science+Business Media New York 2012

In 2000, presidential hopefuls used their websites to raise money, recruit volunteers, organize chat rooms, and develop email lists (Bimber and Davis 2003). In the 2004 presidential primaries, Howard Dean became the first candidate to harness blogs and a social networking portal, Meetup.com, to track, organize, and communicate with voters (see Hindman 2008; Trippi 2004). After an early victory in an online primary, Dean famously raised almost one million dollars from online donations in 1 day (Dionne 2003). Building on Dean's Internet success, George W. Bush and John Kerry used blogs in their 2004 presidential bids to send information to voters (see Williams and Tedesco 2006).

Across the globe, the Internet has also been widely used in campaigns, albeit at a slightly slower pace than in the US (Anstead and Chadwick 2008). In the 1997 British general election, several parties employed the Internet to communicate with voters (Gibson and Ward 1998). By the 2001 general election, almost all parties in the UK had websites, largely used as information platforms and supplementary tools (Ward and Gibson 2003). In Australia, the Australian Labor Party was the first party to establish a website in 1994, followed later by the National Party in 1998. By 2004, over one-third of federal election candidates in Australia had a personal website (Gibson and McAllister 2006). German political parties also turned to the Internet in the 1998 and 2002 National Elections, using websites mostly as static brochures to inform voters (Gibson et al. 2003; Schweitzer 2005). France was slow to jump on the Internet bandwagon, but it was used in the 1995 presidential election. In the early years, marginal parties in France were more likely to use the Internet to communicate with citizens and cut campaign costs (Sauger 2002).

12.1.2 Web 2.0s Evolution in Campaigning

The Internet landscape changed dramatically in the 2000s with the introduction of popular Web 2.0 tools, which are defined as any interactive form of communication on the Internet, such as email, blogs, wikis, podcasts, RSS feeds, microblogs, social networks, and video sharing sites (see Sheun 2008). Not all Web 2.0 tools are the same, however. For example, MySpace and Facebook are social networking sites (SNS), YouTube is a video sharing website, and Twitter is a microblogging service. While the latter tools all have unique features, they have one common characteristic: they connect people who seek to generate and share their own content.

Unlike traditional media and Web 1.0 tools, Web 2.0 tools offer users the opportunity to harness collective knowledge, increase communication, and rely on user-generated content and participation (Cormode and Krishnamurthy 2008). The latter characteristics can profoundly change communication and involvement in political campaigns, as these social tools allow two-way communication between candidates and voters and among the voters themselves. Candidates vying for office can more effectively and efficiently accomplish their campaign goals, which include targeting voters, connecting with them, communicating a message, persuading voters to vote a certain way, and then mobilizing them to the polls. These characteristics and features of Web 2.0 applications lead us to wonder how candidates, parties, and citizens are using these tools in campaigning. It remains unclear how these actors across countries are using Web 2.0 tools in campaigning and to what effect these tools have on citizen's political attitudes and behaviors. Presently, much of the literature on Web 2.0 applications and campaigning focuses on a single country and fails to conduct comparative analyses across many counties (for a notable exception, see Lilleker 2011). In an effort to fill this gap, I ask: How and why are candidates and parties around the globe using Web 2.0 tools in their campaigns? How are citizens in these countries using social media sources during campaigns? How does Web 2.0 tool usage influence citizens' political knowledge, government cynicism, and participation? To answer these questions, this chapter draws on literature examining recent campaigns across the US, UK, Germany, France, Israel, and Australia.

12.2 The Web 2.0 Wave in the US

12.2.1 Obama's use of Web 2.0 Tools

Web 2.0 tools burst onto the campaign scene during the 2008 US presidential election. Many tools, which were not available in the 2004 elections, gained popularity in the 2006 midterm elections (Gueorguieva 2008) and then became the new form of political communication in 2008. Presidential candidates used Facebook, MySpace, blogs, Twitter, YouTube, Flickr, and sophisticated campaign websites. Research shows that Barack Obama's campaign used the Internet and social media much more effectively than John McCain's (e.g., Clayton 2010). For example, in addition to Obama's Facebook and MySpace profiles, his campaign created its own social network, my.barackobama.com or MyBO.com. MyBO.com allowed supporters to create their own profiles, interact with others, share information, organize and advertise local events, and donate funds. Most importantly, Obama communicated with supporters directly, without the filter of mainstream media. McCain followed with a similar social network, McCainSpace, but Obama's campaign used their site differently, targeting voters and organizing get-out-the-vote efforts (Germany 2009).

Along with SNS, Obama also concentrated heavily on YouTube. Throughout the campaign, Obama's staff posted videos of stump speeches, rallies, campaign ads, and supporter endorsements. Candidates no longer had to use mainstream media to reach voters. By the end of the campaign, Obama had posted around 1,800 videos on YouTube, garnering over 19 million views. McCain's campaign only posted 330 videos, receiving about 2 million views (Heffernan 2008; Owyang 2008). Along with campaign-generated material, user-generated material about the campaign was also popular; particularly a pro-Obama music video "Yes We Can" and a satirical video "I Got a Crush...on Obama" became viral hits (see Powell 2010;

Wallsten 2010). Of course, not all user-generated video sought to help the candidates' image, such as a video of McCain's remarks at an event where he sang "bomb, bomb, … bomb Iran" to the tune of the Beach Boys hit "Barbara Ann."

While a relatively new tool in the 2008 election, Twitter, developed in 2006, was used by both Obama and McCain. Not surprisingly, Obama tweeted more frequently and had more followers on Twitter than McCain (Ancu 2010). Obama largely used Twitter to announce upcoming or past appearances, mobilize voters, and solicit donations (Ancu 2010; Solop 2010). In contrast, McCain tweeted about his campaign ads, campaign website, opponents Obama and Biden, and unsupportive media coverage. Citizen use of Twitter during the election largely included rants or random thoughts about the election or candidates, but some tweets contained policy issues or information about political action. In general, Twitter use was limited to self-expression rather than two-way interaction between candidates and supporters (Ancu 2010).

Overall, Obama's concentration on Web 2.0 tools paid off. His follower and subscriber counts on all social media far outpaced those of McCain's (Owyang 2008). Obama successfully used Web 2.0 tools to communicate and interact with supporters as well as mobilize voters. His campaign eschewed top–down campaigning, as supporters organized themselves, and created and shared their own campaign content on social networks.

12.2.2 Candidate use of Web 2.0 Tools

Along with candidate Obama, many other US candidates down the ticket also used Web 2.0 tools in recent elections. But who used Web 2.0 sources? What factors encouraged candidates to use social media? In the 2006 midterm elections, Facebook use among Congressional candidates was often determined by candidate party affiliation, budgets, incumbency status, competitiveness of the race, and district demographics (Williams and Gulati 2007). By 2008, a majority of Congress members used Facebook, increasing dramatically from 2006. In the 2008 elections, House candidates who were Democrats, challengers, open seat candidates, better financed, running in competitive races, and running in districts with more whites, college graduates, and youth were more likely to have a Facebook profile (Williams and Gulati 2009). Along with Facebook, Congressional candidates also used YouTube. In 2008, major party Senate candidates were more likely than House candidates to have YouTube channels. Similar to Facebook use, YouTube adoption and activity was often influenced by budget, competitive races, incumbency status, and district demographics (Gulati and Williams 2010).

Web 2.0 tools also played a role in the 2010 US midterm elections. Williams and Gulati (2011) show that a majority of major party candidates in the House adopted Facebook, YouTube, and the latest Web 2.0 tool—Twitter. In general, candidates who adopted these Web 2.0 tools had bigger budgets and more familiarity with online media. Across these applications, however, there were differences in adoption. For example, candidates who were Republicans and in more competitive races were more likely to adopt YouTube, but there were no party or competitive seat differences for Facebook and Twitter. As Williams and Gulati (2011) note, Twitter, developed in 2006, was a new tool in the 2010 midterm elections. Several scholars find that Twitter activity among Congress members is often influenced by party affiliation, budget, and district demographics (Lassen and Brown 2011; Williams and Gulati 2010).

12.2.3 Citizen use of Web 2.0 Tools

The public did not ignore the increasing use of Web 2.0 tools by presidential and congressional candidates. According to a Pew report, television (77%) was still the most common source for election news in the 2008 presidential election, followed by newspapers (28%) and the Internet (26%). Of Internet users, 60% of all adult Internet users went online to find news and information about the 2008 campaign (Smith 2009). In addition, online news consumers accessed a number of Web 2.0 sources for campaign information and news, such as blogs, candidate websites, SNS, and video sharing websites (Smith 2009). Respondents report watching online political videos, sharing election news online, engaging politically on SNS, and posting political content (Smith 2009). Confirming that the Internet and social media tools are not a fading fad, Pew reports that about 60% of all adult Internet users went online to find news and information about the 2010 US midterm election (Smith 2011a). Smith (2011b) reports that 22% of online adults used SNS or Twitter to connect with the campaign or election.

12.2.4 Effects of Web 2.0 Tools

As candidates and voters turn to Web 2.0 sources with more frequency, scholars have begun to examine the causal links between social media tools and political attitudes and behaviors. Yet, these studies offer a mix of findings. For example, some scholars find that use of Web 2.0 sources significantly increases offline civic engagement and political participation (Pasek et al. 2009; Steger and Williams 2011; Towner and Dulio 2011a; Zhang et al. 2010), whereas others find that those who get news from social networks and YouTube are not more likely to vote, sign a written petition, or boycott (Baumgartner and Morris 2010; Zhang et al. 2010). Regarding political knowledge, several studies reveal that younger Americans who obtain news and information from social networks learn very little information about politics and candidates (Baumgartner and Morris 2010; Groshek and Dimitrova 2011; Pasek et al. 2009; Towner and Dulio 2010). Conversely, Teresi (2010) provides evidence that political information transmitted through SNS, particularly Facebook, can increase political knowledge (see also Bode 2008).

Examining government trust, Towner and Dulio (2011a) find that respondents exposed to campaign information on YouTube exhibit more cynicism than those exposed to candidates' websites, television network websites, or Facebook (see also Towner and Dulio 2011b). Hanson et al. (2010), however, show that using YouTube for political information has no significant influence of cynicism, but using SNS results in lower levels of cynicism. Finally, Towner and Dulio (2011a) find evidence that exposure to candidate Facebook pages increases political efficacy, whereas others show that social media has no influence (Kushin and Yamamoto 2010). While these research findings are mixed, there is some promise to the notion that Web 2.0 tools have the potential to invigorate certain aspects of democracy.

12.3 The Web 2.0 Wave Around the World

12.3.1 Candidate use of Web 2.0 Tools

The use of Web 2.0 tools in campaigning is not limited to the US, as many parties and candidates across the globe have also turned to social media. But have candidates worldwide adopted Obama's Web 2.0 strategy? As some scholars suggest, Web 2.0 campaign strategies in other counties are not dictated by American practice but rather structural factors, such as the characteristics of political parties and electoral environment norms (Anstead and Chadwick 2008; Lilleker 2011). Comparative analyses are limited, but many examine how differing political characteristics and media environments matter in social media use and activity in campaigning (see Chen 2010; Kissane 2010; Lilleker 2011; Serfaty 2010). Thus, it is important to examine how and why candidates in other countries use Web 2.0 tools. Below, six countries with high Internet proliferation, the US, UK, Germany, France, Israel, and Australia, were selected to illustrate social media usage by candidates and parties in campaigns.

Following the 2008 US presidential election, many speculated that the 2010 UK election would be the first Web 2.0 election. Indeed, Web 2.0 tools were commonly used on parliamentary and non-parliamentary party websites, largely to mobilize voters, encourage activism, and heighten interaction among supporters. Specifically, the Conservative, Labor, Liberal Democrat, Greens, and British National parties (BNP) used Facebook, Twitter, and YouTube during the election, whereas the UK Independence party (UKIP) did not. In addition, how Web 2.0 applications were used differed among parties, with BNP, Conservative, and Liberal Democrats integrating social media into their campaign much more than UKIP, Labor, and Green (Lilleker 2011; Lilleker and Jackson 2010). Focusing on Facebook during 2010 UK election, Sudulich et al. (2010) find that candidates who are Conservative and Liberal Democrats, are incumbents, have a low chance of winning, and have a high level of opponents with a Facebook group were more likely to have a Facebook group. The latter factors, however, did not predict Facebook profile or fan page use. As a relatively new tool, Twitter is gaining prominence as a social media tool in the UK In 2009, 12% of the members of parliament were using Twitter, with a majority of the users from the Labor Party (77.3%).

Examining German party websites in National Elections from 2002 to 2009, Schweitzer (2011) concludes that implementation of Web 2.0 tools increased during this period, but many parties continued to use a top–down approach to campaigning. As an exception, however, the Pirate Party, a minor party, fully accepted Web 2.0 tools, such as chat rooms, discussion forums, and wikis, engaging in two-way communication. This suggests that minor parties can use Web 2.0 tools to overcome offline disadvantages, particularly lack of publicity, financial resources, and staff. In addition, parliamentary websites were much more likely to use Web 2.0 features, whereas non-parliamentary integrated Web 2.0 applications more selectively. For instance, YouTube was commonly used among parliamentary and non-parliamentary parties, but more sophisticated Web 2.0 tools, such as Twitter, blogs, SNS, social booking services, and web feeds were not highly used among many non-parliamentary parties (see also Lilleker 2011).

During the 2007 presidential election in France, for the first time the presidential candidates, Segolene Royal and Nicolas Sarkozy, had elaborate websites with some integration of Web 2.0 tools. Web 2.0 use differed between the candidates, however. For example, Sarkozy's website had few external links to social networks, but Royal included videos, blogs, and links to a video sharing site, Daily Motion (Serfaty 2010). Despite this, Web 2.0 tools were used tentatively in the 2007 presidential elections, with very little real two-way communication and interactivity between candidates and voters (Lilleker 2011).

In Israel, candidates and parties in election campaigns between 2007 and 2009 began to use Web 2.0 tools. Lev-On (2011) notes that almost all parties in the 2008–2009 general election (Knesset) had Facebook profiles for their candidate. In addition, several parties, particularly Likud, Kadima, and the Green Party, also used Twitter to promote political participation and inform supporters of campaign events. YouTube was utilized by a majority of the parties (22 parties), with Likud and Meretz parties posting the most videos on their channels (Lev-On 2011).

During the 2010 Australian federal elections, politicians embraced Web 2.0 tools, using websites with the greatest frequency followed by Facebook profiles and pages, Twitter, YouTube, blogs, MySpace, and Flickr. In fact, Macnamara (2011) finds that social media use among politicians substantially increased from the 2007 elections, with Twitter and Facebook increasing in usage. In contrast to the 2007 federal election (see Chen 2010; Gibson and McAllister 2011), there was little difference in social media usage among the political parties, but Liberals used Web 2.0 tools slightly more than the Labor Party. While Web 2.0 tools were used more frequently in 2010, Macnamara (2011) notes that these tools were primarily employed as one-way communication tools during the election, rather than tools for direct dialog, listening, and collaboration. For example, many politicians used Twitter to broadcast messages, such as statements, announcements, attacks on opponents, campaign slogans, and general political statements.

12.3.2 Citizen use of Web 2.0 Tools

Presently, Internet penetration data show that Internet usage is high among the previously discussed countries: US 78.2%, UK 82.0%, Germany 79.9%, France 69.5%, Israel 70.5%, and Australia 78.3% (Internet World Stats 2011). But are citizens in these countries using the Internet, particularly Web 2.0 tools, for campaign information? According to an Ipsos MORI (2010) poll, residents in Great Britain largely received campaign information about the 2010 general election from traditional sources, such as leaflets (95%), billboards (74%), and letters (62%). Fewer residents relied on online sources, such as SNS (e.g., Facebook, Twitter, MySpace) (17%) and party websites (10%).

During the 2008–2009 election, Israelis received a majority (80%) of their political information from traditional sources, particularly television, radio, and newspapers. Only 34.4% obtained political information about political parties from websites (Cohen 2009). In addition, election-related online activities were limited among citizens, as 7% subscribed to newsletters, 6.4% joined a network group, 1.8% made a financial contribution, and 1.2% created and uploaded a political video (Cohen 2009).

In Australia, McAllister and Pietsch (2010) report that Internet usage for election information has steadily increased from 2% in 2001 to 10% in 2010. Internet usage is still far behind television (36%) as a source for Australian election news, but it is quickly catching up to radio (17%) and newspapers (20%) (McAllister and Pietsch 2010). During the 2010 election campaign, respondents reported reading/accessing party and candidate campaign sites (7.8%), viewing/accessing non-official online video with campaign content (5.4%), posting comments on a blog, and Twitter feed or wall of a SNS (6%) (Australian Election Study 2010).

Despite the increase in Web 2.0 tools around the globe, the above surveys show that citizens' usage of Facebook, YouTube, and Twitter for campaign information and involvement is uncommon. That is, citizens around the globe continue to rely largely on traditional sources for election information.

12.3.3 Effects of Web 2.0 Tools

Web 2.0 tools are emerging quickly in other countries, but the causal effects of social media on citizens' political attitudes and behaviors have been examined only in Australia (and in the US). Initially, scholars were skeptical about the influence of Web 2.0 tools on national election outcomes in the 2007 Australian general election, suggesting that social media had little effect on electoral choices (Kissane 2008). However, Gibson and McAllister (2011) find that Australians using Web 2.0 tools for election information were significantly more likely to vote for the Green Party. Howell and Da Silva (2010) find perceived credibility and vote intention differed significantly among Australian subjects exposed to

YouTube, MySpace, Facebook, and official websites during the 2007 Australian election. Specifically, respondents exposed to the Labor Party website Kevin07, which included blogs and social networking links, were more likely to vote.

12.4 Implications for Democratic Discourse

The mainstream media play a vital role in democracy. In the campaign process, historically, the media act as a liaison between the candidates and citizens, communicating the candidates' messages to the public in a one-way fashion. Today, the Internet drastically undermines the role of mainstream media in campaigning (see Shirky 2008). For example, candidates and citizens no longer have to communicate with each other through the filter of traditional media. Web 2.0 tools allow candidates to communicate directly with voters, whether this is on Facebook, YouTube, or a blog. Using Web 2.0 tools, voters can ask candidates about issue positions and then candidates can respond. Thus, social media facilitate two-way communication between candidates and citizens. The latter cannot be achieved in traditional media, as campaign television ads and citizens' letters-to-the-editor are forms of one-way communication. Web 2.0 applications offer a true forum for democratic deliberation between candidates and citizens.

Web 2.0 applications also allow citizens to connect with other supporters. As Shirky (2008) argues, the Internet and social media allow groups to form without formal institutions and organizations. Online groups are not limited by geographic boundaries or the need for face-to-face interaction. With Web 2.0 tools, candidates can build and organize a network of supporters with little cost and without much oversight and assistance from campaign staff. For example, Obama's campaign used the SNS, MyBO.com, to organize an army of volunteers, giving them the tools to engage in real world activity. On the Internet, citizens can drive the political process themselves, as Web 2.0 applications give them the means to communicate and participate.

While social media offer a platform for two-way communication and group formation, many parties and candidates continue to focus on top–down strategies for delivering information (e.g., press releases, offline paraphernalia, and information about the candidates) while interaction and two-way communication (e.g., microblogs, chats, wikis, and Meetups) are scarce. The latter was evident in campaigning in the US and across the globe. Why do candidates continue to rely on top–down communication? First, it is costly in time and money to maintain Web 2.0 sources. Second, two-way communication force candidates to clarify ambiguous policy positions, which may weaken a candidates' broad appeal. Third, candidates fear losing control over their message and image, as Web 2.0 tools open the door to unfiltered, user-generated content. Fourth, candidates simply may not know how to use Web 2.0 tools for two-way communication. Consequently, top–down, one-way interaction is largely used in campaigns. Web 2.0 tools can promote democratic discourse, but candidates must use these tools to their full potential.

With the rise of Web 2.0 sources, the costs of publishing and distributing are dramatically lowered, ushering in citizen journalism and user-generated content (Shirky 2008). Citizens can blog about elections, comment on a candidate's Facebook page, or upload an amateur video to YouTube at little or no cost. As a result, the range of political content available to consumers has increased, enhancing democratic discourse. Citizen journalists can offer campaign coverage that traditional media may not cover, forcing certain stories into the public consciousness and influencing traditional news. In addition, Web 2.0 tools provide a forum for citizens to openly criticize and scrutinize the government and the established media with little censorship, fulfilling a critical watchdog role (e.g., Wikileaks.org). Public expression is encouraged rather than suppressed, as social media offers a readily available public forum. It is well known that democracy cannot function properly without a genuine public sphere (Barlow 2008). In many ways, Web 2.0 tools provide a platform for open and free expression and a medium for informing citizens about candidates and politics.

Despite the above, user-generated news does not necessarily solve the problem of information bias. When consumers become the gatekeepers of campaign information, they can easily filter out topics that do not interest them or information in which they disagree. Instead, they filter in information that confirms their political beliefs. Scholars show that individuals practice self-selection to avoid exposure to information inconsistent with their political beliefs (e.g., Bimber and Davis 2003; Iyengar et al. 2007; Towner and Dulio 2011b). As Sunstein (2008) argues, filtering and personalization limits citizens' exposure to a diverse range of political topics and viewpoints on the Internet. This decentralization of information exposure can lead to a lack of common experiences and unanticipated encounters, components that are central to a well-functioning democracy.

Web 2.0 applications also give relatively unknown candidates or minor parties the ability to disseminate campaign messages (see Gueorguieva 2008). Consider, for example, the Pirate Party's—a relatively unfamiliar minor party—impressive use of Web 2.0 tools during recent German elections (Schweitzer 2011). The Internet offers a platform for the underfunded and unknown, giving them an opportunity to become viable candidates for office. Nevertheless, many scholars assert that online politics will simply mirror traditional politics. Specifically, the Internet does not expand political discourse, but continues to empower a small, elite group (Hindman 2008). For instance, those candidates with more staff and funds to dedicate to online campaigning will have a distinct advantage over everyone else. In recent U.S. elections, scholars show that better financed candidates are more likely to use Facebook, YouTube, and Twitter (Gulati and Williams 2010; Williams and Gulati 2007, 2009, 2010, 2011). Thus, just as in traditional campaigning, the most popular and well-funded candidate has a clear advantage in an online public forum.

An important role of the media is to provide equal access to both the means and ends of political information. Web 2.0 tools give candidates the unprecedented ability to reach voters—anywhere and anytime. As discussed above, however, not all citizens have equal access to the Internet nor are they all using Web 2.0 sources for campaign information. Many citizens continue to use traditional sources. This may be due to the inequality of Internet access among population segments along racial, age, and other lines (e.g., the "digital divide") (see Mossberger et al. 2008). In many parts of the world, access to computer technology and the Internet is limited (Internet World Stats 2011). During campaigns, political candidates must be mindful of access, connectivity, citizens' capacity to use Web 2.0 tools, and the appropriateness of content for different audiences (e.g., language and literacy skills). If not, population segments may be excluded, thereby harming democracy.

Web 2.0 applications are essential to democratic discourse as they facilitate communication between candidates and voters, broaden the public sphere, offer a platform for lesser-known candidates, and seek to provide voters with equal access to political information. Yet, Web 2.0 tools are unlikely to replace traditional media or tactics. For many citizens, the Internet is a supplemental source for campaign information (see Althaus and Tewksbury 2000; Bimber and Davis 2003), filling the gaps in mainstream content (Barlow 2008). As discussed above, traditional media remain the top information sources (e.g., Cohen 2009; Ipsos MORI 2010; McAllister and Pietsch 2010; Smith 2009). Thus, employing only Web 2.0 tools is not "the solution" to winning elections.

12.5 Conclusion

Today, candidates in the US and around the world are employing Web 2.0 applications to communicate with citizens, transmit their message, raise funds, and organize supporters. Barack Obama showed the world that he could reach an unprecedented number of citizens with social media while organizing them both online and offline. This chapter illustrates, however, that parties and candidates worldwide are not using social media to its full potential, limiting its use to one-way communication with citizens. The latter was evident in recent elections, such as in Germany, France, and Australia. Many campaigns continue to employ Web 2.0 applications as broadcasting tools, similar to radio and television. That is, Web 2.0 tools are simply a means to distribute information to the public and traditional media outlets. Furthermore, this chapter shows that citizens across the globe are using Web 2.0 during campaigns with greater frequency, but they are not abandoning traditional media for social media. This suggests that Web 2.0 applications are not revolutionizing campaigning. Rather, social media is best viewed as an additional source that will support and maybe enhance modes of campaign communication. Indeed, the review of the literature examining the effects of Web 2.0 tools demonstrates that social media is not radically changing political behavior. In fact, the influence of Web 2.0 sources is modest and varied. In only the US and Australia was there some causal evidence suggesting that Web 2.0 usage influences offline political participation and vote choice. Unfortunately, casual relationships between Web 2.0 applications and political attitudes and behaviors remain largely unstudied in other countries.

In a Web 2.0 world, candidates and parties must rethink how they interact and communicate with citizens during campaigns. Instead of merely broadcasting campaign information on Facebook or Twitter, candidates should open a virtual dialog with citizens, encouraging an open forum for feedback and questions. To do this, campaigns must invest more time, money, and staff to social media. A dedicated staff is necessary to respond to voter queries, otherwise questions are not addressed and the democratic process ceases. In addition, following the Obama model, campaigns should give citizens the tools to virtually organize and communicate with other voters using microblogs, chats, wikis, and Meetups. To maintain a consistent campaign message, candidates should establish a quality presence on only a handful of popular social media sites. Rather than splintering their identities across the web, candidates and parties can select the best digital platforms for their campaign. As noted above, a balanced communication strategy, with both social media and traditional tools, is also necessary to reach all voters. Candidates then must continue to buy television airtime and newspaper ad space, while using Web 2.0 tools to communicate with specific audiences.

Although likely a futile proposition, it is important to speculate on the future of Web 2.0 tools. It is expected that candidates will increase their investment in online campaigning and will use Web 2.0 applications with greater frequency. Candidates will likely use a website, Twitter, YouTube, Facebook, LinkIn, Friendfeed, and Ning, as well as newer tools such as Google+ and Tumblr. Web 2.0 tools will be employed to target citizens, communicate with voters, recruit and organize supporters, and raise funds. More campaigns will embrace the "Obama model," establishing a relationship with supporters and allowing supporters to build relationships with each other. As social media develops, candidates may be able to interact with supporters in virtual worlds (e.g., SecondLife) and tailor *every* political message to each voter. In a few years, the Web 2.0 campaign will likely shift into more personalized media ads, market hybrid segmentation, websites tailored to the user, and smart phone applications. Web 2.0 applications are still in their infancy, with many opportunities and advancements ahead in future campaigns.

References

Althaus, S., & Tewksbury, D. (2000). Patterns of Internet and traditional news media use in a networked community. *Political Communication* 17(1):21–45.

Ancu, M. (2010). From soundbite to textbite: Election 2008 comments on Twitter. In J. A. Hendricks and L. L. Kaid (Ed.), *Techno politics in presidential campaigning* (pp. 11–21). New York: Routledge.

Australian Election Study. 2010. Australian National University and the Australian Data Archive. Retrieved from http://aes.anu.edu.au/data

Anstead, N. & Chadwick, A. (2008). Parties, election campaigning, and the Internet: Toward a comparative institutional approach. In A. Chadwick and P. N. Howard (Ed.), *The Routledge handbook of Internet politics* (pp. 56–71). New York: Routledge.

Barlow, A. (2008). *The rise of the blogosphere.* Westport, CN: Praeger.

Baumgartner, J. C., & Morris, J. S. (2010). MyFaceTube politics: Social networking websites and political engagement of young adults. *Social Science Computer Review* 28(1):24–44.

Bimber, B., & Davis, R. (2003). *Campaigning online.* New York: Oxford.

Bode, L. (2008). Don't judge a Facebook by its cover: Social networking sites, social capital and political participation. A pilot study. Presented at the Annual Meeting of the Midwest Political Science Association, Chicago.

Chen, P. (2010). Adoption and use of digital media in election campaigns: Australia, Canada and New Zealand. *Public Communication Review* 1(1):3–26.

Clayton, D. (2010). *The presidential campaign of Barack Obama.* New York: Routledge.

Cohen, M. (2009). Elections migrate online, but voters do not [in Hebrew]. Retrieved from www.haaretz.com/captain/spages/1055638.html

Cormode, G. & Krishnamurthy, B. (2008). Key differences between Web 1.0 and Web 2.0 *First Monday* 13(6). Retrieved from http://firstmonday.org/htbin/cgiwrap/bin/ojs/index.php/fm/article/view/2125/1972

D'Alessio, D. (2000). Adoption of the World Wide Web by American political candidates, 1996–1998. *Journal of Broadcasting and Electronic Media* 44:556–68.

Dionne Jr., E. J. (2003). Dean's grass-roots cash cow. *The Washington Post,* A17.

Germany, J. B. (2009). The online revolution. In D. W. Johnson, (Ed.), *Campaigning for president 2008.* New York: Routledge.

Gibson, R. K., & McAllister, I. (2006). Does cyber-campaigning win votes? Online communication in the 2004 Australian election. *Journal of Elections, Public Opinion, & Parties* 16(3):243–63.

Gibson, R. K., & McAllister, I. (2011). Do online election campaigns win votes? The 2007 Australian "YouTube" election. *Political Communication* 28:227–44.

Gibson, R. K. & Ward, S. J. (1998). U.K. political parties and the Internet: "Politics as usual" in the new media? *The Harvard International Journal of Press/Politics* 3(3):14–38.

Gibson, R., A. Rommele, & Ward, S. (2003). German parties and Internet campaigning in the 2002 federal election. *German Politics* 12(1):79–108.

Groshek, J., & Dimitrova, D. (2011). A Cross-section of voter learning, campaign interest and intention to vote in the 2008 American election: Did Web 2.0 matter? *Studies in Communications* 9:355–75.

Gueorguieva, V. (2008). Voters, MySpace, and YouTube: The impact of alternative communication channels on the 2006 election cycle and beyond. *Social Science Computer Review* 26(3):288–300.

Gulati, G. J., & Williams, C. B. (2010). Congressional candidates' use of YouTube in 2008: Its frequency and rationale. *Journal of Information Technology and Politics* 7(2/3):93–109.

Hanson, G., Haridakis, P. M., Cunningham, A. W., Sharma, R., & Ponder, J. D. (2010). The 2008 presidential campaign: Political cynicism in the age of Facebook, MySpace, and YouTube. *Mass Communication and Society* 13:584–607.

Heffernan, V. (2008). Clicking and choosing. *New York Times,* 22.

Hindman, M. (2008). *The myth of digital democracy.* Princeton University Press.

Howell, G., &. Da Silva, B. 2010. New media, first time voters and the 2007 Australian federal election. *Public Communication Review* 1(1):27–36.

Internet World Stats. (2011). World Internet usage and population statistics. Retrieved from http://www.internetworldstats.com/stats.htm.

Ipsos MORI/Reuters Base. (2010). Reuters Marginal Constituencies poll—Wave 5. Fieldwork April 30–May 2, 2010. Retrieved from http://www.ipsos-mori.com/researchpublications/researcharchive/2606/Reuters-Marginal-Constituencies-poll-Wave-5.aspx?view=print

Iyengar, S., Hahn, K. S., Krosnick, J. A., & Walker, J. (2007) Selective exposure to campaign communication: The role of anticipated agreement and issue public membership. *The Journal of Politics* 70(1):186–200.

Kamarck, E. C. (1999). Campaigning on the Internet in the elections of 1998. In E. C. Kamarck and J. S. Nye Jr. (Ed.), *Democracy.com?* (pp. 99–123). Hollis, NH: Hollis Publishing.

Kamarck, E. C. (2003). Political campaigning on the Internet: Business as usual? In E. C. Kamarck and J.S. Nye Jr. (Ed.), *Governance.com* (pp. 81–103). Washington D.C.: Brookings Institution Press.

Kissane, D. (2008). Chasing the youth vote: Kevin07, Web 2.0 and the 2007 Australian federal election. Paper presented at the Politics: Web 2.0 International Conference, Royal Holloway University, London, UK.

Kissane, D. (2010). A Tale of two campaigns: A comparative assessment of the Internet in French and US Presidential Elections. Paper presented at the Central European University Conference in the Social Sciences. Budapest, Hungary.

Kushin, M. J., & Yamamoto, M. (2010). Did social media really matter? College students' use of online media and political decision making in the 2008 election. *Mass Communication and Society* 13:608–30.

Lassen, D. & Brown, A. (2011). Twitter: The electoral connection? *Social Science Computer Review* 29(4):419–436.

Lev-On, A. (2011). Candidates online: Use of the Internet by parties, candidates and voters in national and local election campaigns in Israel. *Policy & Internet* 3(1):6.

Lilleker, D. G. (2011). *Political campaigning, elections and the Internet*. New York: Routledge.

Lilleker, D. G., & Jackson, N.A. (2010). Towards a more participatory style of election campaigning: The impact of Web 2.0 on the U.K. general election. *Policy & Internet* 2(3):69–98.

Macnamara, J. (2011). Pre and post-election 2010 online: What happened to the political conversation? *Communication, Politics & Culture* 44(2):18–36.

McAllister, I., & Pietsch, J. (2010). Trends in Australian political opinion—results from the Australian Election Study, 1987–2010. Retrieved from http://aes.anu.edu.au/sites/default/files/Trends%20in%20Australian%20Political%20Opinion.pdf

Mossberger, K., Tolbert, C. J., & Stansbury, M. (2008). *Digital citizenship*. Washington, DC: Georgetown University Press.

Owyang, J. (2008, November 3). Snapshot of presidential candidate social networking stats: Retrieved from http://www.web-strategist.com/blog/2008/11/03/snapshot-of-presidential-candidate-social-networking-stats-nov-2-2008/

Pasek, J., More, E., & Romer, D. (2009). Realizing the social Internet? Online social networking meets offline social capital. *Journal of Information Technology and Politics* 6(3–4):197–215.

Powell, L. (2010). Obama and Obama girl: YouTube, viral videos, and the 2008 presidential campaign. In J. A. Hendricks and R. E. Denton, Jr., (Ed.), *Communicator-In-Chief*. Lanham: Lexington Books.

Sauger, N. (2002). First approach practices virtual party French political. In V. Serfaty (Ed.), *The Internet in politics, United States and Europe*. (pp. 179–95). Strasbourg Presses: University of Strasbourg.

Schweitzer, E. J. (2005). Election campaigning online: German party websites in the 2002 national elections. *European Journal of Communication* 20(3):327–51.

Schweitzer, E. J. (2011). Normalization 2.0: Evidence from German online campaigns in the national elections 2002–2009. *European Journal of Communication* 26(4):310–327.

Serfaty, V. (2010). Web campaigns: Popular culture and politics in the U.S. and French presidential elections. *Culture, Language and Representation* 8:115–29.

Shirky, C. (2008). *Here comes everybody*. New York: Penguin Press.

Shuen, A. (2008). *Web 2.0: A strategy guide*. O'Reilly Media, Inc.

Smith, A. (2009). The Internet's role in campaign 2008. Pew Internet & American Life Project. Retrieved from http://pewinternet.org/~/media//Files/Reports/2009/The_Internets_Role_in_Campaign_2008.pdf

Smith, A. (2011a). The Internet and campaign 2010. Pew Internet & American Life Project. Retrieved from http://www.pewinternet.org/~/media//Files/Reports/2011/Internet%20and%20Campaign%202010.pdf

Smith, A. (2011b). 22% of online Americans used social networking or Twitter for politics in 2010 campaign. Pew Internet & American Life Project. Retrieved from http://pewinternet.org/~/media//Files/Reports/2011/PIP-Social-Media-and-2010-Election.pdf

Solop, F. I. (2010). RT @BarackObama We just made history: Twitter and the 2008 presidential election. In J. A. Hendricks and R. E. Denton, Jr., (Ed.), *Communicator-In-Chief* (pp. 37–49). Lanham: Lexington Books.

Steger, W., & Williams, C. (2011). An analysis of social network and traditional political participation in the 2008 U.S. election. Presented at the Annual Meeting of the American Political Science Association, Seattle.

Sudulich, M. L., Wall, M., Jansen, E., & Cunningham, K. (2010). Me too for Web 2.0? Patterns of online campaigning among candidates in the 2010 U.K. general elections. Presented at the Elections, Public Opinion and Parties Annual Conference, University of Essex.

Sunstein, C. R. (2008). *Republic.com 2.0*. Princeton University Press.

Teresi, H. 2010. Friending your way to political knowledge: An experiment of political communication in computer-mediated social networks. Presented at the Annual Meeting of the Midwest Political Science Association, Chicago.

Towner, T. L., & Dulio, D. A. (2010). The Web 2.0 election: Voter learning in the 2008 presidential campaign. In J. A. Hendricks and L. L. Kaid, (Eds), *Techno politics in presidential campaigning* (pp. 22–43). New York: Routledge.

Towner, T. L., & Dulio, D. A. (2011a). The Web 2.0 election: Does the online medium matter? *The Journal of Political Marketing* 10(1 & 2):165–88.

Towner, T. L., & Dulio, D. A. (2011b). An experiment of campaign effects during the YouTube election. *New Media & Society* 13(4):626–44.

Trippi, J. (2004). *The revolution will not be televised*. New York: ReganBooks.

Wallsten, K. (2010). "Yes we can": How online viewership, blog discussion, campaign statements, and mainstream media coverage produced a viral video phenomenon. *Journal of Information Technology & Politics* 7(2):163–81.

Ward, S., & Gibson, R. K. (2003). On-line and on message? Candidate websites in the 2001 General Election. *British Journal of Politics and International Relations* 5(2):188–205.

Williams, A. P., & Tedesco, J. C. (2006). *The Internet election*. Lanhan, Md: Rowman & Littlefield.

Williams, C. B. & Gulati, G. J. (2007). Social networks in political campaigns: Facebook and the 2006 midterm elections. Paper presented at the Annual meeting of the American Political Science Association, Chicago.

Williams, C. B. & Gulati, G. J. (2009). The political impact of Facebook: Evidence from the 2006 midterm elections and 2008 nomination contest. In C. Panagopoulos (Ed.), *Politicking online*. New Brunswick, NJ: Rutgers University Press.

Williams, C. B. & Gulati, G. J. (2010). Communicating with constituents in 140 characters or less: Twitter and the diffusion of technology innovation in the United States Congress. Presented at the Annual Meeting of the Midwest Political Science Association, Chicago.

Williams, C. B. & Gulati, G. J. (2011). Social media in the 2010 congressional elections. Presented at the Annual Meeting of the European Consortium for Political Research, Reykjavik, Iceland.

Zhang, W., Johnson, T. J., Seltzer, T., & Bichard, S. L. (2010). The revolution will be networked: The influence of social networking sites on political attitudes and behavior. *Social Science Computer Review* 28(1):75–92.

Chapter 13
Measuring the Effects of Social Media Participation on Political Party Communities

Robin Effing, Jos van Hillegersberg and Theo W. C. Huibers

13.1 Introduction

Political parties can potentially benefit from Social Media such as Facebook, Twitter, YouTube, Google+, and LinkedIn to improve interactions between their members. For example, multiple studies have indicated that the Social Media strategies of Howard Dean, Barack Obama, and Ségolène Royal contributed to members becoming more engaged (Christakis and Fowler 2009; Citron 2010; Greengard 2009; Lilleker et al. 2010; Montero 2009; Talbot 2008; Ren and Meister 2010; Zhang et al. 2010). In the case of Obama, the members with higher engagement donated more to the party and also were more willing to take an active part in the campaign. In the case of Royal, party membership increased from 120,000 to 200,000 members, 90 % of whom had not previously been members of a political party (Montero 2009).

The Arab revolutions of 2011 are other examples of the impact of Social Media. During the "Arab Spring", voices of normally ignored people could reach and influence people all over the world (Howard and Hussain 2011). These examples show that Social Media can affect party politics and democracy more generally. However, we know little of precisely how—and to what extent—Social Media

R. Effing (✉) · J. van Hillegersberg
Department of Information Systems and Change Management,
School of Management and Governance, University of Twente,
P.O. Box 217, 7500 AE, Enschede, The Netherlands
e-mail: r.effing@utwente.nl

J. van Hillegersberg
e-mail: j.vanhillegersberg@utwente.nl

T. W. C. Huibers
Human Media Interaction, University of Twente, Enschede, The Netherlands
e-mail: t.w.c.huibers@utwente.nl

C. G. Reddick and S. K. Aikins (eds.), *Web 2.0 Technologies and Democratic Governance*, Public Administration and Information Technology 1, DOI: 10.1007/978-1-4614-1448-3_13, © Springer Science+Business Media New York 2012

participation affects politics. Why do certain politicians benefit from Social Media, while others do not? Are social network sites purely reflecting preexisting offline social networks? Yet, these questions remain unanswered.

Society changes with the expansion of science and technology (Latour 2005). Social Media, as products of new technology, have a high impact on society. The Internet has become increasingly social. As of January 2012, Facebook has 800 million registered users, and according to market researcher ComScore (Ray 2010), people are spending even more time on the Facebook than on the Google. The increased use of the mobile Internet by users of smartphones and tablet computers contributed significantly to the adoption and use of Social Media. In the United States, Social Media reach nearly 80 % of active Internet users and currently represents the majority of Americans' time online (Nielsen 2011). In Western Europe, these numbers are even higher. Increasingly, people are connected to each other, without regard to time or place.

As people and politicians increasingly adopt Social Media, measuring the effects of Social Media Participation on party community participation has become more important. However, to our knowledge, effective evaluation methods remain lacking. A systematic literature review that we recently conducted revealed that there is a lack of measurement instruments and most existing instruments in the e-participation field are not capable to evaluate the effects of Social Media. (Effing et al. 2011). Our survey further revealed that the available instruments primarily focus on pre-Social Media Internet tools such as forums, chat, and online surveys (Phang and Kankanhalli 2008; Roeder et al. 2005; Stern et al. 2009). Only a few frameworks are capable of evaluating Social Media participation, such as the e-participation ladder of Macintosh (Grönlund 2009). However, these frameworks are too high level in perspective and not ready to evaluate Social Media participation directly from the available empirical data.

In this chapter, a measurement model is proposed that will be able to measure the community effects of Social Media. Improvements in measurement can guide researchers and politicians about which Social Media to use and which strategies are the most effective.

Therefore, the main question addressed in this chapter is: What determines Social Media Participation and how can the effects on political parties be best measured?

Let us, first define the main elements of this question. Political party communities are relational communities for a professional cause and are not necessarily territorially bounded (McMillan and Chavis 1986). The members of political parties are engaged in their communities because of shared beliefs, goals, or interests.

Grönlund (2009) defines participation as "the specific activity of doing things together". Xie and Jaeger (2008) define political participation as "behaviors aimed at shaping governmental policy, either by influencing the selection of government personnel or by affecting their choices". Participation is doing things together for a shared belief that government policy should change in the parties' direction. Participation is one of the key elements of Social Media. Kaplan and Haenlein (2010, p. 61) define Social Media as: "a group of Internet-based applications that build on the ideological and technological foundations of Web 2.0, and that allow the creation and exchange of User Generated Content." This definition makes clear that Social

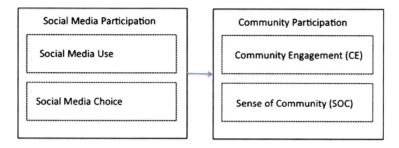

Fig. 13.1 Social media participation model

Media as a term is not a completely new generation of Internet tools. Social Media rely heavily on the concept of Web 2.0. "Web 2.0 is a term that was first used in 2004 to describe a new way in which software developers and end-users started to utilize the World Wide Web; that is, as a platform whereby content and applications are no longer created and published by individuals, but instead are continuously modified by all users in a participatory and collaborative fashion" (Kaplan and Haenlein 2010, p. 60). People collaborate in communities and the Internet evolved into a place where many people have collaborative tools at their fingertips.

To measure the effects of Social Media Participation on Political Communities, we propose a conceptual measurement model based on two concepts: Social Media Participation and Community Participation. To measure Social Media Participation, we developed a standardized instrument termed the Social Media Indicator to assess the use of Social Media by politicians; a set of questions to assess the degree of Social Media participation based on e-participation theory by Macintosh and Smith (2002). Additionally, we integrate established media-choice-theory from Short et al. (1976); Rice (1993), and Te'eni (2001) to include the aspects of the choice and appropriateness of Social Media. For measuring Community Participation, we deploy the following two constructs: Community Engagement (CE) and Sense of Community (SOC) (McMillan and Chavis 1986).

The proposed conceptual measurement model is shown in Fig. 13.1.

Using this model, we aim to discover if, how and to what extent certain Social Media strategies affect the participation of communities' members. This relationship is visualized by the arrow between the concepts of Social Media Participation and Community Participation. This model is a major simplification of the empirical situation. But, as made clear by Blumberg et al. (2011, p. 155), causal studies "cannot observe and measure all the processes that may account for the A-B relationship". While more complex models could be designed, this first version focuses on key factors to measure effects.

We hypothesize that a causal relationship exists between the two concepts. Our grounds to assume this are three-fold:

1. The number of relationships between people tends to increase when people use social network sites, because these sites reveal relationships by making them visible (Boyd and Ellison 2008). Consequently, people connect more easily

with each other. For example, a study of Tomai et al. (2010) showed that members of a virtual community of a school had significantly higher levels of bridging social capital.

2. Online behavior changes offline behavior. For instance, the use of Social Media can reduce transaction costs of communication (Ren and Meister 2010). Consequently, this can lead to other choices in communication channels for certain tasks. While online communication can replace certain forms of offline communication, studies show that online relationships do not replace offline relationships, but augment them (Vergeer and Pelzer 2009).

3. If people are connected online, this contributes to general feelings of attachment to the community: the Sense of Community. People are confronted with their connection to the community at other places and other times, which makes them aware of their existing relationships more frequently. Consequently, this can increase their feeling of being part of the community in general (Tomai et al. 2010). However, we should be aware that an already existing Sense of Community can influence Social Media use. In that case, offline relationships are, partly, mirrored in online relationships and will stimulate the use of Social Media. Therefore, the arrow could also be drawn in both directions.

Given the reasons above, Social Media Participation is assumed to influence Community Participation overtime. By using this model in empirical studies, future outcomes will provide evidence to accept or reject this hypothesis.

The remainder of this chapter is structured as follows: In the next section, we will define Social Media Participation in more detail by operationalizing the constructs of the model. In the third section, we will do the same for Community Participation. In the fourth section, we propose directions for applying the Social Media Participation Model. In the final section, we discuss the study, draw conclusions, and make recommendations for future work.

13.2 Social Media Participation

In this section, we propose a method for the measurement of Social Media Participation by introducing operationalization for the constructs of Social Media Use and Social Media Choice. However, we will first explain underlying theory of Social Media Use. The concept of Social Media Use refers to the upper left construct of our model.

13.2.1 Social Media Use

Effective measurement instruments must be able to produce detailed data to evaluate and compare Social Media use of individual politicians. This is the key reason why we developed our own instrument.

Table 13.1 Social media indicator

Contribution (e-Enabling)
In case of a Blog, how many Blog posts?
In case of a personal Facebook account, how many friends?
How many videos are posted on a personal YouTube channel?
Based on all videos, how many times are they watched?
Based on this YouTube channel, how many subscribers?
In case of a personal Twitter account, how many tweets?
In case of a personal Twitter account, how many followers?
In case of a personal LinkedIn account, how many connections?
Calculate sub score for contribution: Sum of the above.
Interaction (e-Engagement)
In case of a Blog, how many replies?
In case of a personal Twitter account, how many following?
In case of a personal Facebook account, how many likes?
Based on all videos on YouTube, how many comments?
Based on latest 200 tweets of Twitter, how many retweets?
Based on latest 200 tweets, how many replies?
In case of a personal LinkedIn account, how many recommendations?
Calculate subscore for interaction: Sum of the above.
SMI Score (Per member) = Subscore Contribution + Subscore Interaction

The Social Media Indicator (SMI) evaluates the use of Social Media by politicians. The indicator combines *Contribution* (sending information and content) and *Interaction* (discussion, dialog). The indicator comprises a set of standardized questions that will deliver scores that indicate the extent to which individual politicians are using Social Media. The scores can be used to indicate adoption levels of Social Media, but can also be used to assess both levels of contribution and interaction. Therefore, in addition to total SMI scores, the instrument provides scores for *Contribution* and *Interaction*. Currently, the instrument measures the following Social Media tools: Weblog (Blog), Facebook, YouTube, Twitter, and LinkedIn. Overtime, the instrument will be extended with other Social Media tools as well.

The standardized questions of the Social Media Indicator are presented in Table 13.1.

After answering the SMI questions, it is possible to calculate and compare personal SMI scores for each member of a political party. Every act of communication represents one point, because we decided that every person-to-person interaction counts the same, regardless of the medium. A time interval must be defined before collecting the data. Overtime, measurements must be repeated to see how participation develops. For the first measurement, it can be useful to calculate the score on the basis of the entire history of Social Media use by the politicians.

We claim that the SMI that we have devised makes the participation levels of politicians in Social Media both visible and comparable. Three reasons underpin

Table 13.2 Correlations between SMI and voting outcome within the Netherlands

Positive correlation >0.5	Positive correlation >0.3	No correlation found <0.3
Partij voor de Dieren	CDA	PVV
Piratenpartij	PVDA	SGP
	Christenunie	TON
	SP	Nieuw NL
	TON	MenS
	Lijst17	Partij één
	D66	

both reliability and validity of the SMI: (1) an empirical example; (2) solid underlying theory; and (3) public accessibility of data. We will describe each of these next.

First, there is an empirical example available where the SMI has been applied. This is the case of the elections in the Netherlands. The instrument was tested at the national level on all Dutch political parties and all the candidates for the Second Chamber election and it was able to collect data that was used for calculation of statistically significant correlations (Effing et al. 2011).

In the example above, the relation between Social Media and voting outcome were measured by the SMI. Therefore, politician's personal SMI scores were compared with personal votes. Scatterplot diagrams and the calculation of Spearman's rank correlations revealed the following outcomes:

Within 9 parties, out of 16, a positive significant correlation was found between SMI and votes as illustrated in Table 13.2.

The differences in correlations could be a result of differences in target audience, content strategy, and other factors, but these factors are not yet thoroughly explored.

Although the empirical results show that Social Media Use in 9 out of 16 cases has a positive relationship with voting outcome, we could not completely explain what determined the relationship (Effing et al. 2011). This emphasized the need for further research. Also, for six parties, this relationship was not significant. To understand what determines effectiveness in Social Media use, additional interviews with Dutch political parties revealed that the presence of underlying strategies partly determine the variations in the effectiveness of Social Media. Target group differences could also partly explain variations in significance of correlations.

Secondly, the SMI is grounded in established theory. The instrument is based on the frequently cited participation ladder of Macintosh (Grönlund 2009; Medaglia 2007; Sommer and Cullen 2009). Macintosh created a three-step participation ladder, which is useful for describing the participation levels of the Social Media phenomenon at a high level. Other e-participation ladders from the literature might also be useful, but we found Macintosh's model to be most suitable for Social Media. The first step in the ladder is e-Enabling. In this step, party members provide access and information to citizens. The second step is e-Engaging. During this stage, party members give opportunities to citizens to interact with them and start a dialogue. Citizens are frequently consulted on certain projects, decisions, or activities, for instance through forums and polls. The third step is e-Empowering. This step is about members working together with citizens, empowering the citizens with responsibilities, tasks, and options to collaborate with the party's community. Previous efforts at trying to empower citizens often failed (Phang and Kankanhalli 2008; Roeder et al. 2005; Stern et al. 2009). This was due to immature technology and low user adoption rates. As Social Media mature, the challenge remains to discover how Social Media can accomplish e-Empowering. However, e-Empowering is not directly recognizable from the SMI data without additional inquiry. For this reason, we argue that Social Media choice aspects should also be part of the analysis of Social Media participation.

Thirdly, most of the data necessary to calculate the SMI scores are available from open databases. Although certain statistics are not accessible due to privacy settings, the majority of personal data from Social Network Sites are publicly accessible (Boyd and Hargittai 2010). In cases, where authorization is required to access required data, collaboration with parties can be the answer. However, since most of political communication is public debate, this is not a key problem.

In our projects, we listed the top five Social Media, which were representative of the vast majority of all Social Media traffic, based on numbers of advertisement-reach from market researchers. In the Netherlands, for instance, Hyves is one of the largest Social Network Sites, therefore, it should be part of the Social Media Indicator to obtain valid results (Comscore 2011).

Because the SMI score is only an indicator, it is unnecessary and impractical to include all available Social Media tools. Social Media tools with low adoption rates are not included because of their low reach. However, there could be specific reasons to include Social Media that are less common. For instance, political party communities could use the internal Social Medium called Yammer. In that case, this medium may be included. Indicators should be investigated carefully, before being included into the SMI. For instance, the view count of Hyves in the Netherlands is not a valid indicator of participation because artificial users such as search engine spiders heavily skew the results. In such a case, the total apparent score is biased.

Our experience with the SMI has demonstrated that the Social Media Indicator is an effective method for measuring and comparing the degree of use and participation but does not fully explain the differences in effectiveness.

13.2.2 Social Media Choice

"Nothing impacts the success of a Social Media effort more than the choice of its purpose." (Bradley and McDonald 2011) Social Media tools are not effective for everything. For some politicians, participating in Social Media seems to be a goal in itself. Not all communication by Social Media is appropriate for all communication strategies. According to Te'eni (2001, p. 1), "current technology can affect not only how we communicate but also what we communicate." Therefore, we have to take the choice and appropriateness of Social Media into account when determining variations in impact on the dependent concept of Community Participation. This part is illustrated in the left bottom construct of our model (Fig. 13.1). According to Rice (1993, p. 453), appropriateness is "a good match between the characteristics of a medium and one's communication activities".

From our open interviews with Dutch political parties in 2010, we learned that one of the explanatory factors for possible influences were the underlying communication strategies (Effing et al. 2011).

Furthermore, in the cases of Obama, Dean, and Royal, all of them thought thoroughly about both choice of and strategy for using various Social Media for different purposes and target groups (Christakis and Fowler 2009; Citron 2010; Greengard 2009; Lilleker et al. 2010; Montero 2009; Talbot 2008; Ren and Meister 2010; Zhang et al. 2010). The combination of our recent studies and the experiences of Obama, Dean, and Royal make a strong case to include Social Media choice aspects in our measurement model.

An extensive body of literature is available from the communication and Information Systems fields, which focuses on the choice, capacities, strategies, and appropriateness of media. After a literature review, based on the relevance and frequency of citations, we selected the theories of Social Presence (Short et al. 1976), Media Appropriateness (Daft and Lengel 1986; Rice 1993), and the Theory of Cognitive and Affective Organizational Communication (Te'eni 2001) to strengthen our model. Although all of those theories have certain shortcomings, they provide a helpful theoretical background for understanding differences in the appropriateness of Social Media. The theories of Social Presence and Media Appropriateness should not be applied too strictly, because users cope effectively with the limitations of digital communication and they invent ways to transmit social cues through these media (Morris and Ogan 1996).

In the selected theories, various communication strategies are presented.

Short et al. (1976), present the following communication activities.

- Exchanging information.
- Problem solving and making decisions.
- Exchanging opinions.
- Generating ideas.
- Persuasion.
- Getting the other on one's side of an argument.
- Resolving disagreements or conflicts.
- Maintaining friendly relations/staying in touch.
- Bargaining.
- Getting to know someone.

In addition, Te'eni (2001) presents the following communication strategies:

- Contextualization (how and why and meta-data): "provision of explicit context in the message" to increase comprehension.
- Affectivity: inclusion of affective components in the message that describe emotions and moods.
- Control [by testing/planning]: redundancy and repeated communication. Timely feedback is essential for effective control.
- Perspective taking: actively considering the receiver's point of view, inquiring of them about their affairs and attitudes and supporting them, sharing common beliefs and talking in a personal style.
- Attention focusing: manipulating the receiver's processing of the message by emphasizing (switching style, highlighting, shouting, pervasive techniques).

Media differ in terms of efficiency and capability of reaching the desired outcome of communication strategies. According to Short et al. (1976), media vary in Social Presence, which is "the degree to which a medium is perceived as conveying the presence of the communicating participants". Social Media differ in terms of capacity to transfer Social Presence.

Apart from Social Presence, media also differ in terms of interaction level. In regards to different forms of media, differences exist in their capacity to handle immediate feedback from the communicating participants and differences in the way social cues can be part of the communication. According to Daft and Lengel (1986, p. 560), "media vary in capacity to process rich information". Information richness is defined as: "the ability of information to change understanding within a time interval" (Daft and Lengel 1986, p. 560). In that sense, the amount of time required for a medium to provide understanding is also considered an important element when considering the richness of a medium.

Rice (1993) was one of the first to apply the theories of Social Presence and Media Richness to new media. Based on the empirical evaluation of Rice (1993), people perceive the following hierarchy in appropriateness of media for communication activities of Short, Williams, and Christie:

1. Face-to-face (most appropriate for 8 out of 10 activities).
2. Phone (most appropriate for time-sensitive information).
3. Meeting (scheduling/organizing, temporal, and physical obstacles.
4. Desktop video.
5. Vmail.
6. Text.
7. E-Mail/(New media) (appropriate for exchanging information and time-sensitive information, asking questions, staying in touch).

Types of Social Media, as specific forms of new media, have different levels of appropriateness for different communication strategies (Kaplan and Haenlein 2010).

To develop a classification scheme for our measurements, we now present our Social Media Appropriateness Matrix. On the left vertical axis, we present the degree to which Social Media have the ability to facilitate direct feedback and

Fig. 13.2 Social media
appropriateness matrix

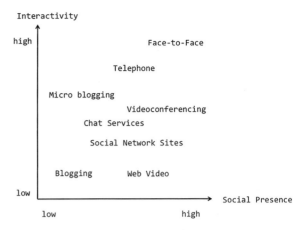

interactivity. Social Media differ in the potential time it takes to receive immediate feedback. On the right horizontal axis, we present the extent to which Social Media can be perceived as personal. This axis relates to Social Presence. In Fig. 13.2, we present our Social Media Appropriateness Matrix, which compares different types of Social Media from the perspective of appropriateness for communication. The labels within the matrix are partly based on the definitions given by Kaplan and Haenlein (2010). They do not reflect actual perceived levels from politicians and have not yet been empirically tested.

Social Presence mediated by Social Media is lower than, for instance, face-to-face conversations. However, as Fig. 13.2 shows, videoconferencing with a high-speed connection via Skype can be perceived as a form of higher Social Presence. This is because social cues are made visible through webcam video and voice transmission. Twitter, being mainly a text message micro-blogging system, is assumed to have a lower Social Presence than, for instance, a personal YouTube web video, but has the ability for immediate feedback by followers. Therefore, we classify micro-blogging as an example of higher interactivity. Nevertheless, this feedback level is lower than in face-to-face or telephone communication. Social Network Sites, such as Facebook, offer opportunities to generate a certain level of Social Presence. Social Presence is increased due to the creation of personal profiles with interests, maintaining networks of relationships, and sharing personal content, such as pictures.

This Social Media Appropriateness matrix, in combination with communication strategies, provides a classification scheme to evaluate Social Media strategies in structured, semi-open interviews. Repeating those interviews overtime will provide results about changing strategies overtime.

At this point, we have discussed all relevant constructs of the left part of the SMPM (Fig. 13.1): Social Media Participation. Now, we will elaborate on the concept of Community Participation.

13.3 Community Participation

We divide the concept Community Participation into two constructs. The first construct is Community Engagement. The second construct is Sense of Community. We explain each of these next.

13.3.1 Community Engagement

To evaluate the level of general offline and online community engagement, we collect data about individual members' activity within the community. Community Engagement represents the upper right construct in our model (Fig. 13.1). Community participation addresses more than the online environment alone. Data collection of one or more of the following indicators at the overarching level of community is required:

- Time spent.
- Presence at meetings.
- Money donated.
- Number of Legislature Bills, requests, or ideas contributed.
- Other activity indicators.

Asking survey questions to retrieve these data is possible, but could deliver biased results. The reason is that asking respondents directly will influence them, because they then become aware of their (lack of) engagement. Unobtrusive methods are preferable to obtain similar data, such as document or database analysis.

Next to the data mentioned above, basic social networking analysis can provide data about how community members are interconnected. For example, the community may be formed around one powerful leader, while in other cases, the community power is distributed among many politicians. Political friends tend to influence each other. Christakis and Fowler (2009) showed that being connected to each other in a social network influences political party campaigns, voting and cosponsorship within politics. Making basic network diagrams of a party network can help to understand how communication, power, and influence within a party are distributed. In addition, subgroups, powerful leaders, or disengaged members tend to become visible. The investigation of those elements and networks can be repeated overtime to see how the community engagement develops or collapses.

Community Participation also relies on softer factors such as Sense of Community, which will be discussed below.

13.3.2 Sense of Community

Measurement of participation within political communities involves more than measuring Community Engagement. The Sense of Community largely covers the psychological aspect of Community Participation. This construct is visualized in the bottom right part of our model (Fig. 13.1).

Chavis especially contributed to the scholarly literature in regard to Sense of Community (McMillan and Chavis 1986; Chavis and Pretty 1999; Chavis et al. 2008). The concept of Sense of Community has been used in numerous social studies (Chavis et al. 2008). Sense of Community (SOC): "is a feeling that members have of belonging, a feeling that members matter to one another and to the group and a shared faith that members' needs will be met through their commitment to be together." (McMillan and Chavis 1986, p. 9)

It consists of four elements (McMillan and Chavis 1986, p. 9):

1. Membership: "the feeling of belonging or of sharing a sense of personal relatedness."
2. Influence: "a sense of mattering, of making a difference to a group and of the group mattering to its members."
3. Reinforcement/integration and fulfillment of needs: "the feeling that members' needs will be met by the resources received through their membership of the group."
4. Shared emotional connection: "the commitment and belief that members have shared and will share history, common places, time together and similar experiences."

It is difficult to view the four elements in isolation because the elements influence each other.

Examples of Sense of Community studies are broadly available in the literature to explain the dynamics within various communities, such as neighborhoods, youth gangs, kibbutz, churches, workplaces, schools, universities, recreational clubs, and Internet communities. The Sense of Community theory does not limit itself to a certain type of community and is therefore useful to describe and compare various types of community. McMillan and Chavis (1986), p. 19 argue that "because of their common core, although our four elements will be of varying importance depending on the particular community and its membership. These elements, then, can provide a framework for comparing and contrasting various communities".

The last few decades have seen frequent testing and refinements in measuring Sense of Community. "Researchers do not appear ready to settle on a definitive and consistent SOC measure" (Chavis and Pretty 1999, p. 636). One of the most refined measurement instruments is the so-called SCI-2 (Chavis et al. 2008). It consists of 24 statements that individuals can respond to on a Likert scale. The SCI-2 was used in a survey of 1,800 people and the measure's reliability was found to be very high (coefficient alpha $= 0.94$). This SCI-2 instrument is effective in evaluating how strongly members feel attached to their political party's community. More importantly, it is possible to measure how community attachment develops overtime, if measurements are repeated.

Table 13.3 Suggestions to apply the social media participation model

Measurement construct	Overarching measurement concept	Data collection
1. Social media indicator	Social media participation	Quantitative monitoring of SMI scores of members by observing or by social listening with technical data-mining tools.
2. Social media choice	Social media participation	Qualitative, structured in-depth interviewing with a selection of members based on communication strategies and social media appropriateness matrix.
3. Community engagement	Community participation	Quantitative inquiry of selected indicators augmented with basic, low-level social network analysis.
4. Sense of community	Community participation	Quantitative survey with the SCI-2 (Chavis et al. 2008), which is a standardized questionnaire to evaluate belonging, influence, reinforcement and shared emotional connection.

Now that the measurement model for measuring Social Media and Community Participation has been described, we will propose a method to apply the model in future research projects.

13.4 Application of the Social Media Participation Model

Based on the Social Media Participation Model, it is possible to design a causal study to reveal relationships between Social Media Participation and Community Participation. For example, to discover how the use of Social Media affects the community of a political party at a local municipality. In this section, we propose guidelines for using the model.

The proposed guidelines for studies applying the Social Media Participation Model are based on comparative case study research (Yin 2008), including both quantitative and qualitative data collection techniques. According to Waters et al. (2009), "longitudinal studies could offer insights into how organizations change their social networking strategies overtime, and case studies should be conducted to help offer insights for other organizations based on efforts that have both succeeded and failed".

Table 13.3 summarizes guidelines for applying the model and underlying measurement constructs, which can be part of longitudinal case studies.

Constructs can be related to each other. SMI scores can be compared with both levels of engagement as the number of Sense of Community. This is particularly important when political parties increase their Social Media activities. When measurements are repeated overtime, they will provide insights into how communities—such as political parties—change by Social Media.

Because multiple influence factors are involved in complex community settings, we suggest a combination of quantitative and qualitative research methods. However, the model can be used for a variety of research designs.

13.5 Conclusion and Discussion

In this chapter, we have aimed to create an understanding of how Social Media Participation affects political party communities, and proposed the Social Media Participation Model (SMPM) as illustrated in Fig. 13.1. In the final section, we will conclude the chapter with a short summary, describe the limitations of the proposed model, and give pointers for future research.

13.5.1 Conclusion

Which forms of Social Media participation influence aspects of the Community Participation the most? By getting results from the SMPM, it will be clear which choice and use of Social Media positively influence member participation within political communities. Our hypothesis is that Social Media participation, using certain strategies and with appropriate media selection, can increase Community Participation in political party communities.

We proposed the SMPM to help understand how Social Media Participation affects community participation. We combined four measurement constructs from theory and practice into one integrated model.

This model is a first step in developing a standardized instrument to compare Social Media Participation with Community Participation. Although the model mainly consists of constructs used in established theories, the model still needs further improvement and empirical testing.

13.5.2 Discussion

The advantages of measuring with the SMPM are that data analysis can be carried out to compare left and right concepts from the model. For instance, correlations can be calculated between SMI scores and SCI scores. Also, we can make different comparisons for different communication strategies (Social Media Appropriateness) and analyze which strategies affect Community Participation the most.

Nevertheless, several limitations exist for our measurement model and its constructs.

First, obtaining results from the Social Media Indicator by observation is still time consuming since appropriate integrated social listening tools are still lacking or are being developed. Currently, social-listening tools, such as Radian6 and Teezir, cover only parts of the necessary data. A second limitation is that due to privacy control, not all Social Media participation data are publicly accessible.

A second limitation is that Sense of Community can consist of various echelons (such as local versus national communities) and therefore can be complex to measure if boundaries between communities are not clear.

The SMPM is based on a linear causal view, while in reality the constructs also influence each other in cycles. This is the third limitation.

A final limitation, presented here, is that not all politicians are willing to use Social Media for various reasons. As addressed earlier in this chapter, Social Media does not replace other channels of interaction but augment them. The Social Media Participation model does focus entirely on the effects of Social Media and does not cover other instruments for interacting with and between politicians that could cause changes in Community Participation as well.

13.5.3 Future research

Future results obtained by using this model should bring us further knowledge about which Social Media strategies are most effective for political party communities, and prove the reliability and validity of the model. By applying the proposed model and methods, we have designed a longitudinal study at the council of the municipality of Enschede, which has more than 160,000 citizens and is located in the eastern part of the Netherlands. We plan to conduct a series of tests based on this measurement model. They will show us how and to what extent Social Media changes communities operating within Enschede's city council. It is hoped that design principles for effective Social Media implementations, can be derived from the empirical results.

This measurement model is part of a larger research project. In this project, we also investigate other types of communities, such as churches. With a broad selection of cases of the use of social media in not-for-profit communities, interesting comparisons can be made. With future outcomes, relevant advice can be given to political parties about how to improve their interaction with their communities by using Social Media.

Next to our own future studies, we also encourage other scholars to test and refine this research model. A more refined cause-and-effect model could help to increase understanding of the effects of Social Media Participation on Community Participation. At this point, questions remain about how Social Media affects politics, all over the world.

Acknowledgments The research projects mentioned in this chapter are initiated, supported, and funded by the School of Creative Technology at Saxion University of Applied Sciences in Enschede.

References

Blumberg, B., Cooper, D. R. & Schindler, P. S. (2011). *Business research methods.* Third European Edition, McGraw-Hill Higher Education.

Boyd, D. M., & Ellison, N. B. (2008). Social network sites: definition, history, and scholarship. *Journal of Computer-Mediated Communication, 13*(1), 210–230.

Boyd, D. M., & Hargittai, E. (2010). Facebook privacy settings: Who Cares? *First Monday, 15*(8), 1–22.

Bradley, A. J. & McDonald, M. P. (2011). Social media success is about purpose (not technology), *Harvard Business Review.* Retrieved November 3, 2011, from http://blogs.hbr.org/cs/2011/11/social_media_success_is_about.html?utm_source=pulsenews&utm_medium=referral&utm_campaign=Feed%3A+harvardbusiness+%28HBR.org%29

Chavis, D. M., Lee, K. S., & Acosta J. D. (2008). The sense of community (SCI) revised: The reliability and validity of the SCI-2. Paper presented at the 2nd international community psychology conference, Lisboa, Portugal.

Chavis, D. M., & Pretty, G. M. H. (1999). Sense of community: Advances in measurement and application. *Journal of Community Psychology, 27*(6), 635–642.

Christakis, N. A., & Fowler, J. H. (2009). *Connected: The surprising power of our social networks and how they shape our lives.* Portsmouth: Little, Brown and Company.

Citron, D. K. (2010). Fulfilling government 2. 0' s promise with robust privacy protections. *Arguendo, The George Washington Law Review, 78*(4), 822–845.

Comscore (2011), Nederland wereldwijd nummer 1 in bereik van Twitter en LinkedIn in maart 2011—comScore, Inc. Retrieved November 3, 2011, from http://www.comscore.com/dut/Press_Events/Press_Releases/2011/4/The_Netherlands_Ranks_number_one_Worldwide_in_Penetration_for_Twitter_and_LinkedIn

Daft, R. L., & Lengel, R. H. (1986). Organizational information requirements, media richness and structural design. *Management Science, 32*(5), 554–571.

Effing, R., van Hillegersberg, J., & Huibers, T. (2011). Social media and political participation: Are facebook, twitter and YouTube democratizing our political systems? In E. Tambouris, A. Macintosh, & H. de Bruijn (Eds.), *Electronic Participation, Third IFIP WG 9.5 International Conference, Delft, The Netherlands,* LNCS Vol. 6847, Springer, 25–35.

Greengard, S. (2009). The first internet president. *Communications of the ACM, 52,* 16–18.

Grönlund, Å. (2009). ICT is not participation is not democracy—eParticipation development models revisited. *ePart 2009* (pp. 12–23).

Howard, P. N., & Hussain, M. M. (2011). The role of digital media. *Journal Of Democracy, 22*(3), 35–48.

Kaplan, A. M., & Haenlein, M. (2010). Users of the world, unite! The challenges and opportunities of social media. *Business Horizons,* (53), 59–68.

Latour, B. (2005). *Reassembling the Social.* Oxford: University Press Oxford.

Lilleker, D. G., Pack, M., & Jackson, N. (2010). Political parties and Web 2.0: The liberal democrat perspective. *Political Studies, 30*(2), 105–112.

Macintosh, A., & Smith, E. (2002). Citizen participation in public affairs. *EGOV 2002,* pp. 256–263.

Medaglia, R. (2007). Measuring the diffusion of eParticipation: A survey on Italian local government. *Information Polity, 12,* 265–280.

McMillan, D. W., & Chavis, D. M. (1986). Sense of community: A definition and theory. *Journal of Community Psychology, 14*(1), 6–23.

Montero, M. D. (2009). Political e-mobilisation and participation in the election campaigns of Ségolène Royal (2007) and Barack Obama (2008). *Quaderns Del Cac, 33*(December), 27–34.

Morris, M., & Ogan, C. (1996). The Internet as Mass Medium. *Journal of Computer-Mediated Communication,* 1(4).

Nielsen, (2011). Webinar: State of social media 2011. Retrieved October 30, 2011, from http://www.nielsen.com/us/en/insights/events-webinars/2011/state-of-social-media-2011.html

Phang, C. W., & Kankanhalli, A. (2008). A framework of ICT exploitation for e-Participation initiatives. *Communications of the ACM, 51*(12), 128–132.

Ray, A. (2010). The implications of consumers spending more time with facebook than Google. *Forrester Blogs*. Retrieved November 26, 2010, from http://blogs.forrester.com/augie_ray/

Ren, J., & Meister, H. P. (2010). Drawing lessons from Obama for the European context. *The International Journal of Public Participation, 4*(1), 12–30.

Rice, R. E. (1993). Media appropriateness using social presence theory to compare traditional and new organizational media. *Human Communication Research, 19*(4), 451–484. Wiley Online Library.

Roeder, S., Poppenborg, A., Michaelis, S., Märker, O. & Salz, S. R. (2005). Public budget dialogue: An innovative approach to E-Participation. *TCGOV 2005*. pp. 48–56.

Short, J., Williams, E., & Christie, B. (1976). *The Social Psychology of Telecommunications.* Chichester: Wiley.

Sommer, L., & Cullen, R. (2009). Participation 2.0: A case study of e-participation within the New Zealand government New Zealand New Zealand abstract. *42nd Hawaii International Conference on System Sciences 20089.*

Stern, E., Gudes, O., & Svoray, T. (2009). Web-based and traditional public participation in comprehensive planning: A comparative study. *Environment And Planning, 36*(6), 1067–1085.

Talbot, D. (2008). How Obama really did it: The social-networking strategy that took an obscure senator to the doors of the white house. *Technology Review*. Retrieved from http://www.technologyreview.com/web/21222/

Tomai, M., Rosa, V., Ella, M., Acunti, A. D., Benedetti, M., & Francescato, D. (2010). Computers & Education virtual communities in schools as tools to promote social capital with high schools students. *Computers & Education, 54*(1), 265–274.

Te'eni, D. (2001). A cognitive affective model of organizational communication. *MIS Quarterly, 25*(2), 1–62.

Vergeer, M., & Pelzer, B. (2009). Consequences of media and Internet use for offline and online network capital and well-being. A causal model approach. *Journal of Computer-Mediated Communication, 15*, 189–210.

Waters, R. D., Burnett, E., Lamm, A. & Lucas, J. (2009). Engaging stakeholders through social networking: How nonprofit organizations are using Facebook. *Public Relations Review, 35*, 102—106.

Xie, B., & Jaeger, P. T. (2008). Older adults and political participation on the Internet : A cross-cultural comparison of the USA and China. *Journal of Cross Cultural Gerontologyurnal of Cross Cultural Gerontology, 23*, 1–15.

Yin, R. K. (2008). Case study research: design and methods (4th ed.). Thousand Oaks: Sage Publications, Inc.

Zhang, W., Johnson, T. J., Seltzer, T., & Bichard, S. L. (2010). The revolution will be networked. *Social Science Computer Review, 28*(1), 75–92.

Chapter 14
Social Media for Political Campaigning. The Use of Twitter by Spanish Mayors in 2011 Local Elections

J. Ignacio Criado, Guadalupe Martínez-Fuentes and Aitor Silván

14.1 Introduction

Political communication has a central role in every strategy that seeks access to, or the maintenance of, power. For that reason it is not surprising that in democracies the electoral campaign is the most intense political period of communicative activity (Martínez Nicolás 2007:211). Especially in electoral campaigns, political parties multiply their number of communicators, diversify their channels of communication, and intensify their efforts in order to get their message across to the greatest possible number of receivers, in a marketing effort (Petrocik 1996).

This pattern of political behavior is also repeated in the digital environment. The political parties have found in social networks a new and privileged scenario for their electoral campaign (Anduiza et al. 2010). For the candidates, the social networks also represent a communicative resource of high value as a consequence of its interactive potential, and its philosophy of direct and personal relationships.

However, exporting campaigning activities to the digital arena of the social networks does not only entail extra-marketing efforts for parties and candidates. It also involves potential changes in the focus of these energies. In fact, this new way

J. Ignacio Criado (✉) · A. Silván
Department of Political Science and International Relations, Universidad Autónoma de Madrid, Edificio de Ciencias Jurídicas, Políticas y Económicas, 1ª planta, C/Marie Curie, 1, Ciudad Universitaria de Cantoblanco, 28049 Cantoblanco, Madrid, Spain
e-mail: ignacio.criado@uam.es

A. Silván
e-mail: aitorsilvanrico@gmail.com

G. Martínez-Fuentes
Department of Political Science and Public Administration,
Universidad de Granada, Facultad de Ciencias Políticas y Sociología,
C/Rector López Argueta, s/n, 18071 Granada, Spain
e-mail: gmart@ugr.es

C. G. Reddick and S. K. Aikins (eds.), *Web 2.0 Technologies and Democratic Governance*, Public Administration and Information Technology 1, DOI: 10.1007/978-1-4614-1448-3_14, © Springer Science+Business Media New York 2012

of campaigning is what Zittel has conceptualized as *individualized campaigning:* the use of the Internet to promote the personal dimension of the electoral message and to promote the proximity of the candidate to the elector, increasing his or her capacity of personal interaction and dialogue with the community (Zittel 2007:6–7; Zittel 2009).

Studies such as those of Gibson (2010), Gibson and McAllister (2011), Gueorguieva (2008), Gulati and Williams (2010), Steger et al. (2010) among others, have examined the importance of the social networks and tools of the Web 2.0 (YouTube, MySpace, Facebook, etc.) in the most recent electoral campaigns held in developed democracies. One conclusion that these studies have in common is the fact that there is a growing tendency to use the social networks as a channel of political communication. Nevertheless, little evidence exists about these phenomena beyond this verification. The behavior that parties and candidates show on the social networks; the degree of coherency among them; and the principles of the so-called Web 2.0, are questions that have still barely been addressed in the academic literature (Bode et al. 2011; Golbeck et al. 2010; Lassen and Brown 2010; Gaines et al. 2009; Williams and Gulati 2009, 2010; Yannas et al. 2011). The role of social media in different spheres of electoral political democracies requires greater understanding.

This study seeks to contribute to the accumulated knowledge about electoral campaigns and social networks by means of an empirical study that employs the case study as a methodology. For that reason it focuses on the impact of Twitter on the electoral campaign of the local Spanish elections of May 2011. On the basis of this case study, the following questions are addressed: Which candidates to the mayoralty employed Twitter during their campaign? To what extent did they use Twitter? Did they manage to widen or deepen their network during the campaign? Did they really use Twitter to boost their dialogue with the electors linked to this network? Did the candidates' gender, age, political party, municipality affect this behavior?

This study is presented in six sections. Following this introduction a second section is dedicated to contextualizing the electoral campaign developed in Spain in the recent local elections, justifying at the same time the political opportunity to employ Twitter as a channel of personal interaction with the electorate. The third section identifies the analytical strategy followed in order to address the research questions of this study. The fourth section presents the results of the analysis undertaken. The fifth section discussed the main findings. The paper closes with a sixth section that offers the conclusions of the study.

14.2 The 2011 Local Elections in Spain. Why "individualized campaigning"? and Why Use Twitter To Do So?

Every party's electoral campaign is based on a communication plan of a persuasive character. This program of persuasion is generally oriented toward mobilizing and attracting the vote of three types of electors (Holborok 1996; Scher 1997; Barnes 2005). The first group is that of the 'party faithful', which represents the captive or base vote of the organization. The second group is that of the voters who are susceptible to vary the orientation of their vote between one electoral campaign and the next. These 'non party' electors (Dalton 2002) are the source of the fluctuating or volatile vote, and represent the opportunity for parties to add a strategic percentage of additional votes to their base vote. The third group is that of the electors who generally do not vote.

The effort that the parties dedicate to persuade each of these groups of electors varies in function of the structural and circumstantial conditions of the electoral competition (Vanaclocha 2005). In political contexts where the structural form of the electorate is strongly ideologized and/or intensely identified with a party, the parties dedicate a large part of their resources to mobilizing their 'party faithful'. For that reason they employ campaigns that have a strong ideological or identity bias. On the other hand, in contexts where there is a significant percentage of floating and/or abstaining voters, this becomes a second focus for priority attention. The strategic value of this group's vote achieves the highest level when, circumstantially, the elections are perceived as elections of rupture or change. In these cases, the parties develop campaigns of persuasion that are more centered on the candidates and on their specific projects than on the ideology and identity of the organization.

In Spain party ideology and identity represent determinant factors of the orientation of the vote for the majority of electors. Nevertheless, Spaniards perceive the municipal elections as elections of second order. For this reason in the local political arena they present electoral behavior that is distinct to that demonstrated at national level elections. The particularity of Spanish electoral behavior at municipal level resides in two tendencies: the abstention differential and the dual vote (Molins and Pardos 2005; Montabes Pereira and Ortega Villodres 2011). On the one hand, the municipal elections mobilize the electors to a lesser extent than the general elections. On the other, those electors who go to the polls in the municipal elections tend to consider dimensions of the electoral offer that go beyond ideology or the brand of the party. Among these alternative dimensions may be highlighted the qualities of the candidate for mayor–those who the electors feel closest to, as politicians–and their projects of city management–by those who feel directly affected by them (Martínez Fuentes and Ortega Villodres 2010a).

The Spanish electoral arena that presents the highest rate of floating voter and abstentionism is at local level. Consequently, it is at this stage where these types of electors receive the highest level of attention from the parties. In general terms, the large parties encourage their local groups to run an electoral campaign that sells not only the brand of the party, but also the figure of their mayoral candidate; specifically their personal identification with the local community and their concern with specific problems. As a result, in Spain, the design and implementation of the municipal electoral campaigns has a strongly personalized or presidential nature (Natera 2001; Martínez 2008; Martínez Fuentes and Ortega Villodres 2010b; Criado and Martínez Fuentes 2010, 2011).

In particular, the municipal elections of May 2011 opened up a scenario, for the largest Spanish parties, that especially favored the design of strategies of electoral competition orientated to the floating voter and the abstentionist elector by campaigns that were centered principally on the promotion of candidates to the mayoralty. Why? In first place, the party brand was not particularly attractive on this occasion. In second place, the municipal competitions were not perceived as 'second order' elections. On the other hand, all the preelectoral polls coincided in the prediction that a significant number of citizens were going to punish with their vote, or abstention, both the party who govern the nation (The Socialist Workers's Party–PSOE, in their Spanish initials) and their President. This is why this election was seen as 'primaries' for the following general elections. In sum, the 2011 municipal elections were viewed as elections of change.

In the large Spanish cities, in particular, these local groups decided to adapt to the circumstances by adopting the technique of "individualized campaigning" as a campaign strategy. To put this campaign model into practice, a significant number of candidates looked to the 'online' social networks. The existing high degree of social receptivity in Spain to the political use of the social networks helps to explain this decision. This was highlighted by an opinion survey undertaken by Intelligence Compass (2010) months before the holding of the elections. 96 % of Spanish politicians who used social networks were found to consider them to be channels of either 'significant' or 'outstanding' importance in their contact strategy with citizens. In parallel, 86 % of Spanish citizens surveyed stated that politicians should use social networks to maintain themselves in contact with electors.

Three fundamental reasons determined the choice of Twitter as a key social network for this election campaign. The first is the degree of diffusion achieved by this social network. In Spain, more than 60 % of the population are users of the Internet (EUROSTAT 2011). In addition 83 % of Spanish Internet users employ social networks and 25 % subscribe to Twitter. The second is its capacity to facilitate access to nonparty and abstentionist electors. The majority of Internet surfers and users of social networks are concentrated in urban locations where there are larger numbers of young people with higher levels of formal education (INE 2011). In fact, 90 % of young Spaniards aged between 16 and 20 are linked to a social network (Fundación Orange 2011). The third argument is the potential associated with Twitter to endow the campaign with a personal, direct, interactive and speedy style. According to a study undertaken by Cocktail Analysis (2011) among the Spanish users of social networks, many who were surveyed showed a preference for Twitter because of two specific attributes: its speed and direct character. For these reasons, recent comparative studies, such as Hanna et al. (2011), Jaeger et al. (2010), Pole and Xenos (2011), and Tumasjan et al. (2011), have emphasized the use of this resource for electoral purposes.

14.3 Analytical Strategy: Inquiring into Who Tweets?, How Much They Tweet?, and What for?

This section provides the analytical strategy that has guided this study. The objective of our research is to reveal two key facets of the use of Twitter during the electoral campaign of the municipal elections held in Spain in May 2011: namely, the presence and behavior of the candidates in this social network. To achieve this stated goal we raise the following research questions: How many candidates used Twitter during the campaign? Did gender, age, political party, and size of the local community affect this behavior? To what extent did they use Twitter? Did they manage to broaden or deepen their network throughout the campaign? Did they really use Twitter to promote their interaction and dialogue with electors who are linked to this network? We designed the following research strategy with the aim of finding responses to these questions.

In first place, we considered the size of our universe of study. The mayoral posts of 8,808 municipalities were under competition in the May 2011 Spanish local elections. In consequence, we decided to focus our attention on a specific segment of that group. In this way, we decided to limit our object of study to the mayors of large cities who sought to renew their posts by competing as candidates for the mayoralty in the 2011 elections.

The decision to study only mayoral-candidates derives from the fact the local Spanish mayoral political system, classifiable under the formula "strong-mayor-form" (Mauritzen and Svara 2002), provides the mayor with a high level of personal political visibility and influence. Assuming that the use of Twitter in an electoral campaign seeks to exploit the personal facets of the candidate, we understand that the candidates that are at the same time mayors were the best known.

The idea of studying these types of actors, only in the context of large cities, is justified by one reason. Given that in Spain the use of social networks is concentrated in the large urban areas, the mayors who achieved most electoral returns through the use of social networks would be precisely those who led in large cities.

To identify the mayoral-candidates from large Spanish cities who are users of Twitter in electoral campaigns, we decided to track which of them had an official Twitter account on the date of the start of the electoral campaign (6th of May). In this tracking and identification process, we decided not to discriminate if those accounts were managed by the candidate or by personnel from their communication team.

Besides, in order to clarify if determining factors exist in the use of Twitter between mayoral-candidates of large cities, we opted to observe their own attributes and those of their environment. Therefore, we took into consideration the following factors:

- Candidate gender: the general statistics indicate that the users of Twitter are mostly men (National Observatory of Telecommunications and Information Society 2011).
- Age: the general statistics highlight the fact that users of Twitter are mostly young (National Observatory of Telecommunications and Information Society 2011).
- Party to which they pertain: the candidates of the PSOE may have greater incentives to emphasize the personal component of their campaign by using *individualized campaigning*, due to the crisis of popularity of the PSOE and of their national leader.
- Size of their community: the mayoral-candidates of the most populous cities show a greater willingness to use Twitter in their campaigns, as a means of getting closer to their citizens.

Table 14.1 Mayoral-candidates using Twitter during the last electoral campaign

Units of analysis	Twitter accounts	%
55	39	70.9

Source own elaboration

Then, we measured the intensity of use that the mayoral-candidates of large cities made of Twitter during the electoral campaign. For that reason we identified the number of tweets emitted by these candidates between the 6th and 20th May.

Next, we evaluated the density of the network of the mayoral-candidates on Twitter and the effect that the campaign had on it. In first place, we identified the number of profiles that the candidates had as followers at the start and at the end of the campaign. In the same way we identified the number of profiles that the mayoral-candidates followed in Twitter.

Finally, we analyzed if the use the candidates made of the Twitter network in their electoral campaign was coherent with the interactive and conversational logic of the 2.0 philosophy. For that reason we counted the number of tweets sent by the candidate that involved a direct response to a user in this social network. (That is, we identified how many tweets appeared with the 'dialogue balloon' symbol.)

14.4 Results

In this section, the data collected during the fieldwork and its statistical treatment is presented in two separate parts. In the first we discuss the use of Twitter in the electoral campaign. In the second we address the type of use that this network has received, and identify its determinants, throughout the campaign.

14.4.1 Who is Using Twitter as an Instrument for Campaigning?

Table 14.1 shows the initial universe of observed cases and the final universe of the cases studied. In the Spanish municipal elections of 2011, 55 mayors of large cities sought to renew their candidature for the post. After tracking their presence in the Twitter network, we concluded that 39 of them had an operative account at the start of the electoral campaign (around 70 %). Considering that in the previous Spanish municipal elections held in 2007 there was no electoral use of Twitter, our data allowed us to confirm that Twitter is a tool that has a new and high degree of popularity among local Spanish political leaders, at least during the last election campaign.

Table 14.2 The use of Twitter by gender

Gender	Total	Twitter	Media Tweets	Tweets dialogue	% Dialogue	Initial followers	Final followers	Initial following	Final following
Men	43	32	164.29	27.25	16.58	657.73	822.9	359.9	408.54
Women	12	7	118.42	18.42	15.55	803.71	898	205.14	209.33

Source own elaboration

14.4.2 Factors Explaining the Extent and Style of Twitter Use in the Campaign

Do gender, age, party affiliation, and size of the municipality of the candidate, may explain the use of Twitter as a channel of communication in the electoral campaign and its means of employment?

Table 14.2 shows that there were significant differences between men and women in the level of utilization of Twitter during the electoral period under analysis. While 74 % of male candidates had a Twitter account, only 58 % of female candidates made use of this network. Then, these data reflect general population statistics for male/female use of Twitter in Spain.

Gender differences can also be seen in male and female candidates' use of Twitter during the campaign. The average number of messages sent is greater in the case of the men. From its part, the volume and evolution of the candidates' virtual communities also show differences on the gender variable. Men have greater success in adding supporters. They manage to increase the size of their community on the network by 25.11 % on average during the campaign. Additionally, men also pay more attention to the work of listening; thereby more rapidly increasing the quantity of people who follow them (13.51 % in the case of men, against 2.04 % for women).

On the other hand, these data result quite intriguing if we contrast them with the fact that there is no a significant difference between male and female candidates behavior when the volume of 'dialogue' is analyzed (16. 18 % in the case of men, against 15.55 % for women). Since the level of dialogue sustained by female and male candidates cannot explain why male candidates were more successful in adding supporters, opening new lines of research within this framework would be needed to clarify the reasons of this manifestation.

Regarding the independent variable of age, Table 14.3 shows that the candidates who are aged between 35 and 44 have a greater relative presence on Twitter. This data, however, does not allow us to establish a direct relation between the youth of the candidate and the propensity to use Twitter as a channel of communication in the electoral campaign. As can be seen in the table, the second group who have a greater rate of presence on Twitter are candidates who are older than 65. Then, we can conclude that there is no correspondence between our data and general statistics about young/elder population use of Twitter in Spain.

Table 14.3 Data by age

Age	Total	Twitter	Media Tweets	Tweets dialogue	% Dialogue	Initial followers	Final followers	Initial following	Final following
35–44	12	11	190.45	51.27	26.92	459.9	617.6	241.7	360.6
45–54	12	8	154.25	20.25	13.12	851.3	1016.75	263.5	271.75
55–64	19	13	190.81	17.5	0.91	593.1	741.6	226	205.4
More than 65	11	8	61.75	5	8.09	902.9	1073.4	708.75	732

Source own elaboration

The age of the candidates does not appear to clearly explain level of activity on Twitter. Although the level of activity of those older than 65 is very much lower than that of candidates from the younger age groups, there is no growing activity on Twitter as age groups descend. The groups of 35–44 and 55–64 years old show slightly above the average number of messages, while this effect weakens in the age group between 45 and 54. Therefore it might be suggested that age does not determine the development of a specific level of activity in the digital age.

The explanatory capacity of age increases for the dependent variables 'differential of monitoring' and 'differential of supporters' of the candidates between the start and end of the electoral campaign. The youngest age group has patterns of behavior that are very distinct to the rest. In this group, while their number of people followed increased to 34.35 % during the whole campaign, the people who decided to follow them increased to 49.13 %. The results show that this group produces more increments in both categories, and is also unique in having greater growth in the number of people who listen to them. In the remaining groups the growth in followers is much less (between 18.8 and 25.03 %). It is worth emphasizing the data that shows a decrease in the differential in the age group between 55 and 64 years old (−9.11 %). In the other two groups the increases are marginal and barely reach 3 %.

These data invite to take into consideration two possible explanations about the relative success of the youngest candidates. One of them is that they were more successful in adding supporters because they sustained a higher level of dialogue. An alternative one has sociological roots: their success responds to the mere fact they were young–being the candidate's youth considered as an element of identification between the candidate and the majority of the Twitter users.

The third independent variable that is analyzed in this study is the political party to which candidates belong. Of the 39 cases that comprised our final universe of study, 38 correspond to candidates who are members of the Spanish Socialist Worker's Party (PSOE) or the Popular Party (PP). From now on we focus on this double category PSOE-PP.

In this respect, Table 14.4 makes it clear that defending the political colors of the PSOE or of the PP does not affect use of individualized campaigning via Twitter. That is, the candidates of the PSOE and the PP had a similar

Table 14.4 Division by party

Party	Total	Twitter	Media Tweets	Tweets dialogue	% Dialogue	Initial followers	Final followers	Initial following	Final following
PSOE	31	23	165.09	17.63	10.67	699.26	806.68	440.63	453.95
PP	20	15	147.06	39.06	26.56	722	920.1	224.6	274.12

Source own elaboration

Table 14.5 Division by size of municipality

City size	Total	Twitter	Media Tweets	Tweets dialogue	% Dialogue	Initial followers	Final followers	Initial following	Final following
>200.000	28	19	161.84	17.29	10.68	576.57	687.42	383.68	397.84
<200.000	27	20	153.1	35.15	22.95	773.28	986.05	292.25	344.31

Source own elaboration

predisposition to have a presence on Twitter in this electoral campaign (74 % PSOE against 75 % PP). However, to pertain to one or the other party does appear to affect the way in which Twitter was used during the election.

The average number of tweets employed by the candidates of the socialist party was greater than that of the PP candidates. A more marked difference between both groups of candidates was found in the attitude toward dialogue that they adopted in Twitter. In this sense the percentage of dialogue interactions of the PP with the electorate was double that of the PSOE. Furthermore, one can observe large differences in the evolution of the networks of followers of the candidates of both parties. The increase in the network community of the candidates of the PP was also greater than that of the candidates of the PSOE (27.43 % against 15.36 %). The advantage of the PP was also notable in relation to the 'followers of candidates' differential. While the number of accounts followed by the socialist candidates increased throughout the campaign by an average of 3.02 %, in the case of the PP the differential ascended to 22.04 %.

These data are reasonable in electoral terms. The concrete electoral context of demobilization of socialist voters gave the socialist candidates more incentives to make strongest marketing efforts in their management of the social network. Then, they posted more tweets than the popular candidates. However, the political pressure over the socialist party made socialist candidates present themselves more active than interactive in the social network. Popular candidates behaved in the opposite way. They focused on follow new people and dialogue with the electorate, achieving in this way better results in terms of increments in the number of followers.

The last independent variable analyzed in this study relates to the size of the municipality. According to Table 14.5, the larger the size of the municipality of the candidate, the greater his/her propensity to use Twitter as a channel of communication with the electorate. The mayors of the municipalities with more than 200,000 inhabitants have a rate of participation in this social network of 67 %, while those who compete in smaller municipalities have 7 % points more (74 %).

These data seem to be coherent. The bigger the city, the fewer chances the candidates have to interact personally with the electorate and the more useful the social networks may be to do so. In a parallel logic: the smaller the city, the fewer citizens are active in social networks, so the fewer incentives the candidates have to make extra-marketing efforts in the digital environment.

If it can be said that the candidates of the municipalities of less than 200,000 were more active in the use of the network (they made more tweets), it is true that they also had less dialogue with their followers in their virtual community. In fact, the mayors of municipalities of more than 200,000 inhabitants posted a percentage of dialogue messages that was double that of their counterparts of municipalities of lesser size. Other data equally shows that the mayors of larger municipalities took better advantage of the possibilities of Twitter in terms of their network of people followed, and people who were following them. The following activity of the mayors of bigger municipalities increased to 27.51 % during the electoral campaign, against a 19.22 % increase experienced by the number of people followed by the mayors of municipalities with fewer inhabitants. The difference is still greater if we consider that the followers of the candidates of the larger cities increased to 17.81 %, against 3.69 % in the case of the candidates of the less populated cities.

We find a double and basic explanation for these facts. Since in bigger cities the social network is denser, the mayoral candidates in these environments had potentially more opportunities to increase their number of followers. Moreover, since in bigger cities mayoral candidates finally demonstrated themselves more prone to dialogue, they were in fact more attractive to followers.

14.5 Discussion

In this section we emphasize our main research findings. The five points selected have been chosen for their descriptive/explanatory value, and also for their potential to inspire new lines of research.

Although in 2011 the PSOE had greater incentives than the PP to run a local campaign based on the strategy of individualized campaigning, in the large Spanish cities both parties similarly decided that their greatest electoral attraction were their candidates. Then PP and PSOE exported their campaigning activities to the digital arena of Twitter, encouraging their respective mayoral candidates to make extra-marketing efforts in this environment. This fact reveals that the main and major Spanish political parties contribute to the promotion of a visible tendency toward the personalization of local elections. That also invites us to suggest that this party behavior reinforces the already accentuated personalist character of local political leadership in Spain.

In second place, for the Spanish political elites the local political scenario has been a 'test laboratory' of the application of the technique of individualized campaigning through Twitter. This communication tool has achieved notable diffusion among the main candidates to the mayoralty of large Spanish cities. It still remains to be seen to what point the circumstances that surrounded these elections determined the high level of utilization' of Twitter on this occasion. As a result, these findings raise new questions. Is this level of Twitter use an isolated case or will its use continue to increase in municipal and/or national elections that are less marked by the expectation of political change?

The socialist and popular candidates to the mayoralty of the large Spanish cities use Twitter to raise awareness about their electoral message, but also to increase their community of contacts and support through four techniques (namely: broadcasting tweets, following others on the network, ensuring that they are followed, and initiating dialogues with their interlocutors). Nevertheless, they do not all know how to exploit the entirety of the communicative potential that Twitter offers. Those who most strategically employed this tool included: the PP candidates, men, the youngest, and those from the most populous cities.

Without doubt the greatest novelty introduced by the use of Twitter in this electoral campaign was the possibility of establishing direct and fluid dialogues between candidates and electors. Taken together, the data from this study suggests that this possibility was not exhaustively exploited by most candidates. As a whole, the majority of the candidates' interventions on the network were made to broadcast their own messages, and only a small percentage responded to messages of their interlocutors. This reality can be interpreted in two different ways. On the one hand, it might be suggested that the candidates to the mayoralty of the large Spanish cities, in general terms, are still at an early stage in their use of the social network, and for that reason did not know how to make best use of it. On the other hand, it can equally be argued that this process will demand the time, effort, and training of those candidates who are accustomed to a style of unidirectional campaign that is supported by the party, and that focuses on traditional means of communication.

Finally, now we do know that in Spain most mayoral candidates made new marketing efforts to develop their local campaign in Twitter. Throughout this study we have found as well preliminary data to approach the understanding of how these efforts were made and what is their impact on election politics. On the one hand, our work shows that efforts were made in a heterogeneous way, since the candidates' incentives were varied and conditioned by different factors. On the other hand, our study indicates that these dissimilar efforts had an impact in the Spanish model of personalization of local politics. When candidates wished to learn and really exploit the communicative opportunities that social networks offered to them, leadership was still in force but the accent was not posed just in the leaders figure. The emerging way of personalization of Spanish local politics promoted by the best use of social network in the conduction of individualized campaigning is based on the bidirectional relation of influence between leaders and followers, mayoral candidate and electors. That is real leadership, is not it?

14.6 Conclusion

In this chapter, the importance of social media in electoral campaigns has been made clear. For that reason, an initial discussion has explored the relation between political communication and social networks during the time of electoral campaigns, and has highlighted the scarcity of empirical evidence about this phenomenon. Immediately following this analysis, the frame of reference in this case study has been specified. In this way, the presence and the behavior of the mayoral-candidates on Twitter during the recent local election campaign in Spain has been analyzed. This research design is both innovative and unique in Spain. Nevertheless, we consider that its interest transcends the Spanish academic world, given the scarcity of equivalent empirical work at comparative level.

The study has provided statistical results that have allowed us to respond to the questions that were posed at the outset. It has been made clear that Twitter has been used in an electoral campaign by the immense majority of the observed candidates. Equally, the existence of different patterns of use of the network as a channel of electoral political communication has been emphasized. Not all the candidates with a presence on Twitter have exploited the personal and interactive potential of this network in a similar way, nor have they been capable of making their network of support denser by fully employing the resources that it offers. Through investigating the incidence of various factors in the expansion and 'style of use' of Twitter as a campaign tool, we have revealed that gender, size of the population of the candidate's municipality, and party membership seem to have an effect in the behavior on the mayoral candidates in the social network. However, just the two first variables seem to influence the dependent variable "presence of the candidates in Twitter".

These results, taken together, have a merely exploratory value. A nuanced statistical treatment of these data is needed to reveal the insights of the facts they suggest. The consideration of other independent variables is equally required for further steps of research. Nevertheless, the interest of the data already presented is not small, given that they offer some initial clues from which to start investigating the phenomena of the virtualization of electoral campaigns, be it in the study of isolated cases or in comparative studies of different cases.

Therefore, it is expected that future studies can address some of the questions that have been left open by this chapter. Is the use of Twitter in campaigns a passing fashion or will it become consolidated as an electoral strategy of political communication? In this sense, it would be interesting to see the results of various consecutive electoral contests and to monitor this phenomenon over time. Is the use of Twitter more common in local or national election campaigns? Equally valuable would be a comparative analysis between electoral scenarios at distinct levels. What is the role of other social networks in the electoral campaign? We argue that research projects that are more ambitious, and that contrast the electoral use of other social networks such as Facebook, will greatly enrich accumulated knowledge about this question.

References

Anduiza, Eva, Aina Gallego & Marta Cantijoch (2010) 'Online political participation in Spain: the impact of traditional and Internet resources', *Journal of Information Technology and Politics*, 7 (4): 356–368.

Barnes, Samuel H. (2005) 'La movilización política en las democracias contemporáneas: un análisis comparado', in Francisco Llera and Pablo Oñate (eds) *Política comparada. Entre lo local y lo global*. Madrid: Centro de Investigaciones Sociológicas, pp. 23–38.

Bode, Leticia et al. (2011) 'Mapping the Political Twitterverse: Finding Connections between Political Elites. Paper prepared for the *2011 Political Networks Conference, Ann Arbor*.

Cocktail Analysis (2011) *Informe de Resultados. Observatorio Redes Sociales. Tercera Oleada*. Available on line: http://www.tcanalysis.com. Accessed: 21-X-2011.

Criado, J. Ignacio and Martinez Fuentes, Guadalupe (2010) *Blogging político y personalización de la democracia local en España y Portugal. Evidencias presentes y propuestas de futuro*.Madrid: Fundación Alternativas.

Criado, J. Ignacio and Martinez Fuentes, Guadalupe (2011) 'Mayors' usage of blogs in local election campaign: the Spanish case study', *International Journal of Electronic Governance*, 3 (4): 395–413

Dalton, Rusell (2002) 'The decline of party identifications', in Rusell Dalton and Martin Wattemberg (eds) *Parties without partisans: political change in advanced industrial democracies*. Oxfors: Oxford University Press, pp. 19–36.

EUROSTAT (2011). *Europe 2020 Indicators*. Available on line: http://epp.eurostat.ec.europa.eu/portal/page/portal/statistics/themes. Accessed: 21-X-2011.

Fundación Orange (2011). *Informe eEspaña 2010*. Fundación Orange: Madrid. Available on line: http://www.informeeespana.es/docs/eE2011.pdf. Accessed: 21-X-2011.

Gaines, Brian J. & Mondak, Jeffery J. (2009) 'Typing Together? Clustering of Ideological Types in Online Social Networks'. *Journal of Information Technology and Politics*, 6 (3,4), 216–231.

Gibson, Rachel K. (2010) ''Open Source Campaigning?': UK Party Organisations and the Use of the New Media in the 2010 General Election' *Proceedings of the Annual Meeting of the American Political Science Association, Washington DC*.

Gibson, Rachel K. & Ian McAllister (2011) 'Do Online Election Campaigns Win Votes? The 2007 Australian "'YouTube'" Election', *Political Communication*, 28(2), 227–244

Golbeck, J., Grimes, J. M., & Rogers, A. (2010). 'Twitter Use by the U. S. Congress'. *Journal of the American Society for Information Science*, *61*(8), 1612–1621.

Gueorguieva. V. (2008) 'Voters, MySpace, and TouTube: The Impact of Alternative Communication Channels on the 2006 Election Cycle and Beyond'. *Social Science Computer Review*, 26(3), 311–28.

Gulati, Girish J. & Williams, Christine B. (2010) 'Congressional Candidates' Use of YouTube in 2008: Its Frequency and Rationale', *Journal of Information Technology & Politics*, 7(2), 93–109.

Hanna, A., Sayre, B., Bode, L., Yang, J.H., and Shah, D. (2011). 'Mapping the Political Twittervers: Candidates and their Followers in the Midterms'. *Proceedings of the Fifth International Association for the Advancement of Artificial Intelligence (AIII) Conference on Weblogs and Social Media*.

Holbrook, Thomas.M. (1996) *Do campaigns matter?* Thousand Oaks: Sage.

INE (2011) *Estadística de enseñanza universitaria, 30. 05.2011*. Available on line: http://www.ine.es/jaxi/menu.do?type=pcaxis&path=%2Ft13%2Fp405&file=inebase&L=0. Accessed: 21-X-2011.

Intelligence Compass (2010) *Informe sobre Política y redes sociales*. On line: http://intelligencecompass.com/images/Informe%20Pol%C3%ADticos%20y%20Redes%20Sociales.pdf (Accessed 23-XII-2010).

Jaeger, P. T., Paquette, S., & Simmons, S. N. (2010). 'Information Policy in National Political Campaigns: A Comparison of the 2008 Campaigns for President of the United States and Prime Minister of Canada'. *Journal of Information Technology Politics*, 7(1), 67–82.

Lassen, David S., and Brown, Adam R. (2010). 'Twitter: The Electoral Connection?' *Social Science Computer Review*, 29(4): 419–436.

Martínez Nicolás, Manuel, 2007: "Agitación en el campo. Nueve ideas para la investigación sobre comunicación política en España", Política y sociedad, vol. 44 (2), 2007, pp. 209–227

Martínez Fuentes, Guadalupe (2008) 'Local Political Leadership in Spain', *Local Government Studies*,30 (2) : 267–278

Martínez Fuentes, Guadalupe and Ortega Villodres, Carmen (2010a) 'The political leadership factor in the Spanish Local Elections', *Lex Localis, Journal of Local Self-Government*, 8 (2): 147–160.

Martínez Fuentes, Guadalupe and Ortega Villodres, Carmen (2010b) 'Las elecciones municipales de 2007 en Andalucia. Un estudio del comportamiento electoral de los andaluces', *Psicología Política*, núm. 41:7–25.

Mouritzen, Paul. E. M. and Svara, James H. (2002), *Leadership at Apex. Politicians and administrators in Western local governments*. Pittsburg, Pittsburg University Press.

Molins, Joaquim M. and Pardos, Sergi (2005) 'Las elecciones municipales de 2003 en Cataluña. El ruido contra la estructura: lo global y lo local', in Francisco Llera and Pablo Oñate (eds) Política comparada. Entre lo local y lo global. Madrid: Centro de Investigaciones Sociológicas, pp. 91–118.

Montabes Pereira, Juan and Ortega Villodres, Carmen (2011) 'Identificación partidista y voto: las elecciones autonómicas en Andalucía (2004–2008)', *Revista Española de Investigaciones Sociológicas*, 134:27–54.

Natera, Antonio. (2001) *El liderazgo político en las sociedades democráticas*. Madrid, Centro de Estudios Políticos y Constitucionales

Observatorio Nacional de las Telecomunicaciones y de la Sociedad de la Información (ONTSI). (2011). *Las Redes Sociales en Internet*. ONTSI: Madrid.

Petrocik, John R. (1996) 'Issue ownership in presidential elections with a 1980 case study'. *American Journal of Political Science*, 4 (3): 825–850.

Pole, Antoinette, and Xenos, Michael. (2011). 'Like, Comments, and Retweets: Facebooking and Tweeting on the 2010 Gubernatorial Campaign Trail'. *Proceedings of the State Politics and Policy Conference 2011*.

Scher, Richard. K. (1997) *The modern political campaign: Mudslinging, bombast and the Vitality of American Politics*. Armonk: M.E. Sharpe.

Steger, Wayne, Williams, Christine & Andolina, Molly (2010) 'Political Use of Social Networks in 2008'. *Proceedings of the Annual Meeting of the American Political Science Association. Washington DC*.

Tumasjan, Andranik, Sprenger, Timm O., Sandner, Philipp G., and Welpe, Isabell M. (2011). 'Electoral Forecast with Twitter. What 140 Characters Reveal the Political Landscape'. *Social Science Computer Review*, 29(4) 402–418.

Vanaclocha, Francisco (2005): "Los liderazgos en el mercado electoral", in A. Natera & F. Vanaclocha (eds.), Los Liderazgos en el Mercado Político y en la Gestión Pública, Madrid: Universidad Carlos III, 85–108.

Williams, Christine B. and Gulati, Girish J. (2009) 'Social networks in political campaigns: Facebook and Congressional elections 2006, 2008'. Paper presented at the *Annual Meeting of the American Political Science Association*, Toronto, Ontario, Canada.

Williams, Christine B. and Gulati, Girish J. (2010). 'Communicating with Constituents in 140 Characters or Less: Twitter and the Diffusion of Technology Innovation in the United States Congress'. *Proceedings of the Annual Meeting of the Midwest Political Science Association*.

Yannas, Prodromos, Kleftodimos, Alexandros and Lappas, Georgios (2011) 'Online Political Marketing in 2010 Greek Local Elections: The Shift from Web to Web 2.0 Campaigns'. *Proceedings of the 16th International Conference on Corporate and Marketing Communications*, Athens.

Zittel, Thomas (2007) 'Lost in Technology? Political Parties and Online-Campaigning in Mixed Member Electoral Systems'. *Paper for ECPR General Conference, panel on party organisations and new information and communication technologies (ICTs)*, Pisa.

Zittel, Thomas (2009) 'Lost in Technology? Political Parties and Online Campaigning in Germany's Mixed Member Electoral System', *Journal of Information Technology and Politics*, 6 (3/4): 298–311.

Chapter 15
Government–Citizen Interactions Using Web 2.0 Tools: The Case of Twitter in Mexico

Rodrigo Sandoval-Almazan and J. Ramon Gil-Garcia

15.1 Introduction

Web 2.0 represents an evolution in the way that applications and Internet portals present and manage content and information to facilitate higher levels of inter-action among users. These applications foster collaboration and seek to provide services that replace the traditional methods of content creation. In this sense, a particular aspect of Web 2.0 applications and tools refers to the co-creation of Web-based content that Web portal users share with one another. That is, con-sumers of information have started producing some of the information they con-sume. Therefore, Web 2.0 applications could be considered the next stage in the development of Internet-related technologies. Some of these applications are social networks, microformats, social tagging, RSS (syndication), blogs, video blogs, podcasts, wikis, and forums. Examples of commercial sites that deploy these applications are Technorati, Digg, Facebook, Flickr, YouTube, MySpace, Twitter, and Del.icio.us, among others.

Twitter in particular has the potential to change the relationships between Mexican citizens and government. In a population that has low levels of political participation, Twitter presents a different opportunity to share, advocate, and voice opinions about political affairs and public officials in ways that government cannot control. A recent, controversial example of the use of Twitter to actually

R. Sandoval-Almazan (✉)
Universidad Autónoma del Estado de México,
Pino Suarez Sur 607. Col. Americas,
50130 Toluca, Mexico, Mexico
e-mail: rsandovala@uaemex.mx

J. R. Gil-Garcia
Department of Public Administration, Centro de Investigación y Docencia Económicas
Carretera Mexico-Toluca, No. 3655, Col. Lomas de Santa Fe, 01210 México, D.F., Mexico
e-mail: joseramon.gil@cide.edu

C. G. Reddick and S. K. Aikins (eds.), *Web 2.0 Technologies and Democratic Governance*, Public Administration and Information Technology 1, DOI: 10.1007/978-1-4614-1448-3_15, © Springer Science+Business Media New York 2012

circumvent government is when a group of citizens from Mexico City were able to evade arrest for drunk-driving using Twitter's social network by sending the exact location of police checkpoints in the city. These individuals were subsequently apprehended and punished by the police authority (CNN Expansion 2010).

While Web 2.0 can work as a tool to avoid government intervention, it can be also used to monitor government in more positive ways, such as an iPhone app that Mexican citizens developed to reduce corruption. The app compiles local laws about traffic violations and their associated fines so that drivers can use this information if corrupt police officers solicit bribes from them in exchange for reduced fines. Another example is a student from the "Instituto Tecnologico de Estudios Superiores de Monterrey," a private university in Mexico, who sent Twitter messages about military intrusion onto the Monterrey Campus in March 2010, as well as raising awareness about the death of two students. While the military initially identified these two individuals as drug dealers, following the release of this information on Twitter and subsequent investigations, they were later recognized as students of that institution with no nexus with criminal organizations (Hechos 2010). The use of Twitter ensured that the message about what happened reached other students, TV news reporters, and the print media, all of whom challenged the press reports from the state and federal prosecutors and helped bring to light the facts the government wanted to hide. Military incursion into a university, normally forbidden in Mexican law, was widely seen as a violation of the human rights of the students (SDP 2010).

These brief examples illustrate the use and impact of Twitter on citizens and government alike. Recently, government websites are beginning to include these applications. In the case of Mexico, government agencies are using blogs, wikis, forums, RSS, Apis (such as Google Maps), podcasts, videocasts, social bookmarking (like Del.icio.us, Technorati, or Digg), and social networks (Facebook, Hi5, LinkedIn) (Gallupe 2007). All these applications, although they appear very different in purpose and function, share some features such as the collective generation and classification of information and content, the integration of communities, and the production and consumption of socially distributed knowledge. They are all places for interactions among citizens and between citizens and governments. In addition, some of these tools have proven to be potential new mechanisms for political activism [perhaps the best known case is the political campaign of Barack Obama in the U.S. (Diaz 2011)]. They could be used as tools for managing media relations, as is often the case with Twitter, but also as alternative means for disseminating information during social or political crises (like the recent elections in Iran and the coup in Honduras) via tools like YouTube.

In the case of government, these Web 2.0 applications have the potential to generate greater interaction between different social actors and consequently greater citizen participation in government processes. These Government 2.0 applications have started being used at different levels of government and within different policy areas (Grimmelikhuijsen 2010). However, there are few studies assessing the extent of use of these tools and some of their potential impacts.

The term Web 2.0 was coined by O'Reilly (2005), who defines it as "the web as a platform that extends to all connected devices," although these devices are not just limited to being interconnected. Instead, much of their functionality rests on the fact that they use technologies that allow users to build the content and format of the sites. Tapscott and Williams (2006) describe the phenomenon as follows: "The new web is fundamentally different in both its architecture and applications. Instead of a digital newspaper, it is a canvas where every splash of paint contributed by a user enriches the tapestry; whether people are creating, sharing or socializing, the new Web is about participating rather than passively receiving information" (p. 37). O'Reilly says that Web 2.0 is a mechanism for social cohesion and cooperation. However, the term Web 2.0 is still under debate. Wilson et al. (2011) mention that the quantity of concepts included in Web 2.0 has caused confusion and ambiguity about the term. They propose that Web 2.0 must be understood as "the second generation of the Web, wherein interoperable, user-centered web applications and services promote social connectedness, media and information sharing, user-created content, and collaboration among individuals and organizations" (Wilson et al. 2011, p. 2).

Although relatively new, Web 2.0 tools and applications are being used on government websites in several countries. For instance, based on case studies in Germany, De Kool and Van Wamelen (2008) propose six categories for analyzing electronic government using Web 2.0. Eliason and Lundberg (2006) focused their attention on investigating the specific use of Web 2.0 in designing municipal websites as tools to reduce the complexity of sites and better organize content. These researchers gathered data from seven Swiss municipalities in order to evaluate the impact of Web 2.0 (Harfoush 2009).

The future of Web 2.0 in government is promising. INEGI (2011) mentions that mobile government will evolve with new Web 2.0 tools and features. Bannister and Connolly (2011) propose the use of this technology to improve open government initiatives in the US Government, thereby enhancing citizen opportunities to interact with open data and information through crowd sourcing. Different programs of the SOMUS project suggest a promising trend for the use of these tools for citizen-government interaction in the coming years (Näkki et al. 2011). There is potential for Web 2.0 to be useful for governments, but the great question that prevails is whether public sector organizations are able to commit to this new way of interacting with citizens to improve their user-experience and their perceptions of public services (Wilson 2011).

The use of Web 2.0 in the current activities of citizens and governments is a fact. Discarding Web 2.0 should not be seen as an option for governments. However, the way government webmasters and information owners would maintain, distribute, and collect data could dramatically change as a result of the new Web 2.0 citizen interaction capabilities. This chapter explores this kind of interaction, with a particular focus on Twitter. The chapter is organized in five sections, including the foregoing introduction. Section 15.2 presents a literature review on Web 2.0 and the use of Twitter in government settings. Section 15.3 briefly describes the research design and methods used in this study. Section 15.4

illustrates the use of Twitter through three examples in the local, state, and national Mexican contexts. Finally, Sect. 15.5 provides some concluding remarks and suggests ideas for future research.

15.2 The Use of Twitter in Government: A Literature Review

In 2005, Bill Gates, the former CEO of Microsoft, wrote that we now live in an "information democracy" (Soberanes 2011). Twitter could be considered a tool of what has been called the post-broadcast democracy (Wilson 2011). The dispersion of information using an Internet platform, which can be published using a computer or a mobile phone, generates immediate updates, and instantly connects a network of people who can freely and quickly distribute that information, generates an informed network not seen before.

Twitter has over 175 million registered users and 95 million tweets are written daily (Twitter 2011). The web application developed by Jack Dorsey, Evan Williams, and Biz Stone has been online since 2006 and has gained popularity worldwide. Twitter has changed the concept of blogging and has become one of the most used features of Web 2.0. Twitter is a platform for individuals to immediately disseminate brief updates, including URLs that are linked to audio, video, or images. The main differences between Twitter and a traditional blog is that messages (called "tweets") are limited to 140 characters and users can choose to interact in two ways: by sending direct messages (DM) person to person, or sending a message to the general public via a set of subscribers, who can then resend—or "retweet"—the messages to their own network of subscribers.

Although Twitter is relatively new, there are some recent studies that discuss its characteristics and impacts (Monroy-Hernández 2011). Java et al. (2007) compared micro-blogging to regular blogging and found more engagement and reciprocity among Twitter users when compared to conventional bloggers. Honey and Herring (2009) focused on the conversations that can be maintained using this social platform; they found out that using the @ symbol to target messages to specific users makes this service more usable as a collaboration tool. Harfoush (2009) describes the particular use of Twitter in Obama's 2008 presidential campaign, along with the use of other tools such as Facebook and YouTube.

Another important aspect of Twitter is the way users make recommendations to one another. Since the platform is limited to the exchange of short text messages, recommending websites, videos, or photos is a very frequent activity. Phelan et al. (2009) studied the use of Twitter for communicating news and stories at the moment they are occurring. Similarly, Zhao and Rosson (2009) discovered that this aspect of Twitter not only facilitates information sharing, but also helps build common ground and sustain a feeling of connectivity among colleagues and friends, all of which create a new informal medium of communication. In addition, Boyd et al. (2010) studied the retweet function as a tool to promote regular conversations and increase the viral effect of short messages or pictures.

Complementarily, Diakopoulos and Shamma (2010) propose the idea that tweets have a sentiment variable that must be considered for analysis and future studies. The authors proposed that there is a relationship between an event and an effective response shown through a timestamp and a hash tag.

Twitter has been studied within three main areas related to each other: social computing, public administration, and social media. Within social computing, Oates et al. (2006) pose the following question: "Has the Internet demonstrated real potential to improve civil society through a wider provision of information, an enhancement of communication between government and citizen or via better state transparency" (p. 2) "How might Web 2.0 contribute to overcome the obstacles encountered in open government initiatives?". This new trend has its supporters and skeptics; however, the use of different tools as part of government websites indicates the need for research that defines and expands the understanding of this topic.

The study of Web 2.0 tools in public administration is wider than in social computing. Recent research presents several results in the different government levels. Blaiser and Weinberg (2009) research the relationship between the money citizens provide to campaigns to define the digital government. DemoNetare, which is an organization specializing in Web 2.0 tools, has a research focus on services that support network building, technological development and, web-based technologies; some of the projects under their research umbrella are: (1) The use of social network tools, such as Facebook and Twitter, to discuss political issues and candidates fostering e-participation; (2) the use of virtual worlds to promote online participation; and (3) location-based services mainly used by mobile devices (i.e. OneClimate.net) and collaborative writing tools such as wikis and Google docs. One of their reports conclude that citizens are aware of and use these kinds of tools in their daily lives and government must develop strategies to promote the use of Web 2.0 tools (Rose 2009).

Recent research about Congress has provided several highlights about Web 2.0 adoption, such as the low use among elected officials; in the case of the U.S., Web 2.0 is used more by Democrats than Republicans (Chi and Yang 2010). A more detailed study at this level of government was performed by Golbeck et al. (2010), who read and analyzed 6,000 Twitter posts and found that the main activities elected officials undertook were disseminating information (such as news articles or blogs posts) and reporting daily activities; they do not provide new insights about the legislative process or improve transparency. The authors' conclusion was that this tool was only a vehicle for self-promotion, rather than for promoting communication between congress and the people.

More research on the citizen perspective has been conducted by Maciel et al. (2009) from the Democratic Citizenship Community, which creates interaction and communication resources such as citizen profiles, debates, online voting, an information library, a social space, and user help guides for Web 2.0 technologies. As a conclusion of this research, the authors state that "social networks change the way users relate on the Web" (Maciel et al. 2010).

One of the very few research studies about Twitter trust, confidence, and credibility is the research of Juarez (2011b); they propose a category named viewertariat to describe "those who comment on events in real time through social media such as Twitter." This research gathers data from a poll about opinions of Twitter users; according to their findings, some members perform a lay tutelage role, providing information and explanations about polling and elections to fellow citizens who express confusion. According to Ampofo (2011), that mentorship role indicates the continued importance of informed public discussion to some citizens. A second finding is the blurring of elite/non-elite interactions alongside persistent theories about elite conspiracies.

Finally, another contribution to the Twitter research field is the use of this tool to understand and evaluate terrorist attacks. Based on observations of Twitter's role in the civilian response during the recent 2009 Jakarta and Mumbai terrorist attacks, Cheong and Lee (2011) propose a structured framework to harvest civilian sentiment and response on Twitter during terrorism scenarios. Using data mining and filtering methods to provide some graphical visualizations of information could reveal on-the-ground responses to terrorist threats.

Previous research has shown the potential impact of Twitter and provides some clues about the future use of this tool in several government tasks. Twitter has played a role in political activism and changing political systems in Egypt, Tunisia, and Libya (Linders 2011). Twitter can also help during crises and emergency situations (Curtin and Meijer 2006), along with other Web 2.0 features that complement it. Citizen co-production of ideas, content, and solutions for government problems is part of a new participatory channel for government decision-making and has to be considered as a new feature of government interaction (Bannister and Connolly 2011); Twitter is one of the channels to promote this we-government idea (Belanger and Carter 2008).

These elements provide evidence of the impact and current boundaries of Twitter in public administration. However for some authors, the idea of using this Web 2.0 tool goes beyond what presently exists. For instance, Dutton (2009) develops the model of a state created as a result of the interactions of all these technologies. Juarez (2011a) argues that this kind of technology creates a new space for politics, making a virtual place for people to gather and interact with more freedom, mobility, and speed.

15.3 Research Design and Methods

In order to do research on Web 2.0 tools like Twitter, online research has become the best way to collect, compare, and analyze data. However, very few methodologies and research models have been developed to this end, creating confusion about validity and the degree to which we can trust research findings based on data collected online (Linders 2011). E-research may make tasks easier (or sometimes even automates them), but it also raises a whole range of methodological and epistemic issues (Estalella and Ardevol 2011). Using innovative data collection strategies, however, does not necessarily compromise the validity of the findings. Gallupe (2007) mentions that current information systems (IS) research seems more concerned with "how" the research is conducted than "what" research is conducted and "why." Hewson (2008) develops the concept of Internet-mediated research (IMR): "Internet-mediated research involves the gathering of novel, original data to be subjected to analysis in order to provide new evidence in relation to a particular research question" (p. 58). This kind of research, though, like any other study, requires careful planning, design, and piloting. Its most obvious advantage is cost and time efficiency. In order to provide evidence to argue that government and citizens use social media (specifically, Twitter) to achieve public goals, we present three Mexican cases that illustrate the power of Twitter in terms of citizen participation and its influence on government decision-making. The cases were selected because of their visibility and to provide examples from the local, state, and national contexts in the discussion.

15.4 Twitter and Citizen Participation: Three Powerful Stories

The following three cases studies each show a different use of Twitter within citizen-government interaction. One example will focus on relationships among citizens and the Mexican congress with the #InternetNecesario; the second example is citizen information sharing and government reaction to misinformation in the state of Veracruz; the third and last example is the use of Twitter by a citizen of a rich county within the State of Mexico named Huixquilucan with the username @vecinodeTeca. These examples will qualitatively describe the use of Twitter for interaction at three different government levels: the federal, state, and local level.

15.4.1 The Case of #InternetNecesario in the Mexican Congress

Cyberactivism is not a new trend (Oates et al. 2006). However in Mexico it has gained attention with the case of #InternetNecesario. Mexican taxes are assessed every year and the Mexican Congress creates a bill of taxes for reducing, maintaining, or creating new taxes. They proposed to tax Internet use for the first time in 2009. The bill was approved in the low chamber. However, the president of the Mexican Chapter of the Internet Society, Alejandro Pisanty, made a statement against this bill via Twitter. He posted the message "promote, not tax" using the hashtag #InternetNecesario (Indispensable Internet), imitating a Venezuelan movement with the same name in the previous year. The tweet went out on Monday 19 October 2009, at 22:00 hours.

This post fostered an unprecedented attention among Twitter users in Mexico, with more than 10,000 users posting and re-posting through the online platform and supporting Pisanty's complaint. Approximately 100,000 messages were posted during the 10 days of protest according to TrendStats This online protest became a trending topic in a few hours, reaching fifth place in the worldwide top trending topics.

This unusual online social protest persuaded Senator Francisco Javier Castellon Fonseca (@SenadoCastellon) to promote a hearing with some representatives of the Mexican Twitter community and members of the Mexican senate. The hearing happened on 22 October 2009 and included the Chairman of the Senate, Carlos Navarrete (PRD). Twelve representatives of the online community talked with the senators; the citizens expressed their disagreement with the telecommunications tax proposed by the low chamber and offered proposals for how the legislators could promote the use of the Internet and its advantages.

The meeting was widely covered by traditional media outlets and also streamed online. Maria de las Heras, a well-known Mexican pollster from Milenio Newspaper, published a national poll in which 78 % of Mexicans were against taxing Internet use and considered it a basic need (Riva-Palacio 2009). On the day of the hearing, over 32,864 tweets went out from Twitter users supporting their "virtual representatives" with the senators. During the subsequent days, 11,156 Twitter messages using the hashtag #InternetNecesario were sent daily.

A second stage of the Mexican protest occurred when Twitter followers moved their protest from a virtual space to a physical, face-to-face protest. On the following Sunday, 27 October 2009 they gathered together at "Parque Hundido," an emblematic park in Mexico City. This face-to-face meeting was reproduced in other states like Nuevo León, Yucatán, Jalisco, and Chiapas in the same day.

Finally, after a battle of several weeks, the Internet tax was officially rejected. Only cellular phone communications and satellite and cable television were taxed. The hashtag #InternetNecesario remains active on a protest website (www.internetnecesario.org). The #InternetNecesario case is remarkable because it is an example of a Mexican online protest against a bill. There are no previous e.g., of this kind of crowdsourcing using Twitter with congressmen. A novelty of this interaction is that it comes from a virtual space and occurred in a record time of 1 week to produce a citizen hearing from the Senate, something unprecedented in Mexican politics.

This first approach to interaction among citizens using Twitter as a platform for placing pressure on a political bill leads to different analyzes: the first one is the online protest, and the second is the actors' behavior. The online protest found a perfect forum on Twitter. Mexicans can give their opinion online, without problems of space or mobility. The protest went viral and expanded thanks to the retweet and direct message features. Many Mexican citizens abroad could support the protest using the platform, and others encouraged their friends to use or open a new account in order to participate in the online protest.

The online protest lasted for more than a few hours—something relatively infrequent over Twitter—and took some days to dissolve. The protest evolved and became a face-to-face event in parks across several states in the country. This action reveals a commitment to the movement beyond just sending the messages. Even though there was often a small number of people in the parks—fewer than 200—the protest became more real and sent an important warning to the political class that Twitter could help mobilize the public on important issues.

The second level of analysis includes the actors of the online protest and the hearing at the Senate. It is relevant to mention that this hearing is the first time that a group of citizens without a clear leader or a very specific purpose were able to convene a congressional hearing. Some characteristics of the protest are as follows: (1) politicians paid attention to the Twitter disruption because it combined mass media with the platform; (2) the Senate hearing increased the exposure of the online protest, but also highlighted the legislators who are technologically aware; and (3) the Twitter protest had no particular leadership and the coalition was proposed and formed online using Twitter; and (4) finally, the hearing was transmitted online to not only the Twitter community, but the whole Internet community in Mexico.

There are three citizen interaction points and at least three different Web 2.0 tools in this case. The first interaction was to launch the protest using the Twitter platform and viral information. The second interaction was between the congressmen and the Twitter users, a face-to-face interaction produced directly by the online protest. Finally, the third interaction was the face-to-face meeting of the protest supporters in the parks the next Sunday. The first tool used in this case was Twitter to gather and share the information to foster the online protest. The second tool was streaming video and audio of the hearing with senators. The third tool was the use of YouTube to publish videos of the park protests.

15.4.2 Veracruz Retaliation

Veracruz is a southern state in Mexico where the increase of violence due to problems with drug-dealing has become very important. In this context is the following Twitter case, which reveals the impact of this new kind of communication among citizens. On Thursday, 25 August 2011 the Twitter account of @gilius_22 published a tweet announcing the kidnapping of five children by an armed group. The official hastag, #Verfollow, confirmed, "In the primary school named Jorge Arroyo an armed group kidnapped five kids" (Monroy-Hernández 2011). This message was re-tweeted by twelve more people, among them @VerFollow, an account with more than 5,000 followers that was created by the police department of Veracruz to report violence in the state. The viral influence of this tool spread the news in 2 hours. Furthermore, the failure of the cellular communications that day increased citizen panic, and the smoke of a burning car with a mechanical malfunction near one of the local schools contributed to the fear (Soberanes 2011; Monroy-Hernández 2011).

Many parents went to the schools to pick up their children and save them from this threat, causing massive traffic congestion, chaos, and panic across the city. Several other Twitter users reported other incidents related to schools and to helicopters supposedly flying at a low altitude. Many parents did not take their kids to school the next day and businesses reported a 70 % productivity loss due to the incident (Monroy-Hernández 2011). The hashtag was used 8,354 times that day (Diaz 2011). The governor, Javier Duarte Ochoa, published a Twitter message denying the rumor at 12:00 p.m. Five minutes later, in a second Twitter message, the governor tweeted his support for freedom of expression, but urged people to validate information before acting on it. Three hours later he posted that the government would go after those who spread the rumor on the basis of "terrorism" (Monroy-Hernández 2011).

The same day, the government website published a list of sixteen Twitter accounts involved in the rumor and threatening to take legal action against them. The statement also mentioned the names of those associated with two of the Twitter accounts: @gilius_22 (Gilberto Martínez Vera) and @maruchibravo (María de Jesús Bravo Pagola). By Saturday, both were arrested on charges of terrorism; they have claimed to have been tortured by the police and forced to sign confessions (Juarez 2011a). At the same time, many Twitter users across the country have supported the opposition to the arrests; the hastag #twiterxslibres (free twitter users) increased from 197 mentions to 2,462 in 1 week (Diaz 2011).

The event reached international news outlets and was reported on CNN, the BBC, The Guardian, and the Los Angeles Times, creating pressure against the state prosecutor who finally discharged and released Martinez Vera and Bravo Pagola on 21 September 2011, after 1 month of imprisonment (Martinez 2011). In the meantime, the Veracruz government promoted a bill to punish social disorder caused by any means—including electronic or online—with support from the neighbor state of Tabasco, which has the same law (Juarez 2011a).

There are five lessons from the Veracruz case. The first one is the use of Twitter to promote dangerous or high impact information, which could cause disturbances; however, when Twitter was used similarly in the state of Nuevo Leon, with 250,000 tweets that used the word "shootings," the reaction was not the same as in Veracruz (Monroy-Hernández 2011). The second lesson is the high impact of the social media platforms as a primary information channel for citizens. The Veracruz case shows that faster, mobile, and easy to update tools—like Facebook, email, or Twitter—spread news in order to protect family or persons in extreme measures. Despite the government use of the same tool—the Governor's tweet—the citizens did not trust the official version and they acted according to the unofficial reports. This behavior is consistent with a lack of government legitimacy and trust (Bannister and Connolly 2011; Curtin and Meijer 2006).

The third lesson is related to the impact of social media versus traditional media. Twitter's faster input of information and the spread of that information to Veracruz citizens far surpass the reach of other media sources. A fourth lesson is the controversial concept of collaborating with government. Based on the government's treatment of the individuals involved in spreading what turned out to be misinformation, the ideas of co-production and interaction with government officials are heavily discouraged and are unlikely to occur. Who believes in government after this retaliation? Who wants to help government to share, produce, or disseminate information after this event? Citizens are aware of this kind of danger to collaborate and participate using online tools.

Finally, the fifth lesson is related to the absence of laws that regulate this kind of behavior. We do not have enough information to blame the state government for using the terrorism law to charge the individuals involved, nor should those who spread false information do so without any consequence. However it is clear both government and citizens need clarification of the boundaries and procedures for using Web 2.0 tools to promote responsible social participation.

15.4.3 The Neighbor Case: @VecinodeTeca

The name @vecinodeteca is short for "neighbor from Tecamachalco," a town within the Huixquilucan county in the center state of Mexico. Its population is about 242,167 people according to the 2010 census (INEGI 2011). This anonymous Twitter account of a neighbor in that community has 9,169 followers as of 21 January 2012, eight times more than the official county Twitter account (@mdehuixquilucan) with only 1,373 followers.

According to TweetStats this account sends 33 tweets per day (611 tweets per month, on average); the FollowFriday ranking based on user recommendations ranks this account at 213th in México and 1892nd in the Spanish-speaking ranking. Using the tool TweetStats, @vecinodeteca has had a consistent increase in the number of messages—tweets—and people subscribed to the profile—followers; according to this data, the influence of this citizen is increasing in its community (see Fig. 15.1).

The most commonly used words and phrases from the account's tweets are provided in the cloud analysis (see Fig. 15.2), where we notice that many of the topics are related to other neighborhoods (bosques, interlomas), services (trash, water, streets, drops, park, bridges), or newspapers reporting on state issues (reforma-edomex, universal-edomex). Very few of them are complaints, and one commonly used word (indicated by its size) is the name of the mayor: Alfredo del Mazo, who is directly referenced on several occasions by the users and the administrator of the account.

The use of Twitter to inform public opinion and build an online community produces more groups in the area that try to emulate the same political pressure of @vecinodeteca. Table 15.1 presents other neighborhoods in the area of Huixquilucan, which have started similar efforts via both Twitter and/or Facebook. In Huixquilucan, this citizen interaction effort only uses the features of Twitter, like DM, retweets, or twitpic to enhance communication; it also becomes an alternative communication channel, since followers promote information collected by other sources, like other neighbors, the newsmedia, and the Reforma newspaper. Figure 15.3 shows the impact of retweets of messages from @vecinodeteca, and the persons or organizations that use this account most often.

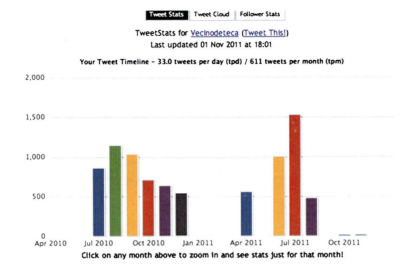

Fig. 15.1 @vecinodeTeca Stats. *Source* tweetsats (November 2011)

Fig. 15.2 @VecinodeTeca TweetCloud. *Source* TweetStats

15.5 Conclusions and Future Research

The use of social media in government is an emerging trend. This chapter provides evidence of the different kinds of interactions that exist or could potentially exist through the use of Twitter in government settings. Empirical data was provided from three cases that each describe a particular situation in which the use of Twitter by citizens promoted policy initiatives and influenced government decision-making at the local, state, and national levels.

Table 15.1 Neighborhood groups using Twitter March–November 2011

	March 2011		November 2011	
	Tweets	Followers	Tweets	Followers
@CdSatelite	4,870	2,052	21,289	9,898
@colonosteca	237	449	357	822
@InterlomasUnido	50	271	50	596
@VozEsmeralda	335	214	1463	724
@lasarboledas	450	196	1,176	797
@famunidas	217	146	292	162

Fig. 15.3 @VecinodeTeca Retweet. Source: TwitterStats November 2011

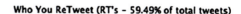
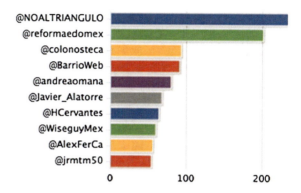

The main findings are consistent with previous studies. For instance, it is not clear whether governments understand the advantages of this kind of technology, and there is not always a clear strategy. Wigand (2010) and (Bertot et al. 2012a, b) describe the different ways government could use this tool to promote transparency or transform interactions with citizens; however, they do not provide empirical evidence. Qualitative data provided in the previous sections support their argument and advance the discussion about further research in this area, particularly the need for a research methodology and metrics for the development of these types of studies.

Opening Twitter accounts and using them strategically to interact with users could influence the interactions between citizens and governments and could be a first step toward other interactions with citizens. However, the development of an integrated strategy to enhance collaboration and participation between citizens and governments should be seen as an essential component. For instance, the use of Twitter without a more comprehensive strategy that includes multiple organizational processes and technologies (such as websites, mobile apps, Facebook, YouTube, blogs, wikis, etc.) could be seen as an isolated effort that becomes an alternative information channel, but will not be used for more complex and fruitful government-citizen interactions.

Further research is needed in several related areas. The first one is to analyze the content of the tweets that are sent by governments to citizens and vice versa. This analysis could reveal greater detail about the real use and interaction that these kinds of tools allow in government settings. A second area is to study the citizen perspective in terms of the use of this kind of tool and the actual interaction with government agencies. The three cases presented in this chapter focus on situations in which citizens are the main actors. However, there is not enough evidence about the interests and motivations of citizens in terms of their use of Web 2.0 tools and applications to interact with government. It is important to understand these motivations and their consequences in public policies and society.

Similarly, a third research area could be to understand the motivations and strategies of public servants and government officials who are using Twitter. There are instances in which a government stopped using its Twitter account completely, or at least some of its features. This selective behavior and its consequences should be analyzed and explained. A fourth research area could be to analyze the impact of Twitter on government communication in the context of other electronic media and Web 2.0 tools and applications (e.g., Facebook, YouTube, email, chats, etc.). This analysis should help to determine the usefulness of this tool as a complement to others and provide guidance for the development of comprehensive strategies. Finally, a fifth research area is related to understanding the actual costs of an integrated social media strategy and the real outcomes or consequences in terms of citizen satisfaction, organizational efficiencies, better coordination, transparency, accountability, and legitimacy.

There is clearly an important trend in terms of using Twitter and other Web 2.0 tools and applications in government to promote more interaction with citizens. Similarly, citizens are increasingly using these tools as participation channels and ways to exercise an influence on government decision-making. Therefore, governments should develop more comprehensive and integrative strategies with the purpose of promoting citizen participation and engagement in a proactive fashion. Being reactive seems not to be a good alternative, since citizens are well aware of these technologies and governments could become important social actors in the current technology-enabled environment. The question is, can governments effectively use these technologies to build networks of citizens and work jointly with them? Time and Twitter will tell us.

References

Ampofo, L., N. Anstead, et al. . 2011. Trust, confidence, and credibility: Citizen responses on Twitter to opinion polls during the 2010 UK general election." *Information Communication and Society* 14(6): 850-871.

Bannister, Frank, and Regina Connolly. 2011. Trust and transformational government: A proposed framework for research. *Government Information Quarterly* 28 (2):137-147. doi:10.1016/j.giq.2010.06.010.

Belanger, France, and Lemuria Carter. 2008. Trust and risk in e-government adoption. *The Journal of Strategic Information Systems* 17 (2):165–176. doi:10.1016/j.jsis.2007.12.002.

Bertot, John Carlo, Paul T. Jaeger, and Justin M. Grimes. 2012a. Promoting transparency and accountability through ICTs, social media, and collaborative e-government. *Transforming Government People Process and Policy* 6 (1):78–91. doi:10.1108/17506161211214831.

Bertot, John Carlo, Paul T. Jaeger, and Derek Hansen. 2012b. The impact of polices on government social media usage: Issues, challenges, and recommendations. *Government Information Quarterly* 29 (1):30–40. doi:10.1016/j.giq.2011.04.004.

Blaser, Britt, David Weinberger, and Joe Trippi. 2009. Digital government through social networks: how citizens can aggregate their money and votes to define digital government: Digital Government Society of North America.

Boyd, Danah, and Eszter Hargittai. 2010. Facebook privacy settings: Who cares? *First Monday* 15 (8):23.

Curtin, Deirdre, and Albert Jacob Meijer. 2006. Does transparency strengthen legitimacy? *Information Polity* 11 (2):109–122.

Cheong, Marc, and Vincent Lee. 2011. A microblogging-based approach to terrorism informatics: Exploration and chronicling civilian sentiment and response to terrorism events via Twitter. *Information Systems Frontiers* 13 (1):45–59. doi:10.1007/s10796-010-9273-x.

Chi, Feng, and Nathan Yang. 2010. Twitter in Congress : Outreach vs Transparency. *Social Sciences*:1–20.

de Kool, D., and J. van Wamelen, J. 2008. Web 2.0: A New Basis for E-Government?

Diakopoulos, Nicholas A., and David A. Shamma. 2010. Characterizing debate performance via aggregated twitter sentiment. Paper presented at the Proceedings of the 28th international conference on Human factors in computing systems, Atlanta, Georgia, USA.

Diaz, Catalina. 2011. Tras detención de tuiteros, disminuye uso del hashtag #verfollow. Milenio Group.

Dutton, William H. 2009. The Fifth Estate Emerging through the Network of Networks. *Prometheus* 27 (1):1–15 %U doi:10.1080/08109020802657453.

Eliason, Emma, and Jonas Lundberg. 2006. The appropriateness of Swedish municipality web site designs. Paper presented at the Proceedings of the 4th Nordic conference on Human-computer interaction: changing roles, Oslo, Norway.

Estalella, Adolfo, and Elisenda Ardevol. 2011. e-research: challenges and opportunities for social sciences. *Convergencia Revista de Ciencias Sociales* 18 (55):87–111.

Expansion, CNN. 2010. Twitter, ¿Enemigo del Alcoholimetro? http://www.cnnexpansion.com/tecnologia/2010/01/18/twitter-enemigo-del-alcoholimetro. Accessed 09 febrero 2011 2012.

Java, Akshay, Xiaodan Song, Tim Finin, and Belle Tseng. 2007. Why we twitter: understanding microblogging usage and communities. ACM.

Gallupe, R. Brent. 2007. The Tyranny of Methodologies in Information Systems Research 1. *Data Base For Advances In Information Systems* 38 (3):20–28. doi:10.1145/1278253.1278258.

Golbeck, Jennifer, Justin M Grimes, and Anthony Rogers. 2010. Twitter Use by the U. S. Congress. *Journal of the American Society for Information Science* 61:1612–1621. doi:10.1002/asi.

Grimmelikhuijsen, Stephan G. 2010. Transparency of Public Decision-Making: Towards Trust in Local Government? *Policy & Internet* 2 (1). doi:10.2202/1944-2866.1024.

Harfoush, Rahaf. 2009. *Yes We Did! An inside look at how social media built the Obama brand* 1st Aufl.: New Riders Press.

Hechos. 2010. Testigo reveló en Twitter balacera frente al ITESM. In *noticias*, ed. noticias: You Tube.

Hewson, Claire. 2008. Internet-mediated research as an emergent method and its potential role in facilitating mixed methods research. In *Handbook of Emergent Methods*, eds. Hesse-Biber, Sharlene Nagy, Leavy, and Patricia, 543–570. **New York**: Guilford Press.

Honey, C., and S. C. Herring. 2009. Beyond Microblogging: Conversation and Collaborationvia Twitter.

INEGI. 2011. Population by State. http://cuentame.inegi.org.mx/monografias/informacion/mex/poblacion/default.aspx?tema=me&e=15. Accessed 1 November 2011 2011.

Juarez, Geraldine. 2011a. Gobierno veracruzano plantea legislación exprés para juzgar a los "tuiteros" presos. Mexico City: Alt1040.

Juarez, Geraldine. 2011b. Se dicta auto de formal prisión a los dos "tuiteros" veracruzanos. In *Alt1040*. Mexico City: Alt1040.

Linders, Dennis. 2011. We-Government: an anatomy of citizen coproduction in the information age. Paper presented at the Proceedings of the 12th Annual International Digital Government Research Conference: Digital Government Innovation in Challenging Times, College Park, Maryland.

Maciel, Cristiano, Lic Roque, nio, and Ana Cristina Bicharra Garcia. 2009. Democratic citizenship community: a social network to promote e-deliberative process: Digital Government Society of North America.

Maciel, Cristiano, Lic Roque, nio, and Ana Cristina Bicharra Garcia. 2010. Interaction and communication resources in collaborative e-democratic environments: The democratic citizenship community. *Info. Pol.* 15 (1,2):73–88.

Martinez, Regina. 2011. Liberan a cibernautas acusados de terrorismo y sabotaje. *Proceso*.

Monroy-Hernández, Andrés. 2011. Gritar fuego con un hashtag o las consecuencias del supuesto twitterrorismo. In *Blog de la Redaccion*. Mexico DF: Revista Nexos.

Näkki, Pirjo, Asta Bäck, Teemu Ropponen, Juha Kronqvist, Kari A Hintikka, and Auli Harju. 2011. Social media for citizen participation Report on the Somus project. In *Vtt Publications*.

Noticias, SDP. 2010. Estudiante Narra por Twitter irrupcion del Ejercito en el Tec de Monterrey. http://sdpnoticias.com/sdp/contenido/nacional/2010/03/22/19/1013808. Accessed febrero 8, 2012 2010.

Oates, Sarah, Diana Marie Owen, and Rachel Kay Gibson. 2006. *The Internet and politics : citizens, voters and activists*. Democratization studies. London; New York: Routledge.

O'Reilly, Tim. 2005. What Is Web 2.0 | O'Reilly Media %U http://oreilly.com/pub/a/oreilly/tim/news/2005/09/30/what-is-web-20.html. O'Reilly.

Phelan, Owen, Kevin McCarthy, and Barry Smyth. 2009. Using Twitter to Recommend Real-Time Topical News. ACM.

Riva-Palacio, Raymundo. 2009. La cruzada de Internet Necesario.

Rose, J. 2009. The role of Social networking software in eParticipation. *DEMOnet Booklet* 28:403–426. doi:10.1177/0894439309341626.

Soberanes, Rodrigo. 2011. Un rumor en 'Twitter' despierta psicosis en Veracruz; desalojaron escuelas. *CNN Mexico*.

Tapscott, Don, and Anthony D. Williams. 2006. Wikinomics: How Mass Collaboration Changes Everything. Portfolio Hardcover.

Wigand, F. D. L. 2010. Twitter in Government: Building Relationships One Tweet at a Time. In *Information Technology: New Generations (ITNG), 2010 Seventh International Conference on*. Las Vegas, NV.

Wilson, David W., Xiaolin Lin, Phil Longstreet, and Saonee Sarker. 2011. Web 2.0: A Definition, Literature Review, and Directions for Future Research. Paper presented at the Americas Conference on Information Systems, Detroit Michigan.

Wilson, Jason. 2011. Playing with politics: Political fans and Twitter faking in post-broadcast democracy. *Convergence: The International Journal of Research into New Media Technologies* 17 (4):445–461.

Zhao, Dejin, and Mary Beth Rosson. 2009. How and why people Twitter: the role that micro-blogging plays in informal communication at work. ACM.

Chapter 16
Secrecy Versus Openness: Democratic Adaptation in a Web 2.0 Era

Jeffrey Roy

16.1 Introduction

Social media and new technologies hold great promise to improve societies and economies, but how do governments deal with risks related to transparency and open data, cyber-security, minority capture in public participation and deliberation, the high failure rate of ICT projects in governments, and the risk of being locked into expensive low-performing systems?

p. 10, The Future of Government: World Economic Forum 2011

As the quote above implies, governmental performance and democratic legitimacy hinge upon successful adaptation within an increasingly networked environment both digitally and socially. The purpose of this chapter is two-fold; first, to sketch out the main structural and cultural tension points between the Westminster model of democratic governance and emerging contours of Web-2.0 stylized reforms associated with likeminded discussions of Gov 2.0; and second, to examine recent reform efforts in Canada and their potential to resolve such tensions.

The chapter is therefore organized as follows. Building upon this brief introduction, section two is a consideration of the inherent tensions between traditional government (within the Westminster Parliamentary paradigm) and new governance dynamics facilitated by networked technologies and online communities (denoted as Web 2.0); the issue of secrecy and information control is examined as central to understanding such tensions. Section three then shifts toward emerging experimentation with openness in government and initiatives predicated on information sharing and a related shift away from control toward collaboration and engagement. By way of conclusion, section four summarizes the resulting challenge for Canadian democratic governance that lies ahead.

J. Roy (✉)
School of Public Administration, Dalhousie University,
Halifax, NS B3H 3J5, Canada
e-mail: roy@dal.ca; jroy44@gmail.com

C. G. Reddick and S. K. Aikins (eds.), *Web 2.0 Technologies and Democratic Governance*, Public Administration and Information Technology 1, DOI: 10.1007/978-1-4614-1448-3_16, © Springer Science+Business Media New York 2012

16.2 Web 2.0 Versus Westminster Democracy: Inherent Tensions

While the Internet initially facilitated the e-government efforts of service integration and communication, Web 2.0 has emerged as a proxy not only for new technological capacities but also for a new social paradigm with sweeping implications for organizations in all sectors. The Wikipedia definition of Web 2.0 is as follows: 'Web 2.0 is a term describing the trend in the use of World Wide Web technology and web design that aims to enhance creativity, information sharing, and, most notably, collaboration among users.'[1] This latter emphasis on user collaboration is the basis of the potential for a new and much more participative ethos among governments, the private and civic sectors and a more empowered, and engaged citizenry (Eggers 2005; Shirky 2008; Williams 2008; Roy 2010).

Consequently, a key challenge for the public sector thus lies balancing three simultaneous sets of forces: (1) in presenting a more integrated front-end face to the user (who may well be seeking simplicity and one point of access); (2) reconfiguring the back-office functions of government in a manner that supports integrative services where warranted (i.e. demanded and deemed beneficial to both users and government); and (3) facilitating new forms of collective intelligence both within and outside of the public sector in accordance with a more networked environment.

In seeking new strategies and mechanisms to adapt and address this multi-faceted challenge, cloud computing and social media are indeed two sides of the same coin: both reflect an era of virtualization and openness in which data and knowledge are increasingly gravitating to online venues for processing, storing, and sharing. Both are intertwined with the emergence of Web 2.0 which denotes a more participative Internet era based less upon one-way communication and more upon collaboration and active engagement (Shirky 2008; Williams 2008; Roy 2010).

Whereas cloud computing—built to some degree upon open source software movements that has challenged and now rivals traditional proprietary models of intellectual property and control, represents the technical architecture of a more open and participative Web (i.e. the tools and systems used by individuals and organizations to undertake tasks), social media personifies the new social and participative architecture (i.e. the creation and sharing of content online). Across both cloud computing and social media spheres, openness and interdependency supersede traditional models of hierarchical control and proprietary ownership (Wyld 2010).

Within such a context, a more agile and mobile public sector is said to be an important dimension of a collective vision for a more knowledgeable, collaborative, and unified society; an enticing perspective on our digital future. One such optimistic vantage point is presented by Accenture Consulting—a value shift to social prosperity brought about through ubiquitous Internet access and the collective intelligence that results:

---

[1] http://en.wikipedia.org/wiki/Web_2

Cooperation, diversity, openness and sharing of knowledge will not only have a dramatic effect on the economy, but also on society as a whole. Society has become more inclusive where people follow the credo of "share and win." The focus shifts away from the individual toward the community and common welfare. People decide to make use of their collective intelligence, build networks and organize their community activities by themselves. This approach toward collective social prosperity fosters new ways of thinking and dealing with information and intellectual property (p. 7, Accenture 2010).

Yet, the reality of realizing such a vision is highly complex—and widely contested, as governments must both navigate between shifting patterns of market and societal behavior and orchestrate a collective path inclusive of and accountable to all. As such, there are important tensions among the initial phases of e-government (a de facto form of e-government 1.0) that centred on service and security and the leveraging of the Internet for information provision and service delivery improvement, and today's emphasis on e-government 2.0 (or Gov 2.0) where new patterns of more networked and participatory governance are more closely intertwined with the dimensions of transparency and trust. Moreover, whereas service reforms took place within, for the most part, existing democratic institutional architectures, democracy becomes more contested via pressures stemming from a more participatory and connected citizenry.

16.2.1 A Culture of Secrecy

Within such a fluid and shifting context, the central issue, that threatens to erode democratically legitimacy in this new era, is the tension between a traditional ethos of governmental secrecy on the one hand, and intensifying pressures for transparency across society on the other hand.

Indeed, a parallel of sorts has emerged between the emergence of e-government and a rhetoric of wider transparency resulting (either in terms of demands from outside of government or promises from government leaders to leverage the Internet to disseminate more widely information), and charges against provincial and federal governments in Canada in terms of endemic secrecy (Roy 2008). These, seemingly contradictory, forces are the result of governments embracing the Internet as a platform for openness in specifically controlled ways—especially in terms of service provision, while resisting other demands and opportunities for transparency that for one reason or another may appear threatening or destabilizing.

One case in point with respect to transparency and accountability is the contrasting efforts of the US federal and Canadian federal governments in terms of communications, awareness, and provision of oversight of federal stimulus spending in recent years. When President Obama signed into law the historically huge stimulus bill of some $800 Billion in federal spending, there was recognition that cronyism and corruption could plague this massive government investment. The Obama administration thus sought to leverage the Internet—creating recovery.gov, a highly sophisticated, interactive website tracking stimulus spending across the country. To ensure the site did not simply function as a political communications tool (more on Canada's approach in a moment), recovery.gov is overseen by an independent, Recovery Accountability and Transparency Board. Mandated by the stimulus bill it has two goals: to provide transparency and to prevent and detect fraud and wasteful spending. The Chairperson is a former Inspector General with considerable experience pursuing government mismanagement and lobbying corruption (an additional 12 Inspector Generals serve alongside).

While the Board's mission is to provide more direct openness and reporting to the public at large, their work also facilitates Congressional scrutiny and oversight. Accordingly, the Administration's own efforts to be transparent provide greater oxygen for political scrutiny and accountability, ideally assisting the White House in avoiding the sort of reactionary media and special interest exposing of questionable conduct only well after the fact (when typically embarrassing details have accumulated to damaging levels). There is an important online dimension here as well—consistent with Web 2.0 and open data principles, as many external and independent watchdog organizations have established their own online tracking tools (leveraging the recovery.gov data sources) in order to better report on results and further mobilize public involvement, raising democratic literary in the process.

In Canada, by contrast, openness and accountability were largely subsumed to communications theatrics, the public interest apparently served by a relentless flow of television and billboard ads extolling the benefits of federal infrastructure investments. Furthermore, when Kevin Page, the Parliamentary Budget Officer, began to probe spending plans and thus requested documentation, such requests were initially thwarted and then met with a farcical mountain of paper (as nearly 5,000 pages of internal Treasury Board documents were delivered, in paper form to Mr. Page's office for review).

This defensive mentality and corresponding preference for communications and inward containment of information is part and parcel of the DNA of Westminster governance—politically and administratively (and how both are intertwined). Here lies the Achilles heel of digital transformation—namely the engrained resistance of representational democracy and its national institutions to openness and power-sharing and the erosion of public engagement and trust that results (Roy 2008, 2011). Such political tendencies also shape the actions of public servants accordingly. One recent study based upon interviews with public servants from across federal and provincial governments summarized the blockage in the following manner:

- *The most significant impediment to government use of social media is the "clay layer" in management and the hierarchical public service culture.*
- *Government has not adapted to the promise of new media to liberate information, foster collaboration and openness and promote organizational change.*
- *The public sector needs organizational change, developing a culture of trust and openness that will allow public servants to take advantage of the benefits that social media offer (executive summary, Fyfe and Crookall 2010).*

Within such an inward and control-oriented setting shunning openness as much as possible, it can hardly be surprising that e-democracy has come to denote little more than hyper-partisan blogging and communications. An examination of the most recent federal election campaign offers evidence in support of such a claim; an analysis of social media usage during the election underscores that far from engaging Canadians in new political channels, Twitter, and Facebook were overwhelmingly communications tools escalating chatter and conflict among party operatives—and thus covered and reported upon by journalists for traditional media outlets in print and on television (Baran 2011).

Rather than widening interest and engagement via more openness and information-sharing; then, social media usage within existing political processes instead tends to limit participation and interest due in large part to a mentality of secrecy that reinforces the cleavage between a mobilized minority of insiders and a disenchanted and disinterested majority. Yet, as pressures for reform and more participatory and transparent mechanisms invariably build in the Internet era, government resistance is gradually giving way to tentative explorations of an alternative approach.

16.3 Toward a New Ethos of Openness?

Social media is rapidly becoming a worldwide phenomenon with profound implications for societies, markets, and governments. In a world of search engines, social media, and open communities devising 'apps' for ubiquitous and mobile Internet devices, companies, and governments are therefore striving to leverage the collective potential of networking. As Shirky and others point out, plummeting costs of organizing collectively coupled with plentiful information and tools for collaborating produce conditions that are ripe for networks (Shirky 2008, 2011).

Yet, as we have seen in the preceding section, governments are not always leading these changes but rather they must find a new role as a catalyst and partner in more outward and networked governance arrangements. What results is a powerful schism for government and public servants between the old and the new. Thomas (2008) provides a useful starting point in framing the schism, by way of contrasting 'government' with 'governance':

> The tensions between centralized government and decentralized governance are heightened by the public mood of mistrust and weak confidence in governments. This fundamental shift towards governance from the traditional processes of government has numerous implications for the future role of the public service, many of which cannot be clearly foreseen at this point (p. 2, Thomas 2008).

Importantly, social media platforms and technologies can be viewed as a means of extending this paradigm via a mainly communications-oriented mentality. Many governments, for instance, have added features to their online portals such as RSS feeds and Twitter updates—important additions but ones that do little to alter the fundamental orientation and organizational of public sector entities. By contrast, Gov 2.0, within an emerging context of Web 2.0 and social media is much more about collaboration, participation, and consultation (much more about governance in Thomas's depiction above). A Web 2.0 ethos ideally aligns more with Thomas's notion of governance, underpinned by a massive expansion of the means to both produce and share information and transform such information flows into creative and applied forms of knowledge. This knowledge generation and the wider shared learning resulting is a key basis of mass collaboration (Tapscott and Williams 2006; Flumian 2009).

The emergence of so-called 'open data' initiatives the world over reflects elements of shared ownership models beginning to gain traction across information, ideas, and infrastructure. Driven by the rise of social media and collective intelligence on the one hand, and the emphasis in recent years on citizen engagement and participatory democracy on the other hand, such strategies are at their core about reframing information as a holding and asset of public sector authorities to a shared basis of not only oversight and accountability, but also direct involvement in the design and delivery of services and solutions.

With respect to the closely related emphasis on 'apps,' there is a more direct technological association with the phenomena of open communities of applications developers devising mini-programs of all sorts to run on various smart phone (and now tablet) devices. The most prominent of such platforms is the Apple operating system and corresponding apps community for the wildly successful i-Phone; at the same time, the growth of Google's Android operating system represents an open source competitor gaining traction and thereby widening the pool of potential participants in Apps communities for both public and private platforms and usages.

Such tensions between proprietary and open source operating systems notwithstanding, the logic of openness and empowerment in the private realm attracted attention from observers in government, notably the aforementioned, former US federal government CIO, Vivek Kundra. While serving as CIO to the Washington DC authority, he oversaw what is believed to be the continent's first experimentation in 'apps for democracy' by inviting citizens to develop new service concepts to improve the quality of life of residents.

Akin to the operating system platforms of private sector actors such as Apple, the Washington DC portal would provide a basis for such mobilization—and a basis for housing the data holdings in an unprecedented raw form. Such holdings, in combination with Web 2.0 tools and methodologies and data sources from elsewhere on the Internet, thereby enabled interested and capable residents to devise their own 'apps' for showcasing and ultimately for widespread adaptation across the community.[2] Several Canadian municipalities joined forces and forged a group of four to promote such efforts nationally—leading to the announcement of an open data by the federal government just prior to the 2011 federal election and BC becoming the first Province during the summer of this same year to launch its own site.[3]

---

[2] http://www.appsfordemocracy.org/

[3] Re the Canadian municipal 'G4' please see—http://cge.itincanada.ca/index.php?cid=314&id=14939

Re the Government of BC Open Data Portal please see—http://www.data.gov.bc.ca/

We can thus point to the partial beginnings of a wider cultural revolution for both democratic politics and public sector operations (and thus the roles and accountabilities of public servants navigating such changes). Though tempting, in some instances, to dismiss open data initiatives in some jurisdictions as little more than open government gimmickry, they, nonetheless, reflect the growing interest in and commitment to openness by an expanding cadre of government managers and elected officials (such as those championing such experiments in the aforementioned jurisdictions).

They are also an important linkage among the advent of cloud computing, mobile Internet devices, and social media. Indeed, another open data pioneer, the City of New York, demonstrates how social media is an enabler of both enhanced service and public engagement. Accordingly, the digital city 'road map' includes four inter-related dimensions: open government; access; industry; and engagement (NYC Road Map for the Digital City 2011). With respect to engagement, seeking to make ample and innovative usage of social media the City has committed to a number of strategic initiatives including online 'listening sessions' across local boroughs in order to encourage input and involvement on the part of the citizenry (ibid.).

As governments seek to experiment in such a manner, an important challenge of moving down a new path of openness and engagement stems from the risks of exposure—especially in a government culture of risk mitigation and political spin (closely intertwined with the sensationalism of traditional media especially via television imagery). The potential for a Wiki-Leaks stylized gotcha mentality is real here, creating a detrimental spiral of cynicism and declining trust in public institutions:

> Revealing previously confidential information—such as the salaries of officials—can, in theory, shift power from the former "holders of secrets" to the newly informed public. But two conditions have to be met for transparency as a source of accountability to work. First, the accountable bodies must be able and willing to provide the information; and second, the public should be able to examine it in the light of an accepted standard. While the first condition is largely met, the second is not…
>
> Of course the public should play a central role in deciding what represents value for money in public services, but the current approach is unlikely to foster any meaningful deliberation or empowerment. What we need more of is public debate, or "good conversations" between professionals and communities to avoid officials losing touch in the first place. The appropriate place to achieve this is local government because circumstances vary in different parts of the country.[4]

This invocation of the importance of conversation underscores a similar theme in the literature on social media and Web 2.0 in the workplace (previous subsection), their commonality being a rethinking of the roles and inter-relationships of public servants, elected officials, and the citizenry. This quote also demands a reflection as to which level of government is best placed to lead participative engagement via social media—since national level entities often have greater

---

[4] http://www.guardian.co.uk/commentisfree/2010/oct/03/transparency-trust-public-sector/print

fiscal resources and digital visibility, whereas local authorities benefit from closer proximity to community constituents and are better able to blend online and offline processes.

Emphasizing these localized advantages, Carr-West outlines four lessons for proceeding with social media innovation within relatively more welcoming confines of local government systems (as opposed to more media centric and adversarial national polities):

> *Free people to innovate: allow council staff and community members to be driven by their passions. Online engagement tools don't require massive IT infrastructures or budgets, they can be pulled together from free web tools. If people want to build something, let them.*
>
> *Try everything: it's no good waiting for the perfect tool. We're in an era of restless technological change and if you try and work out exactly how to match tools to the job, the tools (and possibly the job) will have changed before you even get started.*
>
> *Be open about what you're doing: particularly where it is experimental and be clear about what worked and what did not.*
>
> *Allow good ideas to emerge: wherever they come from and however much they disrupt established hierarchies or ways of working (p. 8, Carr-West 2009).*

In sum, what seems apparent is that social media, open data and other Web 2.0–type platforms and tools are exposing the limits of a government mentality of information containment and control. Instead, new and wider forms of experimentation are emerging where notions of transparency and shared ownership of information are central pillars of a more participative and open ethos.

16.4 Conclusion

The Internet has given rise to the formation of new collaborative communities and civic formations, new business models and indeed entirely new industries, and new service delivery models in the public sector. What remains outstanding is democratic innovation that seeks to fundamentally alter the conduct of politics and the execution of democratic accountability in manners that align with the potential of an online and more participative ethos. The emergence of Web 2.0 and the explosion of increasingly affordable and powerful mobile technologies greatly accentuate this ethos and render extremely problematic any claims that democratic architectures created centuries past can continue to serve us well in our contemporary and rapidly evolving setting.

Such is the great challenge of our time across both established and emerging democracies—namely, innovative and participative approaches to institutional adaptation and redesign. In a sector that traditionally values methodical slowness and structural stability much more so than in private industry (where much of personalized technological empowerment is presently rooted), it is both normal and desirable that a new and more digital version of democracy remains very much a work in progress. At the same time, perfection cannot be the enemy of the good, as it is increasingly urgent to adapt past traditions and mechanisms for today's younger generations that have simply not known a world without Internet connectivity and—paradoxically, a democratization of information and authority in most all sectors of socio economic activity with the notable exception of formalized democratic politics.

The overarching challenge of social media and democratic governance, therefore, lies in fostering more flexible information, knowledge and learning architectures for the public sector as a whole; i.e, facilitating the creation of new and adaptive governance models that are now much more feasible and arguably necessary in an era of ubiquitous and mobile digital technologies on the one hand, and social media engagements on the other hand.

References

Accenture (2010). *Information 2015: Reforming the Paradigm*. New York: Accenture.

Baran, Y. (2011). *Social Media in Campaign 2011: A Noncanonical Take on the Twitter Effect. Policy Options (June)*. Montreal: Institute for Research on Public Policy.

Carr-West, J. (2009). *Local Government 3.0: Local Councils Can Respond to the New Web Agenda*. Local Government Information Unit.

Eggers, W. (2005). *Government 2.0: Using Technology to Improve Education, Cut Red Tape, Reduce Gridlock and Enhance Democracy*, New York, NY: Rowman and Littlefield Publishers.

Fyfe, T., & Crookall, P. (2010). *Social Media and Public Sector Policy Dilemmas*. IPAC.

Flumian, M. (2009). *Citizens as Prosumers: The Next Frontier of Service Innovation*. Ottawa, Canada: nGenera Institute on Governance.

Roy, J. (2008). Beyond Westminster Governance: Bringing Politics and Public Service into the Network Era. *Canadian Public Administration, 5*(4), 54–568.

Roy, J. (2010). Web 2.0 and Canada's Public Sector: Emerging Opportunities and Challenges. In B. W. Wirtz, E-Government—Grundlagen, Instrumente, Strategien. Wiesbaden, Gabler, 2010.

Roy, J. (2011). *Politicians and the Public: Bridging the Great Divide. Policy Options* (October). Montreal: Institute for Research on Public Policy.

Shirky, C. (2008). *Here Comes Everybody: The Power of Organizing Without Organizations*. New York: Penguin Group.

Shirky, C. (2011, February). The Political Power of Social Media. *Foreign Affairs*. Council of Foreign Relations.

Thomas, P. G. (2008, May). Political-Administrative Interface in Canada's Public Sector. *Optimum Online, 38*(2), 21–29.

Tapscott, D. & Williams, A. (2006). *WIKINOMICS—How Mass Collaboration Changes Everything*. New York: Penguin Group.

Williams, A. D. (2008). Government 2.0: Wikinomics and the challenge to government, *Canadian Government Executive* (Ottawa, www.netgov.ca).

Wyld, D. C. (2010). The Cloudy Future of Government IT: Cloud Computing and the Public Sector Around the World. *International Journal of Web & Semantic Technology, 1*(1), 1–20.

World Economic Forum (2011). *The Future of Government: Lessons Learned from Around the World*. World Economic Forum: Global Agenda Council on the Future of Government.

NYC *Roadmap for the Digital City* (2011). The City of New York.

Chapter 17
Blending Social Media with Parliamentary Websites: Just a Trend, or a Promising Approach to e-Participation?

**Aspasia Papaloi, Eleni Revekka Staiou
and Dimitris Gouscos**

17.1 Introduction

The research question discussed in this chapter is how social media can be used by public organizations and especially by parliaments to engage citizens and open up the way to participation.

Digital technologies, especially in the form of Internet and social media, can greatly facilitate communication, since they are used by a large proportion of the population. Social media is easy to use, not costly, can be tailored to the needs of users and organizations, and has a high penetration at age groups of active citizens.

Certain parliaments are currently attempting to use the same communication channels that citizens prefer in order to attract them. Social media is a natural choice. Efforts are needed to integrate these tools in the parliamentary communication channels. Still, as these efforts require time and experience to give tangible results, there is currently a gap between what parliaments can offer and what the public needs.

The two sections that come next briefly discuss the relation between social media, e-participation, electronic parliaments (e-parliaments) and their service offerings, and review some examples of social media use by parliamentary institutions.

A. Papaloi (✉) · E. R. Staiou · D. Gouscos
Laboratory of New Technologies in Communication, Education and the Mass Media,
Faculty of Communication and Media Studies, University of Athens, 5 Stadiou str,
10562 Athens, Greece
e-mail: apapaloi@media.uoa.gr

E. R. Staiou
e-mail: erstaiou@media.uoa.gr

D. Gouscos
e-mail: gouscos@media.uoa.gr

C. G. Reddick and S. K. Aikins (eds.), *Web 2.0 Technologies and Democratic Governance*, Public Administration and Information Technology 1, DOI: 10.1007/978-1-4614-1448-3_17, © Springer Science+Business Media New York 2012

In the following section, the findings of a quantitative research on parliamentary institutions actually using social media are provided and discussed, with a view to assess the current presence of parliaments on social media and their level of interaction with citizens.

In the final part of this chapter a list of issues, factors, and perspectives for a strategic planning approach for the effective use of social media by parliaments is proposed, with a view to contribute to the way toward e-Participation and democratic governance.

17.2 State of Play in e-Participation and e-Parliaments: A Brief Overview

Numerous e-Participation initiatives have been implemented in local, regional, European, and international level. A detailed presentation of all these initiatives and application domains (campaigning, community building, consultation, deliberation, electioneering, information provision, mediation, polling and voting) is beyond the scope of this chapter. Nevertheless, some important points can be highlighted.

At a European context, a study by Panopoulou et al. (2009, p. 23) has brought forward two major findings: (a) interesting activities are being launched that address European countries as a whole in a multi-lingual context; and (b) "*the utilization degree of participation areas may vary according to participation level*", meaning that at a European or international level one-way communication (information provision) is preferred, while at local level two-way communication (e.g., consultation, spatial planning) can be pursued.

On the other hand, implementation of ICTs in parliaments worldwide transforms their traditional picture not only in terms of internal operations, but also in terms of communication with the citizens. The so-called "e-Parliament" premise has been introduced, with a view to applying technology in a way that facilitates everyday work of civil servants and parliamentarians, and at the same time transforms communication between citizens, parliaments, and parliament members in a more direct, transparent, and effective way.

Still, the issue of how and why citizens would be motivated to communicate with parliaments remains open. As noted in the earlier literature (Flickinger et al. 1995; Bakera et al. 1996), motivation to communicate implies rather a need to be informed than a predisposition to support, and obtaining information cannot be assumed to lead to support. However, as more recent research on the UK Parliament (Hansard Society 2011b, p. vi) suggests, knowledge can lead to awareness, interest, and eventually action, and citizens are interested to be informed because they care for an issue or an elected representative (approx. 65%) or want to have a say or take action (approx. 52%) (p. 11). As the Hansard report notes

What exists is demonstrably insufficient to engage the public; social media and changing attitudes mean that new methods of engagement are not optional extras but core parts of a public engagement strategy. They do not replace what is being done; they extend and enhance it. (p.vii)

Under these considerations, electronic services offered by parliaments online can be classified according to taxonomies including (Papaloi and Gouscos 2010, p. 107): Parliament-to-Parliament (P2P) services; Parliament-to-Members of the Parliament (P2MP) services;, Parliament-to-Citizen (P2C) services such as the Portuguese Parliament's Citizens' Space, with e-services for e-mailing parliamentary groups and representatives, e-petitions, blogs, and others (United Nations & Inter-Parliamentary Union 2010, p. 51); and Citizen-to-Parliament (C2P) services, such as the series of UK-based "MySociety" projects.

17.3 Efforts for e-Participation and e-Parliaments Using Social Media

Social media refers to online platforms whereby *"content and applications are no longer created and published by individuals, but instead are continuously modified by all users in a participatory and collaborative fashion"* (Kaplan and Haenlein 2010, as cited in Effing et al. 2011, p. 28). The key ideas are those of participation and of collaboration (Effing et al. 2011), because these are the main differences from online media built in the web 1.0 approach, where only the developer of a webpage owned the power to change its contents.

Social media have multiple affordances and capabilities. Social media users can interact in a peer-to-peer manner, publish their content alone or in collaboration with others, share it with their contacts, gather and discuss feedback, and eventually create their own markets, audiences, and communities (Blossom 2009). Content can be posted on blogs, wikis, and podcasts, organized with tags and then shared through RSS, social networking sites (SNS), and micro-blogging (twitter) feeds, whereas research efforts are underway for enriching social media with semantic Web facilities (Breslin et al. 2009).

Two independent studies, conducted for the European and the Norwegian Parliament, have reached the conclusion that younger parliamentarians are keener on using social media on their websites (Braghiroli 2011; Sæbø 2011). Additionally, the use of twitter in the Norwegian parliament resulted more in one-way communication rather than bidirectional interaction with the citizens (Sæbø 2011).

The "e-Democracia" project (http://www.edemocracia.gov.br) in Brazil, on the other hand, has aimed at citizens' engagement in the law-making process. This project combines Web 2.0 technologies and social media with offline legislative meetings such as committee hearings and intends to *"reach a broad audience that includes citizens, parliamentarians, civil servants, researchers, non-governmental organizations, and interest groups"* (United Nations & Inter-Parliamentary Union 2010, p. 39).

Another example is that of the US Congressional Committees project, a best practice website for 2010 including only up-to-date data on hearing schedules and other relevant documents, and informing visitors with targeted information. This process was enhanced through *"social media tools to allow users to send comments to the committee, subscribe to RSS and e-newsletters, or follow the work of the committee on twitter to abreast of its latest actions"* (Hansard Society 2011a, p. 16).

Combining e-Participation with social media leads to the concept of e-Participation 2.0, in which e-Participation services use social media technologies in order to include more citizens. These applications can be used by a larger number of users in everyday life (Näkki et al. 2011). As the use of social media is increasing (Buhl 2011), e-Participation 2.0 platforms are introduced in countries such as Germany, where they are used in consultations and citizens' discussion with participants in the order of 100,000.

The challenge for e-Participation 2.0 is to combine open public sector data, offered in an unbiased and usable manner, with social data, i.e., the content created by social media users and containing their personal views. This kind of linking is expected to create a two-way *understanding* (beyond mere interaction) between governments and citizens (Kalampokis et al. 2011).

Social media are cheap or free, highly customizable, easy to use, and allow e-participation projects to reach more people in different age groups. Today's teens, namely tomorrow's adults, are already alphabetized in social media and can use them in their interaction with governments for public service delivery (Osimo 2008, Baumgarten and Chui 2009). As Näkki et al. (2011, p. 53) state, the use of social media tools increases the possibility of participation, regardless of time and place.

Moreover, social media *"bring innovation by aggregating and mobilizing people and knowledge"* (Taufique and Shahriar 2011, p. 60). Ferro and Molinari (2010) explicitly outline e-Participation 2.0 as an innovation process, in need of a *"workable strategy"*. They stress that Policy designers need to reach citizens instead of vice versa, innovative applications need to embrace online users with various means including mobile technologies, and integrate underprivileged and excluded target groups *"by means of heterogeneous set of methods, tools and devices"*, as well as introduce *"stable forms of collection, interpretation and follow-up of the political will that is expressed by the citizens (…)"*.

Still, the actual involvement of citizens in the policy and decision-making process faces a number of roadblocks, regardless of the technologies used, and is by definition a multi-step evolution. Arnstein's classical ladder of citizen participation (Arnstein 1969), for instance, identifies eight discrete rungs from nonparticipation of citizens up to citizen control. What is more, in the author's own words, this typology does not include an analysis of

> the most significant roadblocks to achieving genuine levels of participation. These road-blocks lie on both sides of the simplistic fence. On the powerholders' side, they include racism, paternalism, and resistance to power redistribution. On the have-nots' side, they include inadequacies of the poor community's political socioeconomic infrastructure and knowledge-base, plus difficulties of organizing a representative and accountable citizens' group in the face of futility, alienation, and distrust.

These roadblocks are not automatically alleviated by any technology enabling citizen participation, whether social media-based or not. They have to do with the political culture and democratic will of citizens and powerholders, which can be cultivated, but certainly not enforced, through social media.

What is more, social media and social networks in particular, hide some dangers as well. The main problems regard privacy and danger of the users' personal data, spamming, and identity-related problems such as phishing (Al Hasib 2009). These problems represent a major source of criticism for social media, especially when attempting to develop "serious" applications in domains such as, for instance, education and citizen participation.

Last but not least, while citizen participation attempts to overcome some power divides, e-Participation efforts create some new critical digital divides, and especially so if they are based on more novel technologies such as social media. Not all citizens have access and competence in these tools, and the citizens not included in the social media space should certainly not be excluded from the citizen participation space. As a consequence, social media can be put at the service of e-Participation only in a blended approach, based on the co-existence and co-operation of multiple traditional, online, and social channels that actually include all citizens.

17.4 Current Social Media Use by Parliaments: Research and Findings

17.4.1 Scope, Objectives, and Limitations of the Research

The objective of the research reported in this section has been to investigate, through desk-research work and quantitative assessments, the following aspects of the current use of social media by parliamentary institutions in different countries:

- to what extent parliamentary institutions actually use social media
- to what extent this use of social media can move, from one-way communication between parliamentary institutions and citizens, to two-way interaction between them, as well as to engagement of users building more regular relationships with the accounts, facing them in their role (a) as content feed providers and (b) as parliamentary institutions
- to what extent the level of this use is related to the overall readiness of countries and people for social media.

To this end, the scope of the research has been delimited as follows:

- Three major social media have been included in the research, namely facebook, twitter, and youtube; all three are well established, and can serve all forms of use investigated.
- Countries of the European continent and the Americas have been considered in the research, with a significant level of social media readiness that has been assessed from publicly available statistics for facebook users, Internet users, and population (InternetWorldStats website, http://www.internetworldstats.com) as well as the e-government readiness and networked readiness rankings published, respectively, by the United Nations (UNDESA 2010) and the World Economic

Forum (Dutta and Mia 2011). Only the countries included in both those rankings, and having more than 100,000 facebook users, have been selected for further research.

- For countries with bicameral political systems, both parliamentary chambers have been considered for the research, either as different institutions in case they employ different websites and social media accounts, or as one institution, in case they share the same website and accounts.
- Only parliamentary institutions at a country level (as opposed to parliaments of federated regions or states) have been included in the research. A unique exception to this is the European Parliament, which is a case of special interest.
- Every parliamentary website has been checked for social media links on its homepage, since this is the only easy way for citizens to find a parliament's social media profiles. What is more, requiring a visible reference from the site to social media eliminates any doubts as to if a social media account officially represents a parliamentary institution or not.
- The extent of use of social media by parliamentary institutions and their citizen audience is assessed from quantitative parameters determined for the different social media platforms as follows: for facebook pages, counts of posts, comments, likes, shares, fans, and friends, users talking about the page; for twitter accounts, counts of tweets, accounts following, accounts followed, accounts listing, as well as twitter-wide ranking of the parliamentary account; for youtube channels, counts of uploaded videos, friends and subscriptions, channel views, video views, and subscribers; all these parameters have been studied by manually processing the public contents of social media accounts, plus gathering free online available statistics from websites such as TwitterCounter (http://twittercounter.com), TweetGrader (http://tweet.grader.com) and VidStatsX (http://vidstatsx.com).
- All data have been gathered from periodical snapshots since August 2011, and are updated as of the time of writing (mid-February 2012).

This way of work has faced the following limitations:

- Limited geography: Further research is needed at a global scale, including parliamentary democracies from Oceania, Asia, and Africa. Democracies in developing countries and the Arab world could well provide a different landscape and enrich the findings.
- A limited time horizon: as will be shown below, the use of social media by parliaments is evolving rapidly, without any signs of stabilization for the time being. More calendar time needs to be allocated in further research efforts for monitoring this phenomenon.
- Language of social media content: parliamentary profiles in social media, in their majority, are populated in national languages, which prevent understanding of the posts and the comments made. Still, this has no significant research work, which has focused on quantitative rather than qualitative dimensions.
- Need to focus on the institutional social media presence of parliaments, and not on the individual social media presence of elected representatives. Despite the fact that the latter is often important, it constitutes a different topic.

- Lack of knowledge about the parliaments' own perspectives: what parliaments aim to achieve through social media is not known in all these cases, and thus the success of their effort cannot be assessed. Again, this constitutes a subject of further research.

17.5 Findings on the Extent in Which Parliamentary Institutions Use Social Media

Finding #1.   More than 6 out of 10 from the 77 parliamentary institutions researched in Europe and the Americas have not yet any official accounts in facebook, twitter, or youtube.

In the 58 countries from Europe (European Union and non-EU) and the Americas that have been included in the research, 77 parliamentary institutions (also accounting for countries with bicameral political systems) have been identified and further researched. Out of these 77 institutions, 29 (less than 4 out of 10) have official accounts in at least one of the social media considered (facebook, twitter, and youtube).

Finding #2.   The parliamentary institutions that do have social media accounts usually employ at least two platforms of facebook, twitter, and youtube.

Finding #3.   The year of launch of official accounts on social media is different for different platforms. Official accounts have been launched in youtube as of 2007, in twitter as of 2009, and then in facebook as of 2010.

Finding #4.   Among the parliamentary institutions researched, youtube channels have been launched first but have remained fewer than twitter accounts which were launched afterwards, and may be soon outnumbered by facebook pages which were launched last (Table 17.1).

The shift of social media use focus by parliamentary institutions from youtube (2007 and onwards) to twitter (2009 and onwards) and then to facebook (2010 and onwards) corresponds, in a way, to the conceptual shift in the formality and regularity of the relationships with the audience brought about by these platforms: from relationships of both formal and regular user recurrence (youtube *subscribers*), to relationships with users promising to recur less formally but still regularly (twitter *followers*), to relationships with users claiming to return neither formally nor regularly (facebook *friends*).

Table 17.1 Existing social media accounts per platform, year of launch, and age (as of Feb 2012)

Platform	2007	2008	2009	2010	2011	Total	Avg. age
Youtube	2	1	4	4	1	12	29 m
Twitter	1	–	8	11	4	24	23 m
Facebook	–	–	–	4	17	21	12 m
Total	3	1	12	19	22	57	20 m

Table 17.2 Distribution of account owner activity on social media platforms

Platform	Account activity for years 2007–2011	Activity/month (as per avg. age of each platform)
Youtube	9.500	330
Twitter	139.000	6.000
Facebook	24.000	2.000
Total	172.500	

Finding #5.   The aggregate activity of social media accounts (mainly: upload videos on youtube, tweet, post on facebook) of the parliamentary institutions researched amounts, during the 5 years 2007–2011, to approx. 170.000 actions in total.

Finding #6.   Twitter account owners seem to perform per month approx. 18 times more actions that youtube channel owners, and approx. 3 times more actions than facebook page owners (Table 17.2).

17.6 Findings Related to Citizen Interaction and Engagement

Finding #7.   Of the approx. 24.000 facebook posts made by researched parliamentary institutions during the period of operation of their facebook accounts, approx. 52% have been liked by their users, 10% shared, and 7% commented.

This finding may be a testimony to the view that social media users can claim to like some content much more easily that they decide to share it or comment upon it.

Finding #8.   Of the facebook posts made by researched parliamentary institutions during the period of operation of their facebook accounts, at most 60% can be assumed to have provided at least one user reaction (in the form of like, share, or comment), whereas at least 40% can be assumed to have raised no intention to react.

Table 17.3 Social media recurring users with respect to characteristics of offerings

Platform	Accounts (A)	Months (M)	Items posted (I)	Recurring users (RU)	RU/ (A*M)	RU/ I
Youtube	12 channels	29	9.507 videos	6.925 subscribers	20	0,73
Twitter	24 accounts	23	139.134 tweets	351.808 followers	637	2,53
Facebook	21 pages	12	23.814 posts	414.229 friends	1.644	17,4

From the statistics reported in finding #7, if the probabilities of a post being liked, commented or shared were independent, the probability of a post being neither of the three amounts to approx. 40%. Given that these probabilities are normally not independent (they all have to do with a users' appreciation and interest for a post), the probability of a post not raising any reaction at all is even higher.

Yet another interpretation would be to expect that, out of 10 posts made by a parliamentary institution on their facebook page, at least 4 will not find their way to any user's interest to react. This is a strong indication that parliamentary institutions need to better adopt the contents they post on social media to their users' interests and profiles.

Finding #9.   For the social media accounts of the parliamentary institutions researched, citizens tend much more likely and easily to become fans of a facebook page, less likely and easily to follow a twitter account, and even less likely and easily to subscribe to a youtube channel.

As shown in Table 17.3, a youtube subscriber requires more content and time to be gained than a twitter follower, who requires in turn more than a facebook friend. This is in line with the observation above that users accept less formal and regular relationships (facebook friends) more easily than more formal or regular ones.

Would such a finding be confirmed by further research, it can offer an important lesson learnt for parliament institutions and public bodies attempting to use social media to reach fast a broad audience.

17.7 Findings Related to Social Media Readiness

The term "social media readiness" is proposed herein as a new concept to collectively describe the readiness of a country and the people to use and benefit from social media. This is of course a multi-faceted concept, combining technical, socio-economic, legal, and cultural factors. Still, if such a level of social media readiness exists it has a twofold importance for parliamentary institutions attempting to use social media for interacting with and engaging the citizens: on the one hand, it provides a strength and opportunity (in SWOT terms) to exploit, and on the other it constitutes a milestone against which a public institution such as a parliament should not under-perform.

Table 17.4 Parliamentary institutions ranked against relative levels of (a) social media use and (b) social media readiness at country level

Parliamentary institution	Social media use ranking	Country SM readiness ranking	Ranking comparison
European Union Parliament	1	10	9
United Kingdom Parliament	2	1	−1
Brazil Chamber of Deputies	3	25	22
Peru Congress of the Republic	4	21	17
Equador National Assembly	5	20	15
Colombia Senate	6	13	7
France Senate	7	4	−3
Mexico Senate of the Republic	8	19	11
Ireland National Parliament	9	6	−3
Italy Chamber of Deputies	10	15	5
El Salvador Legislative Assembly	11	18	7
Estonia Parliament	12	9	−3
Panama National Assembly	13	23	10
Paraguay Chamber of Deputies	14	28	14
Dominican Republic Senate	15	24	9

In the context of the research, the social media readiness of the countries included is assessed from ICT (internet, facebook) penetration levels and readiness (networked, e-government readiness) rankings already available. The assessment of each country is done in relative terms, in comparison to the other countries involved, and a final ranking of all countries is produced. At the same time, an independent ranking of all parliamentary institutions included in the research is produced, based on comparing them against all dimensions used to assess social media use. Both rankings are combined in the following table:

As this double ranking shows, there can be institutions that use social media at a relative (w.r.t. other institutions) level (a) similar to the relative (w.r.t. other countries) level of their country's readiness for social media, or (b) higher than their countries readiness level ("over-performing" institutions), or (c) lower than the latter ("under-performing" institutions).

It is thus possible to identify

(a) institutions that already use social media more and better than others to interact with citizens, as well as
(b) institutions that are better (relatively) positioned in social media interaction than their country is (relatively) positioned in social media readiness.

The UK and EU Parliaments ranked first in Table 17.4 fall in case (a), whereas most of the Latin America institutions listed above fall in case (b), and the drivers of their good performance in social media use deserve further consideration and research.

At all cases, parliamentary institutions well performing in social media-based interaction with citizens are candidate champions to be further monitored for findings and good practices.

17.8 Elements of a Social Media-Based Participation Strategy for Parliaments

17.8.1 Wrapping Up the Research Findings

The social media strategy of the parliamentary institutions researched was not known to the authors. Still, results have shown that information dissemination is in place, without yet meeting (and unknown if setting) objectives for active citizen participation and engagement.

In their true spirit, social media are exemplified as platforms to allow people create circles around common interests (Breslin et al. 2009). Nevertheless, the heterogeneous landscape of users (Taufique and Shahriar 2011; Ferro and Molinari 2010) testifies that different target groups need to be 'approached' in different means, according to the channels they can afford and use. Familiarization with legislative procedures and texts is equally important when considering formats of information to be posted on social media, and the vulgarization of content that will be required.

Apart from the issues specific to parliaments' potential use of social media, there are issues for the relation between social media and public strategies that are relevant to all organizations, public and private alike. In the rest of this section, we open up a discussion for some of these issues in more general terms (still, if "organization" is replaced by "parliament" the implications for parliaments are quite clear), and wrap this discussion up with specializing to parliaments that aspire to use social media to engage the public.

17.8.2 Differences Between Traditional and Social Media

Extrovert organizations need to differentiate between traditional (printed, electronic, online) and social media and the purposes and content appropriate for each.

Traditional media are governed by an economy of sparsity, message repetition is limited by costs, whereas printed and broadcast editions have short life windows. Social media, like Web 1.0 online media, is "live" and updatable on a 24×365 basis, and unlike Web 1.0 media they provide to the public a sense of ample space and limitless cross-referencing. Web hosting platforms for file sharing and blogs, as well as Wikipedia lemmas, able to extend in countless dimensions, are examples of these capabilities.

Similar to the so-called grammar, i.e., the communication rules and codes appropriate for traditional media (Kotler et al. 2001), social media have their own different grammar, where rich multimedia, rich linking, usability, and user opinion play an important role. The comment, like, share, and flag buttons appearing on any social media page nowadays manifest exactly this distinction.

Traditional media provide no self-contained opportunity for the audience to communicate with an organization. Even if readers use lateral channels to send letters to newspapers or viewers call on TV shows, there is no room for discussion. Social media provides an inherent, built-in-the-channel capability for real-time two-way communication, which radically departs from the traditional concept of what it meant to communicate. This departure at the same time constitutes an imperative for an organization to learn communicating this way. That is why traditional media can best be used for one-way information dissemination, whereas social media can best be used for listening to, responding to, and ultimately engaging, the public. As also suggested by multiple sources, the most fundamental difference between traditional and social media is that of user feedback, and the conversation and interaction that can be established (Van Wagner 2011; Harler 2010; Singh 2010; Shweta 2011).

17.8.3 Using Social Media for Engaging the Public

Social media brings a new meaning to the concept of a "public strategy": this is no more solely a strategy to manage public opinion and public relations, but also a strategy to benefit from public engagement. Therefore, and although it is not very common for public organizations to use business marketing as such, there are certainly lessons that public bodies can learn to reach a broader audience and pursue a more engaged public. The discussion that follows filters some ingredients of social media-based public strategies from the relevant literature.

Public bodies have an obligation to serve all citizens, rather than a choice in targeting their market, and their strategies need to be inclusive of all citizens accordingly. This implies that an organization has to eavesdrop what people say about it, listen to what people need and put it into *strategy* and *practice*. Yet, the *public* strategy of a *public* organization must, like all strategies, have a clear and accountable goal. Keeping the public informed is a different objective and implies different priorities and actions from having them participate in the decision-making process. The goal of the organization's public strategy is going to define the social media platforms to be used, as well as the ways in which they should be used (The H Agency 2010).

Two important factors for successful presence in social media are to stay active and flexible (Patel 2010). Profiles need to be updated frequently and the organization behind a social media profile needs to respond to questions and discuss with users lively. Flexibility in social media management is equally important; social media platforms change fast and organizations cannot afford to stay too behind.

All people in an organization need to align their culture along with using social media effectively, discussing problems and managing crises. They need to respond early when criticism occurs, in the channels that the public has used to report it and awaits for answers, reply honestly and clearly, and be willing to consider changing what needs to be changed. People in an organization open to social media need to proactively enter the online spaces where members of the public (professionals, activists, and citizens alike) discuss and participate (NARA 2010).

Having a strategy for social media does not mean that success is granted. Defining a strategy and goal must be coupled with defining an idea of success that includes the opinion and interests of the public. The medium is a message, but having this as the only message to the public is not enough. People are not naïve; the public as a whole is perfectly capable to distinguish which organizations are really engaged on their social media presence, and who are only pretending (Government of British Columbia 2010). People will only stay in interactions if they can see some practical added value in return for their feedback. One of the best ways to build and maintain a community is to accept and adopt ideas that come from the people (The H Agency 2010).

17.8.4 From Organizations to Public Bodies: Parliaments as A Particular Case

Public administration, especially under conditions of crisis, faces citizen dissatisfaction and disengagement. ICTs and Web technologies are introduced in the public sector with goals of internal simplification and efficiency, external transparency, as well as promoting interaction, reengagement, and participation of the public.

Within democratic states, parliaments have a particular institutional role. Like all other public bodies they are committed to managing information, with privacy and security, as a core prerequisite of their mission, to be safe-guarded even when they adopt open technologies such as social media. In the U.S., the Government Accountability Office has recently reported (US GAO 2011) the policies that US federal agencies apply to protect public sector information on commercially-operated social media.

However, parliaments, unlike public administrations and other executive agencies, have a legislative role. They run rule-making processes, prepare and vote laws, and monitor government performance. Their direct correspondents are elected and public officials, not citizens, which explains why they are regarded as 'closed' institutions, and their decisions to reorganize with ICTs have more implications at the political than administrative level. This explains why the motto of Fyfe and Crookall (2010) that "*social media are spontaneous and instantaneous, but government is slow and steady*" is particularly true for parliaments. The latter lacks flexibility, nimbleness, and cultural shift (Serrat 2010), since their operation sets out the lasting rules that monitor and constrain government and society.

Using social media, and establishing a public strategy alongside, represents a giant "leap forward" for the culture of a parliament. So much so that opening up social media communication channels with the citizens may have repercussions not only on a parliament's legislative and monitoring role, but also to the very concept of representative, as opposed to immediate, democracy. Also considering that voters' turnout and citizens' distrust are on the rise, the adoption of social media by parliaments needs to be planned and sustained with concrete and balanced goals.

In this context, and taking stock of the need for privacy and security for public and personal information, as well as of the experience that one of the authors has with her professional position in the Hellenic Parliament, we propose that parliaments need to consider the following issues when planning their strategy toward the public, with or without the use of social media:

- issues pertaining to public sector information: what information is of citizens' interest, and in what format (e.g., plain language vs. legal text) it can be published; whether the information published will be used only for awareness or also for gathering citizens' feedback, and so much so in a structured way;
- issues pertaining to personal information: how will citizens' feedback be delivered and what kind of citizens' identification information can be made available to the parliament; how will the parliament manage malevolent comments or security risks
- issues pertaining to accessibility and inclusion: combining equivalent channels of traditional and electronic media for different target groups; considering the profile of citizens interested in being engaged (e.g., citizens knowledgeable about politics or not) and adapting the service offerings accordingly (Clarke 2010, p. 4).

17.8.5 Perspectives to Be Considered by Parliaments

The 2010 World e-Parliament Report clearly states that citizens' information about policy issues and proposed legislation is ranked first (67%) in parliaments' objectives for ICT-based communication with the public; the explanation of the parliamentary function (59%) is ranked second, whereas engagement of more citizens in the political process (54%) comes third (United Nations et al. 2010, p. 38).

MPs' attitudes also play a pivotal role for open, transparent, and accountable communication with the citizens. The current socio-economic disorder calls for a change in communication among parliaments, representatives, and the electorate. The unanswered attacks by users via social media or the blocked comments on social media parliamentary profiles show that parliaments act awkward to this crisis. Generally speaking, parliaments do not seem to have a clear strategy or goals for their presence in social media. They experiment with social media, but when faced with criticism their response may be defensive or neutral. Capabilities for citizens to voice their views are often inactivated, essentially enforcing one-way communication over a two-way channel.

The citizens' perspective needs also to be held into account. Citizens' views and expectations for parliaments are crucial for the use of social media and the actual communication and participation that will take place. As Chrissafis and Rohen (2010) state,

Unless citizens have access to simple, clear facts to form their own opinion they may find it impossible to participate. They need to know to whom to address their views and that their views will be heard. They finally want to do this without having to spend a lot of time. After all, citizens are neither consultants nor legislators and have their daily lives to live. (p. 92).

This point of view succinctly summarizes some factors comprising the citizens' perspective: plain language, presentation of short and clear data, and most of all feedback on their feedback.

17.9 Concluding Thoughts

It is true that conclusions about the potential benefits and risks of the political uses of social media are not firm for the time being (Clarke 2010). Still, parliaments, like all other public bodies, do not seem to have a real choice toward social media; at some point, under technological advancements and public demands, they will more or less have to organize their social media presence.

As in many other e-government efforts, the presence of parliaments in social media with a view to citizen information and participation could perhaps best be approached in a "think big-start small", and "bottom-up, rather than top-down" fashion. Local constituencies could provide testbeds for such a venture, operating as feedback repositories between parliaments and citizens. A number of successful such projects, linking directly members of parliament to their electorate, are already in place (UK-based MySociety projects). In this manner, the role of representative democracy is safeguarded due to the fact that elected representatives are *"accountable to the electorate for their performance in office and integrity of conduct"* (United Nations & Inter-Parliamentary Union 2010, p. 22). Moreover, elected representatives can be expected to be more willing to communicate their activities to their own electoral constituency and engage in two-way interaction, in the context of pilot projects on social media platforms that could offer valuable lessons for the overall presence of parliaments in social media.

References

Al Hasib, A. (2009) Threats of online social networks. *International Journal of Computer Science and Network Security. Vol.9*, No 11, November 2009.

Arnstein, Sherry R. (1969) A Ladder of Citizen Participation. *JAIP*, Vol. 35, No. 4, pp. 216–224.

Bakera, J.R., Bennett, L.L.M., Bennett, S.E. & Flickinger, R.S. (1996) Citizens' knowledge and perceptions of legislatures in Canada, Britain and the United States. The Journal of Legislative Studies, 2(2), pp.44–62

Baumgarten, J. & Chui, M. (2009). *E-Government 2.0.* Retrieved from: http://ww1.mckinsey.com/clientservice/publicsector/pdf/TG_MoG_Issue4_egov.pdf

Blossom, J. (2009). *Content Nation. Surviving and thriving as social media changes our work, our lives and our future.* Indianapolis, Indiana: Wiley Publishing

Braghiroli, S. (2011) E-virgins, e-MEPs and MEP 2.0: Internet-based Political Communication in the European Parliament. *Italian Political Science. Issue 6.*

Breslin, J. G., Passant, A. & Decker, St. (2009) *The Social Semantic Web.* Berlin, Heidelberg: Springer-Verlag

Buhl. H. U. (2011) From Revolution to Participation: Social Media and the Democratic Decision-Making Process. *Business & Informations Systems Engineering.* 4|2011, 195–198.

Chrissafis, T. & Rohen, M. (2010). European eParticipation Developments. *JeDEM* 2(2): 89–98, 2010.

Clarke, A. (2010). *Social media. Political uses and implications for representative democracy.* Publication No. 2010-10-E, Background Paper, Library of the Parliament of Canada.

Dutta, S. & Mia, I. (2011) *The Global Information Technology Report 2010–2011. Transformations 2.0.* World Economic Forum, Geneva.

Effing, R., van Hillegersberg, J. & Huibers, T. (2011). Social Media and Political Participation: Are facebook, twitter and YouTube Democratizing Our Political Systems? In E. Tambouris, A. Macintosh & H. de Bruijn (Eds), *ePart 2011, LNCS 6847,* pp. 25–35, 2011. Delft: IFIP

Ferro, E. & Molinari, F. (2010). Framing Web 2.0 in the Process of Public Sector Innovation: Going Down the Participation Ladder. *European Journal of ePractice, No.9.*

Flickinger, R.S., Bennett, L.L.M. & Bennett, S.E. (1995) Citizen Support for the European Parliament: Knowledge and the Democratic Deficit. Retrieved from: http://aei.pitt.edu/6928

Fyfe, T. & Crookall, P. (2010). *Social media and public sector policy dilemmas.* Retrieved from: http://ipac.ca/documents/correction-June10.pdf

Government of British Columbia (2010). *Guidelines for Conducting Citizen Engagement, Specific to Social media.* Retrieved from: http://www.gov.bc.ca/citz/citizens_engagement/some_guidelines_master.pdf

Hansard Society (2011a). *Parliaments and Public Engagement. Innovation and Good Practice from Around the World.* London: Hansard Society.

Hansard Society (2011b). *Connecting Citizens to Parliament.* London: Hansard Society.

Harler, A. (2010) *6 Differences Between Social Media and Traditional Marketing.* Retrieved from: http://www.socialglitz.com/6-differences-between-social-media-and-traditional-marketing/

Kalampokis, E., Hausenblas, M. & Tarabanis, K. (2011) Combining Social and Government Data for Participatory Decision-Making. In E. Tambouris, A. Macintosh & H. de Bruijn (Eds), *ePart 2011, LNCS 6847,* pp.36–47, 2011. Delft: IFIP

Kaplan, A.M., Haenlein, M. (2010) Users of the world, unite! The challenges and opportunities of Social Media. *Business Horizons,* 59–68.

Kotler, P., Armstrong, G., Saunders, J. & Wong, V (2001) *Principles of Marketing.* Athens: Kleidarithmos (in greek)

Näkki, P., Bäck, A., Ropponen, T., Kronqvist, J., Hintikka, K. A., Harju, A., Pöyhtäri, R. & Kola, P. (2011) *Social media for citizen participation. Report of the Somus Project.* Retrieved from: http://www.vtt.fi/inf/pdf/publications/2011/P755.pdf

Osimo, D. (2008). *Web 2.0 in Government: Why and How?* Retrieved from: http://europa.eu/

Panopoulou, E., Tambouris, E. & Tarabanis, K. (2009). eParticipation Initiatives: How is Europe progressing? *European Journal of ePractice. No 7.* pp. 15–26

Papaloi, A. & Gouscos, D. (2010). E-parliaments and novel parliament-to-citizen services: An initial overview and proposal. In Parycek, P. & Prosser, A. (Eds.), *EDem2010: Proceedings of the 4th International Conference on E-Democracy,* pp. 103–111. Wien: Österreichische Computer Gesellschaft

Patel, K. (2010). *8 steps to creating a social media strategy.* Retrieved from: http://iserviceglobe.com/CaseStudies/Salesforce/ProductPageSalesforceCRM-8StepstoCreatingaSocialMediaStrategy.pdf

Sæbø, Ø. (2011) Understanding twitter Use among Parliament Representatives: A Genre Analysis. In Tambouris, E., Macintosh, A. and de Bruijn, H. (Eds.) *ePart 2011, LNCS 6847,* pp. 1–12, IFIP International Federation for Information Processing

Serrat, O. (2010) *Social Media and the Public Sector. Asian Development Bank.* Retrieved from: http://www.adb.org/documents/information/knowledge-solutions/social-media-and-the-public-sector.pdf

Shweta (2011) *Difference between Traditional, Digital and Social Media Marketing.* Retrieved from: http://marketinomics.com/digital-marketing-2/traditional-digital-and-social-media-marketing/

Singh, P. (2010) *Marketing priority for social media success.* Retrieved from: http://www.khabarmedia.com/article/articledetails/id:6

Taufique, K. M. R. & Shahriar, F. M. (2011) Adoption of online social media innovation: who's inside the spectrum? *Global Conference on Innovations in Management.* London, UK, 2011.

The H Agency (2010). *8 steps to integrate Social Media into your Marketing Plan.* Retrieved from: http://thehagency.com/H-Papers/H-Paper_Integrate_Social_Media.pdf

U.S. Government Accountability Office (GAO) (2011). *Social Media. Federal Agencies Need Policies and Procedures for Managing and Protecting Information They Assess and Disseminate.*

U.S. National Archives and Records Administration (NARA) (2010). *Social Media Strategy.* Retrieved from: http://www.archives.gov/social-media/strategies/social-media-strategy-2010-12-08.pdf

UNDESA (2010) *United Nations E-Government Survey 2010.* United Nations Department of Economic and Social Affairs, New York.

United Nations & Inter-Parliamentary Union (2010). *World e-parliament Report 2010.*

Van Wagner, S. (2011) *Traditional Media vs Social Media.* Retrieved from: http://vwmarketingsolutions.ca/2011/11/traditional-media-vs-social-media/

Printed by Books on Demand, Germany